The Education Feminism Reader

The Education Feminism Reader

Edited by Lynda Stone
With the assistance of Gail Masuchika Boldt

Routledge
New York   London

Published in 1994 by

Routledge
29 West 35 Street
New York, NY 10001

Published in Great Britain by

Routledge
11 New Fetter Lane
London EC4P 4EE

Library of Congress Cataloging in Publication Data

The Education feminism reader edited by Lynda Stone : with the assistance of
Gail Masuchika Boldt.
     p.   cm.
   Includes bibliographical references (p.) and index.
   ISBN 0-415-90800-0. — ISBN 0-415-90793-4 (pbk.)
     1. Feminism and education. 2. Women—Education. 3. Women
teachers. 4. Professional education. 5. Critical pedagogy. 6. Sexism in
education. I. Stone, Lynda.
   LC197.E37   1993
   370.19′345—dc20
                                                                    93-5498
                                                                      CIP

British Library cataloguing in publication information also available.

For the Contributors

CONTENTS

ACKNOWLEDGMENTS

Putting this book together has taken many months, and I have learned a great deal. Three people have made it all possible: Nel Noddings, Jayne Fargnoli, and Gail Boldt. Nel has been my teacher, mentor, and friend. She and I originally conceived of the collection, and her collaboration, then guidance and support ensured the completion of the project. Indeed, her fine reputation as a scholar and educator made it initially possible. Jayne has been a staunch supporter from the beginning, an enthusiastic, open, and extremely helpful editor. Again there is no book without her. Gail Boldt has been more a partner than an assistant in this project. She is talented and thoughtful, a careful thinker, a wonderful comrade. I counted on her for needed refinements—just the right ideas at the right times.

Others have been wonderfully supporting. The first is Maxine Greene; I count myself very lucky to know her and to receive her generous support. The second is Jane Bernard-Powers. She and I just go through a lot together, and this book is a part of our lives as close friends. So often, she too puts the right slant on things. Additionally important are Anne Sanow of Routledge and Glenn Masuchika who provided continuous and able assistance. Thank you to students and colleagues in Hawaii for general encouragement; I also wish in particular to thank the "other feminist," Anne Phelan, as well as Elaine Hadfield and Richard Rapson.

Several contributors to the collection offered valuable ideas and deserve special mention: Madeleine Arnot, Elizabeth Ellsworth, Maxine Greene, Patti Lather, and Patricia Thompson. Others providing assistance and support include Michael Apple, Glorianne Leck, Thomas Popkewitz; Jennifer Gore and Carmen Luke provided a fine model. Thanks also to initial reviewers.

Finally, I want to mention friends and family, especially Kathryn Davis, Suzanne Wolfe, my father, my brother, and his family. My mother died several years ago; I think she would have been proud of this endeavor.

And a special acknowledgment to Karen Maloney and *Harvard Educational Review* for republication permissions.

NOTES TO THE TEXT

Greene, Maxine, "The Lived World," Reprinted by permission of the publisher from Greene, Landscapes of Learning. (New York: Teachers College Press, © 1978 by Teachers College, Columbia University.) All rights reserved. Chapter 15, "The Lived World," pp. 213–224.

Gilligan, Carol, "Woman's Place in Man's Life Cycle," Harvard Educational Review, 49: 4, pp. 431–446. Copyright © 1979 by the President and Fellows of Harvard College. All rights reserved. Reprinted by permission of the publisher.

Dill, Bonnie Thornton, "Race, Class, and Gender: Prospects for an All-Inclusive Sisterhood." This article is reprinted from Feminist Studies, Volume 9, number 1 (1983): 130–150, by permission of the publisher, Feminist Studies, Inc., c/o Women's Studies Program, University of Maryland, College Park, MD 20742.

Walkerdine, Valerie, "Femininity as Performance," Oxford Review of Education, 15: 3, 1987, pp. 267–279. Reprinted by permission of the Editorial Board, Oxford Review of Education, University of Oxford Department of Educational Studies.

Nicholson, Linda J., "Women and Schooling," Educational Theory, 30: 3, 1980, pp. 225–234. Reprinted by permission of the Board of Trustees of the University of Illinois, and the editor of Educational Theory.

Arnot, Madeleine, "Male Hegemony, Social Class and Women's Education," 164: 1, 1982, pp. 64–89. Reprinted by permission of the Editorial Board, Journal of Education, Boston University, School of Education.

Martin, Jane Roland, "Excluding Women from the Educational Realm," Harvard Educational Review, 52: 2, pp. 133–148. Copyright © 1982 by the President and Fellows of Harvard College. All rights reserved. Reprinted by permission of the publisher.

Houston, Barbara, "Should Public Education Be Gender Free?," originally "Gender Freedom and the Subtleties of Sexist Education." Educational Theory, 35: 4, 1985, pp. 359–370. Reprinted by permission of the Board of Trustees of the University of Illinois, and the editor of Educational Theory.

Zambrana, Ruth E., "Toward Understanding the Educational Trajectory and Socialization of Latina Women," The Broken Web: The Educational Experience of Hispanic American Women, eds. Teresa McKenna and Flora Ida Ortiz, pp. 61–77. Reprinted by permission of the publisher, copyright © 1988 by The Tomás Rivera Center, 710 North College Avenue, Claremont, CA 91711.

Grumet, Madeleine, "Conception, Contradiction, and Curriculum," reprinted from Bitter Milk: Women and Teaching, by Madeleine R. Grumet (Amherst: University of Mas-

INTRODUCING EDUCATION FEMINISM

You cannot afford to think of being here to receive an education; you will do better to think of yourselves as being here to claim one . . . [to claim is] to take as a rightful owner; to assert in the face of possible contradiction. . . . The difference is that between acting and being acted upon, and for women it can literally mean the difference between life and death.[1]

In 1977, feminist essayist Adrienne Rich delivered an address to women graduates of Douglass College, Rutgers University, in which she urged them to take charge of their educations and through extension, of the rest of their lives. It is now more than fifteen years since Rich's call, and women, both younger and older, have claimed advances for themselves, particularly in the arenas of education and occupation. In fact, opportunity has become commonplace enough for mainstream, middle-class Euro-American women that many of them wonder today why a claiming was even necessary and what Rich's assertiveness was all about.

This obvious opportunity for some women hides the discrimination that continues in many private and public realms and also masks the unevenness of women's advances. A quick consideration of the conditions of minority single mothers living in urban poverty dispels myths of vast, wide-ranging improvements. Moreover, even in education inequality persists today.[2]

Rich's essay has symbolic importance beyond the practical world of societal opportunity. It now occupies a central place in the feminist academic canon, a manifestation of insights from theorizations about women's lives. Notably these are in empirical "gender studies" and nonempirical "feminist theory."[3] In the larger academy, women's studies programs are almost standard, even if a thorough integration of feminist writings is still a nonrealized ideal in the general college curriculum. Since the occasion of Rich's speech, feminist theory has evolved through multiple phases to a proliferation of multiple views. Subsequently, these are taken up as part of the contextualizing of the present book.

CONTEXT OF DISCRIMINATION

The title *The Education Feminism Reader* names a new theoretical formulation and is itself a claiming in the tradition of Adrienne Rich. The claim for education feminism is important because of the special conditions that surround the lives of women in professional education. "Professional education" is the arena most closely associated with the lives of most of the authors of this collection and with the feminist issues about which they write. It also names as a significant category teaching candidates and education graduate students, precollegiate practicing teachers and administrators, teacher educators and education researchers. The lives of women (and of men) in professional education are similar to, but also different from, those in other spheres of education—of the general academy, governmental, corporate and philanthropic arenas. The structural context[4] of women and of feminism in professional education is especially complex given that as a distinct institution it is highly "feminized," that is, populated primarily by women.

Any institution in which women are predominant, common sense dictates, ought to be relatively free of discrimination against its majority. Such, in subtle and not so subtle ways, is not the case for women in professional education. Discrimination, as I see it, has several institutional locations. A first is in precollegiate schools and comes in the form of the patriarchy within which the practitioner works. Here there still exists traditional control over women "subordinates" largely by male administrative "superiors." The masculinist structures of learning and knowledge also continue to be dominant over recent changes in pedagogy. In spite of caring, cooperative, and connected classrooms and a teacher education literature that includes "critical feminist pedagogy," schools are still bastions of traditional, masculinist epistemology.[5] A second location of discrimination is in colleges and universities in which women education researchers, teacher educators, and education students—both undergraduate and graduate— are found. Here masculinist structures converge from two influences, those arising out of schooling and those devolving from the general academy. Professional schools are most often both "normal schools" and "research institutions," and their women carry the stigma of a double discrimination. First, they are not "teachers" and are mistrusted by the "field" because they do not work in schools. Second, they are not "real scholars" because they are not members of the general academy.

A third form of discrimination, also located in higher education, requires a bit of explanation. This is the devaluing that feminists in professional schools feel from their academic sisters. While this is clearly related to the second form of discrimination, something else operates as well. Feminist scholarship from the "pure" scholars is valued more than that from "applied" scholars—a discrimination either perpetuated directly by academic feminists in their own beliefs and practices or perpetuated indirectly in the overall lack of feminist solidarity. In an interesting twist, feminists sometimes romanticize the work of classroom teachers (even though the former have not chosen to teach children), in a move that further silences those education feminists "caught in the middle." When not romanticized, feminist classroom teachers are included in the discrimination. A hierarchy plays out this way: education feminists read, study, and admire the writings of more general academic feminists but there is almost no counterpractice. Moreover, almost no (or very few) education feminists and academic feminists work together. The former are too fearful of suggesting such work, and the latter "just do not think of it." Thus, there persists a situation that contradicts feminist solidarity in general and that, as is most obvious, is antithetical to basic feminist beliefs and theories.[6]

HISTORICAL STRUCTURES

The institutional discrimination described above is related to two sets of conditions that are interpretable both in historical and historicist terms. Such conditions constitute some of the possible contexts, that is, the various influencing structural environments, surrounding the writings of this book.

Historical structures are of four forms. The first two are "practical," the contexts of education and politics today and in the recent past. The second two are "theoretical," the structures of the general intellectual era within which the present and recent past are embedded and the structures of feminist theory over the same time period. Temporally, these four are understood to evolve and change over time and from historical hindsight to contain some elements of continuity and persistence. Clearly no strong historical notion of cause and effect is indicated. These four, of course, are interrelated. It is also interesting that an ideological comparison of the two sets indicates that a schism has existed between a fairly conservative era of education and politics and a fairly radical era of general and feminist scholarship.

An initiating point: the education feminist scholarship of this book, representative of an emerging and already vigorous field of study and practice, seeks to demonstrate its own evolving history and attempts to influence future education and feminist theory and practice.

The education context. Since the sixties the education context has been one of various functional approaches toward persistent problems in public education: problems of instruction and curriculum, of classroom and schooling organization, of the relationships of teachers, students, parents, and the larger community, of positionings of race, class, and gender, and so forth. The lives of women, coming out of general discriminatory structures, are related to all of these. What underlies these considerations is agreement that across the last thirty years, and in spite of continual efforts at reform (and some improvement for some students), educational inequalities continue. Some learn and some do not, some progress and some do not, some earn the credentials of schooling and some do not. Some fit schools and some do not. Some few appear especially to prosper as students and as human beings, but many more do not.[7] And many who do not are girls and women.

The general state of education today is not commendable. Some pose that almost all students are at risk; studies indicate some of the following relevant facts.[8] Approximately one-quarter of all children in the early years of schooling actually go to school disadvantaged; indeed they often are hungry. In urban secondary education, some estimates are that as high as seventy percent of the young, minority males are dropping out of school. These figures come from the United States, whose citizens do not generally realize that the educational/societal conditions of the schooling of their young are an international disgrace.

What remains persistent is the discrepancy between the general and educational lives of the prosperous and of the poor. A related issue of course, is the ethnic and racial makeup of the poor and what this means for realization of aims of equality and opportunity. And related of course is gender.

The political context. In the eighties and early nineties, the malaise over public education was concretized in a reform movement. What is interesting from historical hindsight is the embeddedness of reform in a time of general political conservatism. What this means is that most reform proposals come from rightist and centrist perspectives—the radical left is confined to the education academy and often reduced to internecine squabbling.[9] Out of this civic context, schooling reforms are explicitly functional and implicitly controlling, centering on matters of instruction, student discipline, and finally school structure. Here the road to good education is paved with method—for instance, with matching learning styles to teaching styles or with the continued ubiquity of objectives and standardized assessment.[10] Good method produces good students who produce good learning through their good behavior. All of this, politically, occurs through appropriation by the right of traditional left rhetoric: the liberal language of the sixties becomes the conservative language of the eighties.

The idea that method and prediction lead in a simple way to better education for more or most persons, however, is recognized as a sham by reformers of the center and left. Their own reform proposals focus on matters of more teacher autonomy and empowerment within a related reform of teacher education. Movements in "teacher personal theorizing" and in reflective teaching are illustrative and particularly interesting when they are added to school structure changes such as "community management" but are juxtaposed to the above method reforms. What results, to my mind, is that teachers believe they are gaining greater control of their professional lives but are doing so only within pre-prescribed boundaries that perpetuate masked but manifest top-down control.[11]

The intellectual context. Embeddedness of education and politics occurs within a more general intellectual era in the west. Today is a transitional time, called variously late and postmodernism. Whatever its label, all agree that the modern search for certainty is over. This change is recognized in the spate of "postisms" that describe both the material and the intellectual worlds: postindustrial, post-Western, postliberal, postcolonial, as well as postanalytic, poststructural, and even postfeminist. Again juxtaposition is necessary, when one poses the recent positivistic reform of education practice against the larger postpositivistic theoretical era. As the above description attests, the results of this contradiction are not benign.

Intellectually, postmodern theorization exhibits the tentativeness and ambiguity of the age. The giving up of certainty that is central to the period changes the ways that science and knowledge and their discourse practices are undertaken and considered. Science is fundamental because its practice characterizes modernism. Over the millennia, observation and proof of a noncontaminated reality have yielded to a world that is theory-laden and constructed. Moreover, the unity of science and knowledge is breaking up as theorists posit changes in notions of truth. Knowledge to most is becoming knowledges, with the multiplicity of formulations that such a notion portends. Nonessentialism, difference, and contingency are constitutive of these formulations, rather than essentialism, sameness, and necessity. Related to this development are two other changes in the use of the language of theory. First is a transition in which language becomes mediation between reality and truth, but then its privileging is also given up. Second is a transition to less certain discourse forms: science begins to look more like story.[12]

The feminism context. Particular to this collection and related to the contexts above is a historical background of feminist theory. The present situation of feminist theory has already been mentioned, a state that mirrors the multiplicity of postmodernism: feminism is feminisms. As one theorist puts this,

> [There are] eco-feminists, anarchist feminists, Marxist feminists, socialist-feminists, lesbian feminists, lesbian separatists, lesbian vanguardists . . . psychoanalytic feminists (be they Freudian, Jungian, Kleinian, Lacanian, or object-relations oriented mothering feminists).[13]

Formulations are named for small groups of theorists seeking to differentiate themselves from one another. Underlying this pluralization, however, are some common tenets and recognizable phases of theorizing.

One way to set out common tenets agreed to across multiple feminisms is to define feminism as both a practical and a theoretical endeavor. From a practical point of view feminisms begin as a form of politics, initially in a "common struggle" against patriarchal discriminations and inequalities, and more recently, in an "uncommon struggle" against matriarchal inequities perpetuated by women against women.[14] The point of these two classifications is recent public recognition by white feminists of their insensitivity to, if not downright denial of, the differences between the relations of minority and third-world women and men from their own cross-gender relationships. The overall struggle against discrimination for the latter women has never been common. Their own unique discrimination is reflected in part in the present volume.

The special character of feminism, well recognized as personal, is connected to its politics. The maxim is "the personal is political." This idea is implemented by redefining the private and public realms within which women live, understanding the power relations operating everywhere, and valuing the experience of each and every woman. Finally, one other tenet is connected to these personal experiences: this is the value of feminist collectivity in the form of solidarity. Historically, solidarity begins with consciousness raising and remains an ideal—whatever its present state among women and among feminists.

From a theoretical point of view, feminism is introduced as a series of "classic" and "new" concepts. Writing by feminists about the first set leads to theorizing about the second. Again, recognizing the common and uncommon struggles aids understanding. Out of a theoretical and masculinist hierarchy existing since ancient times comes discrimination inherent in dualisms such as these: subjective-objective, passive-active, procreative-creative, reproduction-production, body-mind, emotion-cognition (reason), nature-culture, private-public, submission-domination, other-person.[15] While the logic of how this occurs is itself convoluted, the result of these dualistic distinctions within a patriarchy of power is that the first of these concepts is culturally devalued in relation to the second: women are inferior to men. Although the essentialism of these concepts is today under suspicion—the natures and lives of women are not alike—nonetheless these conceptual hierarchies are themselves foundational to the social, epistemological, and ethical ways in which the world has been "sensed." Merely saying that these dualisms no longer matter does not get rid of their influence.

Newer theory responds to essentialism. By essentialism is meant the proposal of womanly and feminist sameness, a proposal that discriminates at the expense of difference and differentiation.[16] As indicated above, the problem is that proposals of sameness, utilized to fight male bias, hide inequalities among women themselves. New concepts are not themselves essentialist dualisms but are instead overlapping sets of ideas around which the continuing uncommon struggles are organized. They are well-recognized after a decade or so of attention by feminist writers: position and location, identity and voice, sexuality and gender, differentiation and commonality, community and solidarity.

In addition to tenets of practicality and to theoretical conceptualizations, historical phases of feminist theory and research are worthy of consideration. Various formulations of this history are extant in the literature.[17] Phases continue and persist, phases that are named as universalist, separatist, essentialist, and particularist. Crossing them are the demarcations and tensions of modernism and postmodernism identified previously.

Universalist feminisms pose that women are biologically and culturally equal to men but are historically denied equality. Equality exists within a monocultural world in which change is defined as equity. Basic to these theories are conceptions of human rationality, of a core that all persons share whether they are man or woman. Given a universal element of nature, woman typically becomes equal when she recognizes this nature and learns to live in the world, that is, the man's world that has been created from this nature.

Separatist feminisms pose that women and men are equal but different and are historically denied equality. Here equality comes in the creation of and valuation of separate spheres for women and men. Typically, in a bicultural world the private, reproductive, domesticated world of women is raised in importance to equal the public, productive, and cultured world of men. One variant suggests that all persons become bicultural.

Essentialist feminisms arise out of universalist and separatist formulations and pose that the realms of women are part of women's gendered histories. Here equality comes in a female sameness, in an essence of gender that is different from the gender of men. Solidarity among women is typically proposed as a vehicle for equality, one that is realized when essential gender difference is acknowledged and equally valued by all men and women.

Particularist feminisms (unarguably the most recent forms of feminist theorizings) begin with a critique of the other three forms, and most notably the essentialist variant. As indicated, herein the attention shifts from the common struggle to the uncommon one. Equality comes out of difference rather than sameness but in particulars—there are no essentials for all women or for all men (or for all persons). Typically, the focus of theory seeks recognition of the diverse lives of women, and especially value for the lives of women of color, minorities and third-world women. One strain of variation values all "local narratives" and deconstructs structures of all types, including those of gender. These feminisms also engage in theorizing that adds a sub-conscious and thus particular critique of the initial core element of human rationality.[18]

HISTORICIST NONSTRUCTURES

Thus far both a situation of present institutional discrimination and a set of historical factors contextualize the chapters that follow. These historical factors, it is emphasized, are no longer elements of necessity: there is no notion of progress or even evolution in a forward sense; there is no telos, no means to a proposed end. In what is *now* defined in a historicist interpretation, new conditions obtain. These are plurality and multiplicity and what is shortly defined as simultaneity. First a comment about historicism itself.

In this late or postmodern time, the term *historicism* is itself variously meaningful.[19] It is, in my view, a critique of history as determinate in any sense. It is explanation that is relational. All ideas, beliefs, ideologies, practices, institutions, etc., are related to the present in its multiplicity of relations—as in those just recorded for education feminism. Each of these relationships also has its own history, best understood in its own sets of relations enduring over time. Historicism is explanation embedded in other relationships as well, relationships to many other possible structural features of social life. For instance, some of these are linguistic or economic. In its poststructural variant, historicism means that structures are "worked through" to particulars of the present. As indicated, there are no essentials, and meaning itself is always fluid, dispersed, and in some sense beyond completion. Language loses its privilege in this strong historicism.

Simultaneity, derivation, and origination

Given the nonessentialism of meanings, a new conception of plurality and change is possible in a notion of simultaneity. Temporal (read historical) meanings of derivation and origination are transformed in this conception. These now occur together—at one and the same time. Both derivation and origination from within a historicist, multiple simultaneity explain something significant about the chapters to follow.

This point is that each piece is both derivative and originative. To see the collection in this way rids it of the standard discrimination accorded scholarship that is applied rather than pure, professional rather than academic, and education feminist rather than academic feminist. The latter pairing, of course, is also in line with the nonessentialist pluralism of current feminist theorizing. This transformation means that each piece stands within a set of relational meanings and each (as all other scholarship) has something to say that connects it to others sayings, as well as something to say that is new. In the frames of postmodernism, scholarship is no longer defined dualistically as generative *or* replicative. This is old meaning, from old science, from old epistemology. Rather, each piece, tied in some ways to what has been done before, is also a particular contribution for its own moment. In its moment, it is nothing else (but never pinned down either).

In lay terms, education feminism is a field in its own right with its own value for its theorists and its practitioners at all levels of the education profession (and for others as well). It is scholarship that is no more derivative nor originative than any other. Its determination of value comes from its relevance for its own sets of conditions and issues. Its moment (given the history of change and multiple evolutions that are documented across the chapters of the book) is present life in professional education.

READING FRAMES

The contexts, the structures and nonstructures, presented thus far in the introduction are various, multiple frames from which to read and understand the chapters that follow. The point requires emphasis: all reading is contextualized and situated; all writing is understood again and again in reading and rereading. Only through some framing of the contents (and their formulations) to follow is the significance of this collection fully realized.

Each writer brings her own frames to the writing, just as each reader brings his or her own frames. The writer constructs ideas in particular ways for various intended audiences. All of these pieces have had previous audiences, and all but two have been published. Now they are read by new audiences in new times. Their meanings, framed by the understandings just described, are open to further interpretation. In turn, the reader interprets from within her or his lenses: here there is fluidity in reconstructed meaning. But here too, it seems to me, the reader has a responsibility to attempt to understand the meanings of the writer. This requires for some readers a temporary state of nonbelief, a recognition of one's own frames—personalizations of various structures, including gender, race, class, language, and culture—and an attempt to understand the frames, the lenses, and then the ideas of others. Nonbelief allows for the learning of something new.

The general frame

The chapters that follow were written by *education feminists* beginning in the late seventies. Their collectivity takes place under this new name—a neologism to identify for a time the coming together of various feminist approaches for professional education. The authors are college and university professors. They teach primarily but not exclusively in programs, departments, schools, and colleges of education located not only in the United States but also in England, Canada, and New Zealand. They are both white women and women of color, members of the intelligentsia but also middle class. They have various allegiances to feminist theorizings and in some cases, formal commitments to women's studies. Their research is both nonempirical and empirical and sometimes combines the two. Their discipline backgrounds are philosophy, psychology, sociology (especially critical sociology), and curriculum studies. Whether they do feminist research or gender studies, they unite in reformist beliefs: they seek for all women societal equality both with men and with each other.

CHAPTER OVERVIEW

What follows is a brief description of each chapter that allows for various selective readings of the book: each educational topic is approachable through a diversity of subtopics and feminist perspectives. In addition, a history of feminist theory is woven through each topical section; pieces are arranged somewhat chronologically. Also the five parts of the book have some chronological order since issues of an essentialized self first interested feminists just as issues of nonessentialized and diverse selves are more currently of interest. The book, overall, is intended as a general reader, bringing together for the first time significant writings of a broad nature in education feminism. Its chapters are to be appreciated in their own rights and in their own times. They are meant to introduce and overview feminist theorizing in professional education: they are not intended to be "the last word" about any topic or issue from any position or perspective. They serve as a resource and introduce many readers to an already vibrant field of feminist scholarship.

The book begins from what historically is one of feminisms' starting points, the issue of self. Two aspects of this issue are identity and gender which name part one of the book; other aspects include experience, voice, subjectivity, and personhood. The education problem, one that includes but extends far beyond professional education, concerns the relationships of girls and women to the educational process, and especially in these chapters, to its underlying theories and values. Here begins the general theme of the fit and nonfit (and generally the latter) of those who are female.

Maxine Greene initiates the collection at the level of experience and reality, which she proposes are obscured for women by societal roles that men have constructed for them. Greene, who is a "mother" of education feminism, demonstrates in this chapter her early positioning as a feminist, the connections in her work to literature and to literary criticism, and a continuous conceptualization of alternatives to dominant masculinist philosophy of education.

Carol Gilligan's classic "Woman's Place in Man's Life Cycle" introduces the important tradition of feminist psychology of self in a critique of standard male-defined theories of human development. Building on object-relations theory, Gilligan's chapter, and the book which followed, is one of the most quoted sources in all of feminist theory. Like others, Gilligan works from now-canonical literary figures such as Virginia Woolf and psychological figures such as Nancy Chodorow.

Bonnie Thornton Dill makes a significant contribution with her sociological history of sisterhood and the feminist movement and their places in African-American women's experience. Dill overviews a conception of sisterhood for Black women, relates the struggle against racial injustice for women and men of color, offers the initial critique of white feminism in this book, and poses strategies for a more all-inclusive sisterhood.

Valerie Walkerdine closes the first part of the book with the initial contribution from England and the latest theorizing in a post-structural, psychoanalytic analysis of girls' identity and performance in school. Walkerdine usefully explores the philosophical backdrop of the "rational self," and its relationship to the traditional passive role of femininity. The schooling example concerns the traditional poor showing of girls in mathematics.

Part two takes up the larger issues of institution rather than person in four important chapters. Education and schooling are institutions within which women have been denied equality. Authors herein claim that this inequality relates to broader male-defined norms arising from the role of the family during industrialization, the definitions of gender and of education, and the relationship of class and gender to schooling.

Linda Nicholson's contribution is identified as the first journal article in education feminism. It begins with a critique of the correspondence theory of schooling and capitalism by adding the family to the equation. Nicholson discusses a major theme from feminist theory, that of the separate spheres—the public sphere of men and the private sphere of women. Schools, in spite of the feminization of teaching have been and remain public—and thus discriminatory.

Madeleine Arnot offers the first "critical" piece of the collection in an important theorizing from British "new sociology of knowledge." Here the relationship of social class is added to that of gendered education. With much distinction, Arnot poses an early critique of social reproduction theory, and concepts like hegemony and contradiction are used. For Arnot, gender becomes a social construction that is at once arbitrary and nonessentialist, and based in difference.

Jane Roland Martin's classic chapter takes up the place of women in the philosophy of education. In an account that later is part of her important book, Martin (also a founder of the field) traces the conception of education from ancient times and finds women excluded. This account is complemented by an analysis of the meanings of education, liberal education, and teaching from recent analytic philosophy of education. To the standard picture are added the gendered lives of women.

Barbara Houston builds from Martin's tradition to ask whether a gender-free education is possible. Various interpretations of the meaning of gender-free are presented, and the general question is situated in an amount of studies of girls in classrooms. Houston develops in important respects the idea of a "gender-sensitive" education, promoting it as especially appropriate for understanding particular educational contexts.

Ruth E. Zambrana adds the perspective of Latina women to issues of education and socialization. In an acknowledged working from Dill's theorizing, Zambrana traces the lack of studies about the lives of women who are *not* white and middle-class and adds her own critique of feminist theory. This is followed by a suggestive model that builds in culture along with the relationships of gender, race, class, and language in understanding the choices for educational lives.

If self and society in the form of education are recognized as the bounding poles external of schooling, internal locations are in the first instance what is taught in school and in the second, who teaches and how. Part three takes up issues of the curriculum, of knowledges that are its bases, and of arrangements for instruction. Individual chapters, of course, work from conceptions of self and contexts of education but take a closer look at what is taught in school. Curriculum is considered in both epistemological and ethical terms.

Madeleine Grumet's chapter introduces yet another strand of educational theory in her "reconceptualization" of curriculum in terms of the lives of women. Herein the term "reproduction" assumes both a biological and a phenomenological sense as it is tied to education. Grumet revisits Chodorow and makes salient psychoanalytic theory prior to that of Walkerdine. Contradiction also plays a part in the curriculum "of the fathers" and in a call for another, feminist, conception.

Nel Noddings introduces the now famous "ethic of caring" in her chapter. Writing in the field of philosophy rather than a more dominant psychology, this senior author in education feminism begins from a moral orientation to education, teaching, and instructional arrangements. She posits the need to change almost every aspect of present schooling, a change that should be centered in the ethical relation between each teacher and student. Two important elements are dialogue and confirmation.

Patricia J. Thompson considers the traditional discipline of girls, home economics, which is significant first because it presents a specific case from the school curriculum and second because of the relationship to vocational education that is set out. Thompson makes the point that the "Hermean," or male, standard is still the norm in home economics. What is needed is a new "Hestian" standard based in the lives of women and girls and the new scholarship on women.

Nona Lyons, known initially for her development of Gilligan's moral theory, extends her work on the ethical domain of schooling to the epistemological domain. Here she begins from an important literature on teaching research and then turns to the significant conceptualization of "women's ways of knowing." Knowledge and learning become not only social but also feminist. Lyons documents with empirical evidence an epistemological interaction between teacher and student.

Part four takes up theorizations of who teaches and how. Again, previous topics intersect but in new ways: questions of identity, conditions of education, theories of knowledge as they influence conceptions of teachers and teaching. Diversity of perspectives continue in the four pieces. These perspectives come from philosophy, history, sociology, and curriculum theory, as well as from empirical and nonempirical research. Each paper, working from many others in the book, presents a critique of standard, nonfeminist theorizations.

Lynda Stone posits a transformation of teaching theory based in an understanding of its philosophical roots. Objective and subjective models of education found analogous conceptions of teaching. Both, however, are male-defined, as Stone's gender critique reveals. A new conception related to the work of Martin and Noddings is proposed, a conception based not in a dualistic, but rather in a relational, feminist epistemology.

Barbara McKellar presents an unusual perspective on the diversity of women teachers, that of a black woman who is a teacher educator in Britain. McKellar documents and discusses the way that structures of both society and knowledge influence the success of black people in education. The central role of black women in the family and wider community is a related topic. Issues for teachers include access to higher education, pedagogical interests, and promotion.

Patti Lather continues the strand of "critical theory" in the book with her important critique of the nature of teacher work as it relates to feminism, Marxism, and capitalism. Lather begins with a review of neo-Marxist research in education and points to the general absence of gender. As a source for theoretical reformulation Lather considers "Marxist feminism," a perspective that takes on issues for teachers that involve the public-private split, subjectivity, and the danger of reductionism.

Jo Anne Pagano's chapter continues the reconceptualist tradition of the marriage of philosophy and psychology begun by Grumet by turning to the topic of women teaching women. Pagano's elegant treatment also utilizes literature in the tradition of Greene and Bogdan through the vehicle of a May Sarton novel. Again identity is revisited, as is women's experience. Pagano utilizes the theorizing of important contemporary feminist theorists such as Elaine Showalter and Luce Irigaray.

Part five, the final part of the book, demonstrates the diversity of studies prevalent in education feminism today. It builds, of course, on earlier topics of identity, education, curriculum, and teaching, but as these are operationalized in particular ways by particular researchers and teachers. This section concerns the present state of feminisms manifested in education feminism (and related fields like multicultural education). Diversity is achieved through studies by and about women of color as well as white women and also through locations that include New Zealand and Canada as well as the United States.

Sue Middleton utilizes the methodology of sociological life history research in her interesting chapter about the school experiences of two feminist teachers in New Zealand. One has a British background and the other is Maori with adopted Pakeha (European-background) parents. Each tells her own story about postwar education and becoming a feminist radical teacher. Each describes her own experience of discrimination and marginality. Middleton concludes with implications for feminist pedagogy.

Elizabeth Ellsworth's chapter is identified as one of the most significant in education feminism today, coming out of critical, post-structural theory. Ellsworth poses a critique of "critical pedagogy" that is based in her own university teaching, a critique of what she came to recognize as subtle repressive elements of empowerment, student voice, dialogue, and critical reflection. What emerges is a pedagogical vision constituted of multiple contexts and perspectives.

Dianne Smith emphasizes diversity of conceptions of critical teaching in a chapter that in juxtaposition to Ellsworth is an account of an African-American womanist professor rather than a white feminist professor. Here again is an actual story of teaching, one this time framed in the literary contributions of Blacks that include Maya Angelou, Linda Brent, bell hooks, Zora Neale Hurston, Alice Walker, and Harriet Wilson. Out of the analysis comes direction for a critical, multicultural pedagogy.

Joyce E. King's chapter is the only one of the collection that is not feminist in intent. Rather it points by implication to present divergences between multicultural and feminist education and to the issue of feminist essentialism. King demonstrates in her own teaching what she calls "dysconscious racism," the taking of white norms of educational equality as givens. This chapter again connects to critical, liberatory pedagogy and raises important issues of race and ethnicity for education feminism.

Deanne Bogdan's chapter reaches back to Greene's beginnings for interest in literature and connects education feminism to the important tradition of feminist literary criticism. Bogdan also works from Ellsworth and presents a story of her own teaching. The writings of Sandra Bartky, Robin Morgan, and Shoshana Felman are clearly influential here. The chapter closes the book with a final reminder of the vivacity and diversity that now characterize education feminism.

The Education Feminism Reader is dedicated to the contributors—it is their book after all.[20] Along with many others who presently labor for feminisms' ideas and practices in professional education, they (we) offer exemplars of this work as a beginning for enduring, transformational change. It is, as Adrienne Rich put it, a time for a new claiming.

Notes

1. Adrienne Rich, "Claiming an Education," in *On Lies, Secrets, and Silence* (New York: Norton, 1979), p. 231.

2. See Executive Summary, "How Schools Shortchange Girls," The American Association of University Women Educational Foundation, 1992.

3. It is interesting to note which disciplinary groups and which theorists name themselves as feminists (or as womanists, etc.). For instance, historians often do "women's history."

4. Structuralists historically posited universal elements of human beings and human life, such as forms of language or forms of social organization. Post-structuralists work through these elements as merely enduring and as particular. More on this subse-

quently. See Cleo Cherryholmes, *Power and Criticism* (New York: Teachers College Press, 1988).

5. On the general issue, see Sandra Harding, *The Science Question in Feminism* (Ithaca: Cornell University Press, 1986). In education, see Jennifer Gore, *The Struggle for Pedagogies* (New York: Routledge, 1993).

6. Of course many of us as individuals within education feminism are appreciated, but this does not negate the general discrimination.

7. See Jonathan Kozol, *Savage Inequalities* (New York: Harper Perennial, 1991).

8. These are general *statistics* mentioned often today. Terms such as "at risk" are socially constructed, often by well-intentioned reformers who have not carefully thought through the discrimination embedded in their language usage. None are natural and given, or even historically progressive in my view.

9. See Michael Apple, "Education, Culture, and Class Power: Basil Bernstein and the Neo-Marxist Sociology of Education," *Educational Theory* 42 (2), 127–145.

10. A recent discussion appears in Nel Noddings, *The Challenge to Care in Schools* (New York: Teachers College Press, 1992).

11. See Thomas Popkewitz, *A Political Sociology of Educational Reform* (New York: Teachers College Press, 1991).

12. Stephen Toulmin, *Cosmopolis: The Hidden Agenda of Modernity* (New York: Free Press, 1990).

13. Sandra Lee Bartky, "Letters to the Editor," *APA Proceedings* 65 (7), p. 57, 1992.

14. See Lynda Stone, "What Certain Knowledge Means for Women," in W. Kohli, ed., *Critical Conversations in Philosophy and Education: From Theory to Practice and Back* (New York: Routledge, forthcoming).

15. The classic paper on this subject is from Sherry Ortner: "Is Female to Male as Nature is to Culture?" in M. Rosaldo and L. Lamphere, eds., *Women, Culture, and Society* (Stanford: Stanford University Press, 1974), pp. 67–87; and Evelyn Fox Keller, "Women and Science" in E. Abel and E. Abel, eds., *The Signs Reader: Women, Gender and Scholarship* (Chicago: University of Chicago Press, 1983), pp. 109–122.

16. See Theresa de Lauretis, "Feminist Studies/Critical Studies: Issues, Terms and Contexts," in *Feminist Studies/Critical Studies* (Bloomington: Indiana University Press, 1986), p. 2.

17. An earlier classic study comes from Allison Jaggar, *Feminist Politics and Human Nature* (Totowa, N.J.: Rowman & Allanheld, 1983).

18. See Genevieve Lloyd, *The Man of Reason: "Male" and "Female" in Western Philosophy* (Minneapolis: University of Minnesota Press, 1984) and Chris Weedon, *Feminist Practice and Post-structural Theory* (Oxford: Basil Blackwell, 1987).

19. Thanks to Tom Popkewitz for discussion on this issue. See also Allan Megill, *Prophets of Extremity: Nietzsche, Heidegger, Foucault, and Derrida* (Berkeley: University of California Press, 1985).

20. A special thank you to Gail Boldt for stimulating conversation and careful reading.

PART I

Self and Identity

1

THE LIVED WORLD

Maxine Greene

"The world," writes Merleau-Ponty, "is not what I think but what I live through."[1] He is describing the ways in which human consciousness opens itself to things, the ways in which—as embodied consciousnesses—we are in the world. He speaks of a perceptual reality that underlies our cognitive structures, of a primordial landscape in which we are present to ourselves.

I want to discuss the lived worlds and perceptual realities of women because I am so sharply aware of the degree to which they are obscured by sex and gender roles. I am convinced that the imposition of these roles makes women falsify their sense of themselves. Muriel Rukeyser says something to this effect when, in one of her poems, she writes of "myself, split open, unable to speak, in exile from myself." And a few lines later, "No more masks! No more mythologies!"[2] In "The Laugh of Medusa" Hélène Cixous describes a "unique empire" that has been hidden"[3] and women who "have wandered in circles, confined to the narrow room in which they've been given a deadly brainwashing." I want to point to some of the deformations due to masking and confinement in the hope that they can be repaired. My concern is for the release of individual capacities now suppressed, for the development of free and autonomous personalities. It seems to me that these require an intensified critical awareness of our relation to ourselves and to our culture, a clarified sense of our own realities.

Now it is clear enough that we encounter each other in everyday life by means of roles and patterns of behavior that are habitualized, consciously or unconsciously learned. But what is everyday life? It is important to recall that it constitutes an *interpreted* reality—"interpreted by men," say Berger and Luckmann, "and subjectively meaningful to them as a coherent world."[4] As soon as we become habituated in the use of language, as soon as we begin transmuting perceived shapes and presences into symbolic forms, we become participants in that world. This means that we begin interpreting our experiences with the aid of a "stock of knowledge at hand," recipes made available by the culture for making sense of things and other human beings, for defining our situation as we live.

It is interesting that Berger and Luckmann talk of a "reality interpreted by *men*," because the constructs normally used for mapping and interpreting the common sense world are largely those defined by males. It seems evident that, whenever they were developed, the dominant modes of ordering and categorizing experiences of private as well as public life have been functions of largely male perspectives because, in Western culture, males have been the dominant group, the ones in power. And I include experiences of family life and childbirth as well as those of work, business, politics, and war. Alfred Schutz says that those who are born in any group tend to accept "the ready-made standardized scheme of the cultural pattern handed down . . . by ancestors, teachers, and authorities as an unquestioned and unquestionable guide in all the situations which normally occur within the social world."[5] In other words, the recipes, the interpretations, are treated as wholly trustworthy; they are taken for granted "in the absence of evidence to the contrary." Inevitably, they are internalized by women as well as by men. Once internalized, even such constructs as those having to do with subordination, natural inferiority, and unequally distributed rights are taken for granted. They are objectified, then externalized. They begin to appear as objective characteristics of an objectively existent world.

When Anaïs Nin writes, "My maternal self is in conflict with my creative self," when she says that creativity and femininity seem incompatible, or that acts of independence are likely to be "punished by desertion,"[6] on some level she is reporting such phenomena as *givens*. On some level, she is unable to recall that they have been constituted, that they are part of an *interpreted* reality, that (as Hélène Cixous puts it) "woman has always functioned 'within' the discourse of man."[7] So it is with the fictional Edna Pontellier in Kate Chopin's *The Awakening*. She is listening to her husband moving about his room, "every sound indicating impatience and irritation."

> Another time she would have gone in at his request. She would through habit, have yielded to his desire; not with any sense of submission or obedience to his compelling wishes, but unthinkingly, as we walk, move, sit, stand, go through the daily treadmill of the life which has been portioned out to us.[8]

She accedes "unthinkingly." This means she takes for granted not simply the reality of male domination and conjugal rights but a vision of life as a treadmill, of fate "portioned out" in a fashion that has nothing to do with choice.

These notions are associated with sex roles, not with the sexuality of the woman concerned, not with the body as an "original source of perspective," the means by which subjectivity enters the world. Because they have to do with roles and not perceived realities, they connect with the everyday or common sense realities in which people live most of their lives. They tend, therefore, to overwhelm or to suppress a variety of alternative interpretations and alternative realities—like those of art, or dream, or play. They do so because the conceived world, the constructed world is so frequently at odds with the perceived world; it is difficult, especially for women, to grant to perceived realities the integrity they deserve.

Consider Edna Pontellier again—beginning her life on a Kentucky plantation, grasping her space at first through a bodily situation that involved a sea of grass through which she could run, about which she could feel. As Merleau-Ponty would see it, the smells and colors of that place were "themselves different modalities of (her) co-existence with the world."[9] The distances, the different points in the spaces of the plantation were "relations between those points and a central perspective," the body of the little girl. In any case, this was where Edna came in touch with the world, where she first grasped it in a here-and-now. And this was where, when ten years old, Edna had a fantasy love affair with a cavalry officer and, when threatened by the stern prayers of her Presbyterian father, ran to take refuge in the grass.

Then the social world takes over; Edna marries, begins playing the role of wife, taking on what the author describes as a "fictitious self." Her awakening occurs at the seashore, when she turns away from the Creole mother-women and responds to a flirtatious young man. For the first time she begins "to realize her position in the universe as a human being." More significantly, she is seduced by the voice of the sea, "inviting the soul to wander for a spell in abysses of solitude; to lose itself in mazes of inward contemplation." She confuses the stirring of a long-suppressed sexuality with a hidden authenticity, the emergence of a true self; at length, in despair at abandonment, in fear of possible promiscuity, in defiance of the "soul's slavery" of domesticity, she swims out to sea and drowns. Her suicide is not only due to repression and depression, although it can be explained that way. It is due to the falsification occasioned by the role she is forced to play, given the late nineteenth century moment, her social class, and her husband's demands. It is, in part, a crisis of meaningfulness: she has no way of grounding what she feels; she has no way of confronting her own relationship to the world.

Merleau-Ponty says, "The experience of perception is our presence at the moment when things, truths, values are constituted for us." He writes that "Perception is a nascent logos; that it teaches us, outside all dogmatism, the true conditions of objectivity itself, that it summons us to the tasks of knowledge and action."[10] It is not simply that perceptual experience is in some sense primordial, that it refers to our original landscapes and the background of our lived lives. Nor is it simply that perception remains foundational to a developing rationality. Perceptual reality ought always to be considered one of the multiple realities available to us: a recognizable set of experiences, once they are reflected back upon, characterized by a distinctive mode of attention, one too many people have repressed or refused.

I believe that the ability to come in touch with "the moment when things, truths, values are constituted for us" permits us to break some of the hold of the taken-for-granted when it comes to the already constituted categories by which we interpret the world. In the case of Edna Pontellier, an ability to remain grounded in her earliest relations to her surroundings might have given her some awareness of the way she had built up a meaningful world. It might have kept her in touch with her own perspective, her own vantage point, and allowed her to resist the arbitrariness and the distortions of some of the roles she was forced to play. The spiritualization of women like Edna, the infantilization, the mystification that convinced her of inevitability; all these might have been allayed if she had been somehow able to realize that she lived in a constructed reality, that it was possible to choose along with others, possible even to transcend.

My sense of the oppressiveness of gender roles does not move me to think about recovering a "natural," spontaneous, untrammelled self uncorrupted by the world. I cannot conceive Edna Pontellier or Anaïs Nin or anyone else existing as a human being apart from social relations and social roles. My point has to do with what William James calls the "sense of our own reality, that sense of our own life which we at every moment possess." He talks about the things that have "intimate and continuous connection" with our lives, things whose reality we do not doubt. And he says that the world of those living realities becomes the "hook from which the rest dangles, the absolute support."[11] Without a sense of those realities, we are likely to lose touch with our own projects, to become "invisible" in Ralph Ellison's sense, to think of ourselves as others define us, not as we create ourselves.

If we can be present to ourselves and look through perspectives rooted in our own reality, we may be in a position to confront arbitrariness and oppression. The alternative may be the narcissism, egotism, touchiness, and the rest that Simone de Beauvoir attributes to powerlessness. Talking about the woman who is shut up in the kitchen or boudoir, de Beauvoir says that since she is deprived "of all possibility of concrete communication with others," she experiences no solidarity. "She could hardly be expected, then, to transcend herself toward the general welfare. She stays obstinately within the one realm that is familiar to her, where she can control things and in the midst of which she enjoys a precarious sovereignty." Such a woman is seldom able to grasp the masculine universe, "which she respects from afar, without daring to venture into it." She develops a magical conception of reality that she projects into the male world; "the course of events seems to her to be inevitable."[12]

I think of the narrator of Grace Paley's story, "The Used-Boy Raisers," listening to her present husband and her ex-husband (whom she names "Pallid" and "Livid") battling over religion. She is drawn into their quarrel when they remind her that she is Jewish; she tells them that she believes in the Diaspora and is against Israel "on technical grounds" because she objects to the Jews being like every other temporal nationality. She says:

> Jews have one hope only—to remain a remnant in the basement of world affairs—no, I mean something else—a splinter in the toe of civilizations, a victim to aggravate the conscience.
> Livid and Pallid were astonished at my outburst, since I rarely express my opinion on any serious matter but only live out my destiny, which is to be, until my expiration date, laughingly the servant of man.[13]

It may be that she is associating her own plight as a woman with what she sees as the proper destiny of the Jews, but what is striking is the presentation of a woman who stays obstinately in her own realm, who submits to what she thinks of as her destiny. She says marriage "just ties a man down"; she organizes the "greedy day" with its tasks of motherhood and domesticity; she watches her husbands from a distance as they move off "on paths which are not my concern."

There are others, so many others, in and out of literature. The difficulty is (as it was for Edna and for Nora in *The Doll's House*) that their justifications are always in the hands of others. They keep waiting for male approval, male gratitude, male support. Without grounding, without a sense of themselves, they live, at best, in a kind of negation. They are not self-conscious enough, self-reflective enough, sisterly enough to undo the work of socialization; their personal development is necessarily frustrated; they are submerged in their roles.

Again, if women are in touch with themselves and in concrete communication with others, they have a ground against which to consider the mystifications that work on them, the inequities that prevail—even today in this presumably liberated time. I believe that it is necessary to look into the darkness, into the terrible blankness that creeps over so many women's lives, into the wells of victimization and powerlessness.

I am never surprised, for some reason, to discover in many books written by women that the death of a female heroine creates no stir in the universe. Consider Edna Pontellier's suicide. There is no sense of recognition, not even a funeral scene. Think of Lily Bart's suicide in *The House of Mirth*. There is a slight, sad stirring on Selden's part; a small leaf has fallen from a tree. Consider *To the Lighthouse* and the death of Mrs. Ramsay, who is the glowing, ambivalent center of the first section of the book. The second, called "Time Passes," deals with dark nights, an empty house, the winds, and the waves. Suddenly, parenthetically, there is the following sentence: "Mr. Ramsey, stumbling along a passage one dark morning, stretched his arms out, but Mrs. Ramsey having died rather suddenly the night before, his arms, though stretched out, remained empty."[14]

I am not saying that all women's deaths go unnoticed in women's novels (although I would note that there is undoubtedly more suicide and madness in women's literature than in men's). I am suggesting that there is no female version of Hamlet in women's literature, no one telling a friend like Horatio to absent herself from felicity a while "to tell my story." Nor, in women's literature, is there normally an Ishmael who escapes to tell, to give the tragedy some meaning under the sky. I suspect that is what Virginia Woolf had in mind when she concocted her fiction about Shakespeare's sister. Contemplating a woman of the sixteenth century with the capacity to render the human condition in a play, Woolf writes that any such woman "would certainly have gone crazed, shot herself, or ended her days in some lonely cottage outside the village, half witch, half wizard, feared and mocked at."[15] Perhaps this is part of our perceived reality too.

But there are other ills, more remediable ills, to be confronted by the woman grounded enough to see. Listen to Virginia Woolf again, this time comparing the difficulties faced by a woman writer with those plaguing men:

> The indifference of the world which Keats and Flaubert and other men of genius have found so hard to bear was in her case not indifference but hostility. The world did not say to her as it said to them, Write if you choose; it makes no difference to me. The world said with a guffaw, Write? What's the good of your writing? Here the psychologists . . . might come to our help, I thought, looking again at the blank spaces on the shelves. For surely it is time that the effect of discouragement on the mind of the artist should be measured, as I have seen a dairy company measure the effect of ordinary milk and Grade A milk upon the body of the rat.[16]

To change the universe of discourse for an instant, listen to Catharine R. Stimpson talking about National Endowment for the Arts grants to men and women:

> If census data show 66 percent of musicians are male, 88 percent of individual NEA grants are to men. On the other hand, if census data show 63 percent of painters and sculptors are male, they got but 60 percent of the individual grants. Of the three sample years, 1972 was the best for women as a whole, which may show an effect of the women's movement and the new consciousness about sex roles. In 1970, women received just under 15 percent of the individual awards, in 1968 about 18 percent. A preliminary conclusion that might be drawn is that NEA has not only reflected but sustained a masculinized ideology of the working artist. Microcosm may nuture macrocosm.[17]

And then Stimpson goes on to talk about the way male perspectives have dominated the arts and distorted "our visions of sex and gender." This is simply because men and women have dissimilar experiences that affect their perceptions of themselves and of each other; until women are given full access to the arts, their range will be limited, their complexities less than they should be. Again, this is part of what has to be confronted, not as part of a "given" and unchangeable reality, but as a problematic application of gender categories, at odds with our sense of what is real.

Again, I am arguing for an intensified awareness of women's own realities, the shape of their own lived worlds. Not only might this make possible a clear perception of the arbitrariness, the absurdity (as well as the inequity) involved in genderizing such fields as the arts, the sciences, and yes, school administration. It might also provoke women into confrontations of their authentic corporeal selves. As is well known, women writers—and, particularly, feminist writers—have diversified approaches to the biosocial nature of women. Please note, I am not now speaking of sex or gender roles; I am speaking of sexuality, the distinctiveness of the body that carries subjectivity into the world. As I do so, I want to try to separate what we think about it from the manifold stereotypes, those that associate it with biological destiny, with evil, with the spiritual, the passive, or the irrational. And, certainly, I want to distinguish it from the kind of male view exemplified by Harry Wilborne in William Faulkner's *The Wild Palms.* In that book, Harry muses "on the efficiency of women in the mechanics, the domiciling of cohabitation. Not thrift, not husbandry, something far beyond that, who (the entire race of them) employed with infallible instinct, a completely uncerebrated rapport for the type and nature of male partner and situation."[18]

Alice Rossi, writing in *Daedalus,* uses a "biosocial perspective" through which to consider some of the new egalitarian ideologies that deny innate sex differences and demand that fathers play equal roles when it comes to child care. Making the point that "Sex is an invariant ascription from birth to death," she goes on to talk about the cultural determinists among social scientists and activists, who (she says) "confuse equality with identity and diversity with inequality." Diversity, she writes, "is a biological fact, while equality is a political, ethical, and social precept."[19]

It is not necessary to recapitulate Rossi's interesting and complex argument to make the point that she, partly on the grounds of studies in endocrinology and physiology, argues for the central place of women in parenting. She talks about innate predispositions on the part of mothers to relate intensely to their infants, about the influence upon women of hormonal cyclicity, pregnancy, and birth. At no time does she recommend that all women have children although she does recommend that women who choose to have children avoid giving them over to communal child-rearing centers, where youngsters may become "neglected, joyless creatures." And she does acknowledge the social deprivation of many women and argue for social support systems of many kinds.

I bring up this article not merely for its intrinsic importance; I bring it up because it seems to me to relate to the themes I have been trying to explore. The confusion Rossi talks about—the confusion of diversity with equality—is a function of the general tendency to permit cultural factors to overwhelm the lived world. Once women come in touch not only with the lived world but with their primordial landscapes and with their corporeal involvements, they cannot avoid coming in touch with their sexuality as well. After all, women's distinctiveness as sexual beings affects the ways in which they grasp the surrounding world; it influences the modalities of their "co-existence" with that world. Domination by our sex *roles*, I am convinced, is what moves so many women to deny or belittle or lament their sexual reality. Current calls for unisexism are heard in the domain of social reality; they have much the same effect as traditional expressions of shame and guilt. The consequence is, very often, that attention is diverted from significant questions of family polity and child care policy to misplaced calls for equity. Nothing I have said—and nothing Alice Rossi has said—is meant to suggest that one way of life is best for all women everywhere; nor has anything been said to suggest that women who choose to bear children should forever give up ideas of working or composing or becoming Shakespeare's sisters. Again, it is a matter of grounding, of rooting choices in perceived realities, and in what women grasp as their own lived worlds.

There is another modern novel that deals with some of this, albeit in a mysterious and troubling way: *Surfacing*, by the Canadian writer, Margaret Atwood. The heroine is Canadian, returning home to the wilderness where she grew up from a long sojourn in the United States. In search of her lost father, she is accompanied by three sophisticated, urban friends, but she is absorbed in the recovery of her own past, her own landscape, as she is in struggling against all labels, falsifications, and, finally, all enclosures. An abortion she has had signifies victimization to her; American hunters on the lake signify male violation and destruction; ordinary language signifies deformation. She dreams of rejecting passivity by having a baby herself "squatting on old newspapers in a corner alone; or on leaves, dry leaves, a heap of them." Alone on her island, she slips out of her clothes, out of human habitation, into inchoateness, a pantheist reality—what she thinks of as her own space, her ritual plunge. And finally:

> This above all, to refuse to be a victim. Unless I can do that I can do nothing. I have to recant, to give up the old belief that I am powerless and because of it nothing I can do will ever hurt anyone. A lie which was always more disastrous than the truth would have been. The word games, the winning and losing games are finished; at the moment there are no others but they will have to be invented, withdrawing is no longer possible and the alternative is death. I drop the blanket on the floor and go into my dismantled room. My spare clothes are here, knife slashes in them, but I can still wear them. I dress, clumsily, unfamiliar with buttons; I reenter my own time.[20]

Her lover appears on the shore, "a mediator, an ambassador, offering me something: captivity in any of its forms, a new freedom?" She knows she must return to words and houses and that they may well fail again. And the only way back she can find is through a freely chosen pregnancy.

This is extreme, of course. The reality explored may be the reality of psychosis; again, salvation lies somewhere in the past, in a retracing of the trail. But the dissonance between the narrator's perceived landscape and the taken-for-granted world of gender roles and power is brutally clear. What happens when ordinary barriers are breached, accepted forms destroyed? If alternative constructs are not devised, madness may be the consequence. Where is the freedom that is not linked to manipulative power? How do we go about remaking the constituted world?

Catharine Stimpson talks about a need for "a compensatory consciousness about sex, gender, and culture," and a recovery of women's contributions to the arts of the past. Carol Gould talks of the importance of demystification and "the elimination of . . . those illusions that bind us to exploitation."[21] Virginia Woolf talks of living "in the presence of reality" and having a "room of one's own." It is clear that the interest in socialization, in sex-typing, and in role differentiation has led to notable discoveries. We understand more than we ever have about what has frustrated the self-identification of women, what has prevented free choosing in an open world. Many of the inquiries have had the effect of moving certain women to a reexamination of their own presuppositions, their own roles. There has been—and there must be—an increasing effort to transform teaching practice, to revise teaching materials, and to invent new approaches to work and play.

I believe all this must be supplemented by the kind of emancipatory thinking that enables women to confront the ways in which they have constructed their social reality and to regain touch with their lived worlds. Like Virginia Woolf, I believe in the power of imaginative literature, of novels that allow one to see "more intensely afterwards," that make the world seem "bared of its covering and given an intenser life."[22] A good work of fiction, writes Sartre, is an "exigence and a gift"; it is also an act of faith.

> And if I am given this world with its injustices, it is not so that I might contemplate them coldly, but that I might animate them with my indignation, that I might disclose them with their nature as injustices, that is, as abuses to be suppressed. Thus, the writer's universe will only reveal itself in all its depth to the examination, the admiration, and the indignation of the reader.[23]

To read Muriel Rukeyser or Grace Paley or Virginia Woolf is to be given a gift, which we can receive if we are attentive, if we are willing to bracket our everydayness, conformity, and fear. Moreover, as Sartre also says, the work of art is an act of confidence in human freedom. Freedom is the power of vision and the power to choose. It involves the capacity to assess situations in such a way that lacks can be defined, openings identified, and possibilities revealed. It is realized only when action is taken to repair the lacks, to move through the openings, to try to pursue real possibilities. One of the strengths of imaginative literature is that it can enable women to assume new standpoints on what they take for granted, to animate certain constructs with their indignation, so that they can see them as sources of the injustice that plagues them, see them, not as givens, but as constituted by human beings and changeable by human beings. The imaginative leap can lead to the leap that is *praxis,* the effort to remake and transcend.

This is another dimension of the effort to define sexual equality in the modern age. The aesthetic and the imaginative can never substitute for social, scientific, or biosocial inquiry, although they may provoke new modes of inquiry because of the manner in which imaginative forms present a reality ordinarily obscured. Without articulation, without expression, the perceived world is in some way nullified; until given significant form, it holds no significance except in the prereflective domain. That is why literature may provide a resource, an inroad into a province of meaning that is associated not so much with the "reality interpreted by men and subjectively meaningful to them," but with the world of the "nascent logos," the world women live. And considering that world, I choose to end with more lines from Muriel Rukeyser, these from "Kathe Kollwitz":

What would happen if one woman told the truth
about her life?
The world could split open.[24]

Notes

1. Maurice Merleau-Ponty, *Phenomenology of Perception* (London: Routledge & Kegan Paul, 1967), pp. xvi, xvii.

2. Muriel Rukeyser, "The Poem as Mask," in *by a Woman writt.* ed. Joan Goulianos (Indianapolis: Bobbs-Merrill, 1973), p. 379.

3. Hélène Cixous, "The Laugh of Medusa," *Signs,* Summer 1976, Vol. 1, No. 4, p. 876.

4. Peter L. Berger and Thomas Luckmann, *The Social Construction of Reality* (Garden City, N.Y.: Anchor Books, Doubleday and Co., 1967), p. 19.

5. Alfred Schutz, *Studies in Social Theory,* Collected Papers II, ed. Arvid Brodersen (The Hague: Martinus Nijhoff, 1964), p. 22.

6. Anaïs Nin, *The Diary of Anaïs Nin,* Vol. III, 1939–44, Jan. 1943, Goulianos, ed., *op. cit.,* p. 303.

7. Hélène Cixous, in Goulianos, ed., *op. cit.,* p. 887.

8. Kate Chopin, *The Awakening* (New York: Capricorn Books, 1964), p. 79.

9. Merleau-Ponty, *The Primacy of Perception* (Evanston: Northwestern University Press, 1964), p. 5.

10. Ibid., p. 25.

11. William James, *Principles of Psychology,* Vol. II (New York: Henry Holt, 1950), p. 297.

12. Simone de Beauvoir, *The Second Sex* (New York: Alfred A. Knopf, 1957), pp. 450–451.

13. Grace Paley, "The Used-Boy Raisers," *The Little Disturbances of Man* (New York: Meridian Fiction, 1960), p. 132.

14. Virginia Woolf, *To the Lighthouse* (London: J. M. Dent, Everyman's Library, 1962), p. 149.

15. Woolf, *A Room of One's Own* (New York: Harcourt, Brace, & World, 1957), p. 51.

16. Ibid., p. 54.

17. Catharine R. Stimpson, "Sex, Gender, and American Culture," in *Women and Men: Changing Roles, Relationships and Perceptions,* ed. Libby A. Cater, Anne Firor Scott, and Wendy Martyna (New York: Praeger Publishers, 1977), pp. 216, 220.

18. William Faulkner, *The Wild Palms* (New York: New American Library, Signet Modern Classics, 1968), p. 53.

19. Alice S. Rossi, "A Biosocial Perspective on Parenting," *Daedalus,* Spring 1977, p. 2.

20. Margaret Atwood, *Surfacing* (New York: Popular Library, 1972) pp. 222–223.

21. Carol C. Gould, "Philosophy of Liberation and the Liberation of Philosophy," in *Women and Philosophy: Toward a Theory of Liberation,* ed. Carol C. Gould and Marx W. Wartofsky (New York: Capricorn Books, 1976), p. 38.

22. Woolf, *op. cit.,* p. 114.

23. Jean-Paul Sartre, *Literature and Existentialism* (New York: Citadel Press, 1965), pp. 62–63.

24. Rukeyser, "Kathe Kollwitz," in Goulianos, ed., *op. cit.,* p. 377.

2

WOMAN'S PLACE IN MAN'S LIFE CYCLE

Carol Gilligan

In the second act of *The Cherry Orchard,* Lopakhin, the young merchant, describes his life of hard work and success. Failing to convince Madame Ranevskaya to cut down the cherry orchard to save her estate, he will go on, in the next act, to buy it himself. He is the self-made man, who, in purchasing "the estate where grandfather and father were slaves," seeks to eradicate the "awkward, unhappy life" of the past, replacing the cherry orchard with summer cottages where coming generations "will see a new life" (Act III). Elaborating this developmental vision, he describes the image of man that underlies and supports this activity: "At times when I can't go to sleep, I think: Lord, thou gavest us immense forests, unbounded fields and the widest horizons, and living in the midst of them we should indeed be giants." At which point, Madame Ranevskaya interrupts him, saying, "You feel the need for giants—They are good only in fairy tales, anywhere else they only frighten us" (Act II).

Conceptions of the life cycle represent attempts to order and make coherent the unfolding experiences and perceptions, the changing wishes and realities of everyday life. But the truth of such conceptions depends in part on the position of the observer. The brief excerpt from Chekhov's play (1904/1956) suggests that when the observer is a woman, the truth may be of a different sort. This discrepancy in judgment between men and women is the center of my consideration.

This essay traces the extent to which psychological theories of human development, theories that have informed both educational philosophy and classroom practice, have enshrined a view of human life similar to Lopahkin's while dismissing the ironic commentary in which Chekhov embeds this view. The specific issue I address is that of sex differences, and my focus is on the observation and assessment of sex differences by life-cycle theorists. In talking about sex differences, however, I risk the criticism that such generalization invariably invites. As Virginia Woolf said, when embarking on a similar endeavor: "When a subject is highly controversial—and any question about sex is that—one cannot hope to tell the truth. One can only show how one came to hold whatever opinion one does hold" (1929, p. 4).

At a time when efforts are being made to eradicate discrimination between the sexes in the search for equality and justice, the differences between the sexes are being rediscovered in the social sciences. This discovery occurs when theories formerly considered to be sexually neutral in their scientific objectivity are found instead to reflect a consistent observational and evaluative bias. Then the presumed neutrality of science, like that of language itself, gives way to the recognition that the categories of knowledge are human constructions. The fascination with point of view and the corresponding recognition of the relativity of truth that has informed the fiction of the twentieth century begin to infuse our scientific understanding as well when we begin to notice how accustomed we have become to seeing life through men's eyes.

A recent discovery of this sort pertains to the apparently innocent classic by Strunk and White (1959), *The Elements of Style*. The Supreme Court ruling on the subject of discrimination in classroom texts led one teacher of English to notice that the elementary rules of English usage were being taught through examples that counterposed the birth of Napoleon, the writings of Coleridge, and statements such as "He was an interesting talker, a man who had traveled all over the world and lived in half a dozen countries" (p. 7) with "Well, Susan, this is a fine mess you are in" (p. 3) or, less drastically, "He saw a woman, accompanied by two children, walking slowly down the road" (p. 8).

Psychological theorists have fallen as innocently as Strunk and White into the same observational bias. Implicitly adopting the male life as the norm, they have tried to fashion women out of a masculine cloth. It all goes back, of course, to Adam and Eve, a story that shows, among other things, that, if you make a woman out of a man you are bound to get into trouble. In the life cycle, as in the Garden of Eden, it is the woman who has been the deviant.

The penchant of developmental theorists to project a masculine image, and one that appears frightening to women, goes back at least to Freud (1905/1961), who built his theory of psychosexual development around the experiences of the male child that culminate in the Oedipus complex. In the 1920s, Freud struggled to resolve the contradictions posed for his theory by the different configuration of female sexuality and the different dynamics of the young girl's early family relationships. After trying to fit women into his masculine conception, seeing them as envying that which they missed, he came instead to acknowledge, in the strength and persistence of women's pre-Oedipal attachments to their mothers, a developmental difference. However, he considered this difference in women's development to be responsible for what he saw as women's developmental failure.

Deprived by nature of the impetus for a clear-cut Oedipal resolution, women's superego, the heir to the Oedipus complex, consequently was compromised. It was never, Freud observed, "so inexorable, so impersonal, so independent of its emotional origins as we require it to be in men" (1925/1961, p. 257). From this observation of difference, "that for women the level of what is ethically normal is different from what it is in men" (p. 257), Freud concluded that "women have less sense of justice than men, that they are less ready to submit to the great exigencies of life, that they are more often influenced in their judgments by feelings of affection and hostility" (pp. 257–258).

Chodorow (1974, 1978) addresses this evaluative bias in the assessment of sex differences in her attempt to account for "the reproduction within each generation of certain general and nearly universal differences that characterize masculine and feminine personality and roles" (1974, p. 43). Writing from a psychoanalytic perspective, she attributes these continuing differences between the sexes not to anatomy but rather to "the fact that women, universally, are largely responsible for early child care and for (at least) later female socialization" (1974, p. 43). Because this early social environment differs from, and is experienced differently by, male and female children, basic sex differences recur in personality development. As a result, "in any given society, feminine personality comes to define itself in relation and connection to other people more than masculine personality does. (In psychoanalytic terms, women are less individuated than men; they have more flexible ego boundaries)" (1974, p. 44).

In her analysis, Chodorow relies primarily on Stoller's research on the development of gender identity and gender-identity disturbances. Stoller's work indicates that male and female identity, the unchanging core of personality formation, is "with rare exception firmly and irreversibly established for both sexes by the time a child is around three" (Chodorow, 1978, p. 150). Given that for both sexes the primary caretaker in the first three years of life is typically female, the interpersonal dynamics of gender identity formation are different for boys and girls. Female identity formation takes place in a context of ongoing relationship as "mothers tend to experience their daughters as more like, and continuous with, themselves. Correspondingly, girls tend to remain part of the dyadic primary mother-child relationship itself. This means that a girl continues to experience herself as involved in issues of merging and separation, and in an attachment characterized by primary identification and the fusion of identification and object choice" (1978, p. 166).

In contrast, "mothers experience their sons as a male opposite" and, as a result, "boys are more likely to have been pushed out of the preoedipal relationship and to have had to curtail their primary love and sense of empathic tie with their mother" (1978, p. 166). Consequently, boys' development entails a "more emphatic individuation and a more defensive firming of ego boundaries." For boys, but not for girls, "issues of differentiation have become intertwined with sexual issues" (1978, p. 167).

Thus Chodorow refutes the masculine bias of psychoanalytic theory, claiming that the existence of sex differences in the early experiences of individuation and relationship "does not mean that women have 'weaker ego boundaries' than men or are more prone to psychosis" (1978, p. 167). What it means instead is that "the earliest mode of individuation, the primary construction of the ego and its inner object-world, the earliest conflicts and the earliest unconscious definitions of self, the earliest threats to individuation, and the earliest anxieties that call up defenses, all differ for boys and girls because of differences in the character of the early mother-child relationship for each" (1978, p. 167). Because of these differences, "girls emerge from this period with a basis for 'empathy' built into their primary definition of self in a way that boys do not" (1978, p. 167). Chodorow thus replaces Freud's negative and derivative description of female psychology with a more positive and direct account of her own:

> Girls emerge with a stronger basis for experiencing another's needs and feelings as one's own (or of thinking that one is so experiencing another's needs and feelings). Furthermore, girls do not define themselves in terms of the denial of preoedipal relational modes to the same extent as do boys. Therefore, regression to these modes tends not to feel as much a basic threat to their ego. From very early, then, because they are parented by a person of the same gender . . . girls come to experience themselves as less differentiated than boys, as more continuous with and related to the

external object-world, and as differently oriented to their inner object-world as well. (1978, p. 167).

Consequently, "issues of dependency, in particular, are handled and experienced differently by men and women" (Chodorow, 1974, p. 44). For boys and men, separation and individuation are critically tied to gender identity since separation from the mother is essential for the development of masculinity. "For girls and women, by contrast, issues of femininity or feminine identity are not problematic in the same way" (1974, p. 44); they do not depend on the achievement of separation from the mother or on the progress of individuation. Since, in Chodorow's analysis, masculinity is defined through separation while femininity is defined through attachment, male gender identity will be threatened by intimacy, while female gender identity will be threatened by individuation. Thus males will tend to have difficulty with relationships, while females will tend to have problems with separation. The quality of embeddedness in social interaction and personal relationships that characterizes women's lives in contrast to men's, however, becomes not only a descriptive difference but also a developmental liability when the milestones of childhood and adolescent development are described by markers of increasing separation. Then women's failure to separate becomes by definition a failure to develop.

The sex differences in personality formation that Chodorow delineates in her analysis of early childhood relationships, as well as the bias she points out in the evaluation of these differences, reappear in the middle childhood years in the studies of children's games. Children's games have been considered by Mead (1934) and Piaget (1932/1965) as the crucible of social development during the school years. In games children learn to take the role of the other and come to see themselves through another's eyes. In games they learn respect for rules and come to understand the ways rules can be made and changed.

Lever (1976), considering the peer group to be the agent of socialization during the elementary school years and play to be a major activity of socialization at that time, set out to discover whether there were sex differences in the games that children play. Studying 181 fifth-grade, white middle-class, Connecticut children, ages 10 and 11, she observed the organization and structure of their playtime activities. She watched the children as they played during the school recess, lunch, and in physical education class, and, in addition, kept diaries of their accounts as to how they spent their out-of-school time.

From this study, Lever reports the following sex differences: boys play more out-of-doors than girls do; boys often play in large and age-heterogeneous groups; they play competitive games more often than girls do, and their games last longer than girl's games (Lever, 1976). The last is in some ways the most interesting finding. Boys' games appeared to last longer not only because they required a higher level of skill and were thus less likely to become boring, but also because when disputes arose in the course of a game, the boys were able to resolve the disputes more effectively than the girls: "During the course of this study, boys were seen quarrelling all the time, but not once was a game terminated because of a quarrel and no game was interrupted for more than seven minutes. In the gravest debates, the final word was always to 'repeat the play,' generally followed by a chorus of 'cheater's proof' " (1976, p. 482). In fact, it seemed that the boys enjoyed the legal debates as much as they did the game itself, and even marginal players of lesser size or skill participated equally in these recurrent squabbles. In contrast, the eruption of disputes among girls tended to end the game.

Thus Lever extends and corroborates the observations reported by Piaget (1932/1965) in his naturalistic study of the rules of the game, where he found boys becoming increasingly fascinated with the legal elaboration of rules and the development of fair procedures for adjudicating conflicts, a fascination that, he noted, did not hold for girls. Girls, Piaget observed, had a more "pragmatic" attitude toward rules, "regarding a rule as good as long as the game repaid it" (1932/1965, p. 83). As a result, he considered girls to be more tolerant in their attitudes toward rules, more willing to make exceptions, and more easily reconciled to innovations. However, and presumably as a result, he concluded that the legal sense which he considered essential to moral development "is far less developed in little girls than in boys" (1932/1965, p. 77).

This same bias that led Piaget to equate male development with child development also colors Lever's work. The assumption that shapes her discussion of results is that the male model is the better one. It seems, in any case, more adaptive since as Lever points out it fits the requirements Riesman (1961) describes for success in modern corporate life. In contrast, the sensitivity and care for the feelings of others that girls develop through their primarily dyadic play relationships have little market value and can even impede professional success. Lever clearly implies that, given the realities of adult life, if a girl does not want to be dependent on men, she will have to learn to play like a boy.

Since Piaget argues that children learn the respect for rules necessary for moral development by playing rule-bound games, and Kohlberg (1971) adds that these lessons are most effectively learned through the opportunities for role-taking that arise in the course of resolving disputes, the moral lessons inherent in girls' play appear to be fewer than for boys. Traditional girls' games like jump rope and hopscotch are turn-taking games where competition is indirect in that one person's success does not necessarily signify another's failure. Consequently, disputes requiring adjudication are less likely to occur. In fact, most of the girls whom Lever interviewed claimed that when a quarrel broke out, they ended the game. Rather than elaborating a system of rules for resolving disputes, girls directed their efforts instead toward sustaining affective ties.

Lever concludes that from the games they play boys learn both independence and the organizational skills necessary for coordinating the activities of large and diverse groups of people. By participating in controlled and socially approved competitive situations, they learn to deal with competition in a relatively forthright manner—to play with their enemies and compete with their friends, all in accordance with the rules of the game. In contrast, girls' play tends to occur in smaller, more intimate groups, often the best-friend dyad, and in private places. This play replicates the social pattern of primary human relationships in that its organization is more cooperative and points less toward learning to take the role of the generalized other than it does toward the development of the empathy and sensitivity necessary for taking the role of the particular other.

Chodorow's analysis of sex differences in personality formation in early childhood is thus extended by Lever's observations of sex differences in the play activities of middle childhood. Together these accounts suggest that boys and girls arrive at puberty with a different interpersonal orientation and a different range of social experiences. While Sullivan (1953), tracing the sequence of male development, posits the experience of a close same-sex friendship in preadolescence as necessary for the subsequent integration of sexuality and intimacy, no corresponding account is available to describe girls' development at this critical juncture. Instead, since adolescence is considered a crucial time for separation and individuation, the period of "the second individuation process" (Blos, 1967), it has been in adolescence that female development has appeared most divergent and thus most problematic.

"Puberty," Freud said, "which brings about so great an accession of libido in boys, is marked in girls by a fresh wave of repression" (1905/1961, p. 220) necessary for the transformation of the young girls' "masculine sexuality" into the "specifically feminine" sexuality of her adulthood. Freud posits this transformation on the girl's acknowledgement and acceptance of "the fact of her castration." In his account puberty brings for girls a new awareness of "the wound to her narcissism" and leads her to develop, "like a scar, a sense of inferiority" (Freud, 1925/1961, p. 253). Since adolescence is, in Erikson's expansion of Freud's psychoanalytic account, the time when the ego takes on an identity that confirms the individual in relation to society, the girl arrives at this juncture in development either psychologically at risk or with a different agenda.

The problem that female adolescence presents for psychologists of human development is apparent in Erikson's account. Erikson (1950) charts eight stages of psychosocial development, in which adolescence is the fifth. The task of this stage is to forge a coherent sense of self, to verify an identity that can span the discontinuity of puberty and make possible the adult capacity to love and to work. The preparation for the successful resolution of the adolescent identity crisis is delineated in Erikson's description of the preceding four stages. If in infancy the initial crisis of trust versus mistrust generates enough hope to sustain the child through the arduous life cycle that lies ahead, the task at hand clearly becomes one of individuation. Erikson's second stage centers on the crisis of autonomy versus shame and doubt, the walking child's emerging sense of separateness and agency. From there, development goes on to the crisis of initiative versus guilt, successful resolution of which represents a further move in the direction of autonomy. Next, following the inevitable disappointment of the magical wishes of the Oedipal period, the child realizes with respect to his parents that to beat them he must first join them and learn to do what they do so well. Thus in the middle childhood years, development comes to hinge on the crisis of industry versus inferiority, as the demonstration of competence becomes critical to the child's developing self-esteem. This is the time when children strive to learn and master the technology of their culture in order to recognize themselves and be recognized as capable of becoming adults. Next comes adolescence, the celebration of the autonomous, initiating, industrious self through the forging of an identity based on an ideology that can support and justify adult commitments. But about whom is Erikson talking?

Once again it turns out to be the male child—the coming generation of men like George Bernard Shaw, William James, Martin Luther, and Mahatma Gandhi—who provides Erikson with his most vivid illustrations. For the women, Erikson (1968)) says, the sequence is a bit different. She holds her identity in abeyance as she prepares to attract the man by whose name she will be known, by whose status she will be defined, the man who will rescue her from emptiness and loneliness by filling "the inner space" (Erickson, 1968). While for men, identity precedes intimacy and generativity in the optimal cycle of human separation and attachment, for women these tasks seem instead to be fused. Intimacy precedes, or rather goes along with, identity as the female comes to know herself as she is known, through her relationship with others.

Two things are essential to note at this point. The first is that despite Erikson's observation of sex differences, his chart of life-cycle stages remains unchanged: identity continues to precede intimacy as the male diagonal continues to define his life-cycle conception. The second is that in the male life cycle there is little preparation for the intimacy of the first adult stage. Only the initial stage of trust versus mistrust suggests the type of mutuality that Erikson means by intimacy and generativity and Freud by genitality: The rest is separateness, with the result that development itself comes to be identified with separation and attachments appear as developmental impediments, as we have repeatedly found to be the case in the assessment of women.

Erikson's description of male identity as forged in relation to the world and of female identity as awakened in a relationship of intimacy with another person, however controversial, is hardly new. In Bettelheim's discussion of fairy tales in *The Uses of Enchantment* (1976), an identical portrayal appears. While Bettelheim argues, in refutation of those critics who see in fairy tales a sexist literature, that opposite models exist and could readily be found, nevertheless the ones upon which he focuses his discussion of adolescence conform to the pattern we have begun to observe.

The dynamics of male adolescence are illustrated archetypically by the conflict between father and son in "The Three Languages" (Bettelheim, 1976). Here a son, considered hopelessly stupid by his father, is given one last chance at education and sent for a year to study with a famous master. But when he returns, all he has learned is "what the dogs bark" (1976, p. 97). After two further attempts of this sort, the father gives up in disgust and orders his servants to take the child into the forest and kill him. The servants, however, those perpetual rescuers of disowned and abandoned children, take pity on the child and decide simply to leave him in the forest. From there, his wanderings take him to a land beset by furious dogs whose barking permits nobody to rest and who periodically devour one of the inhabitants. Now it turns out that our hero has learned just the right thing: he can talk with the dogs and is able to quiet them thus restoring peace to the land . The other knowledge he acquires serves him equally well, and he emerges triumphant from his adolescent confrontation with his father, a giant of the life-cycle conception.

In contrast, the dynamics of female adolescence are depicted through the telling of a very different story. In the world of the fairy tale, the girl's first bleeding is followed by a period of intense passivity in which nothing seems to be happening. Yet in the deep sleep of Snow White and Sleeping Beauty, Bettelheim sees that inner concentration that he considers to be the necessary counterpart to the activity of adventure. The adolescent heroines awaken from their sleep not to conquer the world but to marry the prince. Their feminine identity is inwardly and interpersonally defined. As in Erikson's observation, for women, identity and intimacy are more intricately conjoined. The sex differences depicted in the world of the fairy tales, like the fantasy of the woman warrior in Maxine Hong Kingston's (1977)' recent autobiographical novel (which in turn echoes the old stories of Troilus and Cressida and Tancred and Chlorinda) indicate repeatedly that active adventure is a male activity, and if women are to embark on such endeavors, they must at least dress like men.

These observations about sex difference support the conclusion reached by McClelland that "sex role turns out to be one of the most important determinants of human behavior. Psychologists have found sex differences in their studies from the moment they started doing empirical research" (1975, p. 81). But since it is difficult to say "different" without saying "better" or "worse," and since there is a tendency to construct a single scale of measurement, and since that scale has been derived and standardized on the basis of men's observations and interpretations of research data predominantly or exclusively drawn from studies of males, psychologists have tended, in McClelland's words, "to regard male behavior as the 'norm' and female behavior as some kind of deviation from that norm" (1975, p. 81). Thus when women do not conform to the standards of psychological expectation, the conclusion has generally been that something is wrong with the women.

What Horner (1972) found to be wrong with women was the anxiety they showed about competitive achievement. From the beginning, research on human motivation using the Thematic Apperception Test (TAT) was plagued by evidence of sex differences that appeared to confuse and complicate data analysis. The TAT presents for interpretation an ambiguous cue—a picture about which a story is to be written or a brief story stem to be completed. Such stories in reflecting projective imagination are considered to reveal the ways in which people construe what they perceive—that is, the concepts and interpretations they bring to their experience and thus presumably the kind of sense that they make of their lives. Prior to Horner's work, it was clear that women made a different kind of sense than men of situations of competitive achievement, that in some way they saw the situation differently or the situation aroused in them some different response.

On the basis of his studies of men, McClelland (1961) had divided the concept of achievement motivation into what appeared to be its two logical components, a motive to approach success ("hope success") and a motive to avoid failure ("fear failure"). When Horner (1972) began to analyze the problematic projective data on female achievement motivation, she identified as a third category the unlikely motivation to avoid success ("fear success"). Women appeared to have a problem with competitive achievement, and that problem seemed, in Horner's interpretation, to emanate from a perceived conflict between femininity and success, the dilemma of the female adolescent who struggles to integrate her feminine aspirations and the identifications of her early childhood with the more masculine competence she has acquired at school. Thus Horner reports, "When success is likely or possible, threatened by the negative consequences they expect to follow success, young women become anxious and their positive achievement strivings become thwarted" (1972, p. 171). She concludes that this fear exists because for most women, the anticipation of success in competitive achievement activity, especially against men, produced anticipation of certain negative consequences, for example, threat of social rejection and loss of femininity."

It is, however, possible to view such conflicts about success in a different light. Sassen (1980), on the basis of her reanalysis of the data presented in Horner's thesis, suggests that the conflicts expressed by the women might instead indicate "a heightened perception of the 'other side' of competitive success, that is, the great emotional costs of success achieved through competition, or an understanding which, while confused, indicates an awareness that something is rotten in the state in which success is defined as having better grades than everyone else" (Sassen, 1980). Sassen points out that Horner found success anxiety to be present in women only when achievement was directly competitive, that is, where one person's success was at the expense of another's failure.

From Horner's examples of fear of success, it is impossible to differentiate between neurotic or realistic anxiety about the consequences of achievement, the questioning of conventional definitions of success, or the discovery of personal goals other than conventional success. The construction of the problem posed by success as a problem of identity and ideology that appears in Horner's illustrations, if taken at face value rather than assumed to be derivative, suggests Erikson's distinction between a conventional and neohumanist identity, or, in cognitive terms, the distinction between conventional and postconventional thought (Loevinger, 1970; Inhelder and Piaget, 1958; Kohlberg, 1971; Perry, 1968).

In his elaboration of the identity crisis, Erikson discusses the life of George Bernard Shaw to illustrate the young person's sense of being co-opted prematurely by success in a career he cannot wholeheartedly endorse. Shaw at seventy, reflecting upon his life, describes his crisis at the age of twenty as one caused not by lack of success or the absence of recognition, but by too much of both:

> I made good in spite of myself, and found, to my dismay, that Business, instead of expelling me as the worthless imposter I was, was fastening upon me with no intention of letting me go. Behold me, therefore, in my twentieth year, with a business training, in an occupation which I detested as cordially as any sane person lets himself detest anything he cannot escape from. In March, 1876, I broke loose. (Erikson, 1968, p. 143)

At which point Shaw settled down to study and to write as he pleased. Hardly interpreted as evidence of developmental difficulty, of neurotic anxiety about achievement and competition, Shaw's refusal suggested to Erikson, "the extraordinary workings of an extraordinary personality coming to the fore" (1968, p. 144).

We might on these grounds begin to ask not why women have conflicts about succeeding but why men show such readiness to adopt and celebrate a rather narrow vision of success. Remembering Piaget's observation, corroborated by Lever, that boys in their games are concerned more with rules, while girls are more concerned with relationships, often at the expense of the game itself; remembering also that, in Chodorow's analysis, men's social orientation is positional and women's orientation is personal, we begin to understand why, when Anne becomes John in Horner's tale of competitive success and the stories are written by men, fear of success tends to disappear. John is considered by other men to have played by the rules and won. He has the *right* to feel good about his success. Confirmed in his sense of his own identity as separate from those who, compared to him, are less competent, his positional sense of self is affirmed. For Anne, it is possible that the position she could obtain by being at the top of her medical school class may not, in fact, be what she wants.

"It is obvious," Virginia Woolf said, "that the values of women differ very often from the values which have been made by the other sex" (1929, p. 76). Yet, she adds, it is the masculine values that prevail. As a result, women come to question the "normality" of their feelings and to alter their judgments in deference to the opinion of others. In the nineteenth-century novels written by women, Woolf sees at work "a mind slightly pulled from the straight, altering its clear vision in the anger and confusion of deference to external authority" (1929, p. 77). The same deference that Woolf identifies in nineteenth-century fiction can be seen as well in the judgments of twentieth-century women. Women's reluctance to make moral judgments, the difficulty they experience in finding or speaking publicly in their own voice, emerge repeatedly in the form of qualification and self-doubt, in intimations of a divided judgment, a public and private assessment that are fundamentally at odds (Gilligan, 1977).

Yet the deference and confusion that Woolf criticizes in women derive from the values she sees as their strength. Women's deference is rooted not only in their social circumstances but also in the substance of their moral concern. Sensitivity to the needs of others and the assumption of responsibility for taking care lead women to attend to voices other than their own and to include in their judgment other points of view. Women's moral weakness, manifest in an apparent diffusion and confusion of judgment, is thus inseparable from women's moral strength, an overriding concern with relationships and responsibilities. The reluctance to judge can itself be indicative of the same care and concern for others that infuses the psychology of women's development and is responsible for what is characteristically seen as problematic in its nature.

Thus women not only define themselves in a context of human relationship but also judge themselves in terms of their ability to care. Woman's place in man's life cycle has been that of nurturer, caretaker, and helpmate, the weaver of those networks of relationships on which she in turn relies. While women have thus taken care of men, however, men have in their theories of psychological development tended either to assume or to devalue that care. The focus on individuation and individual achievement that has dominated the description of child and adolescent development has recently been extended to the depiction of adult development as well. Levinson in his study *The Seasons of a Man's Life* (1978) elaborates a view of adult development in which relationships are portrayed as a means to an end of individual achievement and success. In the critical relationships of early adulthood, the "Mentor" and the "Special Woman" are defined by the role they play in facilitating the man's realization of his "Dream." Along similar lines Vaillant (1977), in his study of men, considers altruism a defense, characteristic of mature ego functioning and associated with successful "adaptation to life," but conceived as derivative rather than primary in contrast to Chodorow's analysis, in which empathy is considered "built-in" to the woman's primary definition of self.

The discovery now being celebrated by men in mid-life of the importance of intimacy, relationships, and care is something that women have known from the beginning. However, because that knowledge has been considered "intuitive" or "instinctive," a function of anatomy coupled with destiny, psychologists have neglected to describe its development. In my research, I have found that women's moral development centers on the elaboration of that knowledge. Women's moral development thus delineates a critical line of psychological development whose importance for both sexes becomes apparent in the intergenerational framework of a life-cycle perspective. While the subject of moral development provides the final illustration of the reiterative pattern in the observation and assessment of sex

differences in the literature on human development, it also indicates more particularly why the nature and significance of women's development has for so long
been obscured and considered shrouded in mystery.

The criticism that Freud (1961) makes of women's sense of justice, seeing it as
compromised in its refusal of blind impartiality, reappears not only in the work
of Piaget (1934) but also in that of Kohlberg (1958). While girls are an aside in
Piaget's account of *The Moral Judgment of the Child* (1934), an odd curiosity to
whom he devotes four brief entries in an index that omits "boys" altogether because "the child" is assumed to be male, in Kohlberg's research on moral development, females simply do not exist. Kohlberg's six stages that describe the development of moral judgment from childhood to adulthood were derived
empirically from a longitudinal study of eighty-four boys from the United States.
While Kohlberg (1973) claims universality for his stage sequence and considers
his conception of justice as fairness to have been naturalistically derived, those
groups not included in his original sample rarely reach his higher stages (Edwards,
1975; Gilligan, 1977). Prominent among those found to be deficient in moral
development when measured by Kohlberg's scale are women, whose judgments
on his scale seemed to exemplify the third stage in his six-stage sequence. At this
stage morality is conceived in terms of relationships, and goodness is equated with
helping and pleasing others. This concept of goodness was considered by Kohlberg
and Kramer (1969) to be functional in the lives of mature women insofar as those
lives took place in the home and thus were relationally bound. Only if women
were to go out of the house to enter the arena of male activity would they realize
the inadequacy of their Stage Three perspective and progress like men toward
higher stages where morality is societally or universally defined in accordance with
a conception of justice as fairness.

In this version of human development, however, a particular conception of
maturity is assumed, based on the study of men's lives and reflecting the importance of individuation in their development. When one begins instead with women
and derives developmental constructs from their lives, then a different conception
of development emerges, the expansion and elaboration of which can also be
traced through stages that comprise a developmental sequence. In Loevinger's
(1966) test for measuring ego development that was drawn from studies of females, fifteen of the thirty-six sentence stems to complete begin with the subject
of human relationships (for example, "Raising a family . . .; If my mother . . .;
Being with other people . . .; When I am with a man . . .; When a child won't join
in group activities . . .") (Loevinger & Wessler, 1970, p. 141). Thus ego development is described and measured by Loevinger through conception of relationships as well as by the concept of identity that measures the progress of individuation.

Research on moral judgment has shown that when the categories of women's
thinking are examined in detail (Gilligan, 1977), the outline of a moral conception
different from that described by Freud, Piaget, or Kohlberg begins to emerge and
to inform a different description of moral development. In this conception, the
moral problem is seen to arise from conflicting responsibilities rather than from
competing rights and to require for its resolution a mode of thinking that is contextual and inductive rather than formal and abstract.

This conception of morality as fundamentally concerned with the capacity for
understanding and care also develops through a structural progression of increas-

ing differentiation and integration. This progression witnesses the shift from an egocentric through a societal to the universal moral perspective that Kohlberg described in his research on men, but it does so in different terms. The shift in women's judgment from an egocentric to a conventional to a principled ethical understanding is articulated through their use of a distinct moral language, in which the terms "selfishness" and "responsibility" define the moral problem as one of care. Moral development then consists of the progressive reconstruction of this understanding toward a more adequate conception of care.

The concern with caring centers moral development around the progressive differentiation and integration that characterize the evolution of the understanding of relationships just as the conception of fairness delineates the progressive differentiation and balancing of individual rights. Within the responsibility orientation, the infliction of hurt is the center of moral concern and is considered immoral whether or not it can otherwise be construed as fair or unfair. The reiterative use of the language of selfishness and responsibility to define the moral problem as a problem of care sets women apart from the men whom Kohlberg studied and from whose thinking he derived his six stages. This different construction of the moral problem by women may be seen as the critical reason for their failure to develop within the constraints of Kohlberg's system.

Regarding all constructions of responsibility as evidence of a conventional moral understanding, Kohlberg defines the highest stages of moral development as deriving from a reflective understanding of human rights. That the morality of rights differs from the morality of responsibility in its emphasis on separation rather than attachment, in its consideration of the individual rather than the relationship as primary, is illustrated by two quotations that exemplify these different orientations. The first comes from a twenty-five-year-old man who participated in Kohlberg's longitudinal study. The quotation itself is cited by Kohlberg to illustrate the principled conception of morality that he scores as "integrated [Stage] Five judgment, possibly moving to Stage Six."

[What does the word morality mean to you?] Nobody in the world knows the answer. I think it is recognizing the right of the individual, the rights of other individuals, not interfering with those rights. Act as fairly as you would have them treat you. I think it is basically to preserve the human being's right to existence. I think that is the most important. Secondly, the human being's right to do as he pleases, again without interfering with somebody else's rights.

[How have your views on morality changed since the last interview?] I think I am more aware of an individual's rights now. I used to be looking at it strictly from my point of view, just for me. Now I think I am more aware of what the individual has a right to. (Note 1, p. 29)

"Clearly," Kohlberg states,

these responses represent attainment of the third level of moral theory. Moving to a perspective outside of that of his society, he identifies morality with justice (fairness, rights, the Golden Rule), with recognition of the rights of others as these are defined naturally or intrinsically. The human's right to do as he pleases without interfering with somebody else's rights is a formula defining rights prior to social legislation and opinion which defines what society may expect rather than being defined by it. (Note 1, pp. 29–30)

The second quotation comes from my interview with a woman, also twenty-five years old and at the time of the interview a third-year student at Harvard Law School. She described her conception of morality as follows:

> [Is there really some correct solution to moral problems or is everybody's opinion equally right?] No, I don't think everybody's opinion is equally right. I think that in some situations . . . there may be opinions that are equally valid and one could conscientiously adopt one of several courses of action. But there are other situations which I think there are right and wrong answers, that sort of inhere in the nature of existence, of all individuals here who need to live with each other to live. We need to depend on each other and hopefully it is not only a physical need but a need of fulfillment in ourselves, that a person's life is enriched by cooperating with other people and striving to live in harmony with everybody else, and to that end, there are right and wrong, there are things which promote that end and that move away from it, and in that way, it is possible to choose in certain cases among different courses of action that obviously promote or harm that goal.

> [Is there a time in the past when you would have thought about these things differently?] Oh yeah. I think that I went through a time when I thought that things were pretty relative, that I can't tell you what to do and you can't tell me what to do, because you've got your conscience and I've got mine. . . .

> [When was that?] When I was in high school, I guess that it just sort of dawned on me that my own ideas changed, I felt I couldn't judge another person's judgment . . . but now I think even when it is only the person himself who is going to be affected, I say it is wrong to the extent it doesn't cohere with what I know about human nature and what I know about you, and just from what I think is true about the operation of the universe, I could say I think you are making a mistake.

> [What led you to change, do you think?] Just seeing more of life, just recognizing that there are an awful lot of things that are common among people . . . there are certain things that you come to learn promote a better life and better relationships and more personal fulfillment than other things that in general tend to do the opposite and the things that promote these things, you would call morally right.

These responses also represent a reflective reconstruction of morality following a period of relativistic questioning and doubt, but the reconstruction of moral understanding is based not on the primacy and universality of individual rights, but rather on what she herself describes as a "very strong sense of being responsible to the world." Within this construction, the moral dilemma changes from how to exercise one's rights without interfering with the rights of others to how "to lead a moral life which includes obligations to myself and my family and people in general." The problem then becomes one of limiting responsibilities without abandoning moral concern. When asked to describe herself, this woman says that she values

> having other people that I am tied to and also having people that I am responsible to. I have a very strong sense of being responsible to the world, that I can't just live for my enjoyment, but just the fact of being in the world gives me an obligation to do what I can to make the world a better place to live in, no matter how small a scale that may be on.

Thus while Kohlberg's subject worries about people interfering with one another's rights, this woman worries about "the possibility of omission, of your not helping others when you could help them."

The issue this law student raises is addressed by Loevinger's fifth "autonomous" stage of ego development. The terms of its resolution lie in achieving partial autonomy from an excessive sense of responsibility by recognizing that other people have responsibility for their own destiny (Loevinger, 1968). The autonomous stage in Loveinger's account witnesses a relinquishing of moral dichotomies and their replacement with "a feeling for the complexity and multifaceted character of real people and real situations" (1970, p. 6).

Whereas the rights conception of morality that informs Kohlberg's principled level [Stages Five and Six] is geared to arriving at an objectively fair or just resolution to the moral dilemmas to which "all rational men can agree" (Kohlberg, 1976), the responsibility conception focuses instead on the limitations of any particular resolution and describes the conflicts that remain. This limitation of moral judgment and choice is described by a woman in her thirties when she says that her guiding principle in making moral decisions has to do with "responsibility and caring about yourself and others, not just a principle that once you take hold of, you settle [the moral problem]. The principle put into practice is still going to leave you with conflict."

Given the substance and orientation of these women's judgments, it becomes clear why a morality of rights and noninterference may appear to women as frightening in its potential justification of indifference and unconcern. At the same time, however, it also becomes clear why, from a male perspective, women's judgments appear inconclusive and diffuse, given their insistent contextual relativism. Women's moral judgments thus elucidate the pattern that we have observed in the differences between the sexes but provide an alternative conception of maturity by which these differences can be developmentally considered. The psychology of women that has consistently been described as distinctive in its greater orientation toward relationship of interdependence implies a more contextual mode of judgment and a different moral understanding. Given the differences in women's conceptions of self and morality, it is not surprising that women bring to the life cycle a different point of view and that they order human experience in terms of different priorities.

The myth of Demeter and Persephone, which McClelland cites as exemplifying the feminine attitude toward power, was associated with the Eleusinian Mysteries celebrated in ancient Greece for over two thousand years (1975, p. 96). As told in the Homeric *Hymn to Demeter* (1971), the story of Persephone indicates the strengths of "interdependence, building up resources and giving" (McClelland, 1975, p. 96) that McClelland found in his research on power motivation to characterize the mature feminine style. Although McClelland says, "it is fashionable to conclude that no one knows what went on in the Mysteries, it is known that they were probably the most important religious ceremonies, even partly on the historical record, which were organized by and for women, especially at the onset before men by means of the cult of Dionysus began to take them over" (1975, p. 96). Thus McClelland regards the myth as "a special presentation of feminine psychology" (1975). It is, as well, a life-cycle story par excellence.

Persephone, the daughter of Demeter, while out playing in the meadows with her girl friends, sees a beautiful narcissus which she runs to pick. As she does so, the earth opens and she is snatched away to Pluto, who takes her to his underworld kingdom. Demeter, goddess of the earth, so mourns the loss of her daughter that she refuses to allow anything to grow. The crops that sustain life on earth shrivel and dry up, killing men and animals alike, until Zeus takes pity on man's suffering and persuades his brother to return Persephone to her mother. But before she leaves, Persephone eats some pomegranate seeds, an act that insures that she will spend six months of every year in the underworld.

The elusive mystery of women's development lies in its recognition of the continuing importance of attachment in the human life cycle. Woman's place in man's life cycle has been to protect this recognition while the developmental litany intones the celebration of separation, autonomy, individuation, and natural rights. The myth of Persephone speaks directly to the distortion in this view by reminding us that narcissism leads to death, that the fertility of the earth is in some mysterious way tied to the continuation of the mother-daughter relationship, and that the life cycle itself arises from an alternation between the world of women and that of men. My intention in this essay has been to suggest that only when life-cycle theorists equally divide their attention and begin to live with women as they have lived with men will their vision encompass the experience of both sexes and their theories become correspondingly more fertile.

Note

1. Kohlberg, L. *Continuities and discontinuities in childhood and adult moral development revisited.* Unpublished manuscript, Harvard University, 1973.

References

Bettelheim, B. *The uses of enchantment.* New York: Knopf, 1976.

Blos, P. The second individuation process of adolescence. In A. Freud (Ed.), *The psychoanalytic study of the child* (Vol. 22). New York: International Universities Press, 1967.

Chekhov, A. *The cherry orchard.* (Stark Young, trans.). New York: Modern Library, 1956. (Originally published, 1904.)

Chodorow, N. Family structure and feminine personality. In M. Rosaldo and L. Lamphere (Eds.), *Women, culture, and society.* Stanford, Calif.: Stanford University Press, 1974.

———. *The reproduction of mothering.* Berkeley: University of California Press, 1978.

Edwards, C. P. Societal complexity and moral development: A Kenyan study. *Ethos,* 1975, 3, 505–527.

Erikson, E. *Identity: Youth and crisis.* New York: Norton, 1968.

Freud, S. Female sexuality. In J. Strachey (Ed.), *The standard edition of the complete psychological works of Sigmund Freud* (Vol. 21). London: Hogarth Press, 1961. (Originally published, 1931.)

———. Some psychical consequences of the anatomical distinction between the sexes. In J. Strachey (Ed.), *The standard edition of the complete psychological works of Sigmund Freud* (Vol. 19). London: Hogarth Press, 1961. (Originally published, 1925.)

———. Three essays on sexuality. In J. Strachey (Ed.), *The standard edition of the complete psychological works of Sigmund Freud* (Vol. 7). London: Hogarth Press, 1961. (Originally published, 1905.)

Gilligan, C. *In a different voice: Women's conceptions of the self and of morality.* Harvard Educational Review, 1977, 47, 481–517.

The Homeric Hymn (C. Boer, trans.). Chicago: Swallow Press, 1971.

Horner, M. Toward an understanding of achievement-related conflicts in women. *Journal of Social Issues,* 1972, 28 (2), 157–174.

Inhelder, B., and J. Piaget. *The growth of logical thinking from childhood to adolescence.* New York: Basic Books, 1958.

Kingston, M. H. *The woman warrior.* New York: Vintage Books, 1977.

Kohlberg, L., and R. Kramer. Continuities and discontinuities in childhood and adult moral development. *Human Development,* 1969, 12, 93–120.

Kohlberg, L. From is to ought: How to commit the naturalistic fallacy and get away with it in the study of moral development. In T. Mischel (Ed.), *Cognitive development and epistemology.* New York: Academic Press, 1971.

Lever, J. Sex differences in the games children play. *Social Problems,* 1976, 23, 478–487.

Levinson, D. *The seasons of a man's life.* New York: Knopf, 1978.

Loevinger, J., and R. Wessler. *The meaning and measurement of ego development.* San Francisco: Jossey-Bass, 1970.

McClelland, D. *The achieving society.* New York: Van Nostrand, 1961.

———. *Power: The inner experience.* New York: Irvington Publishers, 1975.

Mead, G. H. *Mind, self, and society.* Chicago: University of Chicago Press, 1934.

Perry, W. *Forms of intellectual and ethical development in the college years.* New York: Holt, Rinehart & Winston, 1968.

Piaget, J. *The moral judgment of the child.* New York: Free Press, 1965. (Originally published, 1932.)

Riesman, D. *The lonely crowd.* New Haven: Yale University Press, 1961.

Sassen, G. Success-anxiety in women: A constructivist theory of its sources and its significance. *Harvard Educational Review,* 1980, 50, 13–24.

Strunk, W., and E. B. White. *The elements of style.* New York: Macmillan, 1959.

Sullivan, H. S. *The interpersonal theory of psychiatry.* New York: Norton, 1953.

Vaillant, G. *Adaptation to life.* Boston: Little, Brown, 1977.

Woolf, V. *A room of one's own.* New York: Harcourt, Brace & World, 1929.

3

RACE, CLASS, AND GENDER: PROSPECTS FOR AN ALL-INCLUSIVE SISTERHOOD

Bonnie Thornton Dill

The concept of sisterhood has been an important unifying force in the contemporary women's movement. By stressing the similarities of women's secondary social and economic positions in all societies and in the family, this concept has been a binding force in the struggle against male chauvinism and patriarchy. As we review the past decade, however, it becomes apparent that the cry "Sisterhood is powerful!" has engaged only a few segments of the female population in the United States. Black, Hispanic, Native American, and Asian American women of all classes, as well as many working-class women, have not readily identified themselves as sisters of the white middle-class women who have been in the forefront of the movement.

This article examines the applications of the concept of sisterhood and some of the reasons for the limited participation of racially and ethnically distinct women in the women's movement, with particular reference to the experience and consciousness of Afro-American women. The first section presents a critique of sisterhood as a binding force for all women and examines the limitations of the concept for both theory and practice when applied to women who are neither white nor middle class. In the second section, the importance of women's perception of themselves and their place in society is explored as a way of understanding the differences and similarities between Black and white women. Data from two studies, one of college-educated Black women and the other of Black female household workers, are presented to illuminate both the ways in which the structures of race, gender, and class intersect in the lives of Black women and the women's perceptions of the impact of these structures on their lives. This article concludes with a discussion of the prospects for sisterhood and suggests political strategies that may provide a first step toward a more inclusive women's movement.

THE LIMITATIONS OF SISTERHOOD

In a recent article, historian Elizabeth Fox-Genovese provided a political critique of the concept of sisterhood.[1] Her analysis identifies some of the current limitations of this concept as a rallying point for women across the boundaries of race and class. Sisterhood is generally understood as a nurturant, supportive feeling of attachment and loyalty to other women that grows out of a shared experience of oppression. A term reminiscent of familial relationships, it tends to focus upon the particular nuturant and reproductive roles of women and, more recently, upon commonalities of personal experience. Fox-Genovese suggests that sisterhood has taken two different political directions. In one, women have been treated as unique, and sisterhood was used as a basis for seeking to maintain a separation between the competitive values of the world of men (the public-political sphere) and the nurturant values of the world of women (the private-domestic sphere). A second, more recent and progressive expression of the concept views sisterhood as an element of the feminist movement that serves as a means for political and economic action based upon the shared needs and experiences of women. Both conceptualizations of sisterhood have limitations in encompassing the racial and class differences among women. These limitations have important implications for the prospects of an all-inclusive sisterhood.

Fox-Genovese argues that the former conceptualization, which she labels bourgeois individualism, resulted in "the passage of a few middle-class women into the public sphere" but sharpened the class and racial divisions between them and lower-class minority women.[2] In the latter conceptualization, called the politics of personal experience, sisterhood is restricted by the experiential differences that result from the racial and class divisions of society.

> Sisterhood has helped us, as it helped so many of our predecessors, to forge ourselves as political beings. Sisterhood has mobilized our loyalty to each other and hence to ourselves. It has given form to a dream of genuine equality for women. But without a broader politics directed toward the kind of social transformation that will provide social justice for all human beings, it will, in a poignant irony, result in our dropping each other by the wayside as we compete with rising desperation for crumbs.[3]

These two notions of sisterhood, as expressed in the current women's movement, offer some insights into the alienation many Black women have expressed about the movement itself.

The bourgeois individualistic theme present in the contemporary women's movement led many Black women to express the belief that the movement existed merely to satisfy needs for personal self-fulfillment on the part of white middle-class women.[4] The emphasis on participation in the paid labor force and escape from the confines of the home seemed foreign to many Black women. After all, as a group they had had higher rates of paid labor force participation than their white counterparts for centuries, and many would have readily accepted what they saw as the "luxury" of being a housewife. At the same time, they expressed concern that white women's gains would be made at the expense of Blacks and/or that having achieved their personal goals, these so-called sisters would ignore or abandon the cause of racial discrimination. Finally, and perhaps most important, the experiences of racial oppression made Black women strongly aware of their group identity and consequently more suspicious of women who, initially at least, defined much of their feminism in personal and individualistic terms.

Angela Davis, in "Reflections on the Black Woman's Role in the Community of Slaves," stresses the importance of group identity for Black women. "Under the impact of racism the black woman has been continually constrained to inject herself into the desperate struggle for existence. . . . As a result, black women have made significant contributions to struggles against racism and the dehumanizing exploitation of a wrongly organized society. In fact, it would appear that the intense levels of resistance historically maintained by black people and thus the historical function of the Black liberation struggle as harbinger of change throughout the society are due in part to the greater objective equality between the black man and the black woman."[5] The sense of being part of a collective movement toward liberation has been a continuing theme in the autobiographies of contemporary Black women.

> Ideas and experiences vary, but Shirley Chisholm, Gwendolyn Brooks, Angela Davis and other Black women who wrote autobiographies during the seventies offer similar . . . visions of the black woman's role in the struggle for Black liberation. The idea of collective liberation . . . says that society is not a protective arena in which an individual black can work out her own destiny and gain a share of America's benefits by her own efforts. . . . Accordingly, survival, not to mention freedom, is dependent on the values and actions of the groups as a whole, and if indeed one succeeds or triumphs it is due less to individual talent than to the group's belief in and adherence to the idea that freedom from oppression must be acted out and shared by all.[6]

Sisterhood is not new to Black women. It has been institutionalized in churches. In many Black churches, for example, membership in the church entitles one to address the women as "sisters" and the men as "brothers." Becoming a sister is an important rite of passage that permits young women full participation in certain church rituals and women's clubs where these nurturant relationships among women are reinforced.[7] Sisterhood was also a basis for organization in the club movements that began in the late 1800s.[8] Finally, it is clearly exemplified in Black extended family groupings that frequently place great importance on female kinship ties. Research on kinship patterns among urban Blacks identifies the nurturant and supportive feelings existing among female kin as a key element in family stability and survival.[9]

While Black women have fostered and encouraged sisterhood, we have not used it as the anvil to forge our political identities. This contrasts sharply with the experiences of many middle-class white women who have participated in the current women's movement. The political identities of Afro-American women have largely been formed around issues of race. National organizations of Black women, many of which were first organized on the heels of the nineteenth-century movement for women's rights, "were (and still are) decidedly feminist in the values expressed in their literature and in many of the concerns that they addressed, yet they also always focused upon issues that resulted from the racial oppression affecting *all* black people."[10] This commitment to the improvement of the race has often led Black women to see feminist issues quite differently from their white sisters. And racial animosity and mistrust have too often undermined the potential for coalition between Black and white women since the women's suffrage campaigns.

Many contemporary white feminists would like to believe that relations between Black and white women in the early stages of the women's movement were characterized by the beliefs and actions of Susan B. Anthony, Angelina Grimke, and some others. The historical record suggests, however, that these women were more exceptional than normative. Rosalyn Terborg-Penn argues that "discrimination against Afro-American women reformers was the rule rather than the exception within the women's rights movement from the 1830's to 1920."[11] Although it is beyond the scope of this article to provide a detailed discussion of the incidents that created mistrust and ill-feeling between Black and white women, the historical record provides an important legacy that still haunts us.

The movement's early emphasis upon the oppression of women within the institution of marriage and the family and upon educational and professional discrimination reflected the concerns of middle-class white women. During that period, Black women were engaged in a struggle for survival and a fight for freedom. Among their immediate concerns were lynching and economic viability. Working-class white women were concerned about labor conditions, the length of the working day, wages, and so forth. The statements of early women's rights groups do not reflect these concerns, and "as a rigorous consummation of the consciousness of white middle-class women's dilemma, the (Seneca Falls) Declaration all but ignored the predicament of white working-class women, as it ignored the condition of Black women in the South and North alike."[12]

Political expediency drove white feminists to accept principles that were directly opposed to the survival and well-being of Blacks in order to seek to achieve more limited advances for women. "Besides the color bar which existed in many white women's organizations, black women were infuriated by white women's accommodation to the principle of lynch law in order to gain support in the South (Walker, 1973) and the attacks of well-known feminists against anti-lynching crusader, Ida Wells Barnett."[13]

The failure of the suffrage movement to sustain its commitment to the democratic ideal of enfranchisement for all citizens is one of the most frequently cited instances of white women's fragile commitment to racial equality. "After the Civil War, the suffrage movement was deeply impaired by the split over the issue of whether black males should receive the vote before white and black women. . . . In the heated pressures over whether black men or white and black women should be enfranchised first, a classist, racist, and even xenophobic rhetoric crept in."[14] The historical and continued abandonment of universalistic principles in order to benefit a privileged few on the part of white women is, I think, one of the reasons why Black women today have been reluctant to see themselves as part of a sisterhood that does not extend beyond racial boundaries. Even for those Black women who are unaware of the specific history, there is the recognition that under pressure from the white men with whom they live and upon whom they are economically dependent, many white women will abandon their "sisters of color" in favor of self-preservation. The feeling that the movement would benefit white women and abandon Blacks or benefit whites at the expense of Blacks is a recurrent theme. Terborg-Penn concludes, "The black feminist movement in the United States during the mid 1970's is a continuation of a trend that began over 150 years ago. Institutionalized discrimination against black women by white women has traditionally led to the development of racially separate groups that address themselves to race determined problems as well as the common plight of women in America."[15]

Historically, as well as currently, Black women have felt called upon to choose between their commitments to feminism and to the struggle against racial injustice.

Clearly they are victims of both forms of oppression and are most in need of encouragement and support in waging battles on both fronts. However, insistence on such a choice continues largely as a result of the tendency of groups of Blacks and groups of women to battle over the dubious distinction of being the "most" oppressed. The insistence of radical feminists upon the historical priority, universality, and overriding importance of patriarchy in effect necessitates acceptance of a concept of sisterhood that places one's womanhood over and above one's race. At the same time, Blacks are accustomed to labeling discriminatory treatment as racism and therefore may tend to view sexism only within the bounds of the Black community rather than to see it as a systemic pattern.[16] On the one hand, the choice between identifying as Black or female is a product of the "patriarchal strategy of divide-and-conquer"[17] and therefore, a false choice. Yet, the historical success of this strategy and the continued importance of class, patriarchal, and racial divisions perpetuate such choices both within our consciousness and within the concrete realities of our daily lives.

Race, of course, is only one of the factors that differentiate women. It is the most salient in discussions of Black and white women, but it is perhaps no more important, even in discussions of race and gender, than is the factor of class. Inclusion of the concept of class permits a broader perspective on the similarities and differences between Black and white women than does a purely racial analysis. Marxist feminism has focused primarily upon the relationship between class exploitation and patriarchy. While this literature has yielded several useful frameworks for beginning to examine the dialectics of gender and class, the role of race, though acknowledged, is not explicated.

Just as the gender-class literature tends to omit race, the race-class literature gives little attention to women. Recently, this area of inquiry has been dominated by a debate over the relative importance of race or class in explaining the historical and contemporary status of Blacks in this country. A number of scholars writing on this issue have argued that the racial division of labor in the United States began as a form of class exploitation that was shrouded in an ideology of racial inferiority. Through the course of U.S. history, racial structures began to take on a life of their own and cannot now be considered merely reflections of class structure.[18] A theoretical understanding of the current conditions of Blacks in this country must therefore take account of both race and class factors. It is not my intention to enter into this debate, but instead to point out that any serious study of Black women must be informed by this growing theoretical discussion. Analysis of the interaction of race, gender, and class falls squarely between these two developing bodies of theoretical literature.

Black women experience class, race, and sex exploitation simultaneously, yet these structures must be separated analytically so that we may better understand the ways in which they shape and differentiate women's lives. Davis, in her previously cited article, provides one of the best analyses to date of the intersection of gender, race, and class under a plantation economy.[19] One of the reasons this analysis is so important is that she presents a model that can be expanded to other historical periods. We must be careful, however, not to take the particular historical reality that she illuminated and read it into the present as if the experiences of Black women followed some sort of linear progression out of slavery. Instead, we must look carefully at the lives of Black women throughout history in order to define the peculiar interactions of race, class, and gender at particular historical moments.

In answer to the question: Where do Black women fit into the current analytical frameworks for race and class and gender and class? I would ask: How might these frameworks be revised if they took full account of black women's position in the home, family, and marketplace at various historical moments? In other words, the analysis of the interaction of race, gender, and class must not be stretched to fit the proscrustean bed of any other burgeoning set of theories. It is my contention that it must begin with an analysis of the ways in which Black people have been used in the process of capital accumulation in the United States. Within the contexts of class exploitation and racial oppression, women's lives and work are most clearly illuminated. Davis's article illustrates this. Increasingly, new research is being presented that grapples with the complex interconnectedness of these three issues of race, gender, and class in the lives of Black women and other women of color.[20]

PERCEPTIONS OF SELF IN SOCIETY

For Black women and other women of color, an examination of the ways in which racial oppression, class exploitation, and patriarchy intersect in their lives must be studied in relation to their perceptions of the impact these structures have upon them. Through studying the lives of particular women and searching for patterns in the ways in which they describe themselves and their relationship to society, we will gain important insights into the differences and similarities between Black and white women.

The structures of race and class generate important economic, ideological, and experiential cleavages among women. These lead to differences in perception of self and their place in society. At the same time, commonalities of class or gender may cut across racial lines, providing the conditions for shared understanding. Studying these interactions through an examination of women's self-perceptions is complicated by the fact that most people view their lives as a whole and do not explain their daily experiences or world view in terms of the differential effects of their racial group, class position, or gender. Thus, we must examine on an analytical level the ways in which the structures of class, race, and gender intersect in any woman's or group of women's lives in order to grasp the concrete set of social relations that influence their behavior. At the same time, we must study individual and group perceptions, descriptions, and conceptualizations of their lives so that we may understand the ways in which different women perceive the same and different sets of social structural constraints.

Concretely, and from a research perspective, this suggests the importance of looking at both the structures that shape women's lives and their self-presentations. This would provide us not only with the means of gaining insight into the ways in which racial, class, and gender oppression are viewed but also with a means of generating conceptual categories that will aid us in extending our knowledge of their situation. At the same time, this new knowledge will broaden and even reform our conceptualization of women's situations.

For example, how would our notions of mothering, and particularly mother-daughter relationships, be revised if we considered the particular experiences and perceptions of Black women on this topic? Gloria I. Joseph argues for, and presents a distinctive approach to the study of Black mother-daughter relationships, asserting that

> to engage in a discussion of Black mothers and daughters which focused on specific psychological mechanisms operating between the two, the dynamics of the crucial bond, and explanations for the explicit role of patriarchy, without also including the important relevancy of racial oppression . . . would necessitate forcing Black mother/daughter relationships into pigeonholes designed for understanding white models.
>
> In discussing Black mothers and daughters, it is more realistic, useful, and intellectually astute to speak in terms of their roles, positions, and functions within the Black society and that society's relationship to the broader (White) society in America.[21]

Unfortunately, there have been very few attempts in the social sciences to systematically investigate the relationship between social structure and self-perceptions of Black women. The profiles of Black women that have been appearing in magazines like *Essence,* the historical studies of Black women, fiction and poetry by and about Black women, and some recent sociological and anthropological studies provide important data for beginning such an analysis. However, the question of how Black women perceive themselves with regard to the structures of race, gender, and class is still open for systematic investigation.

Elizabeth Higginbotham, in a study of Black women who graduated from college between 1968 and 1970, explored the impact of class origins upon strategies for educational attainment. She found that class differences within the Black community led not only to different sets of educational experiences, but also to different personal priorities and views of the Black experience.[22] According to Higginbotham, the Black women from middle-class backgrounds who participated in her study had access to better schools and more positive schooling experiences than did their working-class sisters. Because their parents did not have the economic resources to purchase the better educational opportunities offered in an integrated suburb or a private school, the working-class women credited their parents' willingness to struggle within the public school system as a key component in their own educational achievement. Social class also affected college selections and experience. Working-class women were primarily concerned with finances in selecting a college and spent most of their time adjusting to the work load and the new middle-class environment once they had arrived. Middle-class women, on the other hand, were freer to select a college that would meet their personal, as well as their academic, needs and abilities. Once there, they were better able to balance their work and social lives and to think about integrating future careers and family lives.

Among her sample, Higginbotham found that a larger proportion of women from working-class backgrounds were single. She explained this finding in terms of class differences in socialization and mobility strategies. She found that the parents of women from working-class backgrounds stressed educational achievement over and above other personal goals.[23] These women never viewed marriage as a means of mobility and focused primarily upon education, postponing interest in, and decisions about, marriage. In contrast, women from middle-class backgrounds were expected to marry and were encouraged to integrate family and educational goals throughout their schooling.

My own research on household workers demonstrates the ways in which class origins, racial discrimination, and social conceptions of women and women's work came together during the first half of the twentieth century to limit work options and affect family roles and the self-perceptions of one group of Afro-American women born between 1896 and 1915.[24] Most of them were born in the South and migrated to the North between 1922 and 1955. Like the majority of Black working women of this period, they worked as household workers in private homes. (During the first half of the twentieth century, labor force participation rates of Black women ranged from about 37 percent to 50 percent. Approximately 60 percent of Black women workers were employed in private household work up until 1960.)[25]

The women who participated in this study came from working-class families. Their fathers were laborers and farmers, their mothers were housewives or did paid domestic work of some kind (cooking, cleaning, taking in washing, and so forth). As a result, the women not only had limited opportunities for education, but also often began working when they were quite young to help support their families. Jewell Prieleau (names are pseudonyms used to protect the identity of the subjects), one of eight children, described her entrance into work as follows: "When I was eight years old, I decided I wanted a job and I just got up early in the morning and I would go from house to house and ring doorbells and ask for jobs and I would get it. I think I really wanted to work because in a big family like that, they was able to feed you, but you had to earn your shoes. They couldn't buy shoes although shoes was very cheap at that time. I would rather my mother give it to the younger children and I would earn my way."

Queenie Watkins lived with her mother, aunt, and five cousins and began working in grammar school. She described her childhood jobs in detail:

> When I went to grammar school, the white ladies used to come down and say "Do you have a girl who can wash dishes?" That was how I got the job with the doctor and his wife. I would go up there at six o'clock in the morning and wash the breakfast dishes and bring in scuttles of coal to burn on the fireplace. I would go back in the afternoon and take the little girl down on the sidewalk and if there were any leaves to be raked on the year, I'd rake the leaves up and burn them and sweep the sidewalk. I swept off the front porch and washed it off with the hose and washed dishes again— for one dollar a week.

While class position limited the economic resources and educational opportunities of most of these women, racial discrimination constricted work options for Black women in such a way as to seriously undercut the benefits of education. The comments of the following women are reflective of the feelings expressed by many of those in this sample:

> When I came out of school, the black man naturally had very few chances of doing certain things and even persons that I know myself who had finished four years of college were doing the same type of work because they couldn't get any other kind of work in New York.
>
> In my home in Virginia, education, I don't think was stressed. The best you could do was be a school teacher. It wasn't something people impressed upon you you

could get. I had an aunt and cousin who were trained nurses and the best they could do was nursing somebody at home or something. They couldn't get a job in a hospital. I didn't pay education any mind really until I came to New York. I'd gotten to a certain stage in domestic work in the country and I didn't see the need for it.

Years ago there was no such thing as a black typist. I remember girls who were taking typing when I was going to school. They were never able to get a job at it. In my day and time you could have been the greatest typist in the world but you would never have gotten a job. There was no such thing as getting a job as a bank teller. The blacks weren't even sweeping the banks.

For Black women in the United States, their high concentration in household work was a result of racial discrimination and a direct carry-over from slavery. Black women were in essence "a permanent service caste in nineteenth and twentieth century America."[26] Arnold Anderson and Mary Jean Bowman argue that the distinguishing feature of domestic service in the United States is that "the frequency of servants is correlated with the availability of Negroes in local populations."[27] By the time most of the women in this sample entered the occupation, a racial caste pattern was firmly established. The occupation was dominated by foreign-born white women in the North and Black freedwomen in the south, a pattern that was modified somewhat as southern Blacks migrated north. Nevertheless, most research indicates that Black women fared far worse than their white immigrant sisters, even in the North. "It is commonly asserted that the immigrant woman has been the northern substitute for the Negro servant. In 1930, when one can separate white servants by nativity, about twice as large a percentage of foreign as of native women were domestics. . . . As against this 2:1 ratio between immigrants and natives, the ratio of Negro to white servants ranged upward from 10:1 to 50:1. The immigrant was not the northerner's Negro."[28]

Two major differences distinguished the experiences of Black domestics from those of their immigrant sisters. First, Black women had few other employment options. Second, Black household workers were older and more likely to be married. Thus, while private household work cross-culturally, and for white women in the United States, was often used as stepping-stone to other working-class occupations or as a way station before marriage, for Black American women it was neither. This pattern did not begin to change substantially until World War II.

Table 1 indicates that between 1900 and 1940 the percentage of Black women in domestic service actually increased relative to the percentage of immigrant women, which decreased. The data support the contention that Black women were even more confined to the occupation than were their immigrant sisters. At the turn of the century, large numbers of immigrants entered domestic service. Their children, however, were much less likely to become household workers. Many Black women also entered domestic service at that time, but their children tended to remain in the occupation. It was the daughters and granddaughters of the women who participated in this study who were among the first generation of Black women to benefit from the relaxation of racial restrictions that began to occur after World War II.

Finally, Black women were household workers because they were women. Private household work is women's work. It is a working-class occupation, has low social status, low pay, and few guaranteed fringe benefits. Like the housewife who employs her, the private household worker's low social status and pay are tied to

TABLE 1

Percentage of Females of Each Nativity in U.S. Labor Force Who Were Servants, by Decades, 1900–1940

	1900	1910	1920	1930	1940
Native white	22.3	15.0	9.6	10.4	
Foreign-born white	42.5	34.0	23.8	26.8	11.0
Negro	41.9	39.5	44.4	54.9	54.4
Other	24.8	22.9	22.9	19.4	16.0
Total	30.5	24.0	17.9	19.8	17.2
(N, in thousands)	(1,439)	(1,761)	(1,386)	(1,906)	(1,931)
(Percent of all domestic servants)	(95.4)	(94.4)	(93.3)	(94.1)	(92.0)

Source: George J. Stigler, *Domestic Servants in the United States: 1900–1940*, Occasional Paper no. 24 (New York: National Bureau of Economic Research, 1946), p.7.

the work itself, to her class, gender, and the complex interaction of the three within the family. In other words, housework, both paid and unpaid, is structured around the particular place of women in the family. It is considered unskilled labor because it requires no training, degrees, or licenses and because it has traditionally been assumed that any woman could or should be able to do housework.

The woman themselves had a very clear sense that the social inequities that relegated them and many of their peers to household service labor were based upon their race, class, and gender. Yet different women, depending upon their jobs, family situations, and overall outlooks on life, handled this knowledge in different ways. One woman described the relationship between her family and her employer's as follows: "Well for *their* children, I imagine they wanted them to become like they were, educators or something. But what they had in for my children, they saw in me that I wasn't able to make all of that mark but raised my children in the best method I could. Because I wouldn't have the means to put *my* children through like they could for their children." When asked what she liked most about her work, she answered, "Well what I like most about it, the things that I weren't able to go to school to do for my children. I could kinda pattern from the families that I worked for, so that I could give my children the best of my abilities." A second woman expressed much more anger and bitterness about the social differences that distinguished her life from that of her female employer. "They don't know nothing about a hard life. The only hard life will come if they getting a divorce or going through a problem with their children. But their husband has to provide for them because they're not soft. And if they leave and they separate for any reason or (are) divorced, they have to put the money down. But we have no luck like that. We have to leave our children; sometime leave the children alone. There's times when I have asked winos to look after my children. It was just a terrible life and I really thank God that the children grow up to be nice." Yet while she acknowledged her position as an opposed person, she used her knowledge of the anomalies in her employers' lives—particularly the woman and her female friends—to aid her to maintain her sense of self-respect and determination and to overcome feelings of despair and immobilization. When asked if she would like to switch places with her employers, she replied, "I don't think I would want to change, but I would like to live differently. I would like to have my own nice little apartment with my husband and have my grandchildren for dinner and my daughter and just live comfortable. But I would always want to work. . . . But, if I was to change life with them, I would like to have just a little bit of they money, that's all." While the women who participated in this study adopted different personal styles of coping with these inequities, they were all clearly aware that being black, poor, and female placed them at the bottom of the social structure, and they used the resources at their disposal to make the best of what they recognized as a bad situation.

Contemporary scholarship on women of color suggests that the barriers to an all-inclusive sisterhood are deeply rooted in the histories of oppression and exploitation that Blacks and other groups encountered upon incorporation into the American political economy.[29] These histories affect the social positions of these groups today, and racial ethnic women[30] in every social class express anger and distress about the forms of discrimination and insensitivity that they encounter in their interactions with white feminists. Audre Lorde has argued that the inability of women to confront anger is one of the important forces dividing women of color from white women in the feminist movement. She cites several examples from her own experience that resonate loudly with the experiences of most women of color who have been engaged in the women's movement.[31]

> After fifteen years of a women's movement which professes to address the life concerns and possible futures of all women, I still hear, on campus after campus, "How can we address the issues of racism? No women of color attended." Or, the other side of that statement, "We have no one in our department equipped to teach their work." In other words, racism is a Black women's problem, a problem of women of color, and only we can discuss it.
>
> White women are beginning to examine their relationships to Black women, yet often I hear you wanting only to deal with the little colored children across the roads of childhood, the beloved nursemaid, the occasional second-grade classmate. . . . You avoid the childhood assumptions formed by the raucous laughter at Rastus and Oatmeal . . . the indelible and dehumanizing portraits of Amos and Andy and your daddy's humorous bedtime stories.

bell hooks points to both the racial and class myopia of white feminists as a major barrier to sisterhood.

> When white women's liberationists emphasized work as a path to liberation, they did not concentrate their attention on those women who are most exploited in the American labor force. Had they emphasized the plight of working class women, attention would have shifted away from the college-educated suburban housewife who wanted entrance into the middle and upper class work force. Had attention been focused on women who were already working and who were exploited as cheap surplus labor in American society, it would have de-romanticized the middle class white woman's quest for "meaningful" employment. While it does not in any way diminish the importance of women resisting sexist oppression by entering the labor force, work has not been a liberating force for masses of American women.[32]

As a beginning point for understanding the potential linkages and barriers to an all-inclusive sisterhood, Lorde concludes that "the strength of women lies in recognizing differences between us as creative, and in standing to those distortions which we inherited without blame but which are now ours to alter. The angers of women can transform differences through insight into power. For anger between peers births change, not destruction, and the discomfort and sense of loss it often causes is not fatal, but a sign of growth."[33]

PROSPECTS FOR AN ALL-INCLUSIVE SISTERHOOD

Given the differences in experiences among Black women, the differences between Black and white women, between working-class and middle-class women, between all of us, what then are the prospects for sisterhood? While this article has sought to emphasize the need to study and explicate these differences, it is based upon the assumption that the knowledge we gain in this process will also help enlighten us about our similarities. Thus, I would argue for the abandonment of the concept of sisterhood as a global construct based on unexamined assumptions about our similarities, and I would substitute a more pluralistic approach that recognizes and accepts the objective differences between women. Such an approach requires that we concentrate our political energies on building coalitions around particular issues of shared interest. Through joint work on specific issues, we may come to a better understanding of one another's needs and perceptions and begin to overcome some of the suspicions and mistrust that continue to haunt us. The limitations of a sisterhood based on bourgeois individualism or on the politics of personal experience presently pose a very real threat to combined political action.

For example, in the field of household employment, interest in the needs of a growing number of middle-class women to participate in the work force and thus find adequate assistance with their domestic duties (a form of bourgeois individualism) could all too easily become support for a proposal such as the one made by writer Anne Colamosca in a recent article in the *New Republic*.[34] She proposed solving the problems of a limited supply of household help with a government training program for unemployed alien women to help them become "good household workers." While this may help middle-class women pursue their careers, it will do so while continuing to maintain and exploit a poorly paid, unprotected, lower class and will leave the problem of domestic responsibility virtually unaddressed for the majority of mothers in the work force who cannot afford to hire personal household help. A socialist feminist perspective requires an examination of the exploitation inherent in household labor as it is currently organized for both the paid and unpaid worker. The question is, what can we do to upgrade the status of domestic labor for all women, to facilitate the adjustment and productivity of immigrant women, and to insure that those who choose to engage in paid private household work do so because it represents a potentially interesting, viable, and economically rewarding option for them?

At the same time, the women's movement may need to move beyond a limited focus on "women's issues" to ally with groups of women and men who are addressing other aspects of race and class oppression. One example is school desegregation, an issue that is engaging the time and energies of many urban Black women today. The struggles over school desegregation are rapidly moving beyond the issues of busing and racial balance. In many large cities, where school districts are between 60 percent and 85 percent Black, Hispanic, or Third World, racial balance is becoming less of a concern. Instead, questions are being raised about the overall quality of the educational experiences low-income children of all racial and ethnic groups are receiving in the public schools. This is an issue of vital concern to many racially and ethnically distinct women because they see their children's future ability to survive in this society as largely dependent upon the current direction of public education. In what ways should feminists involve themselves in this issue? First, by recognizing that feminist questions are only one group of questions among many others that are being raised about public education. To the extent that Blacks, Hispanics, Native Americans, and Asian Americans are miseducated, so are women. Feminist activists must work to expand their conceptualization of the problem beyond the narrow confines of sexism. For example, efforts to develop and include nonsexist literature in the school curriculum are important. Yet this work cannot exist in a vacuum, ignoring the fact that schoolchildren *observe* a gender-based division of labor in which authority and responsibility are held primarily by men, while women are concentrated in nurturant roles; or that schools with middle-class students have more funds, better facilities, and better teachers than schools serving working-class populations. The problems of education must be addressed as structural ones. We must examine not only the kinds of discrimination that occur within institutions, but also the ways in which discrimination becomes a fundamental part of the institution's organization and implementation of its overall purpose. Such an analysis would make the linkages between different forms of structural inequality, like sexism and racism, more readily apparent.

While analytically we must carefully examine the structures that differentiate us, politically we must fight the segmentation of oppression into categories such as "racial issues," "feminist issues," and "class issues." This is, of course, a task of almost overwhelming magnitude, and yet it seems to me the only viable way to avoid the errors of the past and to move forward to make sisterhood a meaningful feminist concept for all women, across the boundaries of race and class. For it is through first seeking to understand struggles that are not particularly shaped by one's own immediate personal priorities that we will begin to experience and understand the needs and priorities of our sisters—be they black, brown, white, poor, or rich. When we have reached a point where the differences between us enrich our political and social action rather than divide it, we will have gone beyond the personal and will, in fact, be "political enough."

Notes

The author wishes to acknowledge the comments of Lynn Weber Cannon and Elizabeth Higginbotham on an earlier version of this article.

1. Elizabeth Fox-Genovese, "The Personal Is Not Political Enough," *Marxist Perspectives* (Winter 1979–80): 94–113.
2. Ibid., 97–98.
3. Ibid., 112.

4. For discussions of Black women's attitudes toward the women's movement see Linda LaRue, "The Black Movement and Women's Liberation," *Black Scholar* 1 (May 1970): 36–42; Renee Ferguson "Women's Liberation Has a Different Meaning for Blacks," in *Black Women in White America: A Documentary History,* ed. Gerda Lerner (New York: Pantheon, 1972); Inez Smith Reid, *"Together" Black Women* (New York: Emerson-Hall, 1972); Cheryl Townsend Gilkes, "Black Women's Work as Deviance: Social Sources of Racial Antagonism within Contemporary Feminism" (Paper presented at the Seventy-fourth Annual Meeting of the American Sociological Association, Boston, August 1979).

5. Angela Davis, "Reflections on the Black Woman's Role in the Community of Slaves," *Black Scholar* 2 (December 1971): 15.

6. Mary Burgher, "Images of Self and Race," in *Sturdy Black Bridges,* ed. Roseann P. Bell, Bettye J. Parker, and Beverly Guy-Sheftall (Garden City, N.Y.: Anchor Books, 1979), 118.

7. For a related discussion of Black women's roles in the church, see Cheryl Townsend Gilkes, "Institutional Motherhood in Black Churches and Communities: Ambivalent Sexism or Fragmented Familyhood" (published paper).

8. For a discussion of the club movement among Black women, see, in addition to Lerner's book, Alfreda Duster, ed., *Ida Barnett, Crusade for Justice: The Autobiography of Ida B. Wells* (Chicago: University of Chicago Press, 1970); Rackham Holt, *Mary McLeod Bethune: A Biography* (Garden City, N.Y.: Doubleday, 1964); Jeanne I. Noble, *Beautiful, Also, Are the Souls of My Black Sisters: A History of the Black Woman in America* (Englewood Cliffs, N.J.: Prentice-Hall, 1978); Mary Church Terrell, *A Colored Woman in a White World* (Washington, D.C.: Ransdell Publishing Company, 1940).

9. Carol Stack, *All Our Kin* (New York: Harper & Row, 1970); and Elmer P. Martin and Joan Martin, *The Black Extended Family* (Chicago: University of Chicago Press, 1977).

10. Gilkes, "Black Women's Work as Deviance," 21.

11. Rosalyn Terborg-Penn, "Discrimination Against Afro-American Women in the Woman's Movement, 1830–1920," in *The Afro-American Woman: Struggles and Images,* ed. Sharon Harley and Rosalyn Terborg-Penn (Port Washington, N.Y.: Kennikat Press, 1978), 17.

12. Angela Davis, *Women, Race, and Class* (New York: Random House, 1981), 54.

13. Gilkes, "Black Women's Work as Deviance," 19. In this quotation Gilkes cites Jay S. Walker, "Frederick Douglass and Woman Suffrage," *Black Scholar* 4 (7 June 1973).

14. Adrienne Rich, " 'Disloyal to Civilization': Feminism, Racism, and Gynephobia," *Chrysalis,* no. 7 (1978): 14.

15. Terborg-Penn, 27.

16. Elizabeth Higginbotham, "Issues in Contemporary Sociological Work on Black Women," *Humanity and Society* 4 (November 1980): 226–42.

17. Rich, 15.

18. This argument has been suggested by Robert Blauner in *Racial Oppression in America* (New York: Harper & Row, 1972); and William J. Wilson in *The Declining Significance of Race: Blacks and Changing American Institutions* (Chicago: University of Chicago Press, 1978).

19. Davis, "Reflections on the Black Woman's Role."

20. See Cheryl Townsend Gilkes, "Living and Working in a World of Trouble: The Emergent Career of the Black Woman Community Worker" (Ph.D. diss., Northeastern

University, 1979); and Elizabeth Higginbotham, "Educated Black Women: An Exploration in Life Chances and Choices" (Ph.D. diss., Brandeis University, 1980).

21. Gloria I. Joseph and Jill Lewis, *Common Differences: Conflicts in Black and White Feminist Perspectives* (Garden City, N.Y.: Anchor Books, 1981), 75–76.

22. Higginbotham, "Educated Black Women."

23. Elizabeth Higginbotham, "Is Marriage a Priority? Class Differences in Marital Options of Educated Black Women" in *Single Life,* ed. Peter Stein (New York: St. Martin's Press, 1981), 262.

24. Bonnie Thornton Dill, "Across the Boundaries of Race and Class: An Exploration of the Relationship between Work and Family among Black Female Domestic Servants," (Ph.D. diss., New York University, 1979).

25. For detailed data on the occupational distribution of black women during the twentieth century, see U.S. Bureau of the Census, *Historical Statistics of the United States: Colonial Times to 1970.* H. Doc. 83–78, (Washington, D.C.: GPO, 1973).

26. David Katzman, *Seven Days a Week: Women and Domestic Service in Industrializing America* (New York: Oxford University Press, 1978), 85.

27. Arnold Anderson and Mary Jean Bowman, "The Vanishing Servant and the Contemporary Status System of the American South," *American Journal of Sociology* 59 (November 1953): 216.

28. Ibid., 220.

29. Elizabeth Higginbotham, "Laid Bare by the System: Work and Survival for Black and Hispanic Women," in Amy Swerdlow and Hannah Lessinger, *Race, Class, and Gender: The Dynamics of Control* (Boston: G. K. Hall, 1983); and Bonnie Thornton Dill, "Survival as a Form of Resistance: Minority Women and the Maintenance of Families" (Working Paper no. 7, Inter University Group on Gender and Race, Memphis State University, 1982).

30. The term "racial ethnic women" is meant as an alternative to either "minority," which is disparaging; "Third World," which has an international connotation; or "women of color," which lacks any sense of cultural identity. In contrast to "ethnic," which usually refers to groups that are culturally distinct but members of the dominant white society, "racial ethnic" refers to groups that are both culturally and racially distinct, and in the United States have historically shared certain common conditions as oppressed and internally colonized peoples.

31. Audre Lorde, "The Uses of Anger," *Women's Studies Quarterly* 9 (Fall 1981): 7.

32. bell hooks, *Ain't I a Woman: Black Women and Feminism* (Boston: South End Press, 1981), 146.

33. Lorde, 9.

34. Anne Colamosca, "Capitalism and Housework," *New Republic,* 29 March 1980, 18–20.

4

FEMININITY AS PERFORMANCE

Valerie Walkerdine

INTRODUCTION

As girls at school, as women at work, we are used to performing. We are used, too, to dramaturgical metaphors that tell us that life is a performance in which we do nothing but act out a series of roles[1] or indeed that these roles can be peeled away like layers of an onion to reveal a repressed core, a true self, which has been inhibited, clouded by the layers of social conditioning which obscure it.[2] Such views form much of the common sense of ideas about gender socialisation in relation to education. Girls are conditioned into passivity, the story often goes, this is why they do badly at school. Implicitly, femininity is seen as a series of roles often imposed by agents of socialisation, of whom the worst offenders are taken to be women: mothers and female teachers. But I want to tell a different story, one of female success, one that criticises the idea that socialisation works to render girls and women wimpish, feminine, and passive.

Let me begin with an example, one that can be multiplied many times over. A woman teacher, one of my students, receives a well-deserved distinction for her Master's degree. She received more or less straight 'As' for all her work, but still she cannot believe that the distinction belongs to her. It is as though the person with her name exists somewhere else, outside her body: this powerful person that she cannot recognise as herself. Instead, she feels that she is hopeless, consistently panics about her performance and appears to have little confidence in herself. She can, however, express her views clearly and forcefully and the external examiner in her *viva* thanked her for the tutorial! I am sure this story has resonances for many women. Indeed, I am sure that I related this story because I too have been constantly aware that the Valerie Walkerdine that people speak well of seems to be someone else, someone whom I do not recognise as me.

How come, for many women, the powerful part of themselves has been so split off as to feel that it belongs to someone else? It is not the case that here is a simple, passive, wimp femininity, but with a power that is both desired and strived after, yet is almost too dangerous to be acknowledged as belonging to the woman herself.

In this paper I shall explore this phenomenon, using work from both post-structuralism and psychoanalysis and using data from my research on gender and schooling (Walkerdine et al., 1989) to illustrate my arguments.

PERFORMANCE IN SCHOOL

There is a widespread myth that girls and women perform poorly in school. In the Girls and Mathematics Unit we investigated this issue in relation to mathematics in research, spanning several years and investigating children aged 4 to 15 (Walkerdine et al., 1989). The first way in which I want to deal with the issue of performance is to challenge the idea that femininity equals poor performance and to concentrate rather on the ways in which femininity is read. What I am concerned to demonstrate is the discursive production of femininity as antithetical to masculine rationality to such an extent that femininity is *equated* with poor performance, even when the girl or woman in question is performing well. In other words, I am not talking about some essential qualities of femininity, but the way in which femininity is read as a constellation of signs that mark it off as antithetical to 'proper' performance to an incredible degree. When we first became aware of this, Rosie Walden and I called it "the just or only phenomenon" (Walden and Walkerdine, 1982). By this, we meant that whenever a positive remark was made about girls' performance in mathematics, particularly the strong sense that girls performed well in school up until the transfer at 11, a remark would be brought in which suggested that the performance was to be accounted for by 'something which amounted to nothing'. In other words, no matter how well girls were said to perform, their performance was always downgraded or dismissed in one way or another. These pejorative remarks usually related to the idea that girls' performance was based on hard work and rule-following rather than brains or brilliance (in other words what was supposed to underlie real mathematical performance).[3] This reading of girls' performance was consistent across schools and the age-range. In the younger age-groups it was common for teachers to talk about boys as having 'potential', a term often used to explain their poor performance. Throughout the sample of 39 classrooms, not one teacher mentioned 'potential' within a girl. Quite the contrary, if a girl was performing poorly there was no way she could be considered good; indeed, if she were performing well it was almost impossible for her to escape pejorative evaluations, while boys, it seemed, no matter how poorly they performed, were thought to have hidden qualities:

> Very, very hard worker. Not a particularly bright girl . . . her hard work gets her to her standards.

This typical example of a comment about a girl can be compared with the following comment about a boy, the kind of comment that was never made for girls:

> . . . can just about write his own name . . . not because he's not clever, because he's not capable, but because he can't sit still, he's got no concentration . . . very disruptive . . . but quite bright.

Indeed, it was as though boys did indeed in fantasy possess the 'phallus' [4] while girls represented a fictional 'lack' or absence. For whatever was said about girls, again and again, the presence of certain attributes, like good performance, was read as an indication of a lack of something much more fundamental. Allowances were frequently made for boys who did not perform well academically, however, as in the quote above.

This led me to point out that in engaging with issues concerning the 'truth about women' it is necessary to avoid being caught in an empiricist trap in which we are led to attempt to prove the mathematical equivalence of girls (Walkerdine et al., 1989). For here we are not presented with something as straightforward as 'the evidence of our own eyes'. Here, girls are doing well and yet they are said, in one way or another, 'not to have what it takes', while many boys, whose performance is poor, are said to possess something even when it is not visible in their performance. In order to examine and to understand such a situation, I believe that we have to move away from a simple empiricism to a position in which we understand fact, fiction and fantasy as interrelated. It is to poststructuralism that I turn for an account that will allow us to examine how gender difference is produced in fictional ways that have power in that they are part of the truth-effects of the regulation of children in classrooms. They form a basis of the 'truth about women', in this case the truth that women do not have rational powers of the mind. Such a truth, I shall argue, has to be desperately reasserted for fear that it is not true; only the paranoia of the powerful keeps it in circulation.

RATIONAL POWERS OF THE MIND

Counting girls' performance as evidence is not distinct from the issue for which it is taken to be evidence. We have not only to debate about the data but also to engage with why this decision is made at all, what it means, and what its effects are in terms of practical consequences for girls' education. Classically (within philosophy, for example), the truth of such statements has been the subject of epistemological critiques. But what the latter do is treat truth as though it were a timeless matter, separating the conditions of the production of truth from that truth itself. The question that I want to pose is not 'Are the arguments true?' but 'How is this truth constituted, how is it possible, and what effects does it have?' Such questions, derived from the methodology of genealogy utilised by Foucault, can help us begin to take apart this truth about girls. Only if we understand its historical production and its effectivity, can we begin to go beyond it. We shall argue that we can chart the historical antecedents of the position that females do not possess a capacity for reason or have 'mathematical minds' and so document how and why the arguments in support of that position have such a force now and how we might challenge them.

The argument, in a nutshell, is that ideas about reason and reasoning cannot be understood historically outside of considerations about gender. Since the Enlightenment, if not before, reason, or the _cogito,_ has been deeply embroiled with attempts to control nature. The rationality of the _cogito_ is taken to be a kind of rebirth of the rational self, in this case without the intervention of a woman. The rational self was in this sense a profoundly masculine one from which the woman was excluded, her powers being not only inferior but also subservient. The 'thinking' subject was male; the female provided both the biological prop to procreation and to servicing the possibility of 'man'.

The development of science from the seventeenth century was intimately connected to the control of nature by man. From the nineteenth century, particularly with the work of Darwin, the human was also accorded the status of natural (rather than God-given). 'Human nature' therefore became the object of a scientific inquiry that from its inception was deeply patriarchal. It legitimated doctrines that existed previously within philosophy, and with the transformation of this doctrine into a science, the female body and mind both became the objects of the scientific gaze.[5] In this way it began to be possible to make 'true' statements about the female nature, no longer an object of debate but resolvable by resort to evidence. Yet what counts as 'female nature' does not preexist the development of those doctrines, bodies of knowledge, and scientific practices that produced it as its object. In this sense, the truth of scientific statements is not discovered: it is produced.

Moreover, we can monitor the effects of such 'facts' on the fate of particular girls and women. For example, the legitimation of their exclusion and of practices of discrimination could now be based on fact; the *proven* inferiority of girls and women. It was quite common in the nineteenth century to exclude women from higher education and the professions on the grounds that they were swayed by their emotions and not, therefore, invested with the capacity to make rational judgments. It is by argument such as this that the sexed body (the seat of 'nature') becomes the site for the production and explanation of mind; since the very differentiation between men's and women's bodies is central to the approach, there is no way that reason can ever be gender-neutral.

Discussions about failure have focused on a minority of girls.[6] Of course, it is not surprising that later science 'discovered' the 'female intellect'.[7] Thus women, taken also to possess the capacity to reason, were allowed to enter the competition. If they had *enough* ability. But this means that the terms of the debate are never changed; it is still up to women to prove themselves equal to men. I have tried to show why we should not unquestionably accept these terms but should question their very foundation. We are not duty-bound to accept existing truth conditions. We would argue that showing the truth about girls to be a production in which there are no *simple* matters of fact is a central and strategic part of our struggle.

If those successes for which girls have struggled are refused as data, then it continues to be possible to explain, as a fault within women themselves, the relatively small number of women in the professions (except the caring professions, to which women are 'naturally' suited). 'Brilliant' women are few indeed in number, but women's painstaking attention to detail and their 'capacity for hard work' make them excellent material for the support of a 'brilliant academic male'. For the rational self of the *cogito*, like the reasoning child, cognitive development, 'proper conceptualisation' and rationality are attained naturally: there is work involved. In modern lower school practices, work is downplayed in favour of play. When girls work hard, therefore, there is something wrong. Women's labour (domestic and otherwise) makes intellectual inquiry, as play, relatively easy; it shoulders all the work that makes such creativity possible.

Within both the development of women's education and the rise of child-centred education, there are important shifts in the definition of pedagogy that I have charted elsewhere.[8] However, for the present purposes, let us dwell on the concept of 'the child' (gender unspecified) that is taken to develop within a 'facilitating environment'. The two terms form a couple; a *child* developing in an *environment*.

Further analysis suggests that the mother and the teacher both become part of the environment. They are defined by the very qualities that are opposite of those of 'the child', who is active and inquiring, and whose activity leads to 'real understanding'. The teacher and the mother, by contrast, are not necessary to instruct but to watch, observe, monitor, and facilitate development. The teacher and mother are defined as 'passive' in relation to the child's 'active'. They are nurturant, facilitating, sensitive and supportive, and they know when to intervene but not to interfere.

I have argued elsewhere that this opposition of the passive teacher to the active child is necessary to support the possibility of the illusion of autonomy and control upon which the child-centered pedagogy is founded.[9] In this sense, then, the 'capacity for nurturance' grounded in a naturalised femininity, the object of the scientific gaze, becomes the basis for woman's fitness for the facilitation of knowing and the reproduction of the knower, which is the support for, and yet opposite of, the production of knowledge. The production of knowledge is thereby separated from its reproduction and split along a sexual division that renders production and reproduction the natural capacities of the respective sexes.

The central concepts in the child-centred pedagogy and early mathematics education may themselves be regarded as signifiers, that is, aspects of discourse. That discourse claims to tell the truth about the universal properties of 'the child' who 'has concepts'. In this view, the attempts within psychology and mathematics, for example, may be seen as aspects of the attempt to construct a rationally ordered and controllable universe. We have argued that such an attempt is deeply bound up with the modern form of bourgeois government and the emergence of the modern state. It is also deeply involved with the attempt to describe and therefore regulate 'women', 'children', 'the working class', 'blacks', and 'the mad'.

The purpose of examining the conceptualisations that form the bedrock of modern practices is to draw out the terms that are key to the regime of truth that is constituted in and by the practices. My claim is that the discursive practices themselves, in producing the terms of the pedagogy, and therefore the parameters of practice, produce what it means to be a subject, to be subjected, within these practices. It can be stated that the terms in the discourse, such as *experience, discovery, stage,* etc., are signifiers that take their meaning from their position and function within the discourse itself: they enter as a relation. But this does not mean that there is a simple relation of representation between the material and the discursive. The discourse itself is a point of production and creation. When we say then that *experience* is created as a sign within the practice, or *the child* is produced as a subject, what we are talking about is the production of signs. If language does not represent reality, but rather the regulation of a practice itself produces a particular constellation and organisation of the material and discursive practices, then it can be argued that something is produced. It is in this sense that Foucault's power/knowledge couple can be applied here.

By means of an apparatus of classification and a grading of responses, 'the child' becomes a creation and yet at the same time provides room for a reading of pathology. There are no behaviours that exist outside the practices for producing them, not at any rate in this particular sequence or constellation and with these particular effects. The discursive practice becomes a complex sign system in which signs are produced and read and have truth effects: the truth of children is produced in classrooms. 'The child' is not coterminous with actual children, just as

Cowie (1978) argued that the signifier 'woman' is not coterminous with actual women, but central to the argument is the specification of that relation that is between the signifier and signified. If children become subjects through their insertion into a complex network of practices, there are no children who stand outside their orbit. I use the concept of *positioning*[10] to examine further what happens when such readings are produced and how children become *normal* and *pathological,* fast and slow, rote-learning and real understanding and so forth. In other words the practices provide systems of signs that are at once systems of classification, regulation, and normalisation. These produce systematic differences which are then used as classifications of children in the class. It is the meaning of *difference* that is a central feature in the production of any sign system in terms of the relations with other signs within the discourse. Similarities, that is, those signs that are linked within the discourse, also pile or heap together to provide *evidence* of a related classification. Thus *activity, doing, experience, readiness,* and so forth operate in relations of similarity, while *rote-learning* and *real understanding* are signs of contrastive opposition, of difference. I will attempt to demonstrate that these signs are produced and that often one sign may be taken as an indicator of the presence of another (similarity). Thus, for example, *activity* heralds a sign system, a complex discursive practice, whose terms and limits may be specified. Within this system then, children become embodiments of 'the child', precisely because that is how the practice is set up: they are normal or pathological and so forth. Their behaviour therefore, is an aspect of a position, a multifaceted subjectivity, such that 'the child' describes only their insertion into this, as one of many practices. But the behaviours do not precede the practice, precisely because their specificity is produced in these practices. This is why discourses of developmental psychology themselves can be understood as not simply providing a distortion of a real object, but may be read as evidence of *real understanding,* while *passivity* may be read as coterminous with, or similar to, *rote-learning, rule-following.*

These produce the practices in which 'the child' becomes a sign to be read and in which a normal child is differentiated from a pathological one. 'The child' develops through active manipulation of 'objects' in an 'environment'. Here all of the practices become objects existing in a biologised environment. The Plowden Report is full of illustrations, all of which describe the school, the classroom as an 'environment'. This sets up another aspect of the readings that are to be made. 'The child' is a unique individual, developing at 'his' own pace in an environment. In this way, the classroom therefore becomes the site of such development. However many children there are in a classroom, each is an individual—there is no sense of 'a class'. Indeed, it will be remembered that 'the class' forms a signifier in contrastive opposition to 'the child'. In this way, examining both the texts and practices themselves, it is possible to produce a reading of the pedagogy preexisting object, 'the real child' that they fail to represent or describe adequately. If they are points of production, they have positive and not simply negative effects. In this sense they are our 'raw material', the 'real' of a child is not something that can be known outside those practices in which its subjectivity is constituted. The signified only forms a sign out of fusion with the signifier. The signifier exists as a relation within a discourse. The material can only be known as a relation within a discursive practice. To say, therefore, that 'the child' is a signifier means that it must be united with a signified. Particular children therefore both are—and, that

is, the practices determine what they do anyway—but also they do present behaviours to be read—they may be normal or pathological.

The question remains, of course, what precisely is it that produces these current
truths? I have argued that current claims themselves rest upon a constant 'will to
truth'[11] that investing certainty in 'man', constantly seeks to find its other and
opposite in 'woman'. This truth is constantly reproven within classrooms in which
the very apparatuses themselves differentiate between success and its posited
causes. This has profound material effects upon the life chances of girls.

It is suggested above that within current school mathematics practices, certain
fantasies, fears, and desires invest 'man' with omnipotent control of a calculable
universe, which at the same time covers a desperate fear and desire of the other,
'woman'. 'Woman' becomes the repository of all of the dangers displaced from
the child, itself 'father' to the man. As I have argued, the necessity to prove the
mathematical inferiority of girls is not motivated by a certainty but by a terror of
loss. In all these respects, I have wanted to suggest a story in which these very
fantasies, fears, and desires become the forces that produce the actual effectivity
of the construction of fact, of current discursive practices in which these fantasies
are played out and in actual positions in such practices that, since they can be
proven to exist, literally have power over the lives of girls and boys, as in Foucault's power/knowledge couple.

In this case, we could take the signifiers 'child', 'teacher' and 'girl', or the dichotomies 'active/passive', 'rote-learning'/real understanding' as examples. We
can ask how the contradictory positions created within these practices are lived
and how these effect the production of subjectivity, for example, fears, desires,
and fantasies (cf. Walkerdine, 1985).

The first and most important thing to state is that there are no unitary categories
'boys' and 'girls'. If actual boys and girls are created at the intersection of multiple
positioning, they are inscribed as masculine and feminine. It follows, therefore,
that girls can display 'real understanding' or boys 'nurturance'. What matters is
what the effects of these positions are.

At first sight, it seems curious that such qualities could be displayed inside a
pedagogy designed not only specifically to produce their opposite but also to avoid
their appearance at all costs. It is important that in this respect the pathologisation
of these qualities, linked to the fear of totalitarianism and authoritarianism, has
related to certain developments in post-Freudian psychoanalysis, notably the work
of Klein. As much as their appearance is dreaded, however, it is also needed. Such
ascriptions frequently are correlated with 'helpfulness', in which helpful children
become an important part of the maintenance of calm, order and the smooth
regulation of the classroom. Our research demonstrated that it is as common for
female teachers to fear such qualities as to want them.

In the classroom discourse itself, there appears to be an overt message concerning activity, exploration, openness and so forth, derived from the child-centred
pedagogy. Our work in the primary classrooms suggests however, that the discourse of good behaviour, neatness, and rule-following exists *covertly* alongside
overt messages. It would have to be covert because it is the exact opposite of what
is supposed to take place. Moreover, all of those aspects—good behaviour, neatness and rule-following—are taken to be harmful to psychological and moral
development. Thus, they act as a fear- and guilt-inducing opposite. It is not surprising that teachers cannot afford to acknowledge the presence of such qualities

in the classroom or, if they do, to pathologise their appearance in girls, while failing to recognise that they are demanding the very qualities they simultaneously disparage. This possibility allows us to explore how girls come to desire in themselves qualities that appear the opposite from those of 'the child' that the pedagogy is set up to produce. Clearly, further investigations would have to engage with the classroom production of such contradictions, examining both the overt pedagogy and its covert shadow.

It is common in some psychoanalytic discourses, for example, to counterpose 'fantasy' to 'reality', and yet it is this division that appears most questionable. After all, if it is the case that some girls respond to the covert regulation of the classroom, we cannot say that such behaviour is pathological with respect to the real. It is precisely that certain aspects of the regulation of the practices are themselves suppressed. Simultaneously, the 'reality' of the child-centred pedagogy seems to be the object of an elaborate fantasy. It appears that here in the practices there circulates a vast and complex network of meanings, in which the play of desire, of teachers for children, of children for each other, envy, jealousy, rivalry, and so forth are continually created and re-created. It is not necessary to counterpose fantasy to reality, but to demonstrate how fantasies themselves are lived, played out, and worked through in their inscriptions in the verticality of discourses and practices.

I have begun to explore what this might mean elsewhere[12] but here we can take the analysis a little further, using the distinctions between *work* and *play* and between *rote-learning/rule-following* and *real understanding*. Work forms a relation in the 'old discourse'. In the new, children learn through doing, activity and *play*. Work forms an opposition of this. Work is bad because it relates to sitting in rows, regurgitating 'facts to be stored', not 'concepts to be acquired,' through active exploration of the environment. Work, then, forms a metaphoric relation with rote-learning and rule-following. Each describes a practice, a mode of learning that is opposite and antithetical to the 'joy of discovery'. Play is fun. There are also other aspects of work, that could be further elaborated—it leads to resistance. Children regulated in this way do not become self-regulating. But *work* is also a category to be outlawed by a system of education set up in opposition to child labour. It constitutes a category that frees 'the child' to be something distinct, playful, not an adult, outside the field of productive labour, innocent, natural. Related therefore is a series of values, fantasies, fears, desires that are incorporated into the discursive practices. These multiple connecting significations weave in and out of different discursive practices. It follows that *work,* as constituted as an opposite of *play,* can be recognised as a difference, as everything that does not signify play. It can also be recognised as a danger point, a point to be avoided. It is pathologised. It is learning by the wrong means, it is not 'natural' to 'the child'. If any child is observed 'doing work' this is likely to be understood as a problem. Hence, the distinction between 'rote-learning' and 'real understanding' discussed earlier. First, what happens when a child produces high attainment as well as producing behaviour to be read as *work*? If play is the discourse of the school, through what discourse do children read their performance? If 'real understanding' is co-terminous with the fantasy of possession of total power and control, how is it distinguished and what is the relation of this to 'getting the right answer', 'being certain' etc.? How does *possession* of *real understanding* provide fantasy, a chimera which has to be constantly and continually provided to exist out of a terror that lurking around every corner is its Other, rote-learning, work? Why is there such pressure, remorseless and unrelenting, to 'prove' that real understanding causes real attainment, and moreover that certain children have 'it' and that others just so surely do not, despite high attainment? What is invested?

One of the features of the apparatuses and technologies of the social, the modern production of truth through science, is that *proof* and practices for the production of evidence are central to the production of a truth, the certainty of 'real understanding' is ceaselessly proved in practices even though the evidence is often ambiguous. Here we want to dwell not so much on the evidence itself, as to question the motivation to provide proof, in particular of the opposition of *work* and *play*, rote and real.

Now, if the power of control over the universe in mathematical discourse is a fantasy, I am not setting out to demonstrate the *real* of the proof that girls *really can do* math or boys actually do not have real understanding. Rather, it is how those categories are produced as signs that we are interested in and how they 'catch up' the subjects, position them, and, in positioning, create a truth. For is not girls' bid for the 'understanding' of the greatest threat of all to a universal power or a truth that is invested in a fantasy of control of 'women'? Teachers will often go to great lengths to demonstrate that boys have real understanding. By the metaphoric chain created, *activity* is frequently read as a sign of understanding. Understanding, then, is evidenced by the presence of some attributes and the absence of others. It is activity—playing, utilisation of objects (Lego, for example), rule-breaking (rather than following) and so this can encompass naughtiness to the point of displays of hostility and conflict towards the teacher. All of these and more are taken to be evidence. Conversely, good behaviour in girls, working hard, helpfulness, neat and careful work are all read as danger signs of a lack. The counter-evidence—hard work in boys and understanding in girls is also produced as evidence, but when it is, other positions come into play (see Walkerdine, 1984). Evidence of real understanding, therefore, depends first upon a set of practices in which real understanding is the goal of an explicit framework of the 'activities' set up, as in all of the examples given here. Second it is assumed that the correct accomplishment is the result of understanding and that failure is produced through a lack of requisite experience, readiness, concepts. Third, the likelihood to favour one explanation of success over another depends upon other characteristics that define a real learner. Although boys frequently do not achieve terribly well, evidence of failure itself is produced as evidence in support of understanding.

In these pedagogic practices, facilitating and nurturant Others (teachers, mothers) are necessary to the facilitation of a 'natural' sequence of development in 'the child'. But this means that the designation 'child' sits uncomfortably on actual little girls. If 'women' is other to rationality, how is 'girl' lived, as child or potential women? These contradictions are lived out by girls in pedagogic practices.

Let us explore two aspects of this. First, girls' attainment, relative to boys', is not, in itself, in any simple or general sense the problem. Rather, the pointed cause invests the attainment with value as reproduction (rote-learning, rule-following) and not production (real understanding). It follows, therefore, that this attainment itself, while the object of much agonising about the poor performance of girls, is precisely that combination that is required for the entry of girls into the 'caring professions', in this case specifically the profession of teaching young children. Recruitment to elementary teacher training in Britain requires advanced qualifications, but usually a lower standard (poor pass marks, for example) than for university entrance.

Second, the production of reasoning requires an investment of desire in knowing, as illustrated by the phrase 'attracted to ideas', for example. Rational argument requires the transformation of conflict into discourse, such that the nurturant other facilitates an illusion of autonomy or control by the other, rendering invisible the power of parenting and teaching. In addition, mathematical reasoning presumes mastery of a discourse in which the universe is knowable and manipulable according to particular mathematical algorithms. This, along with the production of hard 'facts', is usually understood as the very basis of certainty. However, conversely, we might understand it as the fear, the necessity of proof against the terror of its other, that is, loss of certainty, control, and attempted control of loss; we might understand it as the impossibility of the object of desire, 'women', and elaborate fantasies to control consequent desire and avoid dependency or powerlessness.

It is the location of this feared and frightening other that is important to understand with respect to those classifications, particularly when they relate to girls' performance. Yet, as argued above, the very contradictions in the practice set girls up to achieve the very thing that is simultaneously desired and feared—passivity. It is feared in 'children' and yet is the very quality desired in nurturant care-givers, women as mothers and teachers.

SPLITTING THE DIFFERENCE

If women being powerful within mathematical and pedagogic practices is so threatening, it is hardly surprising that many women are fearful of recognising power within themselves. No wonder the woman I mentioned in the Introduction has such difficulty in establishing that the person with a distinction is actually herself. What she lives as a psychic problem is a profoundly social one, but a social one in which psychic processes are at the heart of the matter. Women's success appears to present such a threat to masculine rationality and to the bourgeois and patriarchal power that it underpins that it is very dangerous for women to admit their own power. How is that deep contradiction lived for such women? Is femininity a performance, a defence against the frightening possibility of stepping over the gender divide?

In this section of the paper I shall explore this issue, first with reference to the work of Wendy Hollway (1982, 1989), who has discussed splitting in couple relations and the work of women psychoanalysts who have attempted to address this point, particularly Joan Riviere's (1985) work on womanliness as masquerade.

Wendy Hollway analyses adult heterosexual couple relations in terms of the way in which rationality and emotionality are split between partners, with the woman being taken to 'hold' the emotionality for the couple, a quality that the man also projects her into so that she can be the emotional one, meaning that as long as it is located in her, he does not have to come to terms with his own emotional vulnerability. Similarly, the man can hold rationality for the couple. Hollway analyses in great detail how this is achieved by the couple. The concept of splitting that she uses is derived from Kleinian psychoanalysis.[13] In Klein the split-off part of (in this case) 'man' is projected into and held by 'woman' and similarly, rationality in women cannot easily be accommodated and therefore has to be experienced as though it belonged to someone else. To put the argument in this way is completely different from the essentialist view of femininity, in which certain characteristics simply do not belong to women, or a socialisation account that treats the social as though it were added on to the psychic rather than seeing them as produced together.[14] Lacan argued 'woman' exists only as a symptom of male fantasy.[15] What he meant was that the fantasies created under patriarchy (or the Law of the Father or Symbolic Order, as he calls it) create as their object not women as they really are but fantasies of what men both desire and fear in the Other. Women, then, become the repositories of such fantasies, and the effect for the psychic development of women themselves is extremely damaging and complex. Many psychoanalysts have attempted to engage with the problem presented by femininity under patriarchy. Freud tended to naturalise women's procreative function as a normal solution to the problem posed by the gendered splitting of rationality and emotionality. He did not investigate in great depth the elaborate fantasies that uphold the patriarchal and bourgeois order that I am suggesting are projected onto women. It is not surprising, then, that many women analysts who discovered the terrible confusions in their women patients around their power tended to essentialise them. The analysis I am suggesting here makes the essentialising tendency impossible. It is also the case that there is no easy division between fantasy and an observable reality since the social contains the elaborate fictions and fantasies of which I have written.

If masculinity and femininity may both be seen as defenses against the qualities held by other, then there can be no natural division of the sexes, but a complex order through which difference is held in play. Joan Riviere (1985) presents an interesting analysis of femininity in relation to cases of women patients. In her paper entitled 'Womanliness as Masquerade', she gives the example of a woman academic who after giving an academic paper has to flirt with men, often picking a 'fatherly' type as object of her flirtation. Riviere suggests that such flirtation provides her with reassurance that she is, after all, a woman. It acts as a masquerade, and elaborate defence against her fear that her femininity is a mere charade. If the male gaze, in Lacan's terms, constructs the object of the gaze as a masquerade, what lies beneath the masks? Lacan would have us believe that there is nothing, or a confusion. However, we could equally well ask what it is that the fantasy of the phallus holds up. In the academic scenario it appears that the fantasy of femininity is kept in place by the discursive truths that define and regulate the evaluation of women's performance. The struggle both to perform academically and to perform as feminine must seem at times almost impossible. No wonder that some of us split them apart in various ways or have different conscious and unconscious methods for dealing with the unbearable contradiction.[16]

To maintain this requires a tremendous amount of social and psychic labour. Luce Irigaray (1985) points clearly to these phallic fantasies and suggests that there is another libidinal organisation for women that cannot be spoken in the present Symbolic Order. However, where Lacan presents women as a lack, Irigaray presents her as having Other desires screaming to be spoken. The feminine performance in this view is not only a defence against masculinity, but against a powerful and active sexuality quite unlike that defined under patriarchy, although of course precisely that which is pathologised as bad or mad. Irigaray celebrates the plurality of women as the plurality of a sexual pleasure that does not have a goal of a single orgasm nor a single site of pleasure. Bronwyn Davies (1988) has explored women's sexual fantasies and suggests too that those fantasies are unlike the ones to which women are subjected. I am suggesting, therefore, that to become the object of those fantasies—the ones which render women as the object of the male gaze—requires a tremendous amount of work to cover over not an essential femininity but a different set of desires and organisation of pleasures (cf. Foucault) than those that can either clearly be articulated at the moment or are sanctioned in the practices in which femininity circulates as sign.

PEDAGOGIC STRATEGIES?

If girls' and women's power is a site of struggle, constantly threatening the tenuous grasp of male academic superiority, then any engagement with these issues in practice cannot rest upon a rationalistic base of choice or equal opportunities. Not only must the fiction of the gendered splitting be taken apart, but the psychic struggle engaged in by girls and women to live out the impossibly contradictory positions accorded to us must be addressed, as must the paranoias of the powerful that understand women's success as a (conscious or unconscious) threat to their position of superiority, shaky as it is. This requires a strategy that engages with the educational politics of subjectivity, a politics that refuses to split the psychic from the social and attempts to understand the complexity of defence and resistance and to find ways of dealing with those for teachers and students alike. Equal opportunities and models based on choice simply cannot engage with the complexity of the issues I have tried to spell out in this paper. Indeed, the danger is that when such strategies fail, as they do, educators will resort to essentialistic arguments, as they do, to explain, for example, the failure of girls to take 'non-traditional' subjects. Such essentialism is completely unwarranted but working on fiction, fantasy, and contradiction is to work in dangerous and threatening territory. It is that territory that we have to move into if we are to proceed in the struggle that recognises that women, after all, can be very powerful indeed.

Notes

1. See, for example Hartnett et al. (1979).
2. Social conditioning is a term that is commonly used and, although it may once have referred to social learning theory, I think that its roots in behaviourism are often forgotten.
3. This idea is discussed more fully in Walkerdine (1988) and Walkerdine et al. (1989).
4. This is a term used by Lacan (1977) to indicate not the real penis but the idea of male and patriarchal power invested in the possession of a penis. Possession of the phallus is both a metaphor and a fantasy.
5. In Walkerdine et al. (op. cit.) we discuss in more length the way in which physiological evidence is used to support the contention that educating girls would be physiologically dangerous, by in the end, affecting their capacity and desire to have children.
6. Of course, not all girls fail. (The discussions about failure concentrate on the failure of girls and women to enter higher-level careers requiring math and to obtain higher

level passes in the subject, but the issue is generalised so that explanations for this are sought with respect to all girls (see Walkerdine et al., op. cit.).

7. Higher education began to be open to women when the caring professions began to be based on the idea of the amplification of capacities for maternal nurturance (see Walkerdine et al., op. cit.).

8. Walkerdine (1984).

9. Walkerdine and Lucey (1989).

10. See Walkerdine et al. (1989) for a further discussion.

11. Cf. Foucault (1979).

12. Walkerdine et al., op.cit.

13. See for example, Mitchell (1986).

14. Henriques et al. (1984).

15. Lacan, op. cit.

16. One example of a little girl coping with the contradictions of being both her father's feminine little baby and a tomboy are discussed in Walkerdine (1985).

References

Cowie, E. (1978). Women as sign, *m/f*, 1.

Davies, B. (1988). Romantic love and female sexuality, Unpublished paper.

Department of Education and Science (1967). *Children and their Primary Schools* (The Plowden Report) (London, HMSO).

Foucault, M. (1979). *Discipline and Punish* (Harmondsworth, Penguin).

Hartnett, U., G. Boden and M. Fuller, (1979). *Sex Role Stereotyping* (London, Tavistock).

Henriques, J., W. Hollway, C. Urwin, C. Venn and V. Walkerdine (1984). *Changing the Subject* (London, Methuen).

Hollway, W. (1982). Identity and gender difference in adult social relations, Ph.D. thesis, University of London.

Hollway, W. (1989). *Subjectivity and Method in Psychology: gender, meaning and science* (London, Sage).

Irigaray, L. (1985). *This Sex which is not One* (Ithaca, Cornell University Press).

Lacan, J. (1977). *Ecrits: a selection* (London, Tavistock).

Mitchell, J. (Ed.) (1986). *The Selected Melanie Klein* (Harmondsworth, Penguin).

Riviere, J. (1985). Womanliness as masquerade, in: V. Burgin, J. Donald and C. Kaplan (Eds.). *Formations of Fantasy* (London, Methuen).

Walden, R. and V. Walkerdine (1982). Girls and Mathematics: the early years, *Bedford Way Papers*, 8.

Walkerdine, V. (1984). Developmental psychology and the child-centered pedagogy, in: Henriques et al., op. cit.

Walkerdine, V. (1985). Video replay: families, films and fantasy, in: Burgin, Donald and Kaplan (Eds) *Formations of Fantasy* (London, Methuen).

Walkerdine, V. (1988). *The Mastery of Reason* (London, Routledge).

Walkerdine, V. & The Girls and Mathematics Unit (1989). *Counting Girls Out* (London, Virago).

Walkerdine, V. and H. Lucey. (1989). *Democracy in the Kitchen* (London, Virago).

PART II

Education and Schooling

5

WOMEN AND SCHOOLING

Linda J. Nicholson

The decade of the 1970s produced a wide assortment of criticisms of schooling. Martin Carnoy, Ivan Illich, Joel Spring, Neil Postman, and others contributed to a significant body of literature that analyzed from a critical standpoint many of the accepted practices and previously unquestioned values of this institution. Many of the themes expressed in the literature received a full articulation in a book published in 1976, *Schooling in Capitalist America* by Samuel Bowles and Herbert Gintis.[1] Bowles and Gintis, like many of their predecessors, took up as their task the delegitimation of schooling. They argued that schools in a capitalist society not only do not fulfill the functions they are widely believed to fulfill, but on the contrary carry out tasks odious from the standpoint of a democratic ideology. For example, Bowles and Gintis showed that, contrary to accepted belief, schools do not provide the arena in which the industrious and smart make their way to the top of the social ladder. Rather these two economists marshaled a variety of statistics to make the argument that to the degree economic success can be correlated with educational levels, this correlation is not a function of cognitive competence.[2] Schools, rather than providing a fair means for channeling young people of different capacities into different classes, legitimize existing class divisions constructed on the basis of differences in inheritance. Second, schools in a capitalist society do not and cannot for Bowles and Gintis satisfy the Deweyan ideal of imparting beliefs and skills that simultaneously contribute to an individual's self-development while making him or her socially useful. Any needs for self-development or self-expression are, according to Bowles and Gintis, inevitably sacrificed in a capitalist society when they run into conflict with the integrative function of schooling. This integrative function entails that schools not only impart the necessary beliefs and skills demanded by the market economy, but that they also create the type of personality structures necessary for functioning in primarily hierarchical and authoritarian work situations. Like other radical critics of education, such as Illich, Bowles and Gintis pointed to the "hidden curriculum" of schools and argued its dominance over the explicit curriculum. They pointed to the ways in which the social relations of the classroom parallel the social relations of the work world, from student lack of control over curricula and classroom activities paralleling worker lack of control in the factory, to the wage as external means of motivation in the factory paralleling the grade as external

means of motivation in the classroom. They argued that this correspondence between the social relations of the economy and the social relations of the classroom
needed to be understood historically. Whereas a beginning industrial society
needed only a certain amount of homogeneous character training amply provided
by the one-room schoolhouse, the twentieth-century corporation, with its elaborate hierarchical stratification of jobs, required, they claimed, the creation of a
variety of personality types, from those trained in simple obedience to those accustomed to internalizing the goals of the institution. The complexly structured
twentieth-century public school, with its elaborate tracking systems justified by
elaborate IQ testing, was constructed and operates they argued, to create such a
diversely motivated workforce.

The theses of Bowles and Gintis, as well as those of their radical predecessors,
gave theoretical grounding to certain suspicions intuitively held by many activists
of the 1960s. One of the most important progeny of the activist movements of
the 1960s has been the women's movement of the 1970s, which like its predecessors has felt a certain antagonism between its values and goals and the values and
goals of the institution of schooling. What I would like to attempt in this essay is
the beginnings of a theoretical grounding for this felt antagonism similar to the
theoretical grounding provided by the 1970s radical critics. As the women's movement itself provided a needed expansion of focus of the political movements of
the 1960s, so also do I believe that a theoretical analysis of schooling from the
perspective of gender can provide a necessary enlargement to the analysis of the
radical critics of schooling. An analysis such as that of Bowles and Gintis persua-
sively illustrated certain aspects of the relationship between schools and the economy in a capitalist society. What, however, also needs analysis is the relation
between schooling, the economy, and the family in modern capitalist society. One
danger with an analysis such as that of Bowles and Gintis is that it tends to be
mechanistic, i.e., it tends to replicate a crude form of Marxism where all social
phenomena, in this case schools, are seen as direct epiphenomena of the economy.
This mechanism can, I believe, be avoided through an analysis that draws attention to the historically changing relation between the economy and the family in
modern capitalist society and deals with the question of why modern capitalism
needed an institution like schools to perform a socializing function. In other words
one cannot merely make the claim that schools in a capitalist society socialize the
young into the values and practices of capitalism; one must also ask why capitalism needed a socializing agent like schools to perform such a function. Why for
example did the family become no longer sufficient? Second, while the analysis of
the earlier critics of schooling to some extent did account for race, and to a greater
extent for class differences, the analysis did not account for the role of schools in
contributing to gender differentiation and in reproducing the sexual division of
labor. Many have pointed to the role of schools in supplementing the traditional
sex role socialization that takes place within the family. I believe, however, that
we need to go beyond an analysis of the socialization practices that take place
within both family and schools and analyze how the process of dual socialization
of family and schools as a structural feature of modern society is itself important
in maintaining sex role differentiation. In other words, we again need to ask why
schools arose as an additional socializing agent to the family and how the development of a dual system of socialization has been and continues to be crucial in
maintaining sex roles.

Much recent work on the family has emphasized the modern family as a social unit increasingly set off and isolated from the emerging realm of "society." Hannah Arendt in *The Human Condition* early talked about the rise of the "social" in modern western society. She noted that the emergence of this realm as a realm separate and distinct from our modern "private realm" of home and family was importantly allied with the removal of the "economic" from within the household to the exterior of public space. In classical Athens what we would now call "economic" concerns were concerns of the household; our term economy derives from the Greek "oikos," meaning household. In classical Athens those activities associated with the taking care of life's basic necessities, the production of food, and the reproduction of the species were the concerns of the household, hidden there as the underside, most bestial aspects of human existence. Today only the reproduction of the species, sexuality, remains at home; the production of food has become a public phenomenon. For Arendt, this growing publicity of production or labor has totally transformed the modern world; what emerged was "society."

> The laboring activity, though under all circumstances connected with the life process in its most elementary biological sense, remained stationary for thousands of years, imprisoned in the eternal recurrence of the life process to which it was tied. The admission of labor to public stature, far from eliminating its character as a process . . . has, on the contrary, liberated this process from its circular, monotonous recurrence and transformed it into a swiftly progressing development whose results have in a few centuries totally changed the whole inhabited world.[3]

Arendt's description of the labor process as becoming in the modern world increasingly "public" and making possible the rise of "society" seems particularly true of the last few centuries. What we often call "industrialization" is this very removal of labor from the interior of the household to the exterior of the public world. What has emerged with industrialization is not only the realm of "society" but also, in part in opposition, the realm of the "private." "Privacy" no longer refers as with the Greeks to some lack but in the modern world denotes some good.[4] As expressed by the romantic tradition of the eighteenth and nineteenth centuries, one's inner life began to represent a bulwark against what came to be perceived as the less than human nature of society.

> At the same time the conflict between the individual and society took on a new meaning. On one side appeared "society"—the capitalist economy, the state, the fixed social core that has no space in it for the individual; on the other, personal identity, no longer defined by its place in the social division of labour. On one side the objective social world appeared, perceived at first as "machinery" or "industry," then throughout the nineteenth century as "society" and into the twentieth as "big business," "city hall," and then as "technology" or "life." . . . In opposition to this harsh world that no individual could hope to affect, the modern world of subjectivity was created.[5]

Our contemporary sense of subjectivity and privatization cannot, however, be viewed as merely a consequence of industrialization. Both phenomena seem also allied with the increasing isolation and separation of the family that appears a progressive development from the ending of the middle ages. Even our modern concept of the family, as a unit that refers even in its extended form to the primarily biological component of husband, wife, and children, represents a restriction on the medieval concept of kin. As Philippe Aries points out in *Centuries of Childhood*, the biological unit that corresponds to our concept of "family" was prior to the fifteenth century only an unimportant subgroup within a more extended network, linking those sharing a common ancestry.[6] Lawrence Stone in his history of the English family during the period 1500–1800 stresses also the progressive delineation of the "family" as a unit separate and distinct from the external community. Stone traces the progressive dominance of three major family types during this period, from what he calls the "Open Lineage" to the "Restricted Patriarchal Nuclear Family" to the "Closed Domestic Nuclear Family," a progression indicating a steady isolation of family from external society.

> The second type of family which first overlapped and then very slowly replaced the Open Lineage Family over a period of about a century and a half, and then only in certain social strata, was what I call—to stress the differences the Restricted Patriarchal Nuclear Family. This type which began in about 1530, predominated from about 1580 to 1640, and ran on to at least 1700, saw the decline of loyalties to lineage, kin, patron and local community as they were increasingly replaced by more universalistic loyalties to the nation state and its head, and to a particular sect or church. As a result, "boundary awareness" became more closed off from external influences, either of the kin or of the community. . . . After 1640 a series of changes in the state, the society and the church undermined the patriarchal emphasis, while continuing the decline of external pressures on the increasingly nuclear family. The result was the evolution among the upper bourgeoisie and squirearchy of a third type, the closed Domesticated Nuclear Family, which evolved in the late seventeenth century and predominated in the eighteenth. This was the decisive shift, for this new type of family was the product of the rise of Affective Individualism. It was a family organized around the principle of personal autonomy, and bound together by strong affective ties. Husbands and wives personally selected each other rather than obeying parental wishes, and their prime motives were now long-term personal affection rather than economic or status advantage for the lineage as a whole. . . . But the four key features of the modern family—intensified affective bonding of the nuclear core at the expense of neighbors and kin; a strong sense of individual autonomy and the right to personal freedom in the pursuit of happiness; a weakening of the association of sexual pleasure with sin and guilt; and a growing desire for physical privacy—were all well established by 1750 in the key middle and upper sectors of English society. The nineteenth and twentieth centuries merely saw their much wider social diffusion.[7]

What is important to stress in this growing social demarcation between the realms of privacy and subjectivity enclosed within home and family and the external world of society is that the realms became in an important sense gender coded. This phenomenon is apparent in the relation between family and government that emerged from the sixteenth to the nineteenth centuries. As Stone points out, there was within the upper classes a fluctuating loyalty between kin and state during the Middle Ages. From the sixteenth century on, the power of the state became solidified as it increasingly assumed responsibility for regulating property, providing military protection, and serving as general guardian and regulator of the interactions of its subjects.[8] This transfer of power was accompanied by an ideological campaign: duty to country and sovereign became a moral imperative.

As Stone also notes, an important tool used by the state in transferring loyalty from kin to itself was an emphasis on the power of the husband and father within the nuclear family.

> What seems to have happened is that a diffuse concept of patriarchy inherited from the middle ages that took the form of "good lordship" meaning dominance over kin and clientage—was vigorously attacked by the state as a threat to its own authority. Patriarchy was now reinforced by the state, however, in the much more modified form of authoritarian dominance by the husband and father over the woman and children within the nuclear family. What had previously been a real threat to the political order was thus neatly transformed into a formidable buttress to it.[9]

The relation of each family unit to the state was likened to the relationship of the individual members of the family to its male head. As stated in 1609 by James I, "Kings are compared to fathers in families: for a king is truly *parens patriaie,* the politic father of his people."[10] This simultaneous strengthening of the power of the male head of family and the state could work in so far as the male head was seen as the representative of the family to the state. This idea that the male head of household represented the family in the political world continued into the nineteenth century and can indeed be said to have lasted until the granting of women's suffrage. This masculinization of the political world is itself merely an example of the more general gender coding that has accompanied the separation of family from society, intensifying until by the nineteenth century what was in existence at least in the United States a very strict demarcation of "sexual spheres." Ellen Dubois describes this development:

> However, only men emerged from their familial roles to enjoy participation in the public sphere. Women on the whole did not. Women were of course among the first industrial workers, but it is important to remember that they were overwhelmingly unmarried women for whom factory work was a brief episode before marriage. Adult women remained almost entirely within the private sphere, defined politically, economically, and socially by their familial roles. Thus, the public sphere became man's arena; the private, woman's. This gave the public/private distinction a clearly sexual character. This phenomenon, canonized as the nineteenth-century doctrine of sexual spheres, is somewhat difficult for us to grasp. We are fond of pointing out the historical durability of sexual roles into our own time and miss the enormous difference between the twentieth century notion of sexual roles and the nineteenth century idea of sexual spheres. The difference is a measure of the achievements of nineteenth century feminism.[11]

In sum, by the nineteenth century there existed within the United States a strong separation between the realm of the family and home, judged women's sphere, and the external world of "society," including business and politics, the realm of men. This separation of spheres was more than gender coded; it was also divided by differences in values and practices. As noted, the home during the eighteenth and nineteenth centuries became progressively viewed as the realm of privacy and subjectivity, the only place where the expression of feeling and emotion were appropriate. It also became viewed as not only an emotional but also a moral refuge against what progressively became viewed as the immorality of the external, public world. Women as guardians of the home became guardians of the "inner life" and guardians of morality. This latter assignment is manifested in the curious alliance that Ann Douglas points to in the nineteenth century between a certain class of middle-class American women and the clergy, themselves newly removed from authority in the public realm.[12] With the increasing removal of productive activities from the home to the factory, the tasks of the household and thus the tasks of women became redefined. The activity of consumption arose as a semi-skilled occupation, with women receiving approval for their wisdom as shoppers. The cult of motherhood that flourished in the nineteenth century was allied to a new conception of this role as requiring its own skills. Allied to the growth of such "womanly tasks" was also a new conception of "femininity" as "silly," "dependent," "decorative," and "sentimental." Not only did femininity now come to be viewed as importantly constituted by frailness, smallness in size, weakness, and delicacy but masculinity importantly became viewed as its opposite. The differences between men and women became stressed. The laces and frills that adorned the dress of the eighteenth century gentlemen were significantly absent from the attire of his nineteenth century counterpart.

These sharply contrasting conceptions of "femininity" and "masculinity" can be seen as both symbolic and constitutive of the sharp separation between family and society that had arisen in this country by the nineteenth century. Consequent to a society divided into separated spheres was the need for differences in character traits reflective of these differences in spheres. Only in a society where it is theoretically possible for a woman not to be at home does the maxim "a woman's place is at home" make sense. Moreover, only in a society where the activities of the "home" are viewed as importantly different from the activities that take place outside the home does it make sense to view the personalities of the persons who carry out such different activities as themselves necessarily different in kind.

This separation of spheres of private and public life, governed by differences in norms and practices and staffed by persons differentiated in personality, provides, I believe, an important framework for understanding modern Western schooling. Modern Western schooling arose as a necessary conduit institution between the increasingly separated realms of family and society. As these two realms became distinguished in terms of both practices and norms, what arose was the need for an institution to socialize young people, primarily young boys, out of the family and into the public world. In other words, insofar as there arose a social realm governed by practices and values different from those of the home and family, the family became insufficient as a socializing agent. Certainly, some socialization functions of the family were and remain necessary. In the home children learn how to become boys and girls and thus prospective men and women. They also learn all those habits of daily living that do not pertain to a job or public role. The socialization of character traits and skills required for these latter activities have become, however, the province of the schools.

There are several advantages in understanding the socializing functions of modern schooling in terms of the separation between private and public that are not provided by an explanation that only appeals to capitalism. In the United States and Western Europe the process of industrialization and the development of capitalism represent one process. This is not, however, the case for countries such as Russia where industrialization has taken place outside of a capitalist framework. Thus to account for similarities in schooling between such countries and those of Western Europe and the United States it may be necessary to appeal to similarities in a public/private separation attendant upon industrialization that an appeal to capitalism alone could not provide.

There is an additional, most important reason for greater attention to the fact of public/private separation in explanations of modern schooling. If we think of schooling as being merely the institution by which capitalism socializes its young, we are in danger of committing a crucial mistake. It is true that the development of capitalism has been inseparably linked with the split between public and private. What is also true is that the public/private split has not been gender neutral. As I earlier noted, the private sphere has been traditionally the sphere of women, the public sphere, the sphere of men. Insofar as young women have been destined to remain within the private sphere, schooling has been seen for the most part as unnecessary for them. Schooling has been primarily viewed as necessary only for those who are expected to make a transition from the private sphere into the public sphere, and this has been true primarily for young men. Thus without attention to the separation between private and public in modern society, we will not be able to understand the gender bias of modern schooling.

To say that modern western schooling has had a "gender bias" is not to say that young girls and women have had no place in this institution. The story is more complex than that. A degree of this complexity is illustrated in the nineteenth century's feminization of the teaching profession. The expansion of mass public schooling in the latter part of the nineteenth century put a heavy drain on the revenues of many town governments. One means of combatting this drain was to hire women as teachers. Thus Phyliss Stock reports:

> As local education costs rose in the 1870s and 1880s committees that had previously preferred male teachers discovered that women, who earned about 60% of male salaries at best, were appropriate teachers of children. They were gentler, more patient, tender and motherly than men. Teaching was now recognized as women's natural profession.[13]

Stock illustrates an aspect of the thinking involved in a report of a committee hiring a county superintendent of schools that stated: "As there is neither honor nor profit connected with this position, we see no reason why it should not be filled by a woman."[14] The oddity involved in this feminization of the teaching profession was that it occurred in a society that firmly believed that a woman's place was at home and that women's minds were inferior to men's. One means of dealing with this oddity was to create the role of the "schoolmarm," an unmarried woman somewhat "mannish" in character and appearance. Women were thus allowed to leave the home only at the price of giving up their femininity. This has been a familiar demand made on women entering traditional male arenas and is illustrated also in public opinion regarding university women in the late nineteenth and early twentieth centuries. In England such women were known as "bluestockings" and "If they had male friends, it was assumed they were not serious about their studies; if they did not, they were considered unmarriageable."[15]

Thus to say that schools have had a "gender bias" is not to say that schools have excluded women. It is rather to say that schooling has been primarily intended for young men and only secondarily for young women. This has been true for the dame and town schools of the eighteenth and nineteenth centuries as well as for the graduate and professional schools of our own time. The form and extent this bias has assumed has depended largely on the actual extent of women's involvement in the public sphere. One further irony of the feminization of the teaching profession of the nineteenth century was that it brought about the need for extending secondary education to large numbers of young women and thus served as a counterbalance against the tendency of that century to deny higher education to young women. That women's relation to schooling parallels their relation to the public world is also illustrated in the nature of women's participation in schooling in the twentieth century. During the course of the twentieth century, women have increasingly become part of the labor force. This increased participation has been in primarily sex-stereotyped occupations such as teaching, waitressing, secretarial, or other "pink-collar" jobs. The percentage of women in administrative or professional positions has remained low and indeed often decreased during the course of the twentieth century. For example the percentage of American women as university faculty members increased from 20% to 26% from 1910 to 1920, to 27% by the outbreak of World War II and then dropped to 24% in 1950 and 22% in 1960 and 1970.[16] Similarly, while the percentages of women to receive secondary and undergraduate education has increased during the twentieth century (with the exception of drops in certain periods such as between 1940 and 1950) by 1970 women still were only receiving 13.3% of Ph.D.'s. This was in spite of the fact that they were receiving 41.5% of all bachelor's degrees and 39.7% of all master's degrees.[17]

That the public world in modern western society has been primarily the world of men has had consequences not only for the gender of schools' participants but also for the values which have predominated; the "masculinization" of the public world has reflected itself in a parallel "masculinization" of schools. In late twentieth century America this again is most expressed in the difference in the norms and values of the lower and higher levels of schooling. As one moves from elementary to graduate and particularly professional schools, one finds an institution less and less "homelike" and increasingly dominated by characteristics associated with the public world and masculinity. Elementary schools are primarily staffed by women and feminine norms predominate. The injunctions preached here, to "share," to be obedient and quiet, are those in which little girls are trained to be adept. It is not surprising that little boys are often failures in this institution. As one moves higher through schools to the graduate and professional level, the norms change. Competition becomes more encouraged than "sharing"; accomplishment becomes more important than effort. It becomes unacceptable to express emotions; crying is never an appropriate response.

The importance of these gender differences in norms affecting women's success in higher education is frequently overlooked. Many academics believe that the reason there are few women in their departments or their universities has to do with past attitudes towards women that are no longer held by most even mildly enlightened people. Thus the failure of women today to acquire the diplomas or satisfy the criteria for tenure must be the responsibility of the individual woman. Affirmative action is understood, within this framework, as a watchguard against the continuation of such past forms of discrimination. If we can insure that no discrimination exists, just principles of merit can be left free to operate. The problem with this viewpoint, held by many, is that it ignores the extent to which the university is not a gender-neutral institution but has and continues to be an institution in which women are still in manifold ways "out of place." As Adrienne Rich notes, in such a context even the self-perception of the "exceptional" woman must be diminished, if only by her description as "exceptional."[18]

The radical critics of education in the 1970s emphasized three primary functions of modern schooling, its functions of channeling, socializing, and legitimizing. In the preceding I have attempted to show how at least two of these functions, channeling and socializing, need to be understood from the perspective of the separation in modern society between the two spheres of private and public life. I have argued that modern schooling, as a mass public institution, arose as a necessary one-way bridge to channel and socialize primarily young men out of the family and into the public sphere. There remains one final argument I would like to make and that is how the "legitimizing" function of schooling is also gender coded and itself importantly constitutive of the separation between private and public.

Unlike one's initial entrance into a family, entrance into the public sphere represents in modern society an accomplishment. Finding employment in a capitalist society is an activity in which one can be more or less successful. The radical critics of education have stressed the important role of schools in channeling children from different classes into different occupations in the economy and legitimizing this channeling on the basis of differences in "intelligence." Some, such as Illich, have noted the important function of schools in legitimizing not only people but also types of knowledge, in indeed often establishing a corner on "knowledge," thereby discrediting many skills and the activities based on them not taught within schools. Again, what I would like to add is the necessity for placing such arguments within the framework of the modern separation between public and private. Such a framework allows us to see the important ways women as a class have been differentially affected by this function of schools. For example, while women, like other social groups, have been channeled to low occupational slots in the public world, there has also been a tendency to keep them as a class out of the public world altogether. A corollary of this exclusion has been a delegitimation of women's knowledge and skills reinforced by the exclusion of these types of expertise from the curriculum of schools. As a consequence, the abilities women do possess are not taken seriously and are not viewed as transferable to the public world.

In describing school's channeling and socializing functions, I may have created an impression of a passive institution, one reflexively responding to the needs of a society separated into a public and private sphere. I have described schooling as if it were a "one-way bridge" making possible the transition of young people from one sphere to the other. What is important to note about bridges, however, is that they do not only service their respective sides; they may also be important in keeping the sides separate. This active function of schools becomes apparent in discussing the legitimizing function of schooling. Schools not only service the needs of the public sphere; they also by their legitimizing function help constitute the public sphere itself as a sphere distinct from the private. An obvious example here is the process by which medicine became a public institution. Home care suffered disrepute in part because the knowledge and skills upon which it was based were delegitimized in the context of the professionalization of medicine. The professionalization of medicine, like the professionalization of other activities, was made possible through the institution of schooling. One point that needs to be stressed about the phenomenon of professionalization is that while it represents in part a process by which the public is separated from the private, it also represents a process by which the public world is also differentiated into rank and status, again often differentially affecting women as a group. A significant phenomenon of the twentieth century is that many "women's" professions have been requiring more education and simultaneously becoming more practiced by men. One example is the field of social work.[19] Another example is the decline of women as principals in elementary schools as this profession requires more certification by advanced degree.[20] One can even note a difference in the occupation of women's hairdressing between the community beauty parlor, staffed almost entirely by women, and the more exclusive, urban hairdressing salon, more "professional" in style and more highly staffed by men.

In conclusion, the arguments of the radical critics of education of the 1970s need to be placed within the context of the modern separation between the two spheres of private and public life. Such a context enables us to see how those functions of schooling that the radical critics focused on, the socializing, channeling, and legitimizing functions, have all been importantly biased along lines of gender. If the job of schools has been to prepare young people for participation in the public sphere, this sphere as primarily masculine has entailed a corresponding gender bias of both the population and the norms of schools. Moreover, not only have schools mirrored the gender population and norms of the public world, they have also been instrumental in separating it from the private. In doing so they have helped constitute the separation of spheres itself, a separation fundamental to our modern sex-role system. Thus the function of schools in reproducing sex-roles goes beyond the employment of stereotyped readers or the maintenance of biases in vocational counseling and extends to the very creation of the separation of spheres upon which these roles have been based.

Notes

1. Samuel Bowles and Herbert Gintis. *Schooling in Capitalist America: Educational Reform and the Contradictions of Economic Life* (New York, Basic Books, 1976).

2. Ibid., pp. 112–113.

3. Hannah Arendt, *The Human Condition* (Chicago: University of Chicago Press, 1958), pp. 46–47.

4. Ibid., p. 38.

5. Eli Zaretsky, *Capitalism, the Family, and Personal Life* (New York: Harper and Row, 1976), p. 57.

6. Philippe Aries, *Centuries of Childhood: A Social History of Family Life*, trans. Robert Baldick (New York: Alfred A. Knopf, 1962), p. 35.

7. Lawrence Stone, *The Family, Sex, and Marriage in England, 1500–1800* (New York: Harper and Row, 1977), pp. 7–9.

8. Ibid., p. 133.

9. Ibid., pp. 153–154.

10. Ibid., p. 152.

11. Ellen Dubois, "The Radicalism of the Woman Suffrage Movement: Notes Toward the Reconstruction of Nineteenth Century Feminism," *Feminist Studies* 3 (1975): 64–65.

12. Ann Douglas, *The Feminization of American Culture* (New York: Alfred A. Knopf, 1977).

13. Phyliss H. Stock, *Better Than Rubies: A History of Women's Education* (New York: G. P. Putnam's Sons, 1978), p. 189.

14. Ibid., p. 188.

15. Ibid., p. 222.

16. Ibid., pp. 223 and 227.

17. Stock, p. 227.

18. Adrienne Rich, "Toward a Woman-Centered University," in *Women and the Power to Change,* ed. Florence Howe (New York: McGraw-Hill, 1975), p. 24.

19. Felice Davidson Perlmutter and Leslie B. Alexander, "Exposing the Coercive Consensus: Racism and Sexism in Social Work," in *The Management of Human Services,* ed. Rosemary C. Sarri and Yeheskel Hasenfeld (New York: Columbia University Press, 1978). See also James Gripton, "Sexism in Social Work: Male Takeover of a Female Profession," *Social Worker-Le Travailleur Social* 42 (1974): 78–89.

20. Roslyn D. Kane, "Sex Discrimination in Education: A Study of Employment Practices Affecting Professional Personnel," Study Report, Vol. 1, April 1976, a publication of the National Center for Educational Statistics, Department of Health, Education, and Welfare. Kane cites a 1928 NEA study that shows that 55% of elementary school principals were women, whereas in 1972 this percentage was less than 20%.

6

MALE HEGEMONY, SOCIAL CLASS, AND WOMEN'S EDUCATION

Madeleine Arnot

At any given time, the more powerful side will create an ideology suitable to help maintain its position and to make this position acceptable to the weaker one. In this ideology the differentness of the weaker one will be interpreted as inferiority, and it will be proven that these differences are unchangeable, basic, or God's will. It is the function of such an ideology to deny or conceal the existence of a struggle. (Horney, 1967, p. 56)

According to Sheila Rowbotham (1973) in *Woman's Consciousness, Man's World*, the concept of male hegemony, like that of female oppression, is not new, but then as she also points out, it is one thing to encounter a concept, quite another to understand it. That process of understanding requires one to perceive the concept of male hegemony as a whole series of separate "moments" through which women have come to accept a male-dominated culture, its legality, and their subordination to it and in it. Women have become colonized within a male-defined world, through a wide variety of "educational moments" that seen separately may appear inconsequential, but which together comprise a pattern of female experience that is qualitatively different from that of men. These educational moments when collated can provide considerable insights into the collective "lived experience" of women as women. For example, in the educational autobiographies of women edited by Dale Spender and Elizabeth Sarah (1980), what emerges is that in education women have "learnt to lose" and more than that they have learnt *how* to lose, even though they may have had the ability to succeed academically. Through such experience, they have learnt to accept that "the *masculine* man is one who achieves, who is masterful: the *feminine* woman is one who underachieves, who defers" (Brewster, 1980, p. 11).

Research into the experience of women in education also raises numerous problems, however, not just in terms of doing the research (e.g., Llewellyn 1980) but also at the level of theorising about education and its relationship to the political and economic context. Here I shall focus upon existing work in British sociology of education to show the differences between two bodies of research into women's education which I call the cultural and political economy perspectives. I will also discuss the relationship between studies of women's education and recent Marxist theories of education. I will examine the interaction between class and male hegemony in education and then attempt to develop a different and very elementary framework within which to conceive of research questions in this area, as a starting point for a more cohesive study of class and gender. The problems raised through attempting to put together theories of two different structures of inequality will at least point to the complexity of combining, in everyday life, the demands of two sets of social relations and their interrelations.

In a previous paper (MacDonald, 1980b) I have argued that both class and gender relations constitute hierarchies in which material and symbolic power are based. Inside these hierarchies, the dialectics of class and gender struggles are waged. If we want therefore to research the role of schools as one social "site" in which the reproduction of the socio-sexual division of labour occurs, then it is necessary to be aware of the nature of these *two* forms of social struggle, the different stakes involved, and how such struggles are "lived through" by individuals who negotiate terms within these power relations and who construct for themselves specific class and gender identities.

The need to describe the processes of gender discrimination in education and its effects—female subordination in the waged and domestic labour forces—is circumscribed by the political commitment to offer suggestions, proposals, and programmes for educational reform that will help liberate women. That political cause should not allow us, however, to stop at the immediate level of ethnographic or quantitative description and prescription. We need to go further and analyse in depth the processes of the *production* of gender differences both inside and outside schools and to analyse the forms of gender reproduction which are inherent in, and not independent of, the patterns of class reproduction, class control, and class struggles.[1] This political and economic context of gender reproduction sets the limits and influences the forms and outcomes of gender struggles. It critically affects the impact of any education reform and its effectiveness. In this paper, therefore, I shall retain my original position:

> In so far as class relations (in other words the division between capital and labour) constitute the primary element of the capitalist social formation, they limit and structure the form of gender relations, the division between male and female properties and identities. I do not believe that one can disassociate the ideological forms of masculinity and femininity, in their historical specificity from either the material basis of patriarchy nor from the class structure. If one definition of femininity or masculinity is dominant, it is the product of patriarchal relations and also the product of class dominance, even though these two structures may exist in contradiction. (MacDonald, 1980b, p. 30)

The analysis of the origins and nature of gender differences will make reference to the existence of a bourgeois and male hegemony that has controlled the development of female education. The concept of hegemony used here refers to a whole range of structures and activities as well as values, attitudes, beliefs, and morality that in various ways support the established order and the class and male interests that dominate it. By putting the concept of hegemony rather than "reproduction" at the fore of an analysis of class and gender, it is less easy in doing research to forget the *active* nature of the learning process, the existence of dialectic relations, power struggles, and points of conflict, the range of alternative practices that may exist inside, or exist outside and be brought into, the school. Further, it allows us to remember that the power of dominant interests is never total nor secure. Cultural hegemony is still a weapon that must be continually struggled for, won, and maintained. Women in this analysis must offer unconsciously or consciously their "consent" to their subordination before male power is secured. They are encouraged "freely" to choose their inferior status and to accept their exploitation as natural. In this sense the production of gender differences becomes a critical point of gender struggle and reproduction, the site of gender control.

CULTURAL AND POLITICAL ECONOMY PERSPECTIVES

In contrast to studies in the United States, where a considerable amount of research has been carried out on gender socialisation, there is relatively little research on girls' and women's schooling in British sociology of education. It is almost as if the "left wing" stance of much British sociology of education has precluded investigation into the area of gender and race relations within schooling, even though these other structures of inequality are contained within, affect, and even exaggerate the effects of class divisions as Westergaard and Resler (1975), Byrne (1978), and King (1971) amongst others have discovered. By and large, the analysis of gender divisions has developed separately from that of class divisions and still seems to have had little or almost no impact upon those who remain within that tradition. Even those who appear to have moved away from a strict "correspondence" model, such as researchers at the Centre for Contemporary Cultural Studies (CCCS) who now argue that one should recognise that schools face *two* directions—towards the family and towards the economy—have done little to rectify the class bias of their analysis. In their new publication, *Unpopular Education,* (1981) the analysis of state educational policy and forms of struggle at particular historical conjunctures very quickly leaves the study of parenthood and the relationship between class- and gender-determined education on the sidelines. Cultural studies, as Angela McRobbie (1980) has argued, are also guilty of being sex-blind since either they equate "working-class culture" only with that of the male working class or they focus specifically on working-class boys and ignore the sexism inherent in their particular form of subcultural "style" or version of masculinity.[2] In terms of classroom ethnography, which is still a major methodological tradition and strand within contemporary British sociology of education, the neglect of gender is even more noticeable and less excusable since it implies that the observer in the classroom is blind to the process of gender discrimination that, according to recent feminist work (e.g., Clarricoates, 1980; Delamont, 1970; Lobban, 1975), occurs most of the time in teacher-pupil interaction, classroom lessons and pupil control in British primary and secondary schools. Fortunately, there is now a growing amount of research, published for example in Deem (1980) and Kelly (1981), which uses a variety of research techniques to investigate the process of gender ascription, labelling, and discrimination in schools.

The development of work on gender in education in Britain, I believe, has employed what I have called the cultural perspective (Arnot, 1981). I have argued that those who use the cultural perspective focus upon the patterns of "sex-role socialization," that is, upon the processes internal to the school that determine and shape the formation of gender identities.[3] Their concern is with educational "underachievement," with the analysis of the overt curriculum and the hidden curriculum, with classroom interaction, with girls' attitudes to schools as well as with teachers' and career officers' attitudes to girls' futures. What this cultural perspective appears to have in common with the political economy model is that it also refers to the processes involved in the "reproduction" of gender. "Reproduction" here is not a Marxist concept, however. Several critical differences distinguish the political economy and cultural perspectives—only a few of which I can cover here. Perhaps the most important difference is that cultural analysis concentrates upon *how* rather than *why* schools function to reproduce the patterns of gender inequality—the focus is therefore upon internal rather than external processes. The origin of these processes lies in the concept of "sex-role ideology" (or some equivalent concept), yet, paradoxically, this ideology is also produced and reproduced in the school. It is thus both the *cause* and the *effect* of gender inequality since each new generation of pupils in turn becomes the new generation of parents, teachers, employers, etc., carrying with them the assumptions of such "sex-role ideology." Therefore, what is portrayed is a vicious circle of attitudes in which the learnt attitudes of one generation constrain the new generation and so on. It is in this sense that the concept of "reproduction" is used.

This work challenges traditional sociology of education to recognise the complexity of factors that are to be found in schools and that produce the educational, and later the social, inequality between men and women. These analyses make it difficult to hold any belief that we have achieved formal equality of opportunity within schools by eradicating overt forms of gender discrimination. Further, this challenge is directed towards state educational policy makers, who tend to gloss over the nature and extent of discrimination in education against women. The political orientation of much of this research is therefore to challenge the success of the programme for equality of opportunity and to demand that women receive genuine equal opportunity with men. With such a political goal and audience, researchers tend therefore not to address themselves to the radical sociological tradition within sociology of education but rather to aim to influence teachers, local educational authorities, and the Department of Education and Science.

There are two results of such an orientation. First, even though it challenges official views of education, much of this literature takes for granted and uses the official ideology that schools are neutral agents in society and the official definition that if women do "underachieve" relative to men, then it is an "educational problem," and an "educational solution" must be sought. Second, this literature does not search too deeply into the class basis of the inequality of opportunity that boys suffer. Educational achievement in Britain is still closely correlated with the class origins of students. The implication then appears to be that girls should match the class differentials of educational achievement and access to occupations that boys experience. Equality of opportunity in this context therefore appears to mean similar class-based inequalities of opportunity for both men and women. One could say, equal oppression!

What the cultural perspective lacks is precisely the cutting edge that caused the development of Marxist reproduction theory in the first place—that of a need to provide a critique of educational policy and practice, to get behind the illusion of education's neutrality and the myth of equality of opportunity, and to explain the relationship of schools to the economy, dominant class interests, and the hierarchical structures of economic and cultural power. Ironically, what the cultural perspective gains by neglecting this analysis of the socioeconomic context of schooling is its optimism, its belief in educational reform and teachers' practice. What it loses is an adequate political analysis of the context in which these reforms would have any impact and the constraints under which schools realistically operate. By failing to provide a critique of liberal ideology and its view of education, much of the research into gender appears to be undertheorised and to have little concern for the *origins* and the conditions of school processes or the *sources* of potential conflict and contradiction within gender socialisation.

Nevertheless, there are also several advantages in such cultural theory, particularly for the development of a feminist analysis of the operation of *male hegemony* in education. What such research can show is the unity of girls' experiences across class boundaries by focussing upon female education as a common experience vis-à-vis that of boys. Clarricoates (1980), for example, concludes from her research of four primary schools that even though femininity varies, "the subordination of women is always maintained."

> All women, whatever their "class" (economic class for women is always in relation to men—fathers and husbands) suffer oppression. It is patriarchy in the male hierarchical ordering of society, preserved through marriage and the family via the sexual division of labour that is at the core of women's oppression, and it is schools, through their different symbolic separation of the sexes, that give their oppression the seal of approval. (Clarricoates, 1980, p. 40)

The advantage of the alternative perspective, that of political economy, is precisely the reverse of cultural theories, since what this perspective can reveal is the *diversity* of class experience and the nature of *class hegemony* in education.[4] What becomes clear from this analysis is that working class boys and girls do actually share some experiences in school such as alienation from the school values of discipline and conformity, estrangement from school culture, and skepticism as to the validity of an ideology that stresses the possibility of individual social mobility. Admittedly most of the research on social class experience in schools has been conducted on boys, showing the homogeneity of their experiences within one social class (e.g., Corrigan, 1979; Hebdige, 1979; Willis, 1977). Empirically, there are very few studies of working class girls or middle class girls (Lambert 1976; McRobbie, 1978; McRobbie and Garber, 1975; Nava, 1981; Sharpe, 1976). As Delamont (1970) and King (1971) amongst others have pointed out, this is an incredibly underresearched area in the sociology of education as a whole. Most of the work in the political economy perspective has been theoretical or at a macro-level of analysis.

What researchers using this perspective have in common is their concern for constructing a theory of class and gender education and for bridging the gap between Marxist theories of class reproduction and theories of gender divisions.[5] Curiously, in this work one finds perhaps more references today to the Marxist theories of social reproduction that were popular in the mid 1970s in British sociology of education than in any other body of current educational literature.[6] The aim of most of this Marxist feminist work is to develop a political economy of women's education that moves out and away from the limitations of a purely cultural theory of gender and which addresses itself to questions about the determinants of girls' schooling as well as its processes and outcomes. The starting point for much of this work has tended to be social rather than cultural reproduction theory, and in particular the theory of Louis Althusser. The reason for this interest in Althusser's (1971) work on ideological state apparatuses is that he makes the distinction between the reproduction of the labour force and the reproduction of the social relations of production. Much of the domestic labour debate has focused attention upon the role of women in fulfilling the former function for capital through biological reproduction of the next generation of workers and the daily reproduction, through servicing, of the work force (e.g., Hall, 1980; Secombe, 1973). The question that concerns Marxist feminist sociologists of education is that of the role of schooling in the social reproduction of the female waged and domestic labour forces. The differential experience of boys and girls for the first time assumes particular importance in the analysis of the social reproduction of a capitalist labour force and capitalist social relations of production. Sexual divisions of labour which segregate women and men and maintain the male hierarchy within the workplace and domestic life come into direct contact with the forms of class oppression and exploitation, as well as with class cultures of resistance, in these two sites.

FEMINISM AND SOCIAL REPRODUCTION THEORY

In the context of patriarchal capitalism, explaining the nature of women's education has also created a variety of problems for the analysis of class reproduction and it is these that encourage a reformulation of that theory.[7] Let me for a moment give two brief examples of how existing accounts of class reproduction through education must be modified to take account of gender difference. If we look at the explanations that have been offered for the rise of mass compulsory schooling in nineteenth-century Britain, we find none of them can adequately account for the fact that girls were educated at all. Why bother to educate girls in preparation for becoming a skilled work force when few women became such workers? Why educate women to be a literate electorate when they did not have the vote? If women were educated to become docile and conforming workers, why did they receive a different curricula from boys—since their class position would have meant that working class boys and girls had similar experiences. According to Davin (1979), none of these explanations of schooling can account for the particular pattern of girls' education. Instead one must recognise that what schools taught was the particular bourgeois family ideology in which women played a special role as dependent wife and mother. Davin argues that it was this need to educate girls into domesticity that encouraged educational policymakers to establish schools for girls as well as boys. By limiting oneself to a strictly "economic" or "political" model of schooling, the saliency of family life within the concept of "social order" would be missed entirely.

If we turn briefly now to the twentieth century, when human capital theory provided the ideological basis for so much of educational planning and decision making, we find that even within this framework we cannot account for the development of women's education. If human capital theory did influence educational development to the extent that, for example, Bowles and Gintis (1976) suggest, then we understand that all children were prepared strictly for their future place in the work force. However, as M. Woodhall (1973) argues, human capital theorists used the concepts of "investment in *man*" and "*man*-power planning," not without reason since they were mainly if not exclusively referring to men. Human capital theorists viewed women's education very differently from that of men: they saw it as "either a form of consumption, or an unprofitable form of investment given the likelihood that women have to leave the labour force after marriage, or may work short hours or in low paying occupations" (Woodhall, 1973, p. 9). The returns in terms of cost-benefit analysis on women's education would therefore be low and hardly worth the effort. According to T. W. Schultz (1970), himself a renowned human capital theorist:

> If one were to judge from the work that is being done, the conclusion would be that human capital is the unique property of the male population—despite all of the schooling of females and other expenditures on them they appear to be of no account in the accounting of human capital. (p. 302–3)

Can one then ignore the differential investment in men's and women's education and the different purposes for which schooling was meant? It must be remembered that the motto "education for production" or "education for economic efficiency and productivity" takes on specific meaning in the ideological climate of patriarchy.

If these explanations of the nineteenth and twentieth century development of schooling are inadequate to account for the rise of girls' schooling, then so are the theories that have used them as a basis for criticism, such as the work of Johnson (1970) and Bowles and Gintis (1976). Theories of class cultural control and the social reproduction of class relations are inadequate precisely because they have lost the sense of the specificity of class experiences in terms of gender. While there are similarities between members of each social class there are also differences, which often can give them common ground and shared experiences with members of another class (with whom they could potentially form alliances). The problem then becomes one of trying to sort out these similarities and differences. Certainly one way in which the analysis can be improved is through the recognition of the dual origins and destinations of female *and* male students—that of the waged and domestic labour forces and the sets of social relations within both the labour process and domestic life. Another way is to recognise that women's position within the hierarchy of class relations is different from that of men. There are far fewer women employers, managers, members of high status professions, and supervisors. Very few women are likely therefore to give orders and enforce obedience. Indeed they are more likely to be what Bernstein (1977) called the agents of "symbolic control" (teachers, social workers) presenting the "soft face" of capital rather than what Althusser (1971) called the "agents of exploitation and repression." Women therefore are not easily described by a concept of class structure that is defined by the distribution of male occupations and male hierarchies of control.

Another problem in theories such as Bowles and Gintis's (1976) is that there is no identification and analysis of the reproduction of the patriarchal basis of class relations in the workplace and in the school. They ignore the fact that so many women number in the ranks in what they call the "secondary labour market" in a segmented labour force. If the principle of capitalist social relations of production is one of "divide and rule," then one cannot ascribe sex segmentation of the labour force as a subsidiary principle of class division. In my view it is a major medium of class control and also the most visible form of the principle of "divide and rule" (see MacDonald, 1981a).

Bowles and Gintis did not really get involved in discussing patriarchal relations within the social relations of production and schooling because of their view that the reproduction of the sexual division of labour occurs primarily in the family, with the mother playing an active role. They argue that it is because the family is semiautonomous and is actively engaged in the reproduction of *gender* divisions and the private-emotional life of the family, that capital has increasingly come to use the educational system as its primary agency for the reproduction specifically of the *class* structure and its relations. The thesis in *Unpopular Education* (CCCS, 1981) is similar; its authors argue that there are different social "sites" for the reproduction of social relations that are hard to disentangle, especially in their combined effects.

> Nonetheless it is useful to think of "the factory" (in shorthand) as the main site of class relations, and the family as strongly organised around relations of gender, sexuality and age. (p. 25)

We have to be careful of this thesis of the physical and social separation of the two sites of reproduction precisely because it tends to result in giving legitimacy to research that ignores gender divisions in schools and workplaces and that assumes the production of gender all happens outside the school and factory walls. Second, this thesis begs the question of the nature of the relationship between class and gender divisions and between processes of class and gender reproduction that occur simultaneously in the family, the school, and the workplace. Third, implicit in this separation is the assumption that the family and the workplace are indeed separate and distinct destinations for both men and women and that their preparation for one location is different from the preparation for the other. But this separation is itself an ideological construction that has originated in the context of bourgeois hegemony (see Hall, 1980). It is extremely difficult to use such a dividing line for the destination of women since for many the distinction is blurred in terms of the location of their productive work (e.g., domestic industries) and their time. The reproduction of family life and the domestic sexual division of labour could just as well be described as the reproduction of class position so far as women are concerned, especially if one wished to include housewives in, rather than exclude them from, a class analysis.

The family is indeed the site of gender reproduction, but it also reproduces class cultures, ideologies, and values that are critical components of class relations. The simultaneous operation of these two processes means that specific class forms of gender divisions are constructed and reproduced in this site. Similarly, the school is another site in which the two processes occur simultaneously. What is especially significant, therefore, is not the separation of the two sites, but rather the nature of family school interrelations. (See David [1978] who argues for the analysis of the "Family-Education Couple.") The transition from the private world of the family and its "lived" class culture into the public world of class divisions and sex segregation is one which is fraught with conflict between the "familiar," received class and gender identities and those taught in the school. It is the process of transition that is the critical point at which we shall understand the ways in which the reproduction of both sets of power relations occurs. At the end of their school days, school children leave as young adults who despite their different class origins are meant to have learnt the more elaborated[8] and abstract definition of masculinity and femininity and to have placed themselves, using such class and gender identities, in the hierarchies of the domestic and waged labour forces.[9]

The development of a Marxist feminist theory of gender education, like cultural theory, has been affected by the assumptions of the body of knowledge that it is criticising. It is unfortunate that much of the political economy of gender education has repeated many of the mistakes of social reproduction theory. I am thinking here of the four major problems that Johnson (1981) argues lie in the social reproduction model requiring some modification of the model if it is to be used at all. He argues that social reproduction theory has a tendency toward functionalism, especially insofar as it does not refer to the reproduction of the contradictions and conflicts that are integral to the social relations of production and the points of class struggle arising during the process of capital accumulation. I would also add that Marxist feminist theories of social reproduction have a very real tendency to ignore any notion of gender struggle and conflict, of forms of gender resistance, of contradictions within the process of the social reproduction of the female waged and domestic work forces, and of the patriarchal relations in the family and the labour processes. They too suffer from inherent functionalism. Social reproduction theories conflate educational conditions with educational outcomes, giving the appearance that the rationales and rhetoric of state policy successfully determine the products of the educational system. This tendency is just as clear in cultural theories of gender as in the Marxist feminist analysis of the sexual division of labour. It would appear from such work that girls become "feminine" without any problems. They acquire the mantle of femininity through the experience of the family and the school and keep it for the rest of their lives. As a result, in searching historically for the common pattern of girls' schooling, there has been an overwhelming emphasis upon the pattern of subordination of girls through education, with very little emphasis upon the patterns of resistance and struggle. And yet one of the greatest women's struggles has been fought over the right of access to and social mobility through the educational system. The fight for the right to be educated represents the most public of gender struggles and yet in contemporary accounts of schooling it is either forgotten or relegated to a marginal event since it was, after all, a struggle by middle class women for middle-class rights and privileges. And yet it had repercussions for all women. Also, in the analysis of contemporary education, the most visible of struggles over education and the most visible set of problems that confronts teachers is that of controlling working-class boys. The degree of attention paid by educationalists to the disciplining of boys, their degree of concern over male delinquency and truancy rates, is reflected in the amount of attention paid to working-class boys in sociological studies. There is considerable neglect of the more "silent" forms of resistance by girls, whether it takes the form of daydreaming (Payne, 1980) or the form of painting their nails in class (Llewellyn, 1980; McRobbie, 1978) or of "nonattendance" at school (Shaw, 1981).

By ignoring gender struggles, Marxist feminist analyses of schooling fall into the trap of social determinism, even while rejecting as totally false other theories of determinism, such as the biological. Hence de Beauvoir can write:

> The passivity that is the essential characteristic of the "feminine" woman is a trait that develops in her from the earliest years. But it is wrong to assert a biological datum is concerned; it is in fact a *destiny* imposed upon her by teachers and by society [my emphasis]. (quoted in Freeman, 1970, p. 36)

Such determinism means that social reproduction theory suffers from a latent pessimism and can leave women, and women teachers particularly, with a sense of fatality and helplessness. In the case of feminism, the "hold" of the system over women seems especially fatalistic in that women are, according to the CCCS (1981), "doubly determined."

> The position of women is doubly determined and constrained: by patriarchal relations and the sexual division of labour within the home and by their patriarchally structured position within waged labour outside. (CCCS, 1981, p. 156)

However, this can be put another way. What we can say is that the "consent" of women is sought to their subordination in both the home and in the waged labour force, and it is on both these fronts that they fight against class and gender control. If we forget to refer to women's struggles, we also lose sight of the victories gained. Not surprisingly then, it is very hard to find an account of the political economy of women's education that points out the gains women have made in forcing their way through the barriers of social prejudice and the obstacles that men have placed in front of them to prevent their appropriation of male culture and of male-dominated professions, status, and power. It must be remembered that access to education can be liberating even within a class-controlled system, since it is not only at the level of class relations that oppression occurs. What the Marxist feminist accounts lose sight of, because of their overriding concern for Marxist class categories, is that patriarchal oppression has its own dynamic and its own "stakes" in gender struggles, and one of the most important ones has been access to, and achievement in, education as a source of liberation.

CONTRADICTIONS IN THEORIES OF GENDER EDUCATION

Let us now for a brief moment look at the theoretical assumptions of the two traditions within the analysis of gender education and notice the contradictions that emerge between the different analyses. It is at these points of contradiction that research possibilities are opened up and new directions can be taken in the analysis of class and gender. Here I shall identify three major contradictions between the cultural and the political economy perspective.

First, let us look at the different analyses of the relationship between the home and the school. Cultural theorists have argued that there is, by and large, a *continuity* between the home and the school. Gender socialisation appears to start at birth and continue undisturbed to adulthood. Gender definitions are not therefore class specific but societal in source and nature. Thus the school's role is to extend and legitimate the same process begun at home whatever the material circumstances of the particular family or community. The political economy perspective, on the other hand, stresses the importance of the *discontinuity* and distance between the culture of the home and the school. Working class culture is seen as markedly different from the bourgeois culture transmitted in the school. The school's role in this latter case is to select from class cultures and to legitimate only some cultural forms and styles. From this perspective school knowledge is seen as attempting to ensure the ratification of class power in an unequal society that is divided by class conflict. If this is the case, it becomes improbable that *one* pattern of gender socialisation into *one* set of gender stereotypes extends across different class cultures and across the divide of family and school. What is more likely is that the family culture and gender definitions of the bourgeoisie are transmitted in the school and it is the middle class child who will experience the least difficulty with gender roles taught in school. This view is given support, not just by personal accounts of women such as Payne (1980), who was a working-class girl sent to a middle-class grammar school, but also by the class history of girls' education. Marks (1976), for example, shows how definitions of masculinity and femininity were prominent categories in the development of an English school system that was class divided. She argued that her analysis had shown that "notions of femininity vary both historically and between social classes; and [are shown] to be dialectically related to the changing roles of women in society" (p. 197).

Purvis's (1980, 1981) historical research also supports this view. She has shown that what was appropriate for one social class in terms of gender was not necessarily appropriate for another. In the nineteenth century, what Purvis found was the imposition by the bourgeoisie of a different concept of femininity for the middle classes (the "perfect wife and mother") from that imposed upon the working class (the "good woman").

> The ideal of the "good woman" may be seen . . . as an attempt by the bourgeoisie to solve the various social problems associated with industrialisation and urbanisation. The "good woman" was a dilution of the higher status ideal of the perfect wife and mother and thus it may be interpreted as a form of "intervention" into working class family life, an attempt to convert and transmit that part of bourgeois family ideology that insisted that a woman's place was in the home, that she was responsible for the quality of family life and that her domestic skills were more important than, say, vocational skills that might be used in waged labour. The "good woman" was, therefore, a form of class cultural control . . . an attack upon the patterns of working class motherhood and parenthood as perceived by the middle classes. (Purvis, 1980, p. 11)

The second contradiction that arises between the cultural and political economy theories is in terms of the expected effect and outcome of the education system. So much of the work on gender which has come out of the cultural perspective has stressed that the difference between Western European definitions of masculinity and femininity lie precisely in the fact that while femininity is defined as "docility, submission, altruism, tenderness, striving to be attractive, not being forceful or bold or physically strong, active or sexually potent" (Loftus, 1974, p. 4), masculinity means being aggressive, independent, competitive and superior, learning to take initiative, and lead an active out-of-doors life, etc. (Belotti, 1975). Yet according to Bowles and Gintis's (1976) version of social reproduction theory or even Althusser's (1971), what working class children, and in particular working class boys, learn through schooling is to obey, to take discipline, to follow rules, and to submit to hierarchy. They learn docility, which according to cultural theory is a "female" gender attribute. How then do boys cope with this difference in social expectations?

It is impossible to answer this question at the present time since there has been so little research on the problem of class and gender as competing power structures within school environments. However, as I have argued above, it is more likely that there is a discontinuity between the home and the school as a result of class divisions. This will mean that working-class boys and girls will have to negotiate their way not just through class identities, but also through gender identities. Bourdieu (1977a) has argued that the response of the working-class boy and man to the "femininity" of bourgeois school culture is one of resistance, through the use of "coarse" language, manners, dress, etc. This reaffirms their class-identity but also protects their masculinity from negation by the "effeminate" style of bourgeois culture. According to Bourdieu, working-class girls, on the other hand, can more easily negotiate school life and its values since the feminine identity derived from their families also stresses docility and passivity. This analysis forgets the importance of the mental-manual division and the hierarchy of knowledge, not just in the school curriculum, but also in the forms of girls' response to schooling. The inversion of the mental-manual division allows working class "lads" to celebrate their masculine identity (Willis, 1977), but also a similar inversion allows working class women to celebrate their femininity through a rejection of male culture that stresses the value of hierarchies (particularly mental over manual work), objective versus subjective knowledge, and individual competition above cooperation (See Spender, 1980b). Paradoxically then, femininity, the supposed essence of docility and conformity can become the vehicle for resisting forms of class reproduction. By playing off one set of social expectations against the other, working-class girls can resist the attempts of schools to induce conformity. Unfortunately, like the forms of resistance of the "lads" that confirm their fate as manual workers, the resistance of girls only leads them to accept even more voluntarily their futures as dependent and subordinate to men, and as semi- or unskilled workers with low pay and insecure working conditions, and often in dead-end jobs. Furthermore, in neither case are the forms of class resistance of working class boys or girls likely to negate their preconceived notions of gender derived from their families. If anything, they may reinforce the patriarchal relations specific to that social class by granting it more social value and potency in class resistance.

The third contradiction between the two bodies of theory lies in their conceptions of the ideology of schooling. According to cultural theories, girls' educational "underachievement" is a result of the fact that girls are "taught how to fail." Horner (1971) described the process of education as one in which girls learn to avoid and "dread success," since it means becoming a failure as women.[11] Alison Kelly (1981) in her study of girls' failure to study or be successful in science in schools, argues that the school actually discourages girls from achieving in these subjects in a variety of different ways. This process, which she calls a "discouraging process," involves either not making science available to girls or putting them off it through conscious advice or unconscious bias in favour of boys. In contrast to this rather negative view of schools, theories of class reproduction have argued that the dominant ideology of education taught through education is that of equality of opportunity. According to these theories, students are encouraged to see failure as individual, resulting from their lack of ability. Now this may be the case today, where class is a hidden category of education practice and where the categories of educational divisions are in terms of high to low academic ability. However, it is still possible to find gender being used as a very explicit allocating device for curriculum design, options, and routes, as well as for classroom organisation, the labelling of pupils, etc., in a way that is no longer socially acceptable with social class. It is also still possible to find girls' failure at school described as natural since "she is only a girl." Female students as a group can expect not to succeed and their collective failure is visible. Indeed as Wolpe (1976) has argued, the official ideology of equality of opportunity was modified to fit the "special needs or interests" of girls, so that it referred to future expectations of domestic life rather than the rewards to be gained from social mobility through better employment prospects. The illusion of meritocracy, which Bowles and Gintis attacked as being prevalent in schools, must be treated with caution therefore since it may only be an illusion of *male meritocracy,* taught to the working class. What is even more interesting is that when the expansion of the universities occurred in Britain in the 1960s, it was with some despair that Hutchinson and McPherson (1976) reported from their studies of Scottish University undergraduates that equality of opportunity had benefitted middle-class women *at the expense* of working-class men. These women had, in their words, "displaced" those working-class men who had successfully made their way through the school system and were knocking upon the university doors. There were therefore two "competing" ideologies of equality of opportunity, not one. No concern was shown for the drastically low numbers of working-class women who reached the university and whose numbers were quoted as being "stable" (hence uninteresting) *despite* the expansion of the university sector. The impression is gained therefore that class equality of opportunity refers to the male working class and gender equality of opportunity to middle-class women. Possibly the fact that working-class women have not gained by this opening up of opportunities is because their subjective assessment of their objective possibilities for entry into higher education and for social mobility has led them to limit their own education aspirations. Their assessment may well have "penetrated" (to use Willis's term) the fact that meritocracy is for men. Perhaps, as Sharpe's (1976) study has suggested, they have accepted a more satisfying alternative—the ambition to become a wife and mother—rather than compete in vain for access to a male world.

DEVELOPING A THEORY OF CULTURAL PRODUCTION

Up until now, I have focussed on some of the problems of using social reproduction theory to develop a feminist account of girls' schooling, and I have pointed out some of the dangers of not addressing oneself to the questions concerning the determinants of schooling under capitalism. Here I shall turn to theories of cultural reproduction, which I think have been ignored by feminists using either the cultural or the political economy perspective. It is possible that cultural reproduction theories have been avoided because the relevance of this work for a theory of gender is not obvious, especially since it appears to refer only to class. However, even though Bernstein's (1977, 1980) research has been adopted (and transformed) in the context of Marxist theories of education developed in the 1970s, I believe that his theory of classification systems, of the social construction of categories and "classes" (in the neutral sense of social groups), can be very useful in developing a general theory of gender differences and relations and in setting out the premises for research in schools. I think that one can develop a theory of gender codes that is class based and that can expose the structural and interactional features of gender reproduction and conflict in families, in schools, and in workplaces. The idea of a gender code relates well to the concept of hegemony since both concepts refer to the social organisation of family and school life where the attempt is made to "win over" each new generation to particular definitions of masculinity and femininity and to accept as natural the hierarchy of male over female, the superiority of men in society. The concept of code also allows one to develop a structural analysis of school culture that avoids seeing the problem of gender inequality as one simply of attitudes that have no material basis. The political and economic distribution of power between men and women in our society is reproduced through the structural organisation of school life, as one of its major agencies; yet schools are also the critical reproductive agencies of class cultures and their principles of organisation. In this sense gender codes can be related to an analysis of class codes in schools.

The first major premise of any theory of gender must be that gender categories are in a very important sense arbitrary social constructs. The arbitrary nature of their contents, both historically and in terms of social class, is the product of "work" carried out by a variety of social institutions and agents (e.g., schools, churches, the mass media—teachers, priests, authors, film producers). The active nature of the production of a category called gender is captured nicely in Eileen Byrne's (1978) definition:

> Gender is the collection of attitudes which society *stitches together* (dress behaviour, attributed personality traits, expected social roles, etc.) to clothe boys and girls [emphasis added]. (p. 254)

Gender classification differs from that of sex in the sense that whereas the former is totally socially constructed, the other is biologically based. What I believe they have in common, however, is that, like the notions of male and female sex, gender is in fact an arbitrary dichotomy imposed upon what is essentially a continuum. The questions we have to ask then are how and why are gender categories constructed in the way they are? We obviously need an historical analysis to sort out the specificity of our particular version of this dichotomy, our principle of classification, so that we can seek the source of that principle in the changing class relations contained within educational history. Further, we need to look for alternative sources of gender division that can be found in those social classes that have not appropriated the medium of the school to transmit their principles of gender difference.

The second premise is that gender classifications are not universal, nor societal, nor are they static or simple. Indeed they are highly complex in the sense that in order to construct two seemingly mutually exclusive categories that can apply to any range of social contexts, considerable work has to be done to pull together, or as Byrne put it, to "stitch together" a diversity of values and meanings. The tension within each category is as great as that between each category. Think for example of the contradiction that women face in trying to make sense of such antagonistic images of femininity as being both dependable and dependent, of being a sexual temptress and sexually passive, of being childlike and mothering, and of being a capable and intelligent consumer as well as being politically and economically inept. Unfortunately, so much of the work identifying stereotypes in masculinity and femininity has focussed on the consistency rather than the contradiction within these categories. The imposed compatibility of different "narrative structures" in which girls have to construct a coherent female identity has to be "worked at" rather than assumed to exist, in order to produce what Althusser might have called a "teeth gritting harmony."

The third major premise is that gender categories are constructed through a concept of gender difference that Chodorow (1979) has argued is essential to the analysis of male hegemony. The hierarchy of men over women is based upon an ideology of gender difference that is manifested in the structural division of men and women's lives, their education, their dress, their morality, and their behaviour, etc. The ideology may be founded upon a theory of supposed natural divisions. This ideology then successfully hides the fact that gender is a cultural variable and one that is constructed within the context of class and gender power relations. The source and nature of the imposition of gender differences is so concealed that the power of the dominant class and the dominant sex is increased by such unconscious legitimation.

Yet how is the consent won to particular arbitrary definitions of masculinity and femininity by both men and women, so that they treat such classifications as natural and inevitable? One of the ways in which male hegemony is maintained is obviously through schooling, where it is most easy to transmit a specific set of gender definitions, relations, and differences while appearing to be objective. The opportunity to transmit a gender code is, however, not open to any social class, but rather to the bourgeoisie who have appropriated, more than any other class, the educational system for themselves. The dominant form of male hegemony within our society is therefore that of the bourgeoisie. That is not to say that the classification of gender used by the working class or the aristocracy has not entered the school. As we have already seen in the work of Willis and McRobbie, it is these categories and definitions of masculinity and femininity from the working class that provide the vehicle for classroom and social class resistance. The aristocratic ideal of masculinity can be found in the English public schools, where the concept of the amateur sportsman, the gentleman, and the benevolent paternal leader are in contrast to the grammar school bourgeois ideals of the hard-working scientist, scholar, or artist. Matched to each ideal is its antithesis of "nonmasculinity"—the complementary ideals of femininity—the hostess, the good wife and mother, the career woman, etc.

If we return very briefly to the separation of home and work discussed earlier, we can now relate it to the production of gender difference through a class-based classification system. Historically, as Davin (1979) and Hall (1980) have shown, the nineteenth century saw the development of the bourgeois family form (with its male breadwinner, its dependent housekeeping wife, and dependent children) and its imposition upon the working class through educational institutions. Implicit in this social construction was the notion of two spheres that distinguished and segregated the world of women and men. This classification of male and female worlds was made equivalent to and imposed upon a further classification— that of work and family (or put another way, the distinction between the public world of production and the private world of consumption). This latter ideological construction, despite having a material basis as the continuing development of the factory and office systems, nevertheless has to be continually reinforced in day-to-day life. In this sense, the division between family and work that so many sociologists of education take for granted can also be seen as an *ideological* division that is part of bourgeois hegemony. The structural imposition of the gender classification upon this other division unites the hierarchy of class relations with that of gender relations since it allows for the exploitation of women by both men and capital. Hence the productive world becomes "masculine" even though so many women work within it, and the family world becomes "feminine" even though men partner women in building a home. As Powell and Clarke (1976) argue, this classification helps create the political and economic "invisibility" of women.

> It is the dominant ideological division between *Home* and *Work* which structures the invisibility of women and not their real absence from the world of work. Their identification solely with the "privatised" world of the family has masked, firstly, the historical (not natural—and for a long time very uneven) removal of work from the home, and secondly the continuing presence of working women. (It also masks the man's presence in the home). Men and women do not inhabit two empirically separated worlds, but pass through the same institutions in different relations and on different trajectories. (p. 226)

In understanding the differential experience of girls and boys in schools, we should pay particular attention to the way in which the school *constructs* a particular relationship between, for example, home and work and how it prepares the two sexes in different ways for these two destinations. Thus boys and girls are meant to learn a different relation to the bourgeois classification of public and private worlds, of family and work, of male and female spheres. Schools teach boys how to maintain the importance of those distinctions and to see their futures in terms of paid work. (There is little if any training for fatherhood in schools.) Boys are trained to acquire the classification in its strongest form, to make the distinction between work and nonwork, masculinity and nonmasculinity. Hence they avoid academic subjects that are considered to be "feminine," "domestic," and personal/emotional. Their masculinity is premised upon maintaining the distinctiveness of the two spheres, since it is in that hierarchy that their power is based. Girls on the other hand, are taught to *blur* the distinction between family and work for themselves, to see an extension of identity from domestic activities to work activities, to extend their domestic skills to earn an income, and to use their employment for the benefit of their domestic commitments, rather than for themselves. Their construction of the work/family division differs from one that they accept as natural for men, and so they too maintain the classification even though it is not directly applicable to themselves. Thus as Powell and Clarke (1976) point out, the dimensions of possible activity for both sexes are constructed around the oppositions of work/nonwork, management/labour, and work/leisure, but in the case of women, the opposition family/nonfamily overshadows all the others.

We can describe through research the ways in which the schools structure the experience of boys and girls in such a way as to transmit specific gender classifications with varying degrees of boundary strength and insulation between the categories of masculine and feminine and a hierarchy of male over female, based upon a specific ideology of legitimation. Through classroom encounters where boys and girls experience different degrees and types of contact with the teacher, through the different criteria for evaluating boys' and girls' behaviour, and through the curriculum texts and the structured relations of the school, limits are set to the degree of negotiation of gender that is possible within the school. In this sense the school *frames* the degree and type of response to that gender code. What is relevant therefore is not just an analysis of the structural aspects of gender codes but also the *form* of interaction within school social relations.[12]

Using a notion of gender code, we can recognize that while the school attempts to determine the identities of its students, it is also involved in a process of transmission in which the student takes an active role. First the student is active in inferring the underlying rules from a range of social relations between men and women (between parents, teachers, pupils, etc.). Students learn to recognise and make sense of a wide range and variety of contradictory and miscellaneous inputs, and the results are not always predictable, especially since they relate these school messages to the alternatives that they have experienced or derived from their families, their peer group, the mass media, etc. The student will undergo a process of actively transforming these various messages and will produce at the end, in a temporary sense, a constellation of behaviour and values that can be called "femininity" or "masculinity." What the school attempts to do is to produce subjects who unconsciously or consciously consent to the dominant version of gender relations. This does not mean, however, that if it fails, patriarchal relations are challenged, since, it must be remembered, in all social classes it is the men who are dominant and hold power.

Men and women become the embodiment of a particular gender classification by internalising and "realising" the principle that underlies it. They externalise their gendered identities, through their behaviour, language, their use of objects, their physical presence, etc. It is through this process of "realisation" that the dialectics of objective structures and social action are created. In the process of producing classed and gendered subjects who unconsciously recognise and realise the principles of social organisation, the reproduction of such power relations is ensured. Thus individuals internalise the objective and external structures and externalise them, albeit transformed but not radically challenged. The potential for rejecting such definitions is inherent within the process, for as Bernstein (1980) argues, the recognition of principles of classification does not determine the realisation (or practice); it can only set the limits upon it. What appears to be a smooth process of repetition is in fact one in which the contradictions, the struggles, and the experience of individuals are suppressed. As Bernstein (1980) has argued, "any classification system suppresses potential cleavages, contradictions and dilemmas."

The fact that there is a dominant gender code (i.e., that of the bourgeoisie) means that there are also dominated gender codes (those of the working class or different ethnic groups). The experience of learning the principles of the dominant gender code is therefore the experience of learning class relations where working-class family culture is given illegitimate and low status at school. The form of class reproduction may occur through the very formation of gender identities that we have been talking about. Further class resistance may be manifested through resistance to gender definitions. However, and this is really a very important point, in neither the dominant nor the dominated gender codes do women escape from their inferior and subordinate position. There is nothing romantic about resisting school through a male-defined working-class culture. It is at this point that women across social class boundaries have much in common.

CONCLUDING REMARKS

Briefly then, I think that any research in the area of women's education should have two essential features. First, it should recognise the existence of both class and male hegemony within educational institutions and the sometimes difficult relationship that exists between them. Second, it should be aware that any set of social relations, such as class or gender relations, constitutes a social dynamic in which the forces of order, conflict, and change are contained. The process of what Freire (1972) called "domestication" in the case of girls implies a dialectic of oppression and struggle against class-based definitions of femininity. It is the dual nature of that struggle that allows women to seek allies simultaneously in their own social class and amongst women in different social classes. Somehow our research must capture the unity *and* the diversity of the educational lives of women.

Notes

1. Production is used here to refer to the act of *social construction* either by institutions such as schools, the mass media, etc., or by individuals.

2. Angela McRobbie is referring here to the work of Paul Willis (1977) and Dick Hebdige (1979).

3. Examples of a "cultural perspective" are Kelly (1981), Frazier and Sadker (1973), Belotti (1975), Delamont (1980), Lobban (1975).

4. Examples of a "political economy perspective" are Barrett (1980), David (1978, 1980), Deem (1978, 1981), MacDonald (1980b, 1981a), Wolpe (1978a, 1978b). For full references see Arnot (1981).

5. By social reproduction theory, I am referring to the work of Althusser (1971) and Bowles and Gintis (1976).

6. It is interesting that despite the development of the cultural theory of gender, the cultural reproduction theory found in Bernstein (1977) and Bourdieu and Passeron (1977b) has not generally been used, or even referred to.

7. The most contentious area, which cannot be treated here, is obviously the appropriateness of using existing Marxist definitions of social class for describing women's

economic and political position. For this debate see, for example, Barrett (1980), Mac-Donald (1981a), West (1978).

8. I am using Bernstein's (1977) concept here to show that in schools, children are taught the middle class cultural definition of gender that appears to be "context independent" and thus neutral and generalisable.

9. This would obviously only occur in times of full employment. In the present context, being "working class" and "female" is often a qualification for unemployment.

10. See B. Bernstein (1977), Introduction.

11. Similar arguments are put forward in contributions to Spender and Sarah (1980).

12. See "On the Classification and Framing of Knowledge," Bernstein (1977).

References

Althusser, L. Ideology and ideological state apparatuses. In L. Althusser (Ed.), *Lenin and philosophy and other essays*. London: New Left Books, 1971.

Arnot, M. Culture and political economy: Dual perspectives in the sociology of women's education. *Educational Analysis*, 1981, *3*, 97–116.

Barrett, M. *Women's oppression today*. London: Verso, 1980.

Belotti, E.G. *Little girls*. London: Writers and Readers Publishing Cooperative, 1975. First published Milan: G. Feltrienelli Editore, 1973.

Bernstein, B. *Class codes and control*. Vol. III, 2nd ed. Boston and London: Routledge and Kegan Paul, 1977.

———. Codes, modalities, and the process of cultural reproduction: A model. *Pedagogical Bulletin* (No. 7). University of Lund, Sweden: Department of Education, 1980.

Bourdieu, P. The economics of linguistic exchange. *Social Science Information*, 1977a, *16*, 6.

Bourdieu, P. and J.C. Passeron. *Reproduction in education, society and culture*. London: Sage Publications Ltd., 1977b.

Bowles, S. and H. Gintis. *Schooling in capitalist America*. Boston and London: Routledge and Kegan Paul, 1976.

Brewster, P. School days, school days. In D. Spender and E. Sarah (Eds.), *Learning to lose*. London: Women's Press, 1980.

Byrne, E. *Women and education*. London: Tavistock, 1978.

Centre for Contemporary Cultural Studies (CCCS). *Unpopular education*. London: Hutchinson, 1981.

Chodorow, N. Feminism and difference: Gender relation and difference in psychoanalytic perspective. In *Socialist Review*, 1979, *9*, 4, 51–70.

Clarricoates, K. The importance of being earnest . . . Emma . . . Tom . . . Jane. The perception and categorization of gender conformity and gender deviation in primary schools. In R. Deem (Ed.), *Schooling for women's work*. Boston and London: Routledge and Kegan Paul, 1980.

Corrigan, P. *Schooling the smash street kids*. New York: Macmillan, 1979.

David, M.E. The family—education couple: towards an analysis of the William Tyndale dispute. In G. Littlejohn et al. (Eds.), *Power and the state*. London: Croom Helm, 1978.

———. *The state, family, and education*. Boston and London: Routledge and Kegan Paul, 1980.

Davin, A. Mind you do as you are told: Reading books for boarding school girls 1870–1902. *Feminist Review,* 1979, *3,* 80–98.

Deem, R. *Women and schooling.* Boston and London: Routledge and Kegan Paul, 1978.

Deem, R. (Ed.) *Schooling for women's work.* Boston and London: Routledge and Kegan Paul, 1980.

Deem, R. State policy and ideology in the education of women, 1944–1980. *British Journal of Sociology of Education,* 1981, *2,* 2, 131–144.

Delamont, S. The contradictions in ladies' education. In S. Delamont and L. Duffin (Eds.), *The nineteenth century woman.* London: Croom Helm, 1978a.

———. The domestic ideology and women's education. In S. Delamont and L. Duffin (Eds.), *The nineteenth century woman.* London: Croom Helm, 1978b.

———. *Sex roles and the school.* London: Methuen, 1970.

Frazier, N. and Sadker, M. *Sexism in school and society.* New York: Harper and Row, 1973.

Freeman, J. Growing up girlish. *Trans-Action,* 1970, *8,* (Nov.–Dec.), 36–43.

Freire, P. *Pedagogy of the oppressed.* Harmondsworth. Penguin, 1972.

Fuller, M. Black girls in a London comprehensive school. In R. Deem (Ed.), *Schooling for women's work.* Boston and London: Routledge and Kegan Paul, 1980.

Hall, C. The history of the housewife. In E. Malos (Ed.,), *The politics of housework.* London: Alison and Busby, 1980.

Hebdige, D. *Subculture: The meaning of style.* London: Methuen, 1979.

Horner, M.S. Femininity and successful achievement: A basic inconsistency. In J. Bardwick, E.M. Douvan, M.S. Horner, and D. Gutmann (Eds.), *Feminine personality and conflict.* California: Brooks Cole Publishing, 1971.

Horney, K. The flight from womanhood. In H. Kelman (Ed.), *Feminine psychology.* Boston and London: Routledge and Kegan Paul, 1967.

Hutchinson, D., and A. McPherson. Competing inequalities: The sex and social class structure of the first year Scottish University student population 1962–1972. *Sociology,* 1976, *10.*

Johnson, R. Educational policy and social control in early Victorian England. *Past and Present,* 49, 96–113.

———. *Education and popular politics.* Milton Keynes: Open University Press, 1981.

Kelly, A. (Ed.), *The missing half.* Manchester: Manchester University Press, 1981.

King, R. Unequal access in education—Sex and social class. *Social and Economic Administration,* 1971, *5,* 3, 167–175.

Lambert, A. The sisterhood. In M. Hammersley and P. Woods. (Eds.), *The process of schooling.* Boston and London: Routledge and Kegan Paul, 1976.

Levy, B. The school's role in the sex-role stereotyping of girls: A feminist review of the literature. *Feminist Studies,* 1972, *1,* 1. Reprinted in M. Wasserman (Ed.), *Demystifying schools.* New York: Praeger Publishers, 1974.

Llewellyn, M. Studying girls at school: The implications of confusion. In R. Deem (Ed.), *Schooling for women's work.* Boston and London: Routledge and Kegan Paul, 1980.

Lobban, G.M. Sexism in British primary schools. *Women Speaking,* 1975, *4,* 10–13.

Loftus, M. Learning sexism and femininity. *Red Tag,* 1974, *7,* 6–11.

MacDonald, M. Cultural reproduction: The pedagogy of sexuality. *Screen Education,* 1979–80, *32/33,* 141–153.

———. Socio-cultural reproduction and women's education. In R. Deem (Ed.), *Schooling for women's work.* Boston and London: Routledge and Kegan Paul, 1980a.

———. Schooling and the reproduction of class and gender relations. In L. Barton, R. Meighan, and S. Walker (Eds.), *Schooling, ideology and the curriculum.* Barcombe, Sussex: Falmer Press, 1980b. Reprinted in R. Dale, G.E. Esland, R. Fergusson, and M. MacDonald (Eds.), *Education and the state: Politics, patriarchy, and practice.* Vol. II. Barcombe, Sussex: Falmer Press, 1981.

————. *Class, gender, and education.* Milton Keynes: Open University Press, 1981a.

————. See Arnot, M., 1981, 1981b.

Marks, P. Femininity in the classroom: An account of changing attitudes. In J. Mitchell and A. Oakley, *The rights and wrongs of women.* Harmondsworth: Penguin, 1976.

McRobbie, A. Working class girls and the culture of femininity. In Women's Studies Group, Centre for Contemporary Cultural Studies, *Women take issue.* London: Hutchinson, in association with the CCCS, 1978.

————. Settling accounts with subcultures: A feminist critique. *Screen Education,* 1980, *34,* (Spring).

McRobbie, A., and J. Garber. Girls and subcultures. In S. Hall and T. Jefferson (Eds.), *Resistance through rituals.* London: Hutchinson, 1975.

Nava, M. Girls aren't really a problem. *Schooling and Culture,* 1981, 9.

Payne, I. Working class in a grammar school. In D. Spencer and E. Sarah (Eds.), *Learning to lose.* London: Women's Press, 1980.

Powell, R., and J. Clarke. A note on marginality. In S. Hall and T. Jefferson (Eds.), *Resistance through rituals.* London: Hutchinson, in association with the CCCS Birmingham, 1976.

Purvis, J. *Towards a history of women's education in nineteenth century Britain: A sociological analysis.* Paper presented at the International Sociological Association Conference, Paris, August 7–8, 1980.

————. *The double burden of class and gender in the schooling of working class girls in nineteenth century Britain.* Paper presented at Westhill College, Conference on the Sociology of Education, unpublished (1981).

Rowbotham, S. *Woman's consciousness, man's world.* Harmondsworth: Penguin, 1973.

Schultz, T.W. The reckoning of education as human capital. In W.L. Hansen (Ed.), *Education, income and human capital.* New York: National Bureau of Economic Research, 1970.

Secombe, W. The housewife and her labour under capitalism. *New Left Review,* 1973, *83,* (Jan.–Feb.), 3–24.

Sharpe, S. *Just like a girl.* Harmondsworth: Penguin, 1976.

Shaw, J. *Family, state, and compulsory education.* Milton Keynes: Open University Press, 1981.

Spender, D. Education or indoctrination? In D. Spencer and E. Sarah (Eds.), *Learning to lose.* London: Women's Press, 1980a.

————. Educational institutions where co-operation is called cheating. In D. Spender and E. Sarah (Eds.), *Learning to lose.* London: Women's Press, 1980b.

West, J. Women, sex, and class. In A. Kuhn and A.M. Wolpe (Eds.), *Feminism and materialism.* Boston and London: Routledge and Kegan Paul, 1978.

Westergaard, J., and H. Resler. *Class in a capitalist society.* Heinemann Educational Books, 1975.

Willis, P. *Learning to labour.* Farnborough, Saxon House: Teakfield Ltd., 1977.

Wolpe, A.M. The official ideology of education for girls. In R. Dale et al. (Eds.), *Education and the state: Politics, patriarchy, and practice* (Vol. II). Barcombe, Sussex: Falmer Press, 1976.

————. Girls and economic survival. *British Journal of Educational Studies,* 1978a, 26, 2, 150–162.

————. Education and the sexual division of labour. In A. Kuhn and A.M. Wolpe (Eds.), *Feminism and materialism.* London: Routledge and Kegan Paul, 1978b.

Woodhall, M. Investment in women: A reappraisal of the concept of human capital. *International Review of Education,* 1973, *19,* 1, 9–28.

7

EXCLUDING WOMEN FROM THE EDUCATIONAL REALM

Jane Roland Martin

In recent years a literature has developed that documents the ways in which intellectual disciplines such as history and psychology, literature and the fine arts, sociology and biology are biased according to sex. The feminist criticism contained in this literature reveals that the disciplines fall short of the ideal of epistemological equality, that is, equality of representation and treatment of women in academic knowledge itself—for example, in scientific theories, historical narratives, and literary interpretations. The disciplines exclude women from their subject matter; they distort the female according to the male image of her; and they deny the feminine by forcing women into a masculine mold. While certain aspects of philosophy have been subjected to feminist scrutiny,[1] the status of women in the subject matter of philosophy of education has not yet been studied. This is unfortunate, for philosophy of education has more than theoretical significance; in dealing with prescriptive questions of education that touch all our lives, it has great practical significance. Furthermore, as a consequence of state teacher certification requirements and the fact that public school teaching is primarily a women's occupation, a large proportion of philosophy of education students are women. It is important to understand, therefore, that, although throughout history women have reared and taught the young and have themselves been educated, they are excluded both as the subjects and objects of educational thought from the standard texts and anthologies: as subjects, their philosophical works on education are ignored; as objects, works by men about their education and also their role as educators of the young are largely neglected. Moreover, the very definition of education and the educational realm adopted implicitly by the standard texts, and made explicit by contemporary analytic philosophers of education, excludes women.

INVISIBLE WOMEN

In an earlier issue of this journal I argued that the common interpretation of Rousseau's educational thought cannot explain what he has to say about the education of Sophie, the prototype of woman.[2] Rather than admit to the inadequacy of the accepted interpretation, the standard texts either ignore Rousseau's account of the education of Sophie or treat it as an aberration in his thought.

Rousseau's account of the education of girls and women is no aberration; on the contrary, it is integral to his philosophy of education. Nor is Plato's account of the education of women in Book V of the *Republic* an aberration; yet a number of the standard texts and anthologies omit all references to Book V. Others neither anthologize nor comment on those sections containing Plato's proposal that both males and females can be rulers of the Just State and that all those who are suited to rule should, regardless of sex, be given the same education.[3] Moreover, the texts that mention Plato's views on the education of women do so in passing or with significant distortion.[4]

A study done by Christine Pierce has shown that translators and commentators have consistently misinterpreted Book V of Plato's *Republic;* they have been unable to comprehend that such a great philosopher sanctioned the equality of the sexes.[5] Few writers of the standard texts in the history of educational philosophy seem able to grasp this either. But other scholars, for example John Dewey and Thomas Henry Huxley, have, like Plato, treated women's education seriously.[6] Nonetheless, only one standard text lists girls and women in its index.[7] The others do not perceive sex or gender to be an educational category, even though many of the philosophers whose thought constitutes their subject matter did.

The standard texts have also ignored what philosophers of education have said about the educative role of women as mothers. In his classic pedagogical work, *Leonard and Gertrude,* Johann Heinrich Pestalozzi presents Gertrude neither—to use his biographer's words—"as the sweetheart of some man nor, in the first place, as the wife of her husband but as the mother of her child."[8] As such, Pestalozzi presents her as the model of the good educator. When the nobleman Arner and his aide visit Cotton Meyer in Gertrude's village, Meyer describes Gertrude as one who understands how to establish schools that stand in close connection with the life of the home, instead of in contradiction to it.[9] They visit Gertrude and closely observe her teaching methods. Arner's aide is so impressed by Gertrude that he resolves to become the village schoolmaster. When he finally opens a school, it is based on principles of education extracted from Gertrude's practice.

Pestalozzi is not discussed in as many of the standard texts as are Plato and Rousseau. Insofar as the texts do include his thought, however, they scarcely acknowledge that he thinks Gertrude's character and activities "set the example for a new order."[10] Pestalozzi's insight that mothers are educators of their children and that we can learn from their methods has been largely ignored in educational philosophy.

Just as the exclusion of women as objects of educational thought by historians of educational philosophy is easily seen from a glance at the indexes of the standard texts, their exclusion as subjects is evident from a glance at the tables of contents in which the works of women philosophers of education have been overlooked. The one exception is Maria Montessori, whose work is discussed at length by Robert Rusk.[11] However, she is neither mentioned nor anthologized in the other texts I have surveyed, including Robert Ulich's massive anthology, *Three Thousand Years of Educational Wisdom.*

Montessori's claim to inclusion in the standard texts and anthologies is apparent, for her philosophical works on the education of children are widely known.

She is not, however, the only woman in history to have developed a systematic theory of education. Many women have been particularly concerned with the education of their own sex. For example, in *A Vindication of the Rights of Woman,* Mary Wollstonecraft challenged Rousseau's theory of the education of girls and developed her own theory.[12] Wollstonecraft, in turn, was influenced by the writings on education and society of Catherine Macaulay, in particular her *Letters on Education.*[13] In numerous books and articles Catharine Beecher set forth a philosophy of education of girls and women that presents interesting contrasts to Wollstonecraft's;[14] and the utopian novel *Herland,* written by Charlotte Perkins Gilman, rests on a well-developed educational philosophy for women.[15]

While Montessori's work was certainly familiar to the authors and editors of the standard texts and anthologies, it is doubtful that Macaulay, Wollstonecraft, Beecher, and Gilman were even known to these men, let alone that they were perceived as educational philosophers. It is possible to cite them here because feminist research in the last decade has uncovered the lives and works of many women who have thought systematically about education. The works of these women must be studied and their significance determined before one can be sure that they should be included in the standard texts and anthologies. This analytic and evaluative endeavor remains to be done.

It should not be supposed, however, that all the men whose educational thought has been preserved for us by the standard texts are of the stature of Plato and Rousseau or that all the works represented in the anthologies are as important as the *Republic* and *Emile.* On the contrary, a reader of these books will find writings of considerable educational significance by otherwise unknown thinkers and writings of questionable educational value by some of the great figures of Western philosophy. Thus, while criteria do have to be satisfied before Macaulay, Wollstonecraft, Beecher, Gilman, and others are given a place in the history of educational thought, they cannot in fairness be excluded simply for being regarded as less profound thinkers than Plato.

The question remains whether the women cited here can be excluded because their overriding interest is the education of their own sex. In view of the fate of Sophie, Gertrude, and Plato's female guardians as objects of educational thought, one can only assume that, had the works of these women been known to exist, they also would have been ignored by the standard texts and anthologies of the field. From the standpoint of the history of educational thought, women thinkers are in double jeopardy: they are penalized for their interest in the education of their own sex because that topic falls outside the field; and, as the case of Montessori makes clear, those who have written about education in general are penalized simply for being women.

DEFINING THE EDUCATIONAL REALM

Lorenne Clark has shown that from the standpoint of political theory, women, children, and the family dwell in the "ontological basement," outside and underneath the political structure.[16] This apolitical status is due not to historical accident or necessity but to arbitrary definition. The reproductive processes of society— processes in which Clark includes creation and birth and the rearing of children to "more or less independence"—are by fiat excluded from the political domain, which is defined in relation to the public world of productive processes. Since the subject matter of political theory is politics and since reproductive processes have been traditionally assigned to women and have taken place within the family, it follows that women and the family are excluded from the very subject matter of the discipline.

The analogy between political theory and educational philosophy is striking. Despite the fact that the reproductive processes of society, broadly understood, are largely devoted to childrearing and include the transmission of skills, beliefs, feelings, emotions, values, and even world views, they are not considered to belong to the educational realm. Thus, education, like politics, is defined in relation to the productive processes of society, and the status of women and the family are "a-educational" as well as apolitical. It is not surprising, then, that Pestalozzi's insight about Gertrude is overlooked by historians of educational philosophy; for in performing her maternal role, Gertrude participates in reproductive processes that are by definition excluded from the educational domain. If Gertrude is outside the educational realm, so is Sophie, for the training Rousseau intends for her aims at fitting her to be a good wife and mother, that is, to carry on the reproductive processes of society.[17] But the exclusion of these processes from education does not in itself entail the exclusion of training *for* them; people could be prepared to carry on reproductive processes through bona fide educational activities even if the processes themselves are outside of education. However, since educational philosophy defines its subject matter only in terms of productive processes, even this preparation is excluded.

We can see the boundaries of the educational realm in the distinction commonly made between liberal and vocational education. Vocational education is clearly intended to prepare people to carry on the productive processes of society.[18] Liberal education, on the other hand, is not seen as preparation for carrying on its reproductive processes. Even though disagreements abound over which intellectual disciplines are proper to liberal education and the way they are to be organized, no one conceives of liberal education as education in childrearing and family life. The distinction between liberal and vocational education corresponds not to a distinction between the two kinds of societal processes but to one between head and hand *within* productive processes. Liberal education is thus preparation for carrying on processes involving the production and consumption of ideas, while vocational education is preparation for processes involving manual labor.

Historians of educational philosophy have no more interest in Sophie than they do in Gertrude, for Rousseau places Sophie in the home and tailors her education to the role he assigns her there. Indeed, educational philosophy has no ready vocabulary to describe the kind of education Rousseau designs for Sophie. It is not a liberal education, for she will learn coquetry and modesty and skill in lace-making, not science, history, literature, or rational thinking.[19] Like vocational education, her training has narrow and clearly specified ends. Yet vocational education programs prepare their graduates to enter the job market, whereas Sophie's education is designed to keep her out of that arena.[20]

Philosophy of education has no ready classification for the training Rousseau would provide women because it falls outside the educational domain. There is, however, a classification for the training Plato would provide the women guardians of his Just State. For Plato, ruling is a matter of knowing the Good, which involves using one's reason to grasp the most abstract, theoretical knowledge possible. Thus, the education he prescribes for the guardian class is a type of liberal education—one that greatly influences educational thought and practice even today. How, then, are we to explain that historians of educational philosophy ignore Plato's theory of the education of women? In a field that excludes the reproductive processes of society from its subject matter and identifies women with these processes, Plato's theory is an anomaly. Plato places women in the public world and prescribes for them an education for the productive processes of society. Although their education falls squarely within the educational realm as defined by the field and can be readily classified, the fact that *women* are to receive this education is lost to view. The position of women in the history of educational philosophy is not an enviable one. Excluded from its subject matter insofar as they are commonly tied by theory to the reproductive processes of society, women are denied recognition even when a particular theory such as Plato's detaches their lives and their education from childrearing and the family.

THE ANALYTIC PARADIGM: PETERS'S CONCEPT OF EDUCATION

Contemporary philosophical analysis has made explicit the boundaries of the educational realm assumed by the standard texts in the history of educational philosophy. In *Ethics and Education*, R. S. Peters writes that education is something "we consciously contrive for ourselves or for others" and that "it implies that something worthwhile is being or has been intentionally transmitted in a morally acceptable manner."[21] Peters distinguishes between two senses of the word "education." As an activity, education must fulfill three conditions—intentionality, voluntariness, and comprehension—for it involves the *intentional* transmission of something worthwhile, an element of *voluntariness* on the part of the learner, and some *comprehension* by the learner both of what is being learned and of the standards the learner is expected to attain.[22] As an achievement, education involves also the acquisition of knowledge, understanding, and cognitive perspectives.[23]

The analytic literature in philosophy of education is filled with discussions of Peters's concept of education, and at various points in his career he has elaborated upon and defended it.[24] Over the years he has come to acknowledge that there are two concepts of education: one encompassing "any process of childrearing, bringing up, instructing, etc." and the other encompassing only those processes directed toward the development of an educated person.[25] Peters considers only the second, narrower concept to have philosophical significance. He has analyzed this concept in one work after another and has traced its implications in his book, *The Logic of Education*. This narrow concept is the basis not only for his own philosophical investigations of education but also for those of his many collaborators, students, and readers.

Peters is no insignificant figure in the philosophy of education. Indeed, his concept of education, which excludes the reproductive processes of society, defines the domain of the now-dominant school of philosophy of education—analytic philosophy of education.[26] Peters has given analytic philosophy of education a research paradigm that defines the types of problems, approaches, and solutions for the field only in terms of the productive processes of society. Thus from its standpoint, when Gertrude teaches her children, she is frequently not engaged in the activity of education. While a good deal of what she does fulfills Peters's condition of intentionality, and although she always acts in a morally acceptable manner, there are many occasions on which the children fail to meet the condition of voluntariness.

At times, however, the children are voluntary learners, as when the neighbor children implore Gertrude to teach them spinning:

> "Can you spin?" she asked.
> "No," they answered.
> "Then you must learn, my dears. My children wouldn't sell their knowledge of it at any price, and are happy enough on Saturday, when they each get their few kreutzers. The year is long, my dears, and if we earn something every week, at the end of the year there is a lot of money, without our knowing how we came by it."
> "Oh, please teach us!" implored the children, nestling close to the good woman.
> "Willingly," Gertrude replied, "come every day if you like, and you will soon learn."[27]

With her own children, however, Gertrude constantly instills manners and proper conduct without their permission:

> "What business was it of yours to tell the Bailiff day before yesterday, that you knew Arner would come soon? Suppose your father had not wished him to know that he knew it, and your chattering had brought him into trouble."
> "I should be very sorry, mother. But neither of you said a word about its being a secret."
> "Very well, I will tell your father when he comes home, whenever we are talking together, we must take care to add after each sentence: 'Lizzie may tell that to the neighbors, and talk about it at the well; but this she must not mention outside the house.' So then you will know precisely what you may chatter about."
> "O mother, forgive me! That was not what I meant."
> Gertrude talked similarly with all the other children about their faults, even saying to little Peggy: "You mustn't be so impatient for your soup, or I shall make you wait longer another time, and give it to one of the others."[28]

There are numerous questions about the transmission of values by the family that philosophy of education could answer: What does "transmit" mean in this context? Which values ought to be transmitted by the family? Should the values transmitted by the family be reinforced by schools or should they be challenged? Do schools have the right to challenge them? Yet as its subject matter is presently defined, philosophy of education cannot ask them, for they are questions about the reproductive processes of society that are inappropriate to raise, let alone answer.

From the standpoint of contemporary analytic philosophy of education, Gertrude's educational activities and those of mothers in general are irrelevant. Indeed, any account of mothering is considered outside the field. For example, Sara Ruddick's recent innovative account of maternal thought, which gives insights into a kind of thinking associated with the reproductive processes of society, has no more place in the field than Pestalozzi's insights about Gertrude in her capacity as mother.[29]

The kind of maternal thought Ruddick describes and Gertrude embodies is the kind Sophie must exhibit if she is to perform well the traditional female role

Rousseau assigned her. As Ruddick makes clear, however, "maternal" is a social, not a biological category: although maternal thought arises out of childrearing practices, men as well as women express it in various ways of working and caring for others.[30] Thus it is something Sophie must learn, not something she is born with. Notice, however, when Sophie learns maternal skills from her mother and in raising her own children, this learning will also fall outside the educational realm. It will lack Peters's voluntariness and intentionality and will be part of the childrearing processes he would have philosophers of education ignore. In sum, the definition of education used by analytic philosophers today excludes the teaching, the training, and the socialization of children for which women throughout history have had prime responsibility.[31]

THE ANALYTIC PARADIGM: HIRST'S CONCEPT OF LIBERAL EDUCATION

Yet Sophie's learning would not be admitted to the educational realm even if it were designed in such a way that it met Peters's criteria of an educational process. It would still include unacceptable goals and content. According to Peters, the goal of education is the development of the educated person, who does not simply possess knowledge, but has some understanding of principles for organizing facts and of the "reason why" of things. The educated person's knowledge is not inert, but characterizes the person's way of looking at things and involves "the kind of commitment that comes from getting on the inside of a form of thought and awareness." This involves caring about the standards of evidence implicit in science or the canons of proof inherent in mathematics and possessing cognitive perspective.[32] At the center of Peters's account of education and the educated person is the notion of initiation into worthwhile activities, the impersonal cognitive content and procedures of which are "enshrined in *public traditions*."[33] Mathematics, science, history, literature, philosophy: these are the activities into which Peters's educated person is initiated. That person is one who has had, and has profited from, a liberal education of the sort outlined by Peters's colleague Paul Hirst in his essay, "Liberal Education and the Nature of Knowledge":

> First, sufficient immersion in the concepts, logic and criteria of the discipline for a person to come to know the distinctive way in which it "works" by pursuing these in particular cases; and then sufficient generalization of these over the whole range of the discipline so that his experience begins to be widely structured in this distinctive manner. It is this coming to look at things in a certain way that is being aimed at, not the ability to work out in minute particulars all the details that can be in fact discerned. It is the ability to recognise empirical assertions or aesthetic judgments for what they are, and to know the kind of considerations on which their validity will depend, that matters.[34]

If Peters's educated person is not in fact Hirst's liberally educated person, he or she is certainly the identical twin.

Hirst's analysis of liberal education has for some time been the accepted one in the field of philosophy of education.[35] In his view, liberal education consists of an initiation into what he takes to be the seven forms of knowledge.[36] Although in his later writings he carefully denies that these forms are themselves intellectual disciplines, it is safe to conclude that his liberally educated people will acquire the conceptual schemes and cognitive perspectives they are supposed to have through a study of mathematics, physical sciences, history, the human sciences, religion, literature and fine arts, and philosophy. These disciplines will not necessarily be studied separately; an interdisciplinary curriculum is compatible with Hirst's analysis. But it is nonetheless their subject matter, their conceptual apparatus, their standards of proof and adequate evidence that must be acquired if the ideal liberal education is to be realized.

In one way or another, then, the intellectual disciplines constitute the content of Peters's curriculum for the educated person. Since the things Rousseau would have Sophie learn—modesty, attentiveness, reserve, sewing, embroidery, lacemaking, keeping house, serving as hostess, bringing up children—are not part of these disciplines and are not enshrined in public traditions, they fall outside the curriculum of the educated person. But this is to say that they fall outside of education itself for, as we have seen, education, in Peters's analysis, is necessarily directed to the development of the educated person. Just as Rousseau's curriculum for Sophie is excluded from the educational realm, curricula in Beecher's domestic economy, Ruddick's maternal thinking, and Nancy Chodorow's mothering capacities would also be excluded.[37] Given the analyses of the concepts of education, the educated person, and liberal education that are accepted in general outline by the field of philosophy of education, no curriculum preparing people for the reproductive processes can belong to a realm that is reserved for the ways of thinking, acting, and feeling involved in *public* traditions. Since girls and women are the ones who traditionally have carried on the reproductive processes of society, it is *their* activities of teaching and learning and *their* curriculum that are excluded from the educational realm. Sophie and Gertrude are as irrelevant to analytic philosophers of education as they are to the writers of texts in the history of educational philosophy.

THE ANALYTIC PARADIGM: THE RATIONALITY THEORY OF TEACHING

I have said that Gertrude teaches her children even though analytic philosophers of education would say she is not educating them. Yet according to Peters, only a fraction of what Gertrude does could be called "teaching." This is because the concept of teaching is so closely linked to the concept of education that, in ruling out so many of Gertrude's activities as instances of education, Peters's analysis also rules them out as instances of teaching.

But quite apart from Peters's criteria, Gertrude fails to qualify as a teacher according to the accepted analysis of the concept of teaching. Perhaps the best brief statement of this analysis—what I have elsewhere called the rationality theory of teaching[38]—is found in a little known essay by Israel Scheffler. Beliefs, Scheffler says,

> can be acquired through mere unthinking contact, propaganda, indoctrination, or brainwashing. Teaching, by contrast, engages the mind, no matter what the subject matter. The teacher is prepared to *explain,* that is, to acknowledge the student's right to ask for reasons and his concomitant right to exercise his judgment on the merits

of the case. Teaching is, in this standard sense, an initiation into open rational discussion.[39]

In this passage Scheffler harks back to the original account of teaching he gave in his earlier book *The Language of Education,* where he states that to teach "is at some points at least to submit oneself to the understanding and independent judgment of the pupil, to his demand for reasons, to his sense of what constitutes an adequate explanation." And he adds:

> Teaching involves further that, if we try to get the student to believe that such and such is the case, we try also to get him to believe it for reasons that, within the limits of his capacity to grasp, are *our* reasons. Teaching, in this way, requires us to reveal our reasons to the student and, by so doing, to submit them to his evaluation and criticism.[40]

Scheffler is not the only contemporary philosopher of education who has emphasized connections between teaching and rationality. Numerous colleagues and critics in the field have elaborated upon and modified his analysis of teaching, and others have arrived independently at conclusions similar to his.[41] The relevant point for the present inquiry is that, according to this analysis of the concept of teaching, the learner's rationality must be acknowledged in two ways: the manner in which the teacher proceeds and the type of learning to be achieved. Thus, the rationality theory holds that to be teaching, one must expose one's reasons to the learner so that the learner can evaluate them and in addition that one's aim must be that the learner also have reasons and attain a level of learning involving understanding.

On some occasions Gertrude does approximate the conception of teaching that the rationality theory embodies. When she tries to get her children to learn that virtue must be its own reward, she cautions them to give away their bread quietly so that no one may see them and reveals to them her reason that "people needn't think you want to show off your generosity."[42] When one son asks her to give him a mouthful of bread for himself since he is giving his portion away, she refuses to do so. He asks for her reason and receives the reply: "So that you needn't imagine we are only to think of the poor after our own hunger is satisfied."[43] Yet one is left wondering what Gertrude would say and do if her children ever questioned the values she instills in them. One suspects that she would quickly resort to appeals to authority, a move of which the rationality theory would not approve.

Consider now the occasion on which Gertrude attempts to transmit her values to some neglected children by washing them, combing their hair, dressing them with care, and scrubbing their house. She neither gives reasons for the values of cleanliness and order in which she so firmly believes nor tries to *acknowledge the rationality* of the children in other ways.[44] And on another occasion when Gertrude invites these children to pray with her own children and then accompanies them to their house with a "cheery parting, bidding them to come again soon,"[45] the intention is that they acquire good habits, but the mode of acquisition is quite divorced from the giving of explanations and the evaluation of reasons. Gertrude expects that through her kindness, good example, and the efficacy of unconscious imitation, these derelict children will adopt her values. She does not seem to care whether they understand the habits and values they are adopting or have proper backing for the associated beliefs they are acquiring.

It must be made clear, however, that the rationality theory does not function as an account of *good* teaching. It is not meant to be prescriptive; rather its function is to tell us what *constitutes* or *counts* as teaching. If Gertrude's actions do not meet its twofold requirement of rationality in the manner in which the teacher proceeds and in the type of learning to be achieved, adherents of the theory will not judge her teaching to be deficient; they will judge her not to be teaching at all. They will do so, moreover, no matter how reasonable or appropriate her actions may be. That Gertrude's actions are appropriate, given the value she places on cleanliness and godliness, the age of the neighbor children, and their condition, will be evident to readers who know young children. The rationality theory is not concerned, however, that teaching be a rational activity in the ordinary sense that the actions constituting it be suited to the ends envisioned. Its sole concern is that the learner's reason be taken into account. Thus there are many contexts in which an activity meeting the requirements of the rationality theory of teaching will not be rational from the standpoint of the demands of the particular context.

In the process of bringing new infants to the point of independence, parents often do things that fit the rationality theory's criteria of teaching. Yet most of the teaching and learning that takes place in relation to the reproductive processes of society do not fit these criteria.[46] Values are transmitted, sex roles are internalized, character traits are developed, skills are acquired, and moral schemes and world views are set in place. Yet, if the teacher's reasons are not revealed or the learner's rationality is not acknowledged, the rationality theory denies the labels of "teacher" and "learner" to the parties involved.

The analysis of teaching that occupies a central position in philosophy of education today embodies a Socratic conception of both teaching and learning. The give and take of Socrates and his friends philosophizing in the marketplace, the Oxford tutor and his tutee, the graduate seminar: these are the intuitively clear cases of teaching and learning on which the analytic paradigm is based. Gertrude teaching her children a song to sing to their father when he returns home or the neighbors to count as they are spinning and sewing, Marmee helping Jo to curb her temper, Mrs. Garth making little Lotty learn her place—the activities and processes of childrearing that have traditionally belonged to women as mothers are at best considered to be peripheral cases of teaching and learning and are more likely not to qualify under these headings at all.[47]

A SERVANT OF PATRIARCHAL POLICY

In defining education and the questions that can be asked about it, the analyses of contemporary philosophy of education make women and their activities and experiences invisible. The question naturally arises whether this matters. As long as women can enter the educational realm in practice—as they can and do today— what difference does it make that educational philosophy does not acknowledge gender as a bona fide educational category? As long as Plato and Rousseau discussed the education of girls and women in major works and Pestalozzi recognized the ability of mothers to teach, what difference does it make that the texts in the history of educational philosophy ignore their accounts and that the paradigms of analytic philosophy of education do not apply to Sophie, Gertrude, or women in general?

It matters for many reasons. When the experience of women is neither reflected nor interpreted in the texts and anthologies of the history of educational philosophy, women are given no opportunity to understand and evaluate the range of ideals—from Plato's guardians to Sophie and Gertrude—that the great thinkers of the past have held for them. When Wollstonecraft and Montessori are ignored in these texts, students of both sexes are denied contact with the great female minds of the past; indeed, they are denied the knowledge that women have ever thought seriously and systematically about education. What is more important is that, when the works of women are excluded from texts and anthologies, the message that women are not capable of significant philosophical reflection is transmitted.

By placing women outside the educational realm or else making them invisible within it, the contemporary paradigms of philosophy of education also contribute to the devaluation of women. Peters's conviction that only the narrow sense of education is worthy of philosophical inquiry keeps us from perceiving the teaching that takes place in childrearing as a serious, significant undertaking; it makes women's traditional activities appear trivial and banal. Similarly, in defining teaching in terms of a very narrow conception of rationality—the giving and understanding of reasons—the rationality theory of teaching makes the educational activities of mothers, and by implication mothers themselves, appear nonrational, if not downright irrational.

In a report on recent contributions to philosophy of education, Scheffler protested that philosophy is not a handmaiden of policy. "Its function is not to facilitate policy," he said, "but rather to enlighten it by pressing its traditional questions of value, virtue, veracity, and validity."[48] Yet by its very definition of its subject matter, philosophy of education facilitates patriarchal policy; for in making females invisible, philosophy of education helps maintain the inequality of the sexes. It reinforces the impression that girls and women are not important human beings and that the activities they have traditionally performed in carrying on the reproductive processes of society are not worthwhile. Furthermore, philosophy's traditional questions of value, virtue, veracity, and validity cannot be asked about the education of females because females are unseen in the educational realm. Thus the enlightenment that philosophy is capable of giving is denied to policies that directly affect girls and women.

I do not know if philosophy can ever be as divorced from policy as Scheffler would have it. But as long as there is no epistemological equality for women in philosophy of education, that discipline will serve patriarchal policy, albeit unintentionally. For when the activities and experiences of females are excluded from the educational realm, those of males provide our norms. Thus, the qualities Socrates displays in his philosophical conversations with his male companions in the marketplace are built into our very definition of teaching even as the ones Gertrude displays in her interactions with her children are overlooked. Similarly, the traditional male activities of science and mathematics, history and philosophy are built into the curriculum of the educated person even as activities traditionally assigned to females are ignored.

Do not misunderstand: I am not suggesting that the curriculum Rousseau prescribed for Sophie should become the norm or that cooking and sewing should be placed on a par with science and history. An education for coquetry and guile is not good for either sex; and, while there is nothing wrong with both sexes learning how to cook and sew, I am not advocating that these skills be incorporated into the liberal curriculum. Nor am I endorsing Pestalozzi's claim that Gertrude's particular mode of teaching should be a model for all to emulate. My point is, rather, that when the activities and experiences traditionally associated with women are excluded from the educational realm and when that realm is defined in terms of male activities and experiences, then these become the educational norms for all human beings.

It has been shown that psychological theories of development have difficulty incorporating findings about females because they are derived from male data.[49] It should now be clear that the paradigms of analytic philosophy of education are also based on male data. The examples that generate the rationality theory of teaching, Peters's concept of education and the educated person, and Hirst's theory of liberal education all derive from male experience. The response of the psychologists to the difficulty presented them by female data is to impose on their female subjects a masculine mold. The response of philosophers of education to female data is similar: Gertrude's teaching is at best defective; education for carrying on the reproductive processes of society is at best illiberal. Thus, the male norms that are implicit in the concepts and theories of philosophy of education today devalue women and thereby serve patriarchal policy. But this is only part of the story. A corollary of this devaluation of women is that men are denied an education for carrying out the reproductive processes of society. In this way, the traditional sexual division of labor is supported.

RECONSTITUTING THE EDUCATIONAL REALM

The exclusion of women from the educational realm harms not only women; the field of philosophy of education itself is adversely affected. As the example of Rousseau's *Emile* illustrates, interpretations of works by major educational thinkers in which the education of both males and females is discussed will be deficient when they are based solely on material concerned with males. My discussion of the rationality theory of teaching—a theory that is quite implausible as an account of the teaching of young children—makes clear that analyses of concepts are likely to be inadequate when the cases that inform them and against which they are tested are derived solely from male experience. Furthermore, when gender is not seen to be a relevant educational category, important questions are begged.

When the educational realm embodies only male norms, it is inevitable that any women participating in it will be forced into a masculine mold. The question of whether such a mold is desirable for females needs to be asked, but it cannot be asked so long as philosophers of education assume that gender is a difference that makes no difference.[50] The question of whether the mold is desirable for males also needs to be asked; yet when our educational concepts and ideals are defined in male terms, we do not think to inquire into their validity for males themselves.

Perhaps the most important concern is that, when the educational realm makes women invisible, philosophy of education cannot provide an adequate answer to the question of what constitutes an educated person. Elsewhere I have argued at some length that Hirst's account of liberal education is seriously deficient—it presupposes a divorce of mind from body, thought from action, and reason from feeling and emotion—and that, since Peters's educated person is for all intents and purposes Hirst's liberally educated person, Peters's conception should be rejected.[51] Simply put, it is far too narrow to serve as an ideal that guides the educational enterprise and to which value is attached: it provides at best an ideal of an educated *mind,* not of an educated *person,* although, to the extent that its concerns are strictly cognitive, even in this sense it leaves much to be desired.

An adequate ideal of the educated person must join thought to action and reason to feeling and emotion. As I pointed out in an earlier section, however, liberal education is designed to prepare people to carry on the productive processes of society, in particular those involving the production and consumption of ideas. Thus Peters's educated person is intended to inhabit a world in which feelings and emotions such as caring, compassion, empathy, and nurturance have no legitimate role to play. To incorporate these into a conception of the educated person would be to introduce traits that were not merely irrelevant to the desired end, but very likely incompatible with it.

Peters's conception of the educated person is untenable, yet the remedy for its narrow intellectualism is unavailable to philosophers of education as long as the criteria for what falls within the educational realm mirrors the distinction between the productive and the reproductive processes of society. An adequate conception of the educated person must join together what Peters and Hirst have torn asunder: mind and body; thought and action; and reason, feeling, and emotion. To do this the educational realm must be reconstituted to include the reproductive processes of society.

It is important to understand that the exclusion of both women and the reproductive processes of society from the educational realm by philosophy of education is a consequence of the structure of the discipline and not simply due to an oversight that is easily corrected. Thus, philosophical inquiry into the nature of those processes or into the education of women cannot simply be grafted onto philosophy of education as presently constituted. On the contrary, the very subject matter of the field must be redefined.

Such a redefinition ought to be welcomed by practitioners in the field, for there is every reason to believe that it will ultimately enrich the discipline. As the experiences and activities that have traditionally belonged to women come to be included in the educational realm, a host of challenging and important issues and problems will arise. When philosophy of education investigates questions about childrearing and the transmission of values, when it develops accounts of gender education to inform its theories of liberal education, when it explores the forms of thinking, feeling, and acting associated with childrearing, marriage, and the family, when the concept of coeducation and concepts such as mothering and nurturance become subjects for philosophical analysis, philosophy of education will be invigorated.

New questions can be asked when the educational realm is reconstituted, and old questions can be given more adequate answers. When Gertrude, Sophie, and Plato's female guardians are taken seriously by historians of educational thought and when Rousseau's philosophy of education is counterbalanced by those of Wollstonecraft, Beecher, and Gilman, the theories of the great historical figures will be better understood. When analyses of the concept of teaching take childrearing activities to be central, insight into that prime educational process will be increased. When the activities of family living and childrearing fall within the range of worthwhile activities, theories of curriculum will be more complete.

It is of course impossible to know now the precise contours of a reconstituted educational realm, let alone to foresee the exact ways in which the inclusion of women and the reproductive processes of society will enrich the discipline of philosophy of education. Yet the need for a redefinition of its subject matter is imperative if philosophy of education is to cease serving patriarchal policy. The promise of enrichment is real.

Notes

This essay was written while I was a fellow at the Mary Ingraham Bunting Institute, Radcliffe College. I wish to thank Naomi Chazan, Anne Costain, Ann Diller, Carol Gilligan, Diane Margolis, Michael Martin, Beatrice Nelson, and Janet Farrell Smith for helpful comments on the original draft.

1. See Kathryn Pyne Parsons, "Moral Revolution," in *The Prism of Sex,* ed. Julia A. Sherman and Evelyn Torton Beck (Madison: Univ. of Wisconsin Press, 1979), pp. 189–227; and Lawrence Blum, "Kant's and Hegel's Moral Rationalism: A Feminist Perspective," *Canadian Journal of Philosophy,* 12(2), 1982, pp. 287–302.

2. Jane Roland Martin, "Sophie and Emile: A Case Study of Sex Bias in the History of Educational Thought," *Harvard Educational Review* 51 (1981), 357–372.

3. See Robert Ulich, ed., *Three Thousand Years of Educational Wisdom* (Cambridge: Harvard Univ. Press, 1948) and his *History of Educational Thought* (New York: American Book, 1945); Robert S. Brumbaugh and Nathaniel M. Lawrence, *Philosophers on Education: Six Essays on the Foundations of Western Thought* (Boston: Houghton Mifflin, 1963); Paul Nash, Andreas M. Kazemias, and Henry J. Perkinson, ed., *The Educated Man: Studies in the History of Educational Thought* (New York: Wiley, 1965); Kingsley Price, *Education and Philosophical Thought,* 2d ed. (Boston: Allyn & Bacon, 1967); Paul Nash, comp., *Models of Man: Explorations in the Western Educational Tradition* (New York: Wiley, 1968); and Steven M. Cahn, comp., *The Philosophical Foundations of Education* (New York: Harper & Row, 1970).

4. For example, although Brumbaugh and Lawrence call Plato "the great educational revolutionist of his time" in part because of his "insistence on the equality of women" (*Philosophers on Education,* p. 38), they say not another word about that insistence. Robert S. Rusk, who presents Plato's position on the education of women in some detail in his anthology, is apparently so distressed by it that he says what any reader of the *Republic* knows to be false, namely, "Plato can only secure the unity of the state *at the cost of sacrificing all differences*" (*The Doctrines of the Great Educators,* rev. 3d ed. [New York: St. Martin's, 1965], pp. 28–29, emphasis added). Nash comments that Plato's model of the educated person applies "only to those rare men *and rarer women* who are capable of understanding the underlying harmony of the universe" (*Models of Man,* p. 9, emphasis added), without acknowledging that Plato himself never makes a comparative judgment of the ability of males and females in his Just State to grasp The Good.

5. Pierce, "Equality: *Republic* V," *The Monist* 57 (1973), 1–11.

6. See, for example, John Dewey, "Is Coeducation Injurious to Girls?" *Ladies' Home Journal* 28 (1911), pp. 60–61; Thomas Henry Huxley, "Emancipation—Black and White," *Lay Sermons, Addresses, and Reviews* (New York: Appleton, 1870; rpt. in Nash, pp. 285–288).

7. Nash, *Models of Man.*

8. Kate Silber, *Pestalozzi* (New York: Schocken Books, 1965), p. 42.

9. John Heinrich Pestalozzi, *Leonard and Gertrude,* trans. Eva Channing (Boston: Heath, 1885), ch. 22.

10. Silber, p. 42.

11. Rusk, ch. 12.

12. Mary Wollstonecraft, *A Vindication of the Rights of Woman* (New York: Norton, 1967); see also Mary Wollstonecraft Godwin, *Thoughts on the Education of Daughters* (Clifton, N.J.: Kelley Publishers, 1972).

13. Catherine Macaulay, *Letters on Education,* ed. Gina Luria (New York: Garland, 1974). For discussions of Macaulay's life and works, see Florence S. Boos, "Catherine Macaulay's *Letters on Education* (1790): An Early Feminist Polemic," *University of Michigan Papers in Women's Studies,* 2 (1976), 64–78; Florence Boos and William Boos, "Catherine Macaulay: Historian and Political Reformer," *International Journal of Women's Studies* 3 (1980), 49–65.

14. For a list of Beecher's published works, see Kathryn Kish Sklar, *Catharine Beecher: A Study in American Domesticity* (New York: Norton, 1973).

15. Charlotte Perkins Gilman, *Herland* (New York: Pantheon Books, 1979).

16. Lorenne M. G. Clark, "The Rights of Women: The Theory and Practice of the Ideology of Male Supremacy," in *Contemporary Issues in Political Philosophy,* ed. William R. Shea and John King-Farlow (New York: Science History Publications, 1976), pp. 49–65.

17. See Susan Moller Okin, *Women in Western Political Thought* (Princeton: Princeton Univ. Press, 1979). ch. 6; Lynda Lange, "Rousseau: Women and the General Will," in *The Sexism of Social and Political Theory,* ed. Lorenne M. G. Clark and Lynda Lange (Toronto: Univ. of Toronto Press, 1979), pp. 41–52; and Martin, "Sophie and Emile."

18. See Marvin Lazerson and W. Norton Grubb, ed., *American Education and Vocationalism* (New York: Teachers College Press, 1974).

19. Rousseau, ch. 5. For the account of liberal education that dominates the thinking of philosophers of education today, see Paul H. Hirst, "Liberal Education and the Nature of Knowledge," in *Philosophical Analysis and Education,* ed. Reginald D. Archambault (London: Routledge & Kegan Paul, 1965), pp. 113–138; rpt. in Paul H. Hirst, *Knowledge and the Curriculum* (London: Routledge & Kegan Paul, 1974). Page references will be to this volume.

20. I recognize that I have omitted from this discussion all reference to home economics education. Briefly, home economics education has historically been classified as vocational education (see Lazerson and Grubb). However, in the form that is relevant to the present discussion, namely, the preparation of women for their place in the home, it lacks the distinguishing mark of other vocational studies in that it is not intended as training for jobs in the marketplace. Furthermore, contemporary philosophy of education has seldom, if ever, recognized its existence.

21. R. S. Peters, *Ethics and Education* (Glenview, Ill.: Scott, Foresman, 1967), pp. 2–3.

22. Ibid., p. 17.

23. Ibid., p. 27.

24. See Peters, "What is an Educational Process?" in *The Concepts of Education,* ed. R. S. Peters (London: Routledge & Kegan Paul, 1967); Paul H. Hirst and R. S. Peters, *The Logic of Education* (London: Routledge & Kegan Paul, 1970); R. S. Peters, "Education and the Educated Man," in *A Critique of Current Educational Aims,* ed. R. F. Dearden, Paul H. Hirst, and R. S. Peters (London: Routledge & Kegan Paul, 1972);

R. S. Peters, J. Woods, and W. H. Dray, "Aims of Education—A Conceptual Inquiry," in *The Philosophy of Education,* ed. R. S. Peters (London: Oxford Univ. Press, 1973).

25. See, for example, Peters, "Education and the Educated Man," p. 8.

26. In this section and the ones to follow I will only be discussing paradigms of analytic philosophy of education. There are other schools within philosophy of education, but this one dominates the field today as the recent N.S.S.E. Yearbook, *Philosophy and Education,* testifies (ed. Jonas Soltis [Chicago: The National Society for the Study of Education, 1981]).

27. Pestalozzi, pp. 87–88.

28. Ibid., p. 44.

29. "Maternal Thinking," *Feminist Studies* 6 (1980), 342–367.

30. Ruddick, p. 346.

31. I do not mean to suggest that these activities have been in the past or are now carried on exclusively by women. On the contrary, both men and women have engaged in them and do now. Our culture assigns women responsibility for them, however.

32. Peters, *Ethics and Education,* p. 8ff.

33. Peters, *Education as Initiation* (London: Evans Brothers, 1964), p. 35, emphasis added.

34. Hirst, "Liberal Education," p. 47.

35. For an extended critique of Hirst's analysis in this respect, see Jane Roland Martin, "Needed: A New Paradigm for Liberal Education," in *Philosophy and Education,* pp. 37–59.

36. In "Liberal Education," p. 46, Hirst listed the seven as: mathematics, physical sciences, human sciences, history, religion, literature and fine arts, and philosophy.

37. See Ruddick; Chodorow, *The Reproduction of Mothering* (Berkeley: Univ. of California Press, 1978); and Catharine M. Beecher, *Suggestions Respecting Improvements in Education* (Hartford, Conn.: Packard & Butler, 1829).

38. Martin, *Explaining, Understanding, and Teaching* (New York: McGraw-Hill, 1970), ch. 5.

39. "Concepts of Education: Reflections on the Current Scene," in Israel Scheffler, *Reason and Teaching* (Indianapolis: Bobbs-Merrill, 1973), p. 62.

40. Israel Scheffler, *The Language of Education* (Springfield, Ill.: Thomas, 1960), p. 57.

41. See, for example, Thomas F. Green, "A Topology of the Teaching Concept," *Studies in Philosophy and Education* 3 (1964–65), 284–319; and his "Teaching, Acting, and Behaving," *Harvard Educational Review* 34 (1964), 507–524.

42. Pestalozzi, p. 55.

43. Ibid., p. 54.

44. Ibid., p. 87.

45. Ibid., pp. 88–89.

46. Philosophy of education is not alone in placing Gertrude and the mothers she represents in the "ontological basement." In ch. 2 of *Worlds Apart* (New York: Basic Books, 1978), Sara Lawrence Lightfoot discusses mothers and teachers but never acknowledges that mothers *qua* mothers teach.

47. These examples of mother-teachers are taken from Louisa May Alcott, *Little Women* (Boston: Little Brown, 1936); and George Eliot, *Middlemarch* (Boston: Houghton Mifflin, 1956).

48. Israel Scheffler, "Philosophy of Education: Some Recent Contributions," *Harvard Educational Review* 50 (1980), 402–406.

49. See Carol Gilligan, "In a Different Voice: Women's Conceptions of Self and Morality," *Harvard Educational Review* 47 (1977), 481–517; "Woman's Place in Man's Life Cycle," *Harvard Educational Review* 49 (1979), 431–446.

50. Jane Roland Martin, "Sex Equality and Education," in *"Femininity," "Masculinity," and "Androgyny": A Modern Philosophical Discussion,* ed. Mary Vetterling-Braggin (Totowa, N.J.: Littlefield, Adams, 1982).

51. Martin, "Needed: A Paradigm for Liberal Education"; "The Ideal of the Educated Person," *Educational Theory,* 31 (1981), 97–109.

8

SHOULD PUBLIC EDUCATION BE GENDER FREE?

Barbara Houston

INTRODUCTION

Discussion of the question Should public education be gender-free? should begin with a sorting out of the different possible meanings of the term *gender-free*.[1] In the context of our discussion, I take there to be the following three distinct meanings. In the first sense, the strong sense, a gender-free education would be one that made active attempts to disregard gender by obliterating gender differentiations that arose within the educational sphere. Ruling out items on IQ tests that gave sex-differentiated results in scores is an example of a gender-free educational practice in this strong sense. Such efforts are sometimes described as attempts to deinstitutionalize sex differences to create a form of gender blindness.[2] Another example of this approach is the elimination of activities, such as wrestling, in which there are thought to be significant gender differences in achievements due to natural and ineradicable biological differences between the sexes.[3]

In the second case, the weak sense, *gender-free* means that gender is ignored, not attended to. Under this meaning a gender-free education is one that refuses to take notice of gender. No longer using gender as an admissions criterion to educational institutions or to specific educational programs is an example of this weak sense of *gender-free*.

In the third sense I take *gender-free* to mean freedom from gender bias. According to this understanding, a gender-free education would be one that eliminated gender bias.

In this latter weakest sense we could all be said to favor gender-free education. Even the traditionalist who holds to false accounts of sex differences and inadequate justification for gender roles within education might well argue that gender differentiations within education are not meant to constitute a gender *bias*. So, the interesting interpretation of our question Should public education be gender-free? is *not* Should public education be free of gender-bias? This question is not

122

at issue, since all positions, at least in their rhetoric, already agree that public education should be free of gender-bias. The question is rather what is the best way to achieve this freedom from gender-bias. Should we undertake to ignore gender or to obliterate gender differentiations, or should we in some way pay deliberate attention to gender?

I assume, in this paper, the viewpoint of an educator who is already committed to sex equality and to equal educational opportunity but who recognizes that a number of practical questions and policy matters are still undetermined with respect to the question of whether we should or should not institute a kind of gender blindness. I shall argue that, in the present circumstances, the adoption of either a weak or a strong version of the gender-free strategy is problematic in two different ways. It is problematic, first, because the use of either version of the strategy is likely to cause us to miss, or even to reinforce, the more subtle forms of gender bias. Through an examination of three prevalent forms of gender bias and actual examples of the gender-free strategy, I shall show that a general adoption of this strategy would likely ensure that females continue to have unequal educational opportunity. The strategy is problematic in a second way, because both versions of it presuppose an ideal of sex equality that prematurely forecloses on important questions central to the issue. In conclusion, I shall defend a more promising strategy for achieving freedom from gender bias, a strategy first suggested in the work of Jane Roland Martin and labeled by her *gender-sensitive*.[4]

GENDER BIAS: UNEQUAL ACCESS, UNEQUAL OPPORTUNITY FOR PARTICIPATION, AND GENDERIZED VALUATION

That girls and women have had unequal access to educational institutions is news to no one. Undoubtedly, significant progress toward sex equality was made when it was decided that we should ignore gender, that is, no longer pay attention to it in deciding who should get an education, who should be admitted to schools, allowed to study certain subjects, and have access to particular educational activities. Having come to the realization that much sex-segregated education has been both different and unequal, ignoring gender has enabled us to move to coeducation in a stricter sense. For example, no longer do we have home economics and typing for girls only or physical sciences and industrial arts for boys only.

Physical education is an especially interesting case in point. Sex-segregated classes have fostered different and unequal education for boys and girls in this domain.[5] One reasonable attempt to eliminate the gender bias that has developed in physical education has been to adopt both the weak and strong versions of what I have called the gender-free strategy. This approach has urged that we ignore the gender of those in the physical education class and ignore the gender of those on the teams, allowing all to have equal access to the educational resources. Under such a policy, one might expect girls' and women's opportunities to increase. But often quite the opposite is true. Solomon's observations of game interactions in a fifth-grade coed class showed that

> girls tended to be left out of game interactions by the boys. This was true even when the girls had a higher skill level than boys did. Additionally, both girls and boys regarded boys as better players even when the girls were more highly skilled. Boys

123

preferred to pass the ball to an unskilled boy rather than to a skilled girl. Girls tended to give away scoring opportunities to boys. Unskilled girls were almost completely left out of game action. However, both skilled and unskilled girls received fewer passes than boys did.[6]

Of course, it is a good thing to remove access barriers to education, and in this case ignoring gender has allowed us to do that. However, equal participation in the educational process is also a crucial dimension of equal educational opportunity. In this case, the strategy that removes access barriers has also had the effect of bringing about a *greater* loss of educational opportunities for girls.[7]

Research findings suggest that this basketball game, where males keep passing the ball to each other, is a metaphor for all types of mixed-sex classrooms and activities. From the research we have on student-teacher interactions and on student-student interactions, essentially the same picture emerges, though there are some differences dependent upon the race and class of the students.

Studies on teacher-student interactions indicate that within coeducational classrooms, teachers, regardless of sex, interact more with boys, give boys more attention (both positive and negative), and that this pattern intensifies at the secondary and college levels. Girls get less teacher attention and wait longer for it. When they do get attention, it is more likely that the teacher will respond to them neutrally or negatively (though this depends somewhat on the girls' race and class). The reinforcement girls do get is likely to be for passivity and neatness, not for getting the right answer.[8]

Equally distressing is the indication we have from research findings that student interactions with one another also appear to dampen female participation in mixed-sex classes. At the postsecondary level, the brightest women in the class often remain silent; women students are in general likely to be less verbally assertive, they are likely to be called on less than men students, and those who do participate may find that their comments are disproportionately interrupted by teachers and male classmates and that teachers are less likely to develop their points than those made by men students.[9]

Part of the explanation for these classroom inequities may be that the everyday linguistic patterns of how women and men talk together in mixed-sex groupings is carried over into the classroom. In mixed-sex groupings men talk more than women, men talk for longer periods of time and take more turns at speaking; men exert more control over the conversation; men interrupt women more than women interrupt men; and men's interruptions of women more often introduce trivial or inappropriately personal comments that bring women's discussion to an end or change its focus. It is also indicated that what men say carries more weight. A suggestion made by a man is more likely to be listened to, credited to him, developed in further discussion, and adopted by the group than a suggestion made by a woman.[10]

There are also linguistic styles of speech that can affect women's participation opportunities in the classroom. For example, there are certain features that occur more in women's speech than in men's, such as hesitations, false starts, a questioning intonation when making a statement, an extensive use of qualifiers that serve to weaken what is said, and extensive use of modals and forms of speech that are excessively polite and deferential. In addition, in mixed-sex interactive patterns the speech of women is more supportive than that of men, inasmuch as it exhibits an effort to elicit and encourage the contributions of the other speakers to the conversation. Male patterns, on the other hand, include highly assertive speech, an impersonal and abstract style, and "devil's advocate" exchange.[11]

The problem, as one researcher suggests, is that in the school setting these "male" ways of talking are often "equated with intelligence and authority."[12] If someone speaks hesitantly or with numerous qualifiers, she is perceived by her teachers and classmates as unfocused and unsure of what she wants to say. It is also clear that an overly polite style more easily allows interruptions or inattention from both teachers and students.[13] The same points made in a "masculine," assertive way are taken more seriously. But more significant perhaps is the fact that while it is thought to be perfectly proper for boys to "conduct argument, air their views and query information," it is not thought proper for girls to do the same thing.[14] This genderized valuation of classroom talk poses special problems for girls who seek to take on those ways of talking associated with "intelligence and authority."

What are the consequences for girls if the classrooms are male-dominant in this way? Clearly, we think it important that learners be able to talk about their own experiences as a starting point for learning; we regard the classroom as an opportunity for discovering new insights and understandings that need not depend upon received knowledge. Here, we say, "Students can find out things for themselves, they can ask questions, make new connections, describe and explain the world in different ways."[15] Indeed, we even claim they can criticize the received texts. But what if one half of the students are not free to make such explorations, to take up the topics of their choosing, to articulate and validate their own experience? What if this opportunity is blocked for them?

Teacher behavior can directly or inadvertently reinforce those patterns that make it difficult for half the class population not only to talk, particularly to the teacher, but also to have their own experience be perceived as interesting and appropriate topics to discuss. If teachers fail to notice the gender of the student who is talking, if they pay no attention to who is interrupting whom, whose points are acknowledged and taken up, who is determining the topic of discussion, then they will by default perpetuate patterns that discourage women's participation in the educational process.

The *teacher* may well try to ignore gender, but the point is that the *students* are not ignoring it in their sense of how the interactions should go and who is entitled to speak in the educational arena. Gender may be excluded as an *official* criterion, but it continues to function as an *unofficial* factor.

In a recent study designed to measure the effects of efforts to correct sexism in education, a tenth-grade girl said, "If I were a boy I would be more outspoken and confident, but I really don't know why."[16] It has been suggested that "the why is that boys usually know that they are valued whereas girls are not always sure."[17] Although they may not articulate it, students of both sexes have a clear perception of the devaluation of girls in the culture.[18] Obviously, in these circumstances if we simply ignore gender differentiations in the mode in which students can participate in the educational process, we will reinforce the message that girls do not count, or at least they do not count as much.

This suggestion of some of the influences of gender in educational interactions has been necessarily brief. The picture is not nearly as simple as time forces us to sketch it. Nevertheless, although gender bias will vary in texture and complexity depending upon many other factors, notably race and class, our picture points to the fundamental issue with which we should be concerned, namely, the manner in which the school can confirm girls in subordinate positions. This, I would stress, should be a matter of concern regardless of girls' school achievements.

EVALUATION OF THE GENDER-FREE APPROACH

When gender differentiations exist in the opportunity to participate in the educational process, what are we to do to eliminate bias? Within the gender-free strategy there are two approaches, one more radical than the other. We have seen that the first approach, that of deciding to ignore gender by no longer letting it count where it had before, is certainly effective in removing gender as an access barrier. We cannot, however, count on this passive ignoring of gender as an effective means to the elimination of other types of gender bias. In fact, it appears that it may simply have the effect of masking other types of bias, for example, bias in opportunities for participation.

There are two general difficulties with the approach suggested by the weak sense of "gender-free." First, it is doubtful that teachers *can* ignore gender in this sense, because they often do not recognize when gender is exerting an influence. It is startling just how unaware teachers are of the phenomenon we have described. Their perceptions of how they interact with students are often grossly inaccurate. Having claimed that they treat girls and boys equally in the classroom, they are shocked to discover through objective observation measures that they spend over two thirds of their time with boys who comprise less than half the class; or that they reward boys for getting the right answers and girls for neatness; or that they criticize boys for poor work and criticize girls for being assertive; or that they explain a boy's achievements in terms of his abilities and a girl's in terms of the degree of difficulty of the test or in terms of luck.[19] Students, however, are often clear in their perceptions of the gender differences in student-teacher interactions.[20]

But the second and equally important difficulty is that even if the teacher were successful in ignoring gender, it is obvious that students do take cognizance of it. The gender-connected conventions and expectations that students themselves bring to their classroom interactions will continue unaltered, if not actually strengthened, if teachers do not intervene to change the patterns.

Perhaps mindful of these difficulties, the other version of the gender-free strategy would have us press for interventions to eliminate any gender differences in achievements in the hopes of creating in us a kind of gender blindness. As with the first approach, this more active pursuit of gender blindness can be useful. But it is also problematic. There is the very real danger that in restructuring activities we are likely to be unduly influenced by a male valuation scheme. For example, it would have us intervene to eliminate or restructure sports at which either of the sexes had a natural advantage because of physical differences, such as football, in which males are favored, or certain forms of gymnastics work, such as the balance beam, in which girls are favored. The idea behind restructuring sports activities has been to allow girls and boys equal rates of success. There are, however, a number of dubious assumptions at work here, for instance, the assumption that girls' performance levels are accurately perceived and that these levels do determine their opportunities.

But the case is not that simple. The problem is not how well girls do in relation to boys; the problem is that *even when girls do as well as or better than boys at the same activity,* their performance is undervalued by themselves and by others, and their opportunities remain relatively limited.[21] A more radical critique would note that, even if we could straighten out the misperceptions about performance and opportunities, we should still question the further value assumption that only winning matters, rather than the enjoyment of playing or the development of a sporting attitude.[22]

In the case of gender-differentiated speech patterns, a male valuation scheme might well recommend a single classroom speech pattern, an assertive one, and offer girls and women special training in this form of "educated speech." But giving girls lessons in how to be assertive in the classroom can be problematic when it merely puts girls in a double bind in which they must adopt what are perceived as "masculine" speech patterns if they are to succeed. As we have noted earlier, the patterns of speech in boys and men that are regarded as forceful are often regarded as negative and hostile when used by girls and women.[23] More to the point, women's conventional patterns of speech have been demonstrated to be helpful in so far as they foster participation by others and encourage a cooperative development of ideas rather than adversarial relations.[24] If we attempt to eliminate gender differentiations, we will have to bear in mind that often our evaluation of the differences has itself been gender biased.

There are two other significant problems that need to be addressed in our discussion of the interventionists' gender-free approach: How accurate are teachers' perceptions of fairness? And more significantly, what influence can we expect students' efforts to have on teachers' efforts to bring about change?

Even those teachers who undertake to correct genderized patterns of participation have been, in the words of one of them, "spectacularly unsuccessful." Dale Spender notes with dismay how she and others seriously underestimated the amount of attention they gave to boys rather than to girls *even when they were trying to be fair about it.* When teachers feel they are being fair, or even showing favoritism to girls, the empirical evidence shows otherwise. For example, giving 35 percent of one's attention to girls can feel as though one is being unfair to boys. Giving just over one third of one's attention to girls can feel as though one is making a significant effort, even compensating girls.[25]

It is important to notice that students share this perception. For example, when a teacher tries to eliminate gender bias in participation by giving 34 percent of her attention to girls who comprise one half the class, the boys protested: "She always asks girls all the questions"; "She doesn't like boys and just listens to girls all the time."[26] In a sexist society boys perceive that two-thirds of the teacher's time is a fair allotment for them, and if it is altered so that they receive less, they feel they are discriminated against. And of course they resist, and they protest, and teachers often give in in order to foster the cooperation that gives the appearance that they are in control of the classroom. Anyone who has tried to correct the bias will recognize the phenomenon.

In other words, even a strong interventionist strategy may at best achieve a gender-free inequality that gives two-thirds time for attending to males. As Spender notes, even when teachers do want to treat the sexes equally, the difficulty is that "our society and education is so structured that 'equality' and 'fairness' means that males get more attention."[27] Our own existing perceptual frameworks are themselves too gender-biased to provide reliable guides as to whether or not our approaches are actually gender-free. Of course these difficulties will plague all methods we use to get rid of gender discrimination. Their presence represents a powerful argument, however, against the suggestion that the best route to sex equality in education is simply to ignore gender; and, as I shall argue, careful attention to these difficulties can point to a better approach to the problem of the elimination of gender bias.

Thus, as with the weaker version of the gender-free strategy, I find two major difficulties with the stronger version: (1) it fails to aid us in the identification and elimination of genderized valuations; and (2) because of this, in employing the strategy we run a serious risk of encouraging an assimilation of women's identity, interests, and values to men's.

It should be clear that I do not object to all suggestions coming from the gender-free approach. As I have indicated, I think it is useful, indeed imperative, at times to ignore gender in the weak sense, and at other times I think it is useful to try to obliterate gender differentiations to ensure the absence of improper gender influence. It is also clear, however, that both recommendations may, on occasion, fail to eliminate bias. More importantly, on some occasions we may need to use gender as a criterion in designing a practice useful for eliminating gender bias.

For example, we might restructure the basketball game so as to introduce new rules requiring alternate passes to females and males. In other sports such as volleyball, one might introduce a temporary rule change: boys must set up spikes for girls. We may even want to introduce single-sex schooling. Some studies indicate that in certain contexts it may be necessary to have single-sex classrooms for particular subjects such as math or science for a period of time to ensure that in coeducational classrooms girls will have an equal opportunity to participate and attain equal educational results.[28] The point is that these equalizing practices require those involved to be sensitive to gender in a way that appears to be ruled out by the gender-free strategy.

My most general objection then to the gender-free strategy, both the strong and the weak versions, is twofold: (1) it is likely to create a context that continues to favor the dominant group, and (2) it undermines certain efforts that may be needed to realize an equalization of educational opportunities.

The central problem with the gender-free mandate is that it misleadingly suggests that in order to free ourselves of gender bias, we have to stop paying attention to gender. It is singularly odd to call this approach gender-free or gender-blind if it involves paying attention to gender. If we look closely, we find that any significant success of the gender-free strategy would require that one continue to pay scrupulous attention to gender to make sure that the strategy is effective in eliminating bias. Either the strategy recommends this attention to gender or it does not. If it does, its rhetoric is misleading; if it does not, its method is mistaken.

In response to my evaluation of the gender-free strategy, it may be said that I have created a straw strategy. In particular, a gender-free enthusiast might claim that the strategy can be more effectively used than is suggested by my choice of examples. This response to my criticism has some merit. It is never wholly convincing to argue that a strategy or method is a poor one because its use is liable to error. In the wrong hands, or in difficult circumstances, any method for eliminating gender bias will suffer an increased likelihood of failure.

A critic might also contend that any persuasive force my remarks or examples may have is due to my equivocation upon the notion of ignoring gender. Proponents of the gender-free approach would undoubtedly claim that the gender-free strategy, in recommending that we ignore gender, is not recommending that we stop attending to it. But no, my criticism cuts deeper than this. My point is that the gender-free strategy presupposes that we *a priori* decided that gender should have no educational relevance attached to it. This, I contend, could never be decided once and for all *a priori*. The greatest danger of the gender-free approach is that it prematurely forecloses on two important questions: (1) Are there gender-related differences? and (2) How are we to evaluate them?

With the growth of women's studies in the past decade, we are only now beginning to catch a glimmer of the powerful and subtle ways in which gender has been and continues to be a basic social organizing principle in all known societies. In taking gender itself as a matter of study, women's studies has produced a revolutionary means of viewing the form and subject matter of a variety of disciplines. It is too early to pronounce that we know all the forms of gender bias and that we know that they are best eliminated by invoking a gender-free ideal and a gender-free strategy. We need to pay yet *more* attention to gender, not ignore it. We need to inquire further into gender differences, not try to get rid of them.

For the first time in history, we are now actually in a position in which women are beginning to create a study of themselves by themselves. There is now the opportunity for us to articulate systematically, theorize about, and evaluate our own experience. We need this opportunity especially to investigate what is or might be uniquely female experience in order better to understand the human condition. We will not achieve the understanding we seek if we ignore or try to obliterate gender differences, or attend only to those experiences that the genders share in common, without first being sure that we have accurate information about differences and a proper evaluation of them.

ASSUMPTIONS ABOUT GENDER

Thus far I have attempted to show that the gender-free strategy is suspect because both versions of it, the strong and the weak, fail us in the identification and elimination of the type of gender bias I have called gender valuation. I wish now to explain why the strategy has this effect in some cases. The explanation lies in an examination of the assumptions about gender that underlie the strategy and the ideal of sex equality at which it aims.

The ideal of sex equality urged by those who advocate the gender-free strategy is one that gives gender the status eye color now has in our society. In short, gender is taken to be totally irrelevant to social organization. I have no special quarrel with the claim that this is precisely how a good, just society ought to treat gender. My worry is that this ideal is not especially helpful in the detection and elimination of present gender bias.

This difficulty arises, I suspect, because there is a tendency to see gender as a trait of individuals. If gender were simply a characteristic of individuals that was linked to sex, could be easily marked, correlated with achievements, and used as a criterion for qualification or exclusion, then it would make good sense to talk about ignoring gender or treating it as an irrelevant characteristic. However, although we do speak of individuals as gendered, if we see gender solely or primarily as a trait of individuals, we shall be seriously misled.

Gender is also a structure of power; it is a structuring process. As one group of researchers puts it, it is better to "treat gender not just as a matter of existence of two categories of people, male and female, but primarily as a pattern of *relations* among people."[29] They note further: "Relationships between the sexes are not just a matter of distinctions leading to inequalities. They are also relations of power. When we talk about gender we are talking about ways in which social relations get organized in the interests of some groups, overriding the interests of others."[30]

It is equally important to notice that these social relations are systematic, not random, and historical, not static. They change constantly, and they are influenced by other social structuring processes such as race and class. But matters are extremely complex, because the influence of race and class is not in any way straightforward. "Class and gender do not occur jointly in a situation. They abrade, inflame, amplify, twist, negate, dampen and complicate each other. In short, they interact vigorously, often through the schools and often with significant consequences for schooling."[31]

If we want to make any significant difference to the educational opportunities of girls, we shall have to take cognizance of the precise nature of the femininity the school is helping to construct, how it is aided or subverted by race and class influences; and we shall have to map the consequences of alternative interventionist policies. This will not be an easy task. The structuring processes of race, class, and gender have different dynamics, and attempts to remedy unequal educational opportunities from the point of view of one of these interests can have different and even contrary effects for the others. We have learned, for example, that in some cases policies undertaken with class interests in mind have had differential effects for girls and boys.[32] In other instances we have learned that the educational sex segregation of girls, which once served to marginalize them and socialize them to a subordinate role, now works, in some class contexts, to erode their subordination.[33]

Because gender is a set of relations that are constantly changing and are constantly affected by other structuring processes in social relations, the gender-free strategy has to appear somewhat simplistic. It is misleading to think of gender as something that can be ignored or treated as irrelevant. Gender relations can be ignored, but only at the risk of entrenchment; and while they are changeable, it misses the mark to think they can be eliminated. Eliminating gender bias may often be a matter of seeing gender differently rather than becoming blind to it. It is not always a question of making some characteristic of individuals irrelevant; it is often a matter of recognizing that some activities, characteristics, or interests of individuals are more valuable than we thought. We need to learn to assess them independently of their location in gender relations.

A GENDER-SENSITIVE PERSPECTIVE

But there is another, a better approach to the elimination of gender bias, one that is conceptually distinct from the gender-free one, although it does not necessarily foreclose on any particular suggestions recommended by that strategy. Jane Martin has suggested that we employ a gender-sensitive perspective that recommends that we pay attention to gender when it can prevent sex bias or further sex equality.[34] It is a perspective that requires careful monitoring of our gender interactions and urges direct intervention when necessary to equalize opportunities. In considering alternative strategies for eliminating bias, it is Martin's that is, I think, the most defensible.

What differentiates a gender-*sensitive* strategy from a gender-*free* one is that a gender-sensitive strategy allows one to recognize that at different times and in different circumstances one might be required to adopt opposing policies in order to eliminate gender bias.[35] A gender-sensitive perspective is not a blueprint for education that will answer all our questions about particular practices. It is, rather, a perspective that constantly reminds us to question the ways in which students and teachers make sense of and respond to a sexist culture. It is a situational strategy, one that lets the patterns of discrimination themselves determine which particular action to take to eliminate bias. This is an important feature to bear in mind. It is the chief virtue of this perspective, for new, unsuspected types of gender bias will continue to emerge.

We have already seen how a significant school policy on gender relations, namely coeducation, designed to remove access barriers has revealed that women do not have equal participation in the educational process. Once equal participation is achieved, it will become more evident that women do not have an equal say about what knowledge is to be distributed, or about what the styles of pedagogy should be, or about what the goals and ideals of education should be.[36]

A gender-sensitive perspective is a higher-order perspective than that involved in the gender-free strategy. It encourages one to ask constantly: is gender operative here? How is gender operative? What other effects do our strategies for eliminating gender bias have?

A gender-sensitive perspective can also be differentiated from a gender-free strategy by the kinds of questions it leaves open—questions that a gender-free strategy threatens to close, for example, questions about possible differences in learning that might be correlated with gender relations. It is not that a gender-sensitive perspective claims there *are* significant differences, only that there *could be,* given the way in which gender has functioned as a species creator within our culture.

The superiority of the gender-sensitive perspective is secured by the fact that it can yield a methodology that is self-correcting. For it is a view that can acknowledge that gender is a set of relations between the sexes, a process that is constantly organizing and reorganizing our social life. It can recognize the dynamic nature of the gender system, one that exerts pressures, produces reactions, and generates changes.[37] Thus it is a perspective, the only perspective of the three considered, that maintains a constant vigilance and reckoning on the significance gender acquires in particular contexts. Only if we adopt a perspective of this sort will we be able to catch our own errors, alter policies and practices that no longer work, and introduce new policies for new circumstances. It is in this sense that a gender-sensitive perspective can be a self-correcting methodology for realizing the elusive ideal of sex equality.

CONCLUSION

In this paper I have tried to address the transitional problem of moving from a gender-biased education in a sexist culture to an unbiased education that will continue for some time to be influenced by the wider culture. I have argued that the most effective way to deal with gender bias is to adopt a gender-sensitive perspective. It is fundamentally a perspective that encourages a critical and constant review of the meaning and evaluation attached to gender. In this it offers greater hope for the elimination of all types of gender bias than does a gender-free strategy.

Notes

This paper has benefited from my discussions with Susan Franzosa, Jennifer Radden, Janet Farrell Smith, Gillian Michell, and especially Jane Martin and Ann Diller. The original title of this essay is "Gender Freedom and the Subtleties of Sexist Education."

1. One of the common distinctions employed in the literature on sex roles and sex equality is that drawn between sex and gender. When the distinction is drawn, *sex* refers to the biological differences between females and males, and *gender* refers to the social differences between the sexes. The matter is far from simple, however; usage of the terms is often inconsistent, and some have argued that the distinction itself is unsuccessful because of the complex linkage between the biological and the social aspects of sex (see M. Eichler, *The Double Standard: A Feminist Critique of Feminist Social Science* [London: Croom Helm, 1980]). I grant the difficulties and nevertheless employ the distinction in this essay. I use the term *gender-free* precisely because I believe that not only biological differences between the sexes are relevant to the discussion of sex equality in education. I do not wish to beg any questions about the nature or causal explanation of gender differences, but I am interested in the implications we think gender relations should have for educational theory and practice. Hence I invoke the notion of gender, but I use it solely as a descriptive term. For an elaborate clarification of the notions of gender, gender identity, and gender role that attends to educational implications, see M. Ayim and B. Houston, "The Epistemology of Gender Identity: Implications for Social Policy," *Social Theory and Practice* 11, no. 1 (1985): 25–59.

2. So far as I know, the term "gender blindness" was first introduced by Richard Wasserstrom in his paper entitled "Racism and Sexism" in *Philosophy and Women*, ed. S. Bishop and M. Weinzweig (Belmont, Calif.: Wadsworth, 1979).

3. For a discussion of the merits and difficulties with this attempt to pursue gender blindness, see Wasserstrom, "Racism and Sexism"; and Bernard Boxill, "Sexual Blindness and Sexual Equality," *Social Theory and Practice* 6 (Fall 1980): 281–99.

4. Jane Roland Martin, "The Ideal of the Educated Person," *Educational Theory*, 31, no. 2 (Spring 1981): 97–109. For further discussions of Martin's critique of philosophy of education and her views about the best ways to include women in educational theory and practice, see her papers "Sophie and Emile: A Case Study of Sex Bias in the History of Educational Thought," *Harvard Educational Review* 51, no. 3 (1981): 357–72; "Excluding Women from the Educational Realm," *Harvard Educational Review* 52, no. 2 (1982): 133–48; "Sex Equality and Education," in *"Femininity," "Masculinity," and "Androgyny,"* ed. Mary Vetterling-Braggin (Totowa, N.J.: Littlefield, Adams, 1982); and "Bringing Women into Educational Thought," *Educational Theory* 34, no. 4 (Fall 1984): 341–55.

5. This point has been argued in many places. Noteworthy discussions occur in A. Fischel and S. J. Pottker, eds., *Sex-Bias in the Schools* (New Brunswick, N.J.: Rutgers University Press, 1977); T. Saario, C. Jacklin, and J. C. Tittle, "Sex Role Stereotyping in the Public Schools," *Harvard Educational Review* 43, no. 3 (1973): 386–416; and S. D. Eitzen, ed., *Sport in Contemporary Society: An Anthology* (New York: St. Martin's Press, 1979).

6. Quoted in P. Griffin, "Developing a Systematic Observation Instrument to Identify Sex Role Dependent and Sex Role Independent Behavior among Physical Education Teachers" (Ph.D. diss., University of Massachusetts [*University Microfilms International*, No. 8101325], 1980), 10.

7. A. Diller and B. Houston, "Women's Physical Education: A Gender-Sensitive Perspective," in *Women, Philosophy, and Sport,* ed. B. Postow (Metuchen, N.J.: Scarecrow Press, 1983), 251.

8. These studies and their findings are reported in P. Mahoney, "How Alice's Chin Really Came to Be Pressed against Her Foot: Sexist Processes of Interaction in Mixed-Sex Classrooms," *Women's Studies International Forum* 6, no. 1 (1983): 107–115; D. Spender *Invisible Women: The Schooling Scandal* (London: Writers and Readers Publishing Cooperative Society, 1982); D. Spender and E. Sarah, eds., *Learning to Lose: Sexism in Education* (London: Women's Press, 1980); M. Stanworth, *Gender and Schooling: A Study of Sexual Divisions in the Classroom* (London: Hutchinson, 1983); N. Frazier and M. Sadker, *Sexism in School and Society* (New York: Harper and Row, 1973); J. Stacey, S. Bercaud, and J. Daniels, eds., *And Jill Came Tumbling After: Sexism in American Education* (New York: Dell, 1974).

9. For a summary and discussion of these findings, see the report issued by the Project on the Status and Education of Women of the Association of American Colleges, entitled *The Classroom Climate: A Chilly One for Women* (Washington, D.C.: Association of American Colleges, 1982).

10. These findings are reported in D. H. Zimmerman and C. West, "Sex Roles, Interruptions and Silences in Conversations," in *Language and Sex: Difference and Dominance,* ed. B. Thorne and N. Henley (Rowley, Mass.: Newbury House, 1975); Dale Spender, *Man Made Language* (London: Routledge & Kegan Paul, 1980); Dale Spender, "Talking in Class," in *Learning to Lose,* 148–54.

11. For an account of these findings, see M. R. Key, *Male/Female Language: With a Comprehensive Bibliography* (Metuchen, N.J.: Scarecrow Press, 1975); Thorne and Henley, eds., *Language and Sex: Difference and Dominance;* and M. Ayim, "Wet Sponges and Bandaids: A Gender Analysis of Speech Patterns," *Semiotics 1982,* Proceedings of the Seventh Annual Meeting of the Semiotics Society of America (Bloomington, Ind.: Semiotics Society of America).

12. Association of American Colleges, *The Classroom Climate: A Chilly One for Women.*

13. Spender, "Talking in Class," 150.

14. Ibid.

15. Spender, *Invisible Women,* 61.

16. C. Tavris, "How Would Your Life Be Different If You'd Been Born a Boy?" ed. A. Baumgartner, *Redbook* 160 (February 1983): 94.

17. Ibid.

18. Ibid.

19. Spender, *Invisible Women,* 82.

20. E. Sarah, "Teachers and Students in the Classroom: An Examination of Classroom Interaction," in *Learning to Lose.* See also Stanworth, *Gender and Schooling.*

21. Stanworth, *Gender and Schooling.* See also Griffin, "Developing a Systematic Observation Instrument."

22. Diller and Houston, *Women, Philosophy, and Sport,* 252.

23. Spender, *Invisible Women,* 60, 63. For a more general discussion of the genderized valuation of educational traits, see Martin, "The Ideal of the Educated Person."

24. P. Fishman, "Interactional Shitwork," *Heresies, A Feminist Publication on Art and Politics* (May 1977): 99–101.

25. Spender, *Invisible Women*, 55.

26. Ibid., 57.

27. Ibid., 55.

28. J. Finn, J. Reis, and L. Dulberg, "Sex Differences in Educational Attainment: The Process," *Comparative Educational Review* 24, no. 2, pt. 2 (June 1980): 333–52; J. Laviqueur, "Co-education and the Tradition of Separate Needs," in *Learning to Lose*, 180–90.

29. R. W. Connell, R. W. Ashenen, D. J. Kessler, and G. W. Dowsett, *Making the Difference* (Boston: George Allen and Unwin, 1982), 34–35.

30. Ibid., 173.

31. Ibid., 182.

32. Ibid., 181.

33. Ibid., 182.

34. Martin, "The Ideal of the Educated Person."

35. If the complexities of gender relations were acknowledged and taken seriously in education, one should expect those interested in sex equality to recognize that different social contexts can make the same educational policy at one time effective in realizing equality and at another ineffectual. A differential evaluation of the effectiveness of a particular educational policy such as a common curriculum need not make us think the ideal of sex equality has altered, nor should it lead us to doubt either the sincerity or intelligence of feminist reformers who offer differential evaluations of it at different times. For an example of just this sort of a serious misunderstanding of feminist proposals for reform that is based on an ignorance of the complexities of gender, see G. Partington, "Radical Feminism and the Curriculum," *The Salisbury Review* (July 1984): 4–9.

36. Martin, "Excluding Women from the Educational Realm."

37. Connell et al., *Making the Difference*, 180.

9

TOWARD UNDERSTANDING THE EDUCATIONAL TRAJECTORY AND SOCIALIZATION OF LATINA WOMEN

Ruth E. Zambrana

I will keep on working and continue to fight for what I believe is right, and for my people. I have been able to express myself when I had nobody to teach me anything. I think it is a very beautiful thing when a person has within the ability to survive.

—Josephine Turrietta, *Las mujeres*[1]

The overwhelming majority of Latina women have had to teach themselves.[2] An analysis of educational attainment of Latina women reveals that Latinas indeed lag far behind middle-class majority culture Anglo American women. In part, this situation reflects the fact that access to higher education only became a viable option for a significant number of Latinas in the 1960s and 1970s.[3] Nevertheless, the educational experiences of Latinas have received little attention, particularly in the area of higher education.

Although all minority women have experienced some improvement in their educational and occupational achievements, only 10 percent of Mexican American women and 15 percent of Puerto Rican women hold professional or managerial positions. Hispanic women differ from Anglo American women in that they are twice as likely to be operatives and half as likely to be professionals. Moreover, less than one-half of one percent (0.3 percent) of all Spanish-origin women earn $25,000 per year or over.[4] These statistics reflect the reality that most professional Latina women are concentrated in low-level management positions, are trainees, are in community-based organizations, and/or are simply drastically underpaid.

Latinas represent a very diverse group that includes Mexican Americans (60 percent), who are concentrated in the southwest; Puerto Ricans (14 percent), who are concentrated in the northeast; and Cubans (6 percent), who are concentrated in the southeast. In addition, 20 percent of Latinas are immigrants from South and Central America, economic refugees, and/or undocumented workers. Among this last group are a number of Latina professionals who came as adults to the United States. In general, we know very little about the educational experiences of all Latina women. Under what conditions have they attended school? Were their educational experiences positive, or were they made to feel inadequate? If they were made to feel inadequate, did they become passive recipients of information or did they become enraged with the experience? The purpose of this essay is threefold: to provide a brief review and critique of traditional paradigms that have been used to explain the educational experiences of Latina women; to explore dimensions of feminist theory that may contribute to a better understanding of Latina women, as well as the limitations of that theory; and finally, to suggest a psychosocial model for interpreting the nature of experiences within the educational trajectory of Latina women.

A CRITIQUE OF TRADITIONAL PARADIGMS

Latina women have been the subject of very little social science and historical research. Studies of American society generally focus on the majority group and fail to deal with the plight of racial/ethnic minorities, especially Latina women.[5] This critical absence of scholarly work on racial/ethnics is exacerbated by the "problem orientation" of the majority of existing studies. This orientation has a number of important features. First, there is an emphasis on differences of the group with reference to the dominant culture. Second, there is an equally strong emphasis on differences among the groups. Third, the majority of studies do not acknowledge the relationship of these groups to the social structure nor their influence on the larger culture. Fourth, the studies tend to exclude or overlook the roles of women within the culture, or when they are included they offer only myopic and negative views of those roles.[6]

In the 1960s and 1970s a significant number of studies on racial/ethnic communities were generated that, with few exceptions, were purely descriptive and ahistorical. These descriptions emphasized not only problems of "deficiencies" within the communities—that is, according to White middle-class standards—but also the differences in regard to these "problems" between Blacks, Puerto Ricans, Chicanos, and Asians. Focus was on cultural distinctiveness and/or how close these groups approximated the values and norms of the dominant society as measured by upward mobility and acculturation.

The "problem" orientation characterizes a plethora of biased studies of pathology and other disturbances in racial/ethnic communities. This perspective presented distorted views of the lives of racial/ethnics and contributed to their inferior status in the United States. Ladner, when commenting on research on Blacks, noted that "the myths of 'cultural deprivation,' 'innate inferiority,' 'social disorganization,' and the 'tangle of pathology' characterize the writing of many sociologists up to (and including) the present time."[7] This problem orientation has inhibited the emergence of a major paradigm of relations that takes into account the history of racial/ethnic groups' interactions with the majority group in society. By encouraging the identification of the problems of groups in a vacuum, one neglects details of how racial/ethnic groups are in constant conflict, particularly in their ongoing struggles with the dominant group to secure their basic rights and to maintain their own culture.

The most limiting aspect of the majority of studies has been their neglect of the relationship of racial/ethnic groups to the social structure. In his review of the literature on race and ethnicity, Katznelson provides a cogent critique of the limited vision that social theorists have developed in their study of this area. He writes:

> To the extent that this corpus of work has stressed the attitudinal and neglected the structural, it has been tacitly ideological. It has directed attention from differential ethnic and racial distribution of wealth, status and political power, and from an examination of the way in which ethnic and racial groups are linked to each other and to the polity.[8]

As such, these works fail to acknowledge the roles of social structure and social organization in shaping the lives of racial/ethnic minorities. Many authors, unconvinced of the existence and pervasiveness of racism, view people of color as if they had all the options and choices of White, middle-class Americans. Clearly this is not the case, and we must continue to examine the ways in which racism reduces options and limits choice. Further, such works detract attention from the centrality of systematic exclusion (various forms and stages of racism) in the lives of oppressed people. Instead they focus on cultural traits that are identified as the source of a group's ability or inability to succeed and be upwardly mobile in the United States.[9] This approach is most dramatic when one examines the neglect of minorities in relation to social organizations such as schools. Only recently has there been an attempt to examine how the schools hinder the educational achievements of Latinos. In a recent dissertation that examines the relationship between immigrant status and stress among Mexican American boys and girls, it was found that stress in the school environment was related to students' perceptions of lack of interest and support by teachers and counselors.[10]

As a group, Latinos have been troubled by the lack of research depicting their struggles and conflicts. The dearth of scholarship leaves this group vulnerable to stereotypic notions that are easily accepted by others—as well as, perhaps, by themselves—in the absence of empirical research that presents more accurate views of their lives.[11] In this vacuum, perceptions of Mexican American inferiority persist and, as a consequence, continue to justify the inability of members of this group to pursue higher education. Thus, the lack of research hampers the group's mobility efforts. This is particularly true for Latinas, who are often maligned in images that neither acknowledge nor reflect these women's particular difficulties.

Alternately, an examination of existing studies clearly shows that being researched is not in and of itself a real advantage. The lack of a grounded historical perspective has led to the frequent omission of Latinas or else to their identification as a source of their group's problems. The myths vary with the cultures of the groups: Black women are the matriarchs, Latina women are too maternal and submissive to men, and Asian women are passive and content with their roles. Women are either targeted for abuse because they work and contribute to their families, or else they are criticized for not working and having babies. Details on the range of roles and life-styles of Latina women are missing.

Mainstream scholarship has not provided useful paradigms for understanding Latina women. Similarly, much of the recent feminist scholarship merely presents new stereotypes of women's roles, rather than seriously addressing how historical and social structural differences construct a different range of options and choices for women.

FEMINIST THEORY: A LIMITED VISION

Recent descriptions of the historical and material conditions of White women in this country have begun to challenge centuries-old myths of womanhood and femininity. Scholars and activists have begun to use this knowledge to foster social change. Yet, this new feminist scholarship has not been successful in assessing how race and class mediate the experiences of women and result in systematic diversity. Most feminist scholarship is grounded in the experiences and beliefs of White, middle-class women of the majority society and has failed to appreciate the larger context of racial oppression and its impact on the lives of women of color. The historian Phyllis Palmer provides an explanation for this oversight when she notes:

> White academics, in particular, have formulated theories grounded in notions of universal female powerlessness in relation to men, and of women's deprivation to men's satisfaction. Often treating race and class as secondary factors, feminist theorists write from experiences in which race and class are not felt as oppressive elements in their lives.[12]

The feminist scholarship that emerged in the 1970s challenged common notions about women in the humanities and the social sciences and exploded the myth of gender-neutral research. Scholars such as Heidi Hartman called into question basic premises of traditional social theory and empirical research. Prior to this time, male theorists failed to consider women's experiences as a legitimate topic for serious study. Of course researchers had looked at issues such as women in the family and their voting behavior patterns. Such scholarship, however, viewed the differential treatment of males and females in the society as the natural order, rather than the result of their differential positions in the society. With the feminist challenge, women and sexism became central topics of exploration, including mechanisms by which women are socialized to follow specific gender roles, discriminatory barriers that shape women's educational attainment and employment prospects, and sanctions for women who deviate from prescribed gender roles.[13] After centuries of wearing blinders when it came to gender, social theorists were forced to acknowledge that sexist institutions were responsible for maintaining women's place in the family and limiting their participation in the labor market and social institutions outside the home.

Feminist theory has essentially emerged from the experiences of White, upper-middle-class women, and as such it is based on sexual stratification, with little recognition of racial and class stratification. There are also a number of concepts, for example the notions of patriarchy and the public/private dichotomy, which do not fit or aptly describe the reality of Latina women in the U.S. Patriarchy implies that men have power and access to resources. Historically this has not been the case for Latinos. In our case, neither men nor women nor the communities had power. This does not deny the fact that men by virtue of being male were ascribed a higher status in society, but it was the Latino community that was powerless, not only the women. White feminists have neglected to recognize this issue. Second, the notion of public versus private makes an assumption that women were excluded from the work force. Again, this was not the case for women of color and White working-class women. Not by choice, the majority have had to work in poorly paid employment outside the home. There are innumerable differences between the lives of White women and women of color. Recognizing these differences is a first step in better understanding the lives, options, and choices of Latina women.

Nonetheless, some concepts developed by White feminist scholars are powerful in illuminating the conditions of racial/ethnic women. Yet, often it has been the case that concepts developed for White women have had to be modified to provide insights into the lives of women of color. That the historical conditions of racial/ethnic women have differed dramatically from those of White women is an important central thesis. But it must be recognized that rather than simply deviating from the lives of White women, women of color have a radically different material basis for their experiences. This fact is most evident in the areas of paid employment and market work that have consequences for the shape and nature of family life and women's involvement in society. Consequently, it is apparent that gender oppression along with racial and class oppression have shaped the unique positions of women of color. From this perspective, racial and class stratification are essential to understanding the context within which gender roles are developed.

MATERIALS TO CONSTRUCT A THEORY: A BEGINNING MODEL

To establish the conceptual basis needed to construct a model for understanding the educational trajectory of Latina women, one needs to build on recent work in history, observational studies, and the empirical knowledge available.[14] Importantly, such an effort requires an interdisciplinary foundation with a specific focus on a broader reformulation of concepts such as socialization, identity, culture, bicultural socialization, and recognition of institutional dimensions. There is also a need to examine and understand what psychological mechanisms are used by Latina women to reconcile their ascribed status and their own perceptions of their status in society.

In its broadest sense, socialization can be viewed as a process through which a person consciously and unconsciously participates in a number of diverse and complex roles. When the opportunity is present, what are the factors that influence the decision to participate in roles? In other words, the notion of *choices,* and how and why people make them, is critical.

Historically and up to the present, Latinas' choices have been limited due to their ascribed status as minorities and as women within the social structure. Gender, race, class, and language facility can be defined as personal dimensions. Cultural dimensions have also circumscribed choices, resulting in the increased importance of the family as a source of rootedness and increased needs for collective efforts. In many respects, this dimension represents a false choice, as it is related to the lack of acceptance of racial/ethnic minorities in the larger social structure.

This idea may suggest that Latino culture has served a role that has perhaps limited choices, but this role has been reinforced by the exclusionary practices of the dominant culture. Clearly, the Latino culture is a dynamic entity that has changed in response to structural conditions. Baca Zinn has aptly stated that one difficulty in the social science literature is the underlying assumption that culture is static; we must instead view culture as dynamic, historically relevant, and changing.[15]

Culture is a behavioral repertoire that develops as a function of one's historical roots as well as in response to the social conditions under which one lives. Culture helps individuals to better deal with life but does not lock one into a particular life-style if options and choices are available. Culture also, and most importantly, socializes individuals to think and act in particular ways to assure survival. Therefore, culture is a dynamic entity that fosters a sense of self-respect and dignity and contributes to a solid identity. When cultural values are violated (i.e., disregarded or ridiculed), the basic foundation of human experience is shaken. On the other hand, the danger remains that culture is interpreted as determining events rather than mediating events, or as a way of explaining events instead of providing a context in which to perhaps understand them. For example, when one examines the roles in which Latina girls and women participate at home and within the family, it is clear that they have had the opportunity to be active participants and learn many skills, to initiate tasks and be creative and resourceful. This of course does not belie the fact that our cultural values of respect and dignity negatively influence how we are perceived in the dominant culture. In other words, the majority of Latinos, both women and men, are perceived as "nice." Latina women, however, are expected to remain that way and men are expected to assume more assertive characteristics. At this point, the interrelationship or linkage between personal, cultural, and institutional dimensions becomes clearer.

Institutional dimensions have already been aptly described in terms of exclusionary practices in the areas of curriculum, organizational activities, teacher expectations, tracking, and educational counseling.[16] For example, Latina student aspirations dramatically decrease after the ninth grade.[17] Institutions are a major socializing force in a child's life and exhibit all the "isms" of the dominant culture—racism, classism, and sexism. Clearly, these institutions erect barriers that Latina women must confront within the educational system. The psychological effects of the barriers is an area that requires extensive inquiry. One way to conceptualize the psychological component of the perceived barriers is the notion of cultural assault. The following case example may help to illustrate the nature and effect of a cultural assault:

> A 35-year-old Latina woman in graduate school was having difficulty in taking exams and in making verbal reports in class. It was clear that she knew the material but was terrified of expressing or reporting verbally. Upon discussion with her regarding the problem, there was a clear sense of anger, pain, and injustice. After several meetings it became obvious that the nature of past educational experiences of being ridiculed and ashamed of her language and culture had severely damaged her self-esteem and confidence. Those feelings immediately came to the surface under similar circumstances, when she felt put in a position where there was a possibility of shame or ridicule.[18]

The notion of assault or injury to one's sense of identity and self-esteem are complex psychological dimensions. One can speculate that the continuous experience of those assaults leads to stress and tension.

For Latina women, these assaults lead to different patterns of behavior. There will be those women who have a traditional stance and who make themselves subservient to the codes of others. Others may become marginal, find self-worth in the denial of their cultural heritage, and in turn feel guilt and experience self-hatred. Alternately, there are those women who develop a sense of pride in their cultural heritage or ethnic consciousness, are aware that racism, sexism and elitism are integral to the system, and somehow learn the prevailing norms that are different.

The question, then, is under what conditions do these assaults lead to a sense of giving up and under what conditions do they lead to constructive anger and engagement? For example, I have spoken to a number of Latina women who at some point became angry and said, "I'm going to show them that I can do it." The anger enabled them to mobilize all their resources to succeed. What are the costs of using all this anger to succeed? Anger represents one way of coping with our status as a cultural, gender, and ethnic minority. Yet it is only one way of coping. We must also determine what other types of coping mechanisms are used by Latina women as they proceed toward their educational and career goals. Use of social support systems and role modeling constitute another coping mechanism. Role modeling also has a number of dimensions. It implies that the individual has an opportunity to observe and learn new roles that fit with expectations and aspirations, and it implies that the role model incorporates the concept of the individual and her ability to learn and that learning will be useful to her future.

Another case study illustrates the importance of social support and role modeling for young Latina women:

> Maggie was a 25-year-old Puerto Rican woman. She had been in college for five years and had done very poorly. She was about to be expelled. She was living at home with her parents. The father worked in a handbag factory and the mother was a homemaker. Maggie was depressed and unable to move on her goals, which were to complete college and become a teacher. She had been working with Carole, a young, bright, progressive Anglo social worker. Carole asked me to talk with her advisee since she felt she had exhausted all her resources with her and was still unsuccessful. I asked Maggie to come see me. She missed many appointments, was late and quite reticent. We talked at first about her dreams and goals. After about three months, it became clear to me that Maggie was afraid to get good grades because she would become a professional and have to give up her family and community. She also felt stupid because she was shy and the instructor tended to ignore her. I helped Maggie to understand that she could use her education to help others in the community like her and that she had a quiet strength that was valuable. These two themes dominated the next two years. She repeated two college years and obtained all A's and B's. She graduated and two years later successfully completed her master's degree and obtained a teaching position.[19]

In the last ten years I have worked with a number of Latina women who have experienced these fears or who have not achieved the balance of how to retain their own culture and participate in the structure. Social support and role models of successful Latinas have been critical, however, in enabling individuals to handle the situation better and overcome the barriers. Clearly, this positive response requires a fine balance between retaining or maximizing cultural stability and exploring ways of participating in the social structure. Most importantly, these observations and anecdotes suggest that Latina women must see and use social support and resources such as family and friends outside the educational institutions because these settings do not provide the necessary resources required for achievement.

The major question remains. How can Latina women make the transition into a world that is different from theirs? How do they reconcile or learn different values and norms without losing who they are? How do they overcome some of the cultural assaults from their peers, the schools, and the like? Some individuals have attempted to explain these transitions in terms of the concept of bicultural socialization.[20] This approach integrates role modeling as a major determinant of socialization, as well as developing a solid identity in terms of race, gender, and class.

Bicultural socialization is the process by which individuals from an ethnic minority group are instructed in the values, perceptions, and normative behaviors of two cultural systems. There are at least six factors that influence the process.

1. The degree of overlap of commonality between the two cultures with regard to norms, values, beliefs, perceptions, and the like.

2. The availability of culture translators, mediators, and models.

3. The amount and type (positive or negative) of corrective feedback provided by each culture regarding attempts to produce normative behavior.

4. The conceptual style and problem-solving approach of minority individuals and their mesh with prevalent or valued styles of the majority culture.

5. The individual's degree of bilingualism.

6. The degree of dissimilarity in physical appearance from the majority culture, such as skin color and facial features.[21]

This model provides a conceptual framework, but it offers little specific information on the mechanism through which dual socialization occurs. Another related variable is ethnic consciousness, which can be loosely defined as that awareness in the individual, early or later on (is there a critical stage for its development?), that her options and choices are circumscribed by race, class, ethnicity, and gender. In this author's opinion, recognition of these barriers, which can be passed on by family members, role models, siblings, or self-observations, enable the individual to withstand some of the cultural assaults. There is an understanding that the assaults are external and not necessarily related to one's particular abilities, skills, or identity.

Thus the development of a model that attempts to understand the educational trajectory of Latina women must begin with a broad definition of socialization as a group of roles and skills acquired to negotiate the educational system within which they must participate and must also acknowledge that the institutional framework, as well as the social structure, works toward delimiting opportunities and choices. In effect, a reformulation of socialization and its relationship to identity development, and what psychological mechanisms are used to reconcile our own perceptions of ourselves with those of the dominant culture, is sorely lacking. Which coping mechanisms are most widely used by Latina women, and which are the most helpful in mediating their stressful environment? Concepts of ethnic consciousness and bicultural socialization serve as important mediating variables that help the individual to function in two worlds without losing sight of one's status and/or identity in either.

Socialization is also directly influenced by social factors such as institutional settings. Schooling is a powerful determinant in the socialization experiences of Latina women. Two of the most critical elements in the schooling experience are tracking for ability and the types of courses that are available. Data on schools has consistently shown that minority low-income students are more likely to be placed in nonacademic tracks than others; that girls receive less attention and encouragement than boys; and that inner city schools, in particular, have few role models and/or counseling personnel who can encourage the educational aspirations of Latina women. A review of my preliminary data indicates that a substantial number of Latinas feel that their elementary and secondary school experiences failed to prepare them for higher education, and the majority of respondents felt no encouragement to pursue higher education. One respondent remembered her picture being put on a board with the caption beneath it, "A Common Girl."[22]

Thus, institutional factors must be examined as important contributors to the socialization of Latina women, with particular reference to the impediment to, or facilitation of, educational attainment. The focus of inquiry, however, must be on the interactive nature of institutional dimensions on the socialization experiences of Latina women and its influence on the educational aspirations and achievements of Latina women.

This model is, of course, a beginning attempt based on existing knowledge and observations to provide a framework for interpreting Latinas success and lack of success in the educational system. A first step is to operationalize the variables and to test under what conditions they help to explain, under what conditions they fail to explain, and whether their variations are based on class, status, color, and availability of social support systems. Second, the relationship between institutional factors and educational attainment must be examined.

Clearly, we can no longer afford to use our intellectual energy to fight stereotypes and illogical conclusions. Battling these myths has bound racial/ethnic scholars in a research ghetto and has hampered theoretical growth. The double bind has resulted in the inability of scholars to examine the relationship between new research and theory and/or to use new research to modify existing theory or to generate it. In part this dilemma has been perpetuated by a lack of intellectual support by social scientists for new theoretical developments in the field as a whole.

Myths, of course, will continue to exist because of the general lack of knowledge about and interest in racial/ethnics. Our task, however, is to assure that our research is not circumscribed within the parameters set up by the myth. We must move forward in proactive rather than reactive ways to address the issues of concern to Latina women. In the process of creating new approaches to these concerns, we will also debunk the myths. The question, then, is how do we move forward?

First, it seems that there must be clear recognition that the historical conditions of Latina women continue to be different from those of dominant culture women.[23] These material conditions have dictated roles for Latina women whereby they have interacted with social institutions from a different vantage point than White women. The perception of Latina women as deviant, or shy, passive, and unambitious because they are not following prescribed gender roles is at best unfair and clearly ignores the reality of these women's experiences. Latina women actively participate in the outside world of work and community institutions.[24] They observe the treatment of their families, spouses, and children. They are cognizant of the restrictions, limited options, and mythical characteristics ascribed to them and their cultural group. Consequently, they have a vision of life that is broader than dominant culture women. Based on their vision, there is also an impetus to develop and seek community and familial support structures to reinforce their identity.

Thus the analysis of Latina women needs to emerge from a description of their own experiences. Perhaps there will be many similarities with majority culture women based on gender alone. We must cease, however, making assumptions related to personal and institutional variables that have repeatedly been proven erroneous. We must move forward to find answers that reveal the reality that belies the myth.

Notes

I wish to acknowledge the theoretical contributions of Dr. Bonnie Dill and Dr. Elizabeth Higginbotham toward the formulation of many of the concepts in this paper. I worked with these colleagues on the Intersection of Race and Gender Project at the Center for Research on Women at Memphis State University. I also would like to acknowledge the support of the Ford Foundation and the UCLA Academic Senate Faculty Research Fund.

1. N. Elsasser, K. MacKenzie, and Y. Tixier y Vigil, interview with "Josephine Turrietta," *Las mujeres* (Old Westbury, N.Y.: Feminist Press, 1980), 28–35.

2. The terms "Latina" and "Hispanic Woman" will be used interchangeably. These two terms will primarily reflect research and observations of Mexican American and Puerto Rican women.

3. C. M. Haro, "Chicanos in Higher Education: A Review of Selected Literature," *Aztlán: International Journal of Chicano Studies Research* 14, no. 1 (Spring 1983): 35–77.

4. U.S. Congress, House of Representatives Report of the Subcommittee on Census and Population of The Committee on Post Office and Civil Service, 21 April 1983.

5. The term racial/ethnic is used to refer to historically subjugated, racially identifiable ethnic groups in the U.S. Those groups of interest are any collectivity whose membership is derived from a shared racial identity with high visibility in the society and who have a devalued social status, such as Chicanos, Puerto Ricans, and Blacks. See R. Staples and A. Mirande, "Racial and Cultural Variations Among American Families: A Decennial Review of the Literature on Minority Families," *Journal of Marriage and The Family* 42 (Nov. 1980): 887–903.

6. M. Baca Zinn, "Mexican American Women in the Social Sciences," *Signs: Journal of Women in Culture and Society* 8, no. 2 (1982): 259–272; M. J. Vásquez, "Confronting Barriers to the Participation of Mexican American Women in Higher Education," *Hispanic Journal of Behavioral Sciences* 4, no. 2 (1982): 147–165; S. J. Andrade, "Family Roles of Hispanic Women: Stereotypes, Empirical Findings, and Implications for Research," in *Work, Family, and Health: Latina Women in Transition,* ed. R. E. Zambrana (New York: Hispanic Research Center, Fordham University, 1982), 95–106.

7. J. Ladner, *Tomorrow's Tomorrow* (Garden City, N.Y.: Anchor Books, 1972), xxi.

8. I. Katznelson, "Comparative Studies of Race and Ethnicity: Plural Analysis and Beyond," *Comparative Politics* 5, no. 1 (1972): 137.

9. S. Steinberg, *The Ethnic Myth* (New York: Athenaeum, 1981).

10. V. H. Silva-Palacios, "Immigration and Stress Among Mexican Adolescents" (Ph.D. diss., Wright Institute, Los Angeles, 1985).

11. Staples and Mirande, *Racial and Cultural Variations Among American Families.*

12. P. Palmer, "White Women/Black Women: The Dualism of Female Identity and Experience in the United States," *Feminist Studies* 9 (Spring 1983): 154.

13. R. K. Unger, "Advocacy vs. Scholarship Revisited: Issues in the Psychology of Women," *Psychology of Women Quarterly* 7, no. 1 (Fall 1982): 5–17.

14. A. Camarillo, *Chicanos in a Changing Society* (Cambridge: Harvard University Press, 1984); M. Barrera, *Race and Class in The Southwest* (Notre Dame: University of Notre Dame Press, 1979).

15. Baca Zinn, "Mexican American Women in the Social Sciences."

16. T. P. Carter and R. D. Segura, *Mexican Americans in School: A Decade of Change* (New York: College Entrance Examination Board, 1979).

17. V. E. Lee, *Black, Hispanic, and Working-Class Students* (Washington, D.C.: American Council on Education, 1985).

18. Based on personal observations and experiences in academic institutions.

19. See note 18.

20. D. de Anda, "Bicultural Socialization: Factors Affecting the Minority Experience," *Social Work* 29, no. 2 (1984): 101–107.

21. Ibid.

22. A cross-sectional survey conducted by UCLA asked two hundred women of Mexican origin about factors that contribute to the successful completion or noncompletion of higher education degrees. Results are available from the author, the researcher.

23. Elsasser, MacKenzie, and Tixier y Vigil, *Las mujeres;* Barrera, *Race and Class;* Camarillo, *Chicanos in a Changing Society;* M. Baca Zinn, "Mexican Heritage Women: A Bibliographic Essay," *Sage Race Relations Abstracts* 9, no. 3 (Aug. 1984): 1–12.

24. A nationwide study was conducted by the National Network of Hispanic Women. It is a survey of 304 women on the "Work and Family Life Experiences of Professional Hispanic Women." The study was designed to provide (for the first time on a national level) a clear and comprehensive profile of patterns of organizational experiences of upwardly mobile professional Hispanic women; sources of stress and resources for coping with stress; health and mental health status of successful Hispanic women. The report is available from the NNHW in Los Angeles, California.

PART III

Knowledge, Curriculum, and Instructional Arrangement

10

CONCEPTION, CONTRADICTION, AND CURRICULUM

Madeleine Grumet

I suspect that I am about to present a feminist argument, and that's not easy. A feminist argument is unavoidably convoluted:

> It is the argument of whoever is fed up with being a "dead woman"—Jewish mother, Christian virgin, Beatrice beautiful because defunct, voice without body, body without voice, silent anguish choking on the rhythms of words, the tones of sounds, without images; outside time, outside knowledge—cut off forever from the rhythms, colorful, violent changes that streak sleep, skin, viscerals: socialized, even revolutionary but at the cost of the body; body crying, infatuating but at the cost of time; cut-off swallowed up on the one hand the aphasic pleasure of childbirth that imagines itself a participant in the cosmic cycle, on the other, sexuality under the symbolic weight of law, (paternal, familial, social, divine) of which she is the sacrificed support, bursting with glory on the condition that she submit to the denial of nature, to the murder of the body.[1]

This is a secret that everybody knows. It is body knowledge, like the knowledge that drives the car, plays the piano, navigates around the apartment without having to sketch a floor plan and chart a route in order to get from the bedroom to the bathroom. Maurice Merleau-Ponty called it the knowledge of the body-subject, reminding us that it is through our bodies that we live in the world.[2] He called it knowledge in the hands and knowledge in the feet. It is also knowledge in the womb. Eve knew it, but she let on and was exiled from Eden, the world of divine law, for her indiscretion.[3] We, her daughters, have kept silent for so long that now we have forgotten that knowledge from and about the body is also knowledge about the world. The project of this text is to draw that knowledge of women's experience of reproduction and nurturance into the epistemological systems and curricular forms that constitute the discourse and practice of public education. It is an argument drawn from the experience in my own life that is most personal and at the same time most general as it links me to those who share my sex and gender and those who also acknowledge reproductive responsibility for the species. The argument takes off from a commitment in my life for which I accept responsibility with no doubts, hesitations, or second thoughts—parenting—and lands in a field of utter confusion: curriculum. What I hope to show is that the relation between this certain beginning and doubtful end is not accidental but inevitable, the end determining the beginning and the beginning the end.

The reproduction of society, its class structure, cultural variations, institutions, is currently a dominant theme in the sociology of education. Gramsci's concept of hegemony has caught our interest, for it articulates what the experience of our daily lives has led us to suspect, that the forms of our social and individual existences are not merely imposed upon us but sustained by us with our tacit if not explicit consent.[4] I want to take this term, "the reproduction of society," literally.

Now, it is not a new idea that schooling transmits knowledge or that education reproduces culture. But like so much of our language, this phrase, "reproduction," has traveled so far from home that we cannot even tell what part of the country it is from. Curriculum has provided safe shelter for these linguistic orphans so long as they relinquish their specificity and identification with their historical and social sources as they enter the discourse of the academy. I am not advocating that we withhold our hospitality from them, but I am suggesting that it is within their interest and ours that we connect these phrases to their roots and, in so doing, take their figurative function literally. Metaphor matters. If our understanding of education rests on our understanding of the reproduction of society, then the reproduction of society itself rests on our understanding of reproduction, a project that shapes our lives, dominating our sexual, familial, economic, political, and, finally, educational experience.

I want to argue that *what is most fundamental to our lives as men and women sharing a moment on this planet is the process and experience of reproducing ourselves.*

There are two phrases contained within this proposition that I wish to situate within my own understanding. They mark the intersections of action and reflection in my own experience that have generated the themes of this paper. The first is this word "fundamental." I confess to being constantly drawn to the lure of this word. When I was in graduate school, Husserl's call "back to the things themselves" was compelling, drawing me into his phenomenological texts and rigorous, if elusive, method.[5] The method promised clarity, a way of cutting through the thick, binding undergrowth that covers the ground of daily life to reveal a clear path. In 1972 when I went back to school, my children were three, seven, and eight years old, and clear paths were well hidden by the debris of sneakers, play dough, and cinnamon toast and interrupted by endless detours to nursery schools, grocery stores, and pediatricians. In those years, when there was a high probability that at any given moment one of the children was either incubating or recuperating from an ear infection, I found Husserl's stance of the disinterested observer, bracketing the natural attitude, a posture to be practiced and mastered. I am suggesting that there is a dialectical relation between our domestic experience of nurturing children and our public project to educate the next generation. It is important to maintain our sense of this dialectic wherein each milieu, the academic and the domestic, influences the character of the other and not to permit the relation to slide into a simplistic one-sided causality. The presence of the children was just one expression of my situation at that time, coinciding with other themes of my early thirties. It coincided with being the age of my own parents as they appear to me in memories of my own childhood. It coincided with my husband's professional development and our sense of economic security, which offered the family a brief respite from the pursuit of social mobility and class status until the children would be required to derive their sustenance from their own labor rather than ours. It coincided with what was for me a much more difficult bracketing of the natural attitude, the choice not to have more children.

Though any and all of these biographic issues may be probed to understand their relation to this search for the fundamental that kept me riveted to the chair by the dining room table, digging through the dense, often impenetrable passages of Husserl, Merleau-Ponty, and Sartre, they are not the explicit content of this discourse. The dining room table became the locus of this research not because its design was conducive to meditations on eidetic form but because of its proximity to the life world being carried on in the adjoining kitchen. I summon these scenes here because, although I may not directly address them again, they are currents that run through this text, linking the metaphors of epistemology and curriculum to the motives that choose and organize them. I present the passage through these rooms as an alternate route for the argument of this chapter and as a reminder of the many levels of experience that constitute the conceptual order that we employ here to inform, confront, and mystify each other.

This chapter, too, continues this search for the fundamental. The children, the work, the mother, the student are several years older, and the detours are different. The frequent trips to the grocery store have fallen into one "humongous" (as the kids say) trip a week, but the frequency has been retained by daily trips to Geneva, New York, where I go to teach. The path is not any clearer for the passage of time, and every route is a detour. "Back to the things themselves" no longer provides an adequate slogan for the project. The cadence of the command falls too decisively on the things themselves, encouraging an idealism fascinated with essential forms.

The search for origins has capitulated to the pursuit of mediations. The world "as given" is never received as such. The world we have is constituted in the dialectical interplay of our freedom and facticity. What the stripping away of phenomenological reductions reveals most clearly is not the things themselves but the conditions, relations, perspectives through which their objectivity evolves.

If the fundamental is an epistemological chimera, it is also a political ploy that promises cohesion but delivers domination. The fundamental is suspect if it suggests a single way of addressing the project and process of reproduction. To be a gendered human being is to participate in the reproductive commitments of this society, for reproduction is present as a theme in human consciousness without providing a norm for human behavior. Male or female, heterosexual, homosexual, bisexual, monogamous, chaste, or multipartnered, we each experience our sexuality and attachments within a set of conditions that contain the possibility of procreation. Our identities incorporate our position relative to this possibility. They encode our assent, or our refusal, our ambivalence, our desire, our gratification, or our frustration. Whether we choose to be parents or to abstain from this particular relation to children, the possibility of procreation is inscribed on our bodies and on the process of our own development. Even if we choose not to be a parent, we are not exempt from the reproductive process, for we have each been a child of our parents. The intentions, assumptions, emotions, and achievements of educational practice and theory are infused with motives that come from our own reproductive histories and commitments. What is fundamental is not the nuclear family of an orange juice commercial enjoying a suburban breakfast in the family room. What is fundamental is that although there is no one way of being concerned with children, we cannot deny our responsibility for the future whatever form our projects of nurturance assume.

CONCEPTION

Stephen Strasser's concept of dialogic phenomenology more closely approximates the notion of the fundamental that this text addresses.[6] For Strasser, what is fundamental is the interpersonal basis for human experience, and so the primary question is no longer how one comes to constitute a world but how a world evolves for us. The very possibility of my thought, of consciousness, rests upon the presence of a "you" for whom I exist. My thought is a moment suspended between two primordial presences, the "you" who thinks me, and the "you" whom I think.

> My affirmation of the "you" must transcend all doubt for me; it must be characterized as the "primordial faith" upon which all my further cogitos rest. For the nearness of the "you" is a primordial presence, one that makes me believe that relations with other beings also are meaningful. My turning-to a "you" is the most elementary turning-to, one that causes my intentionality to awaken. In short, only the "you" makes me be an "I." That is why, we repeat, the "you" is always older than the "I."
>
> This principle holds for every aspect and all levels of human life. Husserl speaks of primordial faith in connection with the "being given" of the things that are experienced. It is precisely through the mediation of a "you" that I know at all that there are things worth touching, tasting, looking at, listening to. A "you" teaches me also that there exists reality which can be manipulated, "utensils" destined for particular use (Heidegger), matter which I must modify in my work (Marx). Without the active-receptive interplay with a "you" I would not know that my existence has a social dimension (Merleau-Ponty). . . . My "thinking"—no matter what one may mean by it—is never a sovereign act. I cannot think without attuning the mode of my thinking to that which must be thought. . . . But because the "you" is the "first thinkable" I must in the first place attune my thinking to the being of the "you." We may even say that generally speaking, my thinking comes about because there is a "you" that thinks and invites me to a thinking "response." It is the "you" that makes it clear to me for the first time that thinking is possible and meaningful. This also shows the finite, social, and historical character of my cogito.[7]

When Strasser asserts that it is not only the original intentional object but intentionality itself that is generated through human relationships, he is in effect acknowledging that the very ground of knowledge is love. This bonding of thought and relation is consummated in our word "concept." It is derived from the Latin phrase *concipere semina,* which meant to take to oneself, to take together, or to gather the male seed. In this etymology both the child and the idea are generated in the dialectic of male and female, of the one and the many, of love.

What is most fundamental to our lives as men and women sharing a moment on this planet is the process of reproducing ourselves. It is this final phrase, reproducing ourselves, that contains multiple meanings for me. First there is the obvious meaning that refers to the biological reproduction of the species. Then there is the reproduction of culture, the linking of generations, each conceived, born, and raised by another, parenting by extending the traditions and conventions with which it was parented. But by situating reproduction in culture we need not collapse it into the habits, aversions, and appetites that testify to the persuasions of ideology. For reproducing ourselves also brings a critical dimension to biological and ideological reproduction by suggesting the reflexive capacity of parents to reconceive our own childhoods and education as well as our own situations as adults and to choose another way for ourselves expressed in the nurture of our progeny. It is this last, critical interpretation of the phrase that I wish to address here because I see curriculum as expressing this third intention. Curriculum becomes our way of contradicting biology and ideology. The relationship between parent and child is, I suggest, the primordial subject/object relationship. Because these initial relationships are mediated by our bodies and by history, distinct masculine and feminine epistemologies have evolved. Although the initial stages of the parent/child relationship are influenced by the biological processes of conception, gestation, birth, and breastfeeding, the epistemologies that evolve from them do more than merely mirror the biological bonds; they intertwine them with subjective aims representing the power of the human species to negate biology with culture. Hence, these male and female epistemologies and the curricula that extend them into our daily lives stand in a dialectical relation to the original terms of the parent/child bond.

Subjectivity, objectivity, epistemology: Abstraction falls from these terms like a veil, blurring their relation to the men and women who create them, believe them, and use them. We forget that they are lifted from our loins and lungs, from our labor and our love and our libido. And we forget that they in turn pervade our breath, lust, fears, joy, and dreams. The very word "epistemology" is drawn from the Greek word for understanding, *episteme,* and is extended into the word "epistles," or letters that Paul sent to the apostles. In contrast to *gnosis,* a Greek word denoting the immediate knowledge of spiritual truth, epistemology refers to knowledge that is intersubjective, developed through social relations and negotiations. I am interested in understanding the ways in which epistemological categories of subject and object and their implied relations are rooted in the psychosocial dynamics of early object relations as they are experienced by both children and parents. The three interpretations of reproduction—the biological, the ideological, and the critical—never exist independently of one another, and although my discussion of them will be organized in the order just given, often you may hear all three voices.

It is within the infant's social relationships that the terms "subject" and "object" first evolve. Derived from psychoanalysis and cultural anthropology, object relations theory investigates the genesis of personality in the interplay of the aggressive and libidinal drives seeking satisfaction and the social relationships that surround the infant and in which it participates. In *The Reproduction of Mothering* Nancy Chodorow declares that object relations theory eschews both instinctual and cultural determinism. Instead of portraying a passive subject, driven by biology or hypnotized by culture, object relations theory presents biology and social relationships as themes that influence consciousness without subsuming it.[8] Chodorow shows us how the infant transforms the relationships in which he or she participates into psychic structure through the processes of fantasy, introjection, projection, ambivalence, conflict, substitution, reversal, distortion, splitting, association, compromise, denial, and repression.[9] The relationship of curriculum to the experience of the birth and nurturance of children will not proceed, you will be glad to learn, with my psychosexual history, or yours, dear reader. There would be no point in making reference to our own situations, for it is obvious that there are no remote, authoritarian fathers, no binding, seductive mothers among the readers of this feminist study of education. The analysis is structural and thematic and, as such, abuses the specificity of each of us even as it respects our privacy and defenses.

Yet there is one moment I would remember, the day following the birth of my daughter, my first child, when my skin, suffused with the hormones that supported pregnancy, labor, and delivery, felt and smelled like hers, when I reached for a mirror and was startled by my own reflection, for it was hers that I had expected to see there. Over and over again we recapitulate and celebrate that moment, even as we struggle to transcend it.

The child is mine. This child is me. The woman who bears a child first experiences its existence through the transformations of time and space in her own body. The suspension of the menstrual cycle subordinates her body's time to another, contained and growing within her. The pressure of labor and the wrenching expulsion of the infant (the term "delivery" must have been created by those who receive the child, not those who release it) physically recapitulate the terrors of coming apart, of losing a part of oneself. The symbiosis continues past parturition, as the sucking infant drains her mother's swollen breasts of milk, reasserting the dominance of the child's time over the mother's as lactation and sleep as well respond to the duration and strength of the child's hunger and vigor.[10]

In contrast, paternity is uncertain and inferential. Supported and reinforced by the intimacy and empathy of the conjugal relationship, the experience of paternity is transitive, whereas maternity is direct. Paternity, always mediated through the woman, originates in ambiguity. Subject/object relations as experienced on the biological level of the reproduction of the species are concrete and symbiotic for mothers, abstract and transitive for fathers. If the "other" to whom the biological individual is most closely related is the child, then the definition of subjectivity as that which is identical with myself and of objectivity as that which is other than myself originates in an experience of reproduction that differs for men and women. So long as it is woman and not test tubes who bear children, conception, pregnancy, parturition, and lactation constitute an initial relation of women to their children that is symbiotic, one in which subject and object are mutually constituting.[11]

It is important to acknowledge at this point that I am not assuming that all women experience the identification or that all men experience the ambiguity associated here with the anatomical and biological conditions for reproduction. The response to these conditions will vary for different cultures and specific individuals according to the interaction of these conditions with the physical environment, division of labor, organization of families, ritual and legal customs, and so on.

"This child is mine, this child is me" is an index of relation that will vary with every speaker. What it means to be mine, to be me, depends on the way each speaker knows herself. The maternal ego reaches out to another consciousness that is of her and yet not in her, and self-knowledge grows in this process of identification and differentiation with this other, this child, "my child." The process of thinking through the world for and with the child invites a mother to recollect her own childhood and to inspect the boundaries of her own ego. Indeed, as Vangie Bergum's study of women's experiences of becoming mothers suggests, the extension of a mother's own ego identity to another who is her child is a doubling that fosters and intensifies reflexivity.[12]

But what of the mother who is a child herself? Or the mother who is exhausted from the care of too many children, or from strenuous or monotonous work, or from malnutrition? And what about the mother who has been raped or abandoned? "This child is mine, this child is me" is a lullaby sung and chanted, whistled and hummed, keened and whispered, almost, maybe never, uttered.

In order to investigate the interaction of biology and culture in our milieu, I shall turn to the work of Nancy Chodorow, whose book, *The Reproduction of Mothering,* investigates the patterns of parenting that are dominant in our culture. Chodorow's patterns may not provide the score for my song of motherhood or for yours. But the tune of her theory may remind us of our own perhaps unsung tunes and theories. That is the way that general interpretations function in psychoanalysis. The dramas that Freud offered us, Jürgen Habermas points out, were not intended as literal portrayals of our family relations, or as templates for their development.[13] They provided narratives against which the scenes and accounts of the analysand's experience could be perceived in their specificity *and* in their difference. Chodorow's schematic presentation of object relations is a magnificent contribution to those of us who work to understand the relation of gender to the symbol systems that constitute knowledge, curriculum, and schooling. Her work, which describes the constitution of the gendered human subject coming to form in relationships that contain the objects of the child's love and thought, has given us a subject/object schema that permits us to analyze, criticize, and, it is hoped, transform the subject/object relations that organize curriculum and the disciplines.

At the outset of her argument, Chodorow suggests that, even as the biological determinants of mothering have lessened as birth control and bottle feeding have become established, biological mothers have come to have ever-increasing responsibilities for child care. Her observation is reinforced by Bernard Wishy's historical study of child nurture in American culture, which indicates that as urban industrialization drew fathers away from home and the household ceased to be the primary economic unit, the responsibility for moral, social, and emotional development of children devolved upon the women who stayed home to care for them.[14] Our own time has accentuated this process. The economy's demand that working parents be mobile has isolated child nurture from extended kin, isolating mothers and their children from the aunts, uncles, and grandparents who may formerly have shared the tasks and pleasures of nurturance.

These social and economic developments support Chodorow's thesis that the infants of both sexes, though polymorphous and bisexual at birth, as in Freud's view, are immediately introduced into a social field in which they become predominantly matrisexual. Gender identity, which has evolved by the age of three, becomes a precondition for the oedipal crises, and it is the preoedipal relationships of the boy or girl child that, Chodorow argues, are most significant in influencing ego structure, gender, and, ultimately, patterns of parenting in succeeding generations. When the mother is the primary caretaker of her infant, the preoedipal attachment to her precedes the infant's attachment to his or her father and influences it profoundly. Peaking during the first half-year, the infant's symbiotic relation with its mother is upset by the asymmetry in their relation. For the infant there is only the mother, whereas for the mother there are others: husband, other children, the world. She is the first object, the "you" in Strasser's dialogic _cogito,_ and it is within the tension produced by her intermittent presence and absence that the infant evolves as a subject. It is at this developmental juncture that Chodorow distinguishes the mother's response to her sons from her response to her daughters. Acknowledging the sexual gratification that the mother experiences suckling and tending to children of both sexes, she notes that the mother identifies with the daughter but, perceiving her son as sexually other, more closely monitors her contact with her male child:

> Correspondingly, girls tend to remain part of the dyadic primary mother-child relation itself. This means that a girl continues to experience herself as involved in issues of merging and separation, and in an attachment characterized by primary identification and object choice. . . . A boy has engaged and been required to engage in a more emphatic individuation and a more defensive firming of ego boundaries. . . . from very early then, because they are parented by a person of the same gender, girls come to experience themselves as less differentiated than boys, as more continuous with and related to the external object world and as differently oriented to their inner object world as well.[15]

The achievement of masculine gender requires the male child to repress those elements of his own subjectivity that are identified with his mother. What is male is "that which is not feminine and/or connected with women."[16] This is another way in which boys repress relation and connection in the process of growing up. Girls, on the other hand, need not repress the identification with their mothers. Whereas the dyadic structure of preoedipal parent/child relations is extended into the male oedipal period, with the male child transferring his identification from mother to father and repressing the internal preoedipal identifications, the female oedipal crisis is less precipitous and decisive. The dyadic relationship with her mother is sustained rather than repressed, and the father is introduced as a third element, creating what Chodorow calls a relational triangle. For both boys and girls, the father, who is more immersed in the public world, represents an external presence, often called a "reality principle," although that term expresses the very denigration and marginalization of the preoedipal relation that we are trying to rescue from centuries of oblivion and sentimentalization. Identification with the father presents the girl with a means of dealing with the ambivalence she experiences as the intense identification with her mother threatens to subsume her own autonomy. Nevertheless, because that ambivalence, also shared by the male child, is not accompanied by the dramatic repression that accompanies the incest taboo in the male oedipal crisis, the female child sustains the intuitive, emotional, and physical connectedness that the male represses, and for her, external objectivity becomes an alternative postoedipal object relation rather than a substitute for the powerful and emotional experiences of early childhood, which she retains as well. The reciprocity and mutual dependency of a concrete subjectivity, here bonded to the child and a concrete objectivity, the preoedipal other, who is the mother, are sustained for the postoedipal girl; and a more abstract objectivity associated with the external world and the father becomes a third term that mediates the mother/daughter, subject/object relationship.

This story of palpable presence and shadowy absence, of turning to and turning away, is and is not my story. Over and over again it contradicts the intimacies of my own childhood. It obscures my mother's energy and activity in the public world just as it erases my father's attentiveness and care. He walked with me in the dark morning hours when I would not relinquish the world for sleep. She gave speeches and came home late after the meeting, her eyes glowing, showing me the beautiful pin that she had been given to recognize her achievement. The theory fails to notice the photo in our album of my son, sleeping on my husband's chest, and the presence of their father's humor and inflections in our daughters' voices. These moments of familial specificity achieve meaning for me as they both confirm and contradict the relations that Chodorow describes. My father's participation in my infant care, my mother's leadership were both achieved in opposition to the politics of separation and connection that Chodorow presents. Furthermore, the meaning of their actions cannot be separated from this contradiction, for it was in opposition to those norms that my mother talked and my father walked. And sometimes the actors themselves, located somewhere between connection and separation lose their grasp of their own experience. My mother puts my father on the phone to talk to the landlord. My father never talks about his business at home. My son asks about my work and reads my papers, but he is careful not to mention that the research that he is citing in his college classroom was written by his mother.

I reclaim the specificity of my own gender formation as I read these memories of identification and differentiation through the lens of pre- and postoedipal politics. I begin to grasp the dialectic that makes me a particular personality who is, nevertheless, a woman. Because education mediates this passage between the specificity of intimate relations and the generalities of the public world, because cognition requires perpetual negotiation between general concepts and specific perceptions and intuitions, our understanding of our work as educators is enhanced when we grasp the interplay of the general and the specific in the constitution of our own gender identities.

Theory is cultivated in the public world. It is an interpretive and speculative enterprise that the community undertakes to make sense of our collective past, present, and future. Theory grows where it is planted, soaking up the nutrients in the local soil, turning to the local light. A theory of education that is cultivated in the academy, the library, or the laboratory accommodates to its environment. For educational theory to comprehend the experience and implications of reproduction we must generate a dialectical theory that gathers data and interpretation from both the public and the domestic domains.

Psychoanalytic theory abandons mothers and children at the very moment when we make room for Daddy. Though the presence of the father is gathered into the symbolic representation of the third term in the object relations of both mother and child, the entrance of the father and the world he brings with him need not be construed as obliterating the world that mother and child have shared. Too often psychoanalytic theory portrays the mother/child symbiosis as undifferentiated, as if mother and child spent the early days of infancy plastered up against each other, allowing no light, no space, no air, no world to come between them. Mother/child interaction, as the research of Daniel Stern has shown us, is a much more dynamic and differentiated relation than classical psychoanalytic theory would suggest.[17] This is not to dismiss the significant contribution to the life of the mother and the life of the child that the father, the friends, the world provide. A relation to this third term is achieved by both mother and child through their shared history of attachment and differentiation. What we have to remember, however, is that the father does not create the world, although he may enrich and extend it.

In constructivism the symbolic status of the world is acknowledged as the construct that evolves from the interacting and mutually constituting reciprocity of subject and object.[18] Underneath every curriculum, which expresses the relation of the knower and the known as it is realized within a specific social and historical moment, is an epistemological assumption concerning the relation of subject and object. In an attempt to understand how we come to have and share a world, the various epistemologies relegate differing weights to consciousness and facticity. Each epistemology offers a negotiated peace between these two competing terms to account for this intersubjective construct, this ground of all our cognitions, "this world." Materialist epistemologies favor facticity; idealist epistemologies favor consciousness or mind. Whereas both materialist and idealist epistemologies permit the third term to collapse into one or the other poles of the dyad, the constructivist epistemology of Piaget retains the third term as constituted simultaneously by the interaction of the two and as constituting them in turn. Whereas constructivism mirrors the configurations of the symbiosis of the mother/child bond and the extension of that continuity beyond the oedipal crisis in the mother/ daughter relationship, the tenuous father/child bond and harsher repression of the mother/son preoedipal bond reflect the dyadic structure of materialist and idealist epistemologies.

The shift between dyadic and triadic epistemologies marks the contradictory moment that transforms the structure of conception into the structure of curriculum. The paternal relation is first constituted in three terms, as the father's relation with the child is mediated by the mother. The paternal compensation for this contingency is to delete the mother, to claim the child, and to be the cause, moving to a two-term, cause/effect model, where the father is the cause and the child his effect. The original maternal relation, on the other hand, is dyadic, and it is through the process of differentiation as mother and child grasp the world in which they found each other that the third term appears. So where constructivism may represent a preoedipal past for masculine epistemology, it suggests a postoedipal future for feminine epistemologies. This conclusion is mirrored in the collaborative research of Belenky, Clinchy, Goldberger, and Tarule. They develop five categories to describe the epistemological perspectives held by the women they interviewed:

> *Silence*, . . . women experience themselves as mindless and voiceless and subject to the whims of external authority; *received knowledge*, . . . women conceive of themselves as capable of receiving, even reproducing knowledge from the all-knowing external authorities but not capable of creating knowledge on their own; *subjective knowledge*, . . . truth and knowledge are conceived of as personal, private, and subjectively known or intuited; *procedural knowledge*, . . . women are invested in learning and applying objective procedures for obtaining and communicating knowledge; and *constructed knowledge*, . . . women view all knowledge as contextual, experience themselves as creators of knowledge, and value both subjective and objective strategies for knowing.[19]

This study of women's ways of knowing settles on constructivism as the epistemology that celebrates the creativity and responsibility of the knower as well as the context and relations within which knowing takes place and comes to form. Within their developmental argument, these authors make it clear that the constructivist position is an achievement, earned as women bring together the parts of their experience that the politics of gender, of family, school, and science has separated. What I have called masculine epistemology may be found in their categories of received and procedural knowledge and the silence that their politics produces.

Masculine epistemologies are compensations for the inferential nature of paternity as they reduce preoedipal subject/object mutuality to postoedipal cause and effect, employing idealistic and materialistic rationales to compensate as well for the repressed identification that the boy has experienced with his primary object, his mother. The male child who must repress his preoedipal identification with his mother negates it, banishing this primary object from his own conscious ego identity. As his mother is not he, objective reality also becomes not he, and his own gender, more tentative than that of the female, is constituted by the symbolic enculturation of his culture's sense of masculinity, a conceptual overlay that reinforces his own sense that his subjectivity (that preoedipal maternal identification) and objectivity (that primary object, mother) are alienated from each other. Chodorow's point is that masculine identification processes stress differentiation from others, the denial of affective relations, and categorical, universalistic components of the masculine role, denying relation where female identification processes acknowledge it. She concludes that both as infants and as adults, males exist in a sharply differentiated dyadic structure, females in a more continuous and interdependent, triadic one.

If psychoanalytic theory has given too much power to the father, it has taken too much power from the son. The harshness of the son's repression of his preoedipal relation to his mother, though necessary for the development of male gender identity, may be somewhat diminished if that mother is not portrayed as a cloistered recluse, wallowing in regressive fantasies. The mother who is in the kitchen and in the world may nurture both sons and daughters for whom male and female, private and public, knowing and feeling are not so harshly dichotomous and oppositional.

Although Chodorow acknowledges the contributions of biology to the infant's matrisexual experience and subsequent maternal symbiosis, she maintains that the oedipal crisis is culturally specific. She demands that we acknowledge culture, the organization of families and labor, as responsible for the oedipal crisis, which in Freudian theory is attributed to a biological determinism of shifting zones of libidinal expression. For Chodorow the interpretive shift from biology to culture is significant for it acknowledges human agency, assuming that, if biology makes us, we make culture. Culture, she claims, is not a species characteristic but evolves as a response to the repressions demanded by those social relations that prevail in a particular era and milieu. Chodorow argues that the object relations she describes are sustained by a highly rationalized economic system of capitalism that draws men away from parenting and into institutions that require behavioral obedience and an orientation to external authority, thus reinforcing the repressions of the preoedipal experience. Such an argument coincides with the work of critical theorists such as Herbert Marcuse and Christopher Lasch who argue that mass culture, media, and the glorification of the adolescent peer culture have undermined the role of the father as a palpable authority in a child's life, vitiating the oedipal struggle and the autonomy that is the reward of the child who survives it.[20]

Although we must acknowledge the resemblance of this profile of contemporary culture to the world we know, I find its analysis skewed in the weight it gives to the labor and love of the fathers in determining the character of our culture and world. This scheme suggests that the female, domestic, and maternal influence prevails in our time as a consequence of patriarchal default and continues to represent the consequences of female influence as regressive, binding the children left to us to infantilized, undifferentiated, and narcissistic futures. The broad strokes that paint sociology's portrait of culture necessarily present its surface, most visible, and accessible structures for its total reality. The very clarity of the structural scheme that has permitted the generative analogies we draw between object relations and epistemology may mislead us, if it overwhelms us with a description of our situation that is too coherent. In a culture such as ours, where the symbol systems that dominate our social worlds are most often designed, distributed, and credentialed by men, it is not surprising that a sociological portrayal, locating itself in a description of our common situation, depicts a patriarchal order.

An attempt to provide a more complex and dialectical sense of culture is suggested in a study such as Julia Kristeva's *About Chinese Women,* which combines history and sociology to examine the cataclysmic changes in Chinese culture and their impact on the lives of Chinese women.[21] Kristeva describes an era in Chinese history that parallels the preoedipal period of psychological development in the West. Her analysis is interesting because it suggests that despite the 8,000-year-old repression of a putative matrilineal and matrilocal culture, contemporary Chinese women may be able to draw upon the deep streams that have run through their history, linking them to a cultural and historical epoch in which preoedipal symbiosis and continuity of internal and external structures were political realities rather than psychological repressions. Of course, the comparison that I make between Kristeva's and Chodorow's portraits of culture also marks the location of my own perception, as I find the one that deals with my own culture too general because I am so familiar with its complexities and am persuaded by the study of the culture so distant from me.

CONTRADICTION

Although our culture may lack the matriarchal history that might reveal our latent possibilities and the perspectives to reassure us that all is not lost and we have a past ready to reclaim, within us resides the power to imagine, if not remember, the negations of the conditions of our existence.[22] I think we attempt to accomplish this negation in the worlds we construct for our children. The contradiction is not merely altruistic, designed for them, for it also extends the projects of our own development as adults trying to extricate ourselves from our own childhoods and our own children. Unlike other organisms, we do not spawn and die. We not only survive the birth of our children, but from the moment of their conception, their time and ours intermingle, each defining the other. Biology and culture influence our contemporary categories of gender and attitudes toward parenting as well as our epistemologies and curricula. This study of women and curriculum is claiming a space in culture for the women who care for children other than the great empty void assigned to us by the absent fathers and homesick sociologists. It presents a reading of curriculum that attributes the motive of differentiation to the mothers rather than the fathers, whose bureaucracies and collusions extend their own wishes to own and be owned. And if Kristeva finds in archaic Chinese history a female consciousness and promise of transformation contained, yet present, in collective memory, I suggest that our revolutionary female consciousness is lodged not in the recesses of time, but in the work that women do daily teaching children in classrooms.

While claiming, even flaunting, the preoedipal symbiosis of mother and child, we must be suspicious of portrayals of that primal relation that disqualify it as a way of knowing, of learning, of being in the world. If we bury our memories of this relation we knew as children and again as mothers under language, under law, under politics, and under curriculum, we are forever complicit in patriarchal projects to deny its adequacy, influence, and existence. Kristeva maintains that our culture and codes of communication contain not only the linguistic rules and conventions that constitute our postoedipal symbolic systems but also the imagistic, inflected, and gestural semiotic codes that signal the continued presence of our preoedipal pasts in our adult experience.[23] Similarly, the method of this discourse invites us to read the work of women in classrooms as a text of our repressions and compromises. It invites us to read the texts of educational experience and practice as semiotic as well as symbolic systems. Curriculum is a project of transcendence, our attempt while immersed in biology and ideology to transcend biology and ideology. Even in the most conventional scene of classroom practice we can find traces of transformative consciousness, no matter how masked in apparent compliance and convention. This perception invites us to refuse to run the classroom like a conveyance, designed to transport children from the private to the public world, but to make it instead a real space in the middle, where we can all stop and rest and work to find the political and epistemological forms that will mediate the oppositions of home and workplace.

CURRICULUM

The assertion that curriculum is motivated by our projects to transcend the biological and cultural determinations of our reproductive experience seriously undermines the assumption that curriculum design is a rational activity resting on needs assessments, systems analyses, or values clarification. The degree to which our support for open schooling, back-to-basics, moral education, or minimum competency testing is lodged in the relationships of our infantile psychosexual milieu is the degree to which our choices are overdetermined and our praxis vitiated. It would be simple if the relationships were direct, if schooling were just one great funnel into which we poured the entire social, emotional, political contents of our lives. Instead, rather than merely replicating the society from which they spring, schools contradict many of the dominant social and familial themes in our society. The history of education in this country provides countless instances of institutional, curricular, and epistemological configurations that emerge to contradict a particular condition in the culture. The famous ''Olde Deluder Satan

Law," passed in the Massachusetts Bay Colony in 1647, empowered the minister to compel illiterate children to attend his lessons so that they could learn to read Scripture and be saved. It did not merely reflect the colonists' religious fervor and commitment to the Bible. It also revealed the decline of the colonists' religious fervor and the commitment to the Bible. It was compensatory. The very notion of childhood itself, argue both Aries and Wishy, is also compensatory, for it endowed youth with the innocence and protection that adults, adjusting to pluralistic urban centers, lacked in their own daily experience.[24] We do not have to turn back to fourteenth-century Europe or the Massachusetts Bay Colony to discover contradictions. The democratic ethos of American schooling, equality of opportunity leading to social mobility based on achieved rather than ascribed characteristics, belies the actual commitments of the upper and middle classes to retain their class status and the function of the schools in support of their privilege. Racial integration and busing contradict racial distrust and antagonism.[25] Essentialist and "Great Books" curricula contradict our immersion in the imagery of contemporary video, our cultural pluralism, and our infatuation with technology.

Because schools are ritual centers cut off from the real living places where we love and labor, we burden them with all the elaborate aspirations that our love and labor are too meager and narrow to bear. Contradicting the inferential nature of paternity, the paternal project of curriculum is to claim the child, to teach him or her to master the language, the rules, the games, and the names of the fathers. Contradicting the symbiotic nature of maternity, the maternal project of curriculum is to relinquish the child so that both mother and child can become more independent of one another.

Nevertheless, when negation is collapsed into a simple antithesis, a polar contradiction of one extreme by another, the alternative is as restricting as the condition it strives to repudiate. Just as the mother may succumb to the pleasures of sensuality or the shallow comfort of individualism, the father is also menaced by the contradictions he employs to negate conditions of paternity. As a parent, the father contradicts the inferential and uncertain character of his paternity by transforming the abstraction that has been felt as deficiency into a virtue, into virtue itself. Co-opting the word, and transforming it into the law, the fathers dominate communal activity. Tying procreation and kinship to the exchange of capital, the fathers master the pernicious alchemy of turning people into gold, substituting the objectification of persons for the abstraction implied by paternity and amplified by technology and capitalism. The project to be the cause, to see the relation of self and other as concrete, is expressed in monologic epistemologies of cause and effect, of either/or constructions of truth, and of social science that denigrate the ambiguity and dialectical nature of human action to honor the predictability and control of physical and mechanistic phenomena.

Who are these fathers? They are our sons. They are the children the incest taboo estranges from their mothers, repressing their symbiotic experience of connection and identification with the other, the mother, the first object and the conditions of their own sense of self. They are the ones for whom gender identification requires a radical negation that violates the mutual dependency of child and parent, of subject and object. (Hence the "null hypothesis" of social science, which assumes there is no relation between variables and requires substantial quantification before a "significant" relation can be asserted.) Split off from identification with his mother, his primary object, the boy's later identification with his father is supported by his growing capacity to symbolize, to associate signs with experience, genitals with gender, words with power. As a man he will seek to reestablish the connectedness of infancy through work and culture and family; and if he can escape the depersonalizing, bureaucratic alienation of work and the positivistic, objectivizing dehumanization of culture—both of which combine to estrange him from his family—he may succeed. Masculine epistemology reflects this search for influence and control. It is oriented toward a subject/object dyad in which subject and object are not mutually constituting but ordered in terms of cause and effect, activity and passivity.

Masculine curriculum reflects this epistemology, contradicting the ambiguity of paternity, in forms differentiated by class interests. Though more closely identified with class status than women, men of all classes hope to engage in work that will be acknowledged as productive. They seek to be acknowledged as agents, who can claim the crop, the engine, the legal code, the party, the cure, the peace as theirs. For those engaged in manual labor the product, if not fragmented beyond recognition by the assembly line or trick shift, is concrete and tangible. For white-collar workers it becomes more abstract: the plan or the report, or the paycheck. For others it becomes an investment portfolio, an office with a window, a two-year improvement in reading scores. The product, material or symbolic, is public and can be traced, if not to a particular individual, then to the group to which he lends his name.

Competency testing, back-to-basics, and teacher accountability were the expressions of this process/product paradigm in the curriculum trends of the 1970s.[26] They accompanied the historical development of increasing bureaucracy and rationalization of the means of production and, in particular, the repudiation of the educational initiatives of the "sexties," rife with sensuality, ambiguity, rebellion against the paternal order. In the eighties fundamentalist assaults on the curriculum have sought a totalitarian solution for the family's incapacity to reproduce its world view in its children. The attempt to control and shape the child through schooling is also present in the recent criticisms of schooling that have appeared in the proliferating "school reports" of this decade. These documents reinforce the authority of the traditional disciplines and the rationalization of the workplace in their curriculum proposals, demanding higher standards, fewer electives, reliance on the literary canon, more homework, better use of time, merit designations for staff, and higher salaries. No longer rationalizing schooling as the path to success for the entrepreneurial "self-made man" in an era when small business has given way to the corporation, it is the economic prosperity of the nation, no less, that is depicted in some of the reports as resting on the quality of instruction in schools. As we lose ground in our competition with other countries for international markets and military technology because of the greed and mismanagement of corporate production and trade agreements, blame is deflected from the men who establish these policies onto the women who teach the children who fail.[27]

For all the simplistic positivism of the programs of the seventies and the proposals of the eighties, there is a courage in their paternalism that I celebrate. There is courage in their assertions, however self-serving, and in those who designed them. There is courage in their willingness to address the future and to try to shape its character. They are political.

In contrast, even though the curriculum reform that grew out of the counter-culture movement of the seventies was a serious political response to the arbitrary and abstract politics that brought us the Vietnam atrocities and Watergate, its open classrooms, alternative schools, and interdisciplinary curricula came to be seen as attempts to retreat from the world rather than as projects to redesign it. The curriculum of the open classroom mirrors the characteristics that Chodorow identifies as characteristic of women's work rather than men's.[28] Whereas men's work in the office or the factory is contractual, delimited in time, organized around a defined progression toward a finite product, women's work is nonbounded and contingent on others.[29] Women's work is seen as maintenance, repeated in daily chores required merely to sustain life, not to change it.

Ironically, the child-centered philosophy of the open school, the curriculum movement that might have extended the vigor and specificity of maternal nurturance from home to classroom, shifted the stasis attributed to women's work and lives to children. Rachel Sharp and Anthony Green argue that the ethos that supported the individuation of the child was the expectation that, left to his or her own developmental agenda, the child would express an inner nature, realizing what she or he *is*.[30] But they maintain that this ontological view of the child that honors what the child is, rather than what the school will make him become, ultimately served to sustain class differences, masking that teleological agenda and allowing it to function even more efficiently than it had in the traditional setting because its assumptions were no longer explicitly articulated. Their critique suggests that the maternal, ontologic ethos of such schools, its commitment to the "whole child," and apparent willingness to honor the specificity of each child's background and developmental level, masked the patriarchal teleologic project to protect class distinctions and advance the interest of the middle class that proceeded unimpeded by the new "familial" organization and ambience of the classroom. Because the innovations in curriculum often stopped at the classroom door and did not penetrate programs of evaluation or credentialing, the acceptance that they extended to the individual child trapped the poor child in a repertoire of behaviors that did not conform to the standards set to recognize and celebrate middle-class culture. Oblivious to the far-reaching epistemological and political implications of this approach to schooling, the teachers who had transformed their classrooms into places of active exploration and group process failed to create the political and ideological structures required to sustain and enlarge the movement. It disappeared almost as quickly as it came, leaving an empty terrarium, Cuisenaire rods, and an occasional learning center in its wake.

The degree to which schooling continues to imitate the spatial, temporal, and ritual order of industry and bureaucracy indicates the complicity of both men and women in support of paternal authority. That pattern becomes even more obvious in the social arrangement of faculty within schools, where male administrators and department chairmen dominate female teaching staffs, who, secretive and competitive, vie for their fathers' approval while at the same time disregarding the rational schemes and programs that emanate from the central office in favor of a more contextual, idiosyncratic curriculum of their own. Docile, self-effacing, we hand in our lesson plans, replete with objectives and echoes of the current rationale, and then, safe behind the doors of our self-enclosed classrooms, subvert those schemes, secure in their atheoretical wisdom, intuitive rather than logical, responsive rather than initiating, nameless yet pervasive. The programs stay on paper, the administrators' theory barred from practice, the teachers' practice barred from theory by the impenetrable barriers of resistance sustained by sexual politics.

Dorothy Dinnerstein argues that so long as primary parenting remains within the exclusive domain of women, both men and women will seek and support the paternal order as a refuge from the domination of the mother.[31] She maintains that from the early years in which mother is the source of all satisfaction as well as its denial, the audience for our humiliations as well as our triumphs, the supporting, inhibiting, protecting, abandoning agent through whom, and despite whom, we discover the world, we retain a rage at our own dependency and disappointment. The sons *and* the daughters turn to the fathers for relief, they who seem free of her dominion, substituting paternal authority for the maternal order.

It is the female elementary schoolteacher who is charged with the responsibility to lead the great escape. At the sound of the bell, she brings the child from the concrete to the abstract, from the fluid time of the domestic day to the segmented schedule of the school day, from the physical work, comfort, and sensuality of home to the mentalistic, passive, sedentary, pretended asexuality of the school—in short, from the woman's world to the man's. She is a traitor, and the low status of the teaching profession may be derived from the contempt her betrayal draws from both sexes. Mothers relinquish their children to her, and she hands them over to men who respect the gift but not the giver.

Who are these teachers? They are our daughters. Because mothers bear so much of the weight of parenting, as Dinnerstein has pointed out, we are very powerful figures for our children. That power would seem less threatening if it were not confined, however, to the domestic sphere. The discrepancy that children experience between their mother's influence in their home, compared to her influence in the public world, must undermine their comfort and confidence in maternal strength. Though their own intimate experience of her power is not diminished, it becomes suspect if it appears to be confined only to the forms of domestic nurturance. Whereas the sharper repression of the symbiotic tie permits her son to feel safe from her, the stronger identification of the daughter increases her vulnerability, and she turns to her father to escape the maternal presence that threatens to subsume her. Dinnerstein maintains that "both men and women use the unresolved early threat of female dominion to justify keeping the infantilism in themselves alive under male dominion."[32] The infant's rage, projected onto the mother, is reinforced by the disappointments and denials encountered in adult life, whereas the child's aspirations for autonomy along with the enduring desire for dependency are transferred to the father. Identification with paternal authority becomes a spurious symbol of autonomy, while the acquiescence it requires satisfies the unresolved desire to be managed and deny responsibility.

Kim Chernin's study of mother/daughter relationships in *The Hungry Self* suggests another motive for the daughter's emigration to the father's world. Chernin explores the daughter's identification with her mother's experience of stasis, frustration, and disappointment. She sees daughters struggling with their sense of their mothers' unrealized ambitions, unexpressed talents. So the daughter who flees may be attempting to escape her memory of maternal dominion as she simultaneously attempts to compensate her mother for her disappointments by achieving what was denied to her.[33]

The lure of patriarchy is an index to the enduring power of the mother/daughter bond. The symbiotic, concrete, polymorphic, preoedipal attachment of mother and child links our lives across neighborhoods, time zones, and generations. As the woman creates the child, the child completes the woman. Particularly in Western culture, where female sexuality is acknowledged and tolerated only in its capacity for procreation, motherhood bonds sexuality and gender. It legitimizes desire. It permits the woman to reclaim her body and her breasts from their status as erotic objects hitherto perceived only in their capacity to attract and seduce man. It dissolves the stigma of menstruation, inherited from the Old Testament, in the glory of creation. It releases the woman from the guilt of her secret sexuality as it repudiates the myth of the Virgin impregnated by the Word. As the child realizes his or her form within the woman, the woman realizes her form through the child. They constitute each other, subject and object dependent upon each other for both their essence and their existence. Chodorow endows this somewhat idealistic portrait of intersubjectivity with its erotic life when she argues that whereas the male reexperiences the preoedipal intimacy with his mother through coitus with a woman, the female ultimately reexperiences that bond not through the sexual relation to the male but in the intimacy she experiences with the child.[34] This dialectical interdependence obtains not only in the early months of the child's life but throughout its development, for the mother is able to differentiate from the child only insofar as the child is able to differentiate from her. The facticity and freedom of both mother and child are contingent upon their relationship. Psychoanalytic theory celebrates both maternal absence and maternal presence as the basis of ego development. It is argued that it is only in the mother's absence that the child begins to perceive his or her own selfhood so that their intermittent separation is the basis for the first identification of self. Yet the converse is also true. For the willingness and capacity for separation rest upon the prior and anticipated satisfaction of the child's needs for intimacy, dependence, and nurturance. The developmental needs of both mother and child simultaneously sustain and contradict the concrete, symbiotic origins of their relationship. A feminist epistemology reflects this dialectical dependence of subject and object.

Although the presence of open, nongraded classrooms seemed to suggest that a feminine epistemology had penetrated the patriarchal pedagogues of elementary education, the movement has collapsed, its foundations eaten away by technological methods that subvert it as well as by an ethos of individualism that has drained it of social promise and political power. This educational initiative finally failed to address the dilemma that has always plagued public education: the tension between addressing the needs of each individual student and developing the cohesion and identity of the group that contains that student. The project of differentiation that supports ego boundaries and personal strength is too often translated into a laissez-faire individualism that surrenders a vision of the world we might share to a project of individual development that repudiates intersubjectivity and interdependence.

Bonded, interminably, it would seem, to her mother and then to her child, the woman who survives the demands of these relationships to work in the world as a curriculum theorist, school administrator, or teacher is often engaged in the project of her own belated individuation and expression. Furthermore, as I shall argue later, our relations to other people's children are inextricably tied to our relation to our own progeny, actual and possible, and to the attribution of rights and influence that we attribute to that affiliation. If it is our relation to our own children that is contradicted by the curriculum we develop and teach, we must remember that what we develop we teach not to our own but to other people's children. It is with them that the contradictions between the woman's own experiences of childhood and mothering and the curricula she supports appear. Convinced that we are too emotional, too sensitive, and that our work as mothers or housewives is valued only by our immediate families, we hide it, and like Eve, forbidden to know and teach what she has directly experienced, we keep that knowledge to ourselves as we dispense the curriculum to the children of other women. Bonded to the other in a nurturant but inhibiting symbiosis on the species and cultural level, feminine curricula reverse the patterns of species and sociocultural relations emphasizing an asocial and apolitical individuation. It is this monologic intentionality that Kristeva fears will vitiate the hidden, presymbolic power that resides within feminine experience. She fears that we sell out: we escape the binding preoedipal and postoedipal identification with our mothers by identifying with our fathers, striving for access to the word and to time; or we repudiate the dialectic of sexuality, obliterating the other in a fascistic and totalitarian mimicry of power; or we sink into a wordless ecstasy, back into the preoedipal maternal identification, mystical, melancholic, sullen, and suicidal—Virginia walking into the river. Kristeva's warning:

> To refuse both extremes. To know that an ostensibly masculine, paternal (because supportive of time and symbol) identification is necessary in order to have some voice in the record of politics and history. To achieve this identification in order to escape a smug polymorphism where it is so easy and comfortable for a woman here to remain.[35]

Bearing epistemologies and curricular projects that contradict both our psychosocial development as sons and daughters and our procreative experience as fathers and mothers, we find ourselves trapped in the activity we claim as conscious intentionality as we have been in the overdetermined, repressed experience of our early years. This compensatory and simplistic pattern of opposition demeans the dialectic, a title it hardly deserves. To qualify for that designation we would need to interpret our reproductive experience (procreation and nurturance) and our productive practice (curriculum and teaching) each through the other's terms, not obliterating the differences between them but naming their contradictions and reconceiving our commitment to the care and education of children. It is a dialectic that strives not to obliterate differences in a shallow, totalitarian image of equality but to sustain them and work for their integration.

Feminist social theory directs us to reorganize our patterns of infant nurturance, permitting fathers to assume significant nurturant activities and an intimacy with their children that will preclude the harsh, deforming repression of the rich and powerful preoedipal experience. The felt presence of both mothers and fathers in the infant's world may diminish the crippling dichotomy of internal and external, dream and reality, body and thought, poetry and science, ambiguity and certainty. These domestic arrangements clearly remain fantasy unless supported by the economic, religious, and legal systems in which we live. The task when viewed in the structural complexity of our social, political, economic situation appears herculean. Only when we suspend the despair that isolates us from our history and our future can our reproductive capacity reclaim the procreative promise of our species, not merely to conceive but to reconceive another generation.

We, the women who teach, must claim our reproductive labor as a process of civilization as well as procreation. We can continue to escort the children from home to the marketplace as did the *paidagogos,* the Greek slave whose title and function survive in pedagogy, or we can refuse the oppositions and limits that define each place and our love and work within them. The task is daunting and not without its contradictions. These words, for all their intensity, have been sifted through the sieves of academic discourse. The very institutions that I repudiate for their perpetuation of patriarchal privilege are the ones within which I have found the voice that tries to sing the tune of two worlds. This writing has been interrupted and informed by driving the kids to the pool and to soccer practice, by the laundering of sweaty sports socks and mildewed beach towels, by the heat of the summer sun and the soft summons of the night air. As I end this chapter, I am tempted to celebrate both it and myself. But I am chastened by Kristeva:

> To be wary from the first of the premium of narcissism that such integration may carry with it: to reject the validity of the homologous woman, finally virile; and to act, on the socio-political, historical stage, as her negative: that is, to act first with all those who "swim against the tide," all those who refuse—all the rebels against the existing relations of production and reproduction. But neither to take the role of revolutionary (male or female) to refuse all roles, in order on the contrary, to summon this timeless "truth"—formless, neither true or false, echo of our jouissance, of our madness, of our pregnancies—unto the order of speech and social symbolism. But how? By listening, by recognizing the unspoken speech, even revolutionary speech; by calling attention at all times to whatever remains unsatisfied, repressed, new, eccentric, incomprehensible, disturbing to the status quo. A constant alternation between time and its "truth," identity and its loss, history and the timeless, signless, extra-phenomenal things that produce it. An impossible dialectic; a permanent alternation; never the one without the other. It is not certain that anyone here and now is capable of it. An analyst conscious of history and politics? A politician tuned to the unconscious? A woman perhaps . . .[36]

Notes

1. Julia Kristeva, *About Chinese Women,* trans. Anita Burrows (London: Marion Boyars, 1977), p. 15.

2. Maurice Merleau-Ponty, *Phenomenology of Perception,* trans. Colin Wilson (New York: Humanities Press, 1962).

3. In Christine Froula's study of Christian doctrine and its interpretation in Milton's *Paradise Lost,* Eve's transgression is the claim of direct experience, rather than the mediated knowledge that imputes invisibility to authority. See "When Eve Reads Milton: Undoing the Canonical Economy," in *Canons,* ed. Robert von Hallberg (Chicago: University of Chicago Press, 1984).

4. Antonio Gramsci, *Selections from the Prison Notebooks,* trans. and ed. Quinton Hoare and Geoffrey N. Smith (New York: International Publishers, 1971).

5. Edmund Husserl, *Ideas: General Introduction to Pure Phenomenology,* trans. W. R. Boyce Gibson (New York: Collier Books, 1962).

6. Stephen Strasser, *The Idea of a Dialogic Phenomenology* (Pittsburgh: Duquesne University Press, 1969).

7. Ibid., pp. 61–63.

8. Nancy Chodorow, *The Reproduction of Mothering: Psychoanalysis and the Sociology of Gender* (Berkeley: University of California Press, 1978).

9. Ibid., p. 47.

10. In *The Politics of Reproduction* (Boston: Routledge and Kegan Paul, 1981), Mary O'Brien provides a philosophy of birth and brings each of these "moments" to its meaning in the generation of the human species and the human spirit: menstruation, ovulation, copulation, alienation, conception, gestation, labor, birth, appropriation, nurture (p. 47).

11. Shulamith Firestone's startling prophesy that women will seize control of our own bodies and of reproduction, in *Dialectic of Sex* (New York: Bantam Books, 1972), has, despite its specter of a totalitarian technology, challenged us to name the experience, meaning, and politics of heterosexual reproduction as we know it. See Jean Bethke Elshtain's critique of Firestone in *Public Man, Private Woman: Women in Social and Political Thought* (Princeton, N.J.: Princeton University Press, 1981).

12. Vangie Bergum, *Woman to Mother: A Transformation* (South Hadley, Mass: Bergin and Garvey, forthcoming).

13. Jürgen Habermas, *Knowledge and Human Interests*, trans. Jeremy J. Shapiro (Boston: Beacon Press, 1971), pp. 262–63.

14. Bernard Wishy, *The Child and the Republic* (Philadelphia: University of Pennsylvania Press, 1968).

15. Chodorow, *Reproduction of Mothering*, pp. 166, 167.

16. Ibid., p. 174.

17. Daniel Stern, *The Interpersonal World of the Infant* (New York: Basic Books, 1985).

18. Constructivism is the epistemological theory described by Jean Piaget. See *The Grasp of Consciousness*, trans. Susan Wedgwood (Cambridge, Mass.: Harvard University Press, 1976).

19. Mary Field Belenky, Blythe McVicker Clinchy, Nancy Rule Goldberger, and Jill Mattuck Tarule, *Women's Ways of Knowing: The Development of Self, Voice, and Mind* (New York: Basic Books, 1986).

20. See Herbert Marcuse, *Eros and Civilization* (Boston: Beacon Press, 1955); and Christopher Lasch, *The Culture of Narcissism* (New York: W. W. Norton, 1979).

21. Kristeva, *About Chinese Women*.

22. This concept of negation is drawn from Jean-Paul Sartre's association of negativity with the *pour-soi*, the human responsibility to reject determination and shape its own essence, developed in *Being and Nothingness*, trans. Hazel E. Barnes (New York: Washington Square Press, 1966).

23. Extensive development of this distinction can be found in Julia Kristeva, *Revolution in Poetic Language*, trans. Margaret Waller (New York: Columbia University Press, 1984).

24. Philippe Aries, *Centuries of Childhood*, trans. Robert Baldick (New York: Random House [Vintage Books], 1965); Wishy, *Child and Republic*.

25. Although the contradictions as stated here appear to contain a simple opposition of thesis and antithesis, that simple polarity may mask other intervening terms. The polarization of racism and mandated integration masks the issue of economic class. "Back-to-basics" provides another example of an apparent opposition that masks a third term. The slogan responds to the alienating technology of our culture, to the specialized curricula of the fifties and the expressive curricula of the sixties, and to the perceived deficiencies of the high-school graduates of the seventies. The compensatory thrust of "back-to-basics" addresses itself to the failure of the school curriculum to provide adequate instruction in reading, writing, and mathematics and focuses on the profound inadequacies of these high-school graduates. The revelation of these inade-

Yet today it seems innovative—even intrusive—to suggest that the schools should consciously aim at educating people for moral life and that perhaps the best way to accomplish this aim is to conduct the process in a thoroughly moral way. People who should know better continually claim that schools can do only one thing well—the direct teaching of basic skills. In a recent letter that apparently reflects the position espoused in their book (Gann and Duignan 1986), L. H. Gann and Peter Duignan say, "Above all, we should avoid the temptation to regard the school as an instrument that can cure all social ills. The school's job is to teach basic academic skills" (Gann and Duignan 1987). This statement captures a tiny corner of truth, but it ignores the citadel to which this corner belongs.

An honest appraisal of American traditions of schooling reveals that academic skills have long been thought of as a vehicle for the development of character. This was true in colonial days, it was true throughout the nineteenth century, and it was still true the first half of the twentieth century. Schools have always been considered as incubators for acceptable citizens, and citizenship has not always been defined in terms of academic achievement scores. The morality stressed by nineteenth- and early twentieth-century schools contained a measure of hypocrisy, to be sure. Drawing on both Christian doctrine and an ideology of individualism, recommendations on moral education emphasized both self-sacrifice and success through determination, ambition, and competition. The influential Character Development League, for example, stated in the opening paragraph of its *Character Lessons:* "Character in its primary principle and groundwork is *self-control* and *self-giving,* and the only practical method of enforcing this upon the habit of children is to keep before them *examples* of self-control and self-sacrifice" (Carr 1909). *Character Lessons,* however, is liberally laced with success stories, and, indeed, teachers are urged to credit each child for her or his contributions to a "Golden Deed Book." In the closing paragraphs of his Introduction, Carr suggests, "A small prize for the grade having the best "Golden Deed Book" and another to the pupil of the grade having the most Deeds to his credit, will arouse a discriminating interest" (Carr 1909). Thus, educators were urged to encourage both Christian charity and American entrepreneurship. In describing a mid-nineteenth-century school's operations, David Tyack and Elizabeth Hansot comment: "These mid-century themes suggest how deeply the absolutist morality of the evangelical movement became interwoven with a work ethic and ideology favoring the development of capitalism. Just as Christianity was inseparable from Americanism, so the entrepreneurial economic values seemed so self-evidently correct as to be taken for granted. *The school* gave everyone a chance to become hard-working, literate, temperate, frugal, a good planner (italics added; Tyack and Hansot 1982, p. 28).

The school was not expected to cure social ills; in this Gann and Duignan are correct. Rather, it was expected to teach vigorously the values of a society that thought it was righteous. The spirit was evangelical at every level from home and school to national and international politics, where speakers, writers, and statesmen regularly took the position that the United States had a God-given mission to export its righteous way of life to the rest of the world.[2] However wrong we may now consider this arrogant posture, it is clear that hardly anyone thought that the school's major or only job was to teach academic skills. This we did in the service of moral ends, not as an end in itself.

I am certainly not recommending a return to the self-righteous moralizing of the nineteenth century. On the contrary, I would argue for a strong rejection of this attitude, accompanied by a thorough study of its history and ideology. We cannot overcome a perspective, a worldview, as powerful as this one by ignoring it; we have to explore it both appreciatively and critically. Indeed, I would go so far as to suggest that proponents of "basic skills only" may really want to maintain the earlier attitude of Christian-American supremacy and that avoidance of moral issues and social ills is the only currently feasible way to accomplish this. The apparent consensus of earlier times has been lost. Further, attempts to restore the values of a diminishing majority have not been successful. Too many feisty minorities have found their voices and are beginning to suggest alternatives among moral priorities. In such a climate, the only way left for the weakening group in power is to block discussion entirely and hope that hegemonic structures will press things down into the old containers. The need for moral education is apparent to everyone, but concerns about the form it should take induce paralysis. Thus, I suggest that our forebears were right in establishing the education of a moral people as the primary aim of schooling, but they were often shortsighted and arrogant in their description of what it means to be moral.

CARING AS A MORAL ORIENTATION IN TEACHING

Although schools and other institutions have in general withdrawn from the task of moral education (some exceptions will be noted), there is a philosophical revival of interest in practical ethics. Several authors have commented on the arrogance and poverty of philosophical views that conceive of ethics solely as a domain for philosophical analysis.[3] Further, there is increased interest in both ethics of virtue (the modeling or biographical approach advocated in *Character Lessons*; see MacIntyre 1984) and in ethics of need and love. Joseph Fletcher contrasts the latter with ethics of law and rights. "As seen from the ethical perspective," he notes, "the legalistic or moralistic temper gives the first-order position to rights, whereas the agapistic temper gives the first place to *needs*" (Fletcher 1975, p. 45). A blend of these views that tries to avoid both the elitism in Aristotle's ethics of virtue and the dogmatism of Christian agapism is found in the current feminist emphasis on ethics of caring, relation, and response (see Noddings 1984; Gilligan 1982).

As an ethical orientation, caring has often been characterized as feminine because it seems to arise more naturally out of woman's experience than man's. When this ethical orientation is reflected on and technically elaborated, we find that it is a form of what may be called *relational ethics*.[4] A relational ethic remains tightly tied to experience because all its deliberations focus on the human beings involved in the situation under consideration and their relations to each other. A relation is here construed as any pairing or connection of individuals characterized by some affective awareness in each. It is an encounter or series of encounters in which the involved parties feel something toward each other. Relations may be characterized by love or hate, anger or sorrow, admiration or envy; or, of course, they may reveal mixed affects—one party feeling, say, love and the other revulsion. One who is concerned with behaving ethically strives always to preserve or convert a given relation into a caring relation. This does not mean that all relations must approach that of the prototypical mother-child relation in either intensity or intimacy. On the contrary, an appropriate and particular form of caring must be found in every relation, and the behaviors and feelings that mark the mother-child relation are rarely appropriate for other relations; the characteristics of *all* caring relations can be described only at a rather high level of abstraction.

A relational ethic, an ethic of caring, differs dramatically from traditional ethics. The most important difference for our present purpose is that ethics of caring turn the traditional emphasis on duty upside down. Whereas Kant insisted that only those acts performed out of duty (in conformity to principle) should be labeled moral, an ethic of caring prefers acts done out of love and natural inclination. Acting out of caring, one calls on a sense of duty or special obligation only when love or inclination fails. Ethical agents adopting this perspective do not judge their own acts solely by their conformity to rule or principle, nor do they judge them only by the likely production of preassessed nonmoral goods such as happiness. While such agents may certainly consider both principles and utilities, their primary concern is the relation itself—not only what happens physically to others involved in the relation and in connected relations but what they may feel and how they may respond to the act under consideration. From a traditional perspective, it seems very odd to include the response of another in a judgment of our own ethical acts. Indeed, some consider the great achievement of Kantian ethics to be its liberation of the individual from the social complexities that characterized earlier ethics. A supremely lonely and heroic ethical agent marks both Kantian ethics and the age of individualism. An ethic of caring returns us to an earlier orientation—one that is directly concerned with the relations in which we all must live.

A relational ethic is rooted in and dependent on natural caring. Instead of striving away from affection and toward behaving always out of duty as Kant has prescribed, one acting from a perspective of caring moves consciously in the other direction; that is, he or she calls on a sense of obligation in order to stimulate natural caring. The superior state—one far more efficient because it energizes the giver as well as the receiver—is one of natural caring. Ethical caring is its servant. Because natural caring is both the source and the terminus of ethical caring, it is reasonable to use the mother-child relation as its prototype, so long as we keep in mind the caveats mentioned above.

The first member of the relational dyad (the carer or "one caring") responds to the needs, wants, and initiations of the second. *Her* mode of response is characterized by *engrossment* (nonselective attention or total presence to *him*, the other, for the duration of the caring interval) and *displacement of motivation* (her motive energy flows in the direction of the other's needs and projects). She feels with the other and acts in his behalf. The second member (the one cared for) contributes to the relation by recognizing and responding to the caring.[5] In the infant, this response may consist of smiles and wriggles; in the student, it may reveal itself in energetic pursuit of the student's own projects. A mature relationship may, of course, be mutual, and two parties may regularly exchange places in the relation, but the contributions of the one caring (whichever person may hold the position momentarily) remain distinct from those of the cared for. It is clear from this brief description why an ethic of caring is often characterized in terms of responsibility and response.

A view similar in many ways to that of caring may be found in Sara Ruddick's analysis of maternal thinking (Ruddick 1986). A mother, Ruddick says, puts her thinking into the service of three great interests: preserving the life of the child, fostering his growth, and shaping an acceptable child. Similarly, Milton Mayeroff describes caring in terms of fostering the growth of another (Mayeroff 1971). Thus, it is clear that at least some contemporary theorists recognize the thinking, practice, and skill required in the work traditionally done by women—work that has long been considered something anyone with a warm heart and little intellect could undertake. Caring as a rational moral orientation and maternal thinking with its threefold interests are richly applicable to teaching.

CARING AND INSTRUCTIONAL ARRANGEMENTS

Even though the emphasis during this half of the twentieth century has been on intellectual goals—first, on advanced or deep structural knowledge of the disciplines and then, more modestly, on the so-called basics—a few educators and theorists have continued to suggest that schools must pay attention to the moral and social growth of their citizens. Ernest Boyer and his colleagues, for example, recommend that high school students engage in community service as part of their school experience (Boyer 1983). Theodore Sizer expresses concern about the impersonal relationships that develop between highly specialized teachers and students with whom they have only fleeting and technical contact, for example, in grading, recording attendance, disciplining (Sizer 1984). Lawrence Kohlberg and his associates concentrate explicitly on the just community that should be both the source and the end of a truly moral education (Kohlberg 1981, 1984). But none of these concerns has captured either the national interest or that of educators in a way that might bring a mandate for significant change. The current emphasis remains on academic achievement. The influential reports of both the Holmes Group and the Carnegie Task Force, for example, almost entirely ignore the ethical aspects of education (*Tomorrow's Teachers*, 1986; *A Nation Prepared*, 1986). They mention neither the ethical considerations that should enter into teachers' choices of content, methods, and instructional arrangements nor the basic responsibility of schools to contribute to the moral growth of students.

If we were to explore seriously the ideas suggested by an ethic of caring for education, we might suggest changes in almost every aspect of schooling: the current hierarchical structure of management, the rigid mode of allocating time, the kind of relationships encouraged, the size of schools and classes, the goals of instruction, modes of evaluation, patterns of interaction, selection of content. Obviously all of these topics cannot be discussed here. I will therefore confine my analysis to the topic of relationships, which I believe is central to a thorough consideration of most of the other topics.

From the perspective of caring, the growth of those cared for is a matter of central importance. Feminists are certainly not the first to point this out. For John Dewey, for example, the centrality of growth implied major changes in the traditional patterns of schooling. In particular, since a major teacher function is to guide students in a well-informed exploration of areas meaningful to them, learning objectives must be mutually constructed by students and teachers (Dewey [1938] 1963). Dewey was unequivocal in his insistence on the mutuality of this task. Teachers have an obligation to support, anticipate, evaluate, and encourage worthwhile activities, and students have a right to pursue projects mutually constructed and approved. It has long been recognized that Dewey's recommendations require teachers who are superbly well educated, people who know the basic fields of study so well that they can spot naive interests that hold promise for rigorous intellectual activity.

There is, however, more than intellectual growth at stake in the teaching enterprise. Teachers, like mothers, want to produce acceptable persons—persons who will support worthy institutions, live compassionately, work productively but not obsessively, care for older and younger generations, be admired, trusted, and respected. To shape such persons, teachers need not only intellectual capabilities but also a fund of knowledge about the particular persons with whom they are working. In particular, if teachers approach their responsibility for moral education from a caring orientation rather than an ethic of principle, they cannot teach moral education as one might teach geometry or European history or English; that is, moral education cannot be formulated into a course of study or set of principles to be learned. Rather, each student must be guided toward an ethical life—or, we might say, an ethical ideal—that is relationally constructed.

The relational construction of an ethical ideal demands significant contributions from the growing ethical agent and also from those in relation with this agent. There is, clearly, a large subjective component of such an ideal; modes of behavior must be evaluated as worthy by the person living them. But there is also a significant objective component, and this is contributed by the careful guidance of a host of persons who enter into relation with the developing agent. The teacher, for example, brings his or her own subjectivity into active play in the relation but also takes responsibility for directing the student's attention to the objective conditions of choice and judgment; both teacher and student are influenced by and influence the subjectivity of other agents. Hence, in a basic and crucial sense, each of us is a relationally defined entity and not a totally autonomous agent. Our goodness and our wickedness are both, at least in part, induced, supported, enhanced, or diminished by the interventions and influence of those with whom we are related.

In every human encounter, there arises the possibility of a caring occasion (see Watson 1985). If I bump into you on the street, both of us are affected not only by the physical collision but also by what follows it. It matters whether I say, "Oh, dear, I'm so sorry," or "You fool! Can't you watch where you're going?" In every caring occasion, the parties involved must decide how they will respond to each other. Each such occasion involves negotiation of a sort: an initiation, a response, a decision to elaborate or terminate. Clearly, teaching is filled with caring occasions or, quite often, with attempts to avoid such occasions. Attempts to avoid caring occasions by the overuse of lecture without discussion, of impersonal grading in written, quantitative form, of modes of discipline that respond only to the behavior but refuse to encounter the person all risk losing opportunities for moral education and mutual growth.

Moral education, from the perspective of an ethic of caring, involves modeling, dialogue, practice, and confirmation. These components are not unique to ethics of caring, of course, but their combination and interpretation are central to this view of moral education (see Noddings 1984). Teachers model caring when they steadfastly encourage responsible self-affirmation in their students.[6] Such teachers are, of course, concerned with their students' academic achievement, but, more importantly, they are interested in the development of fully moral persons. This is not a zero-sum game. There is no reason why excellent mathematics teaching cannot enhance ethical life as well. Because the emphasis in the present discussion is on human relationships, it should be noted that the teacher models not only admirable patterns of intellectual activity but also desirable ways of interacting with people. Such teachers treat students with respect and consideration and encourage them to treat each other in a similar fashion. They use teaching moments as caring occasions.

Dialogue is essential in this approach to moral education. True dialogue is open; that is, conclusions are not held by one or more of the parties at the outset. The search for enlightenment, or responsible choice, or perspective, or means to problem solution is mutual and marked by appropriate signs of reciprocity. This does not mean that participants in dialogue must give up any principles they hold and succumb to relativism. If I firmly believe that an act one of my students has committed is wrong, I do not enter a dialogue with him on whether or not the act is wrong. Such a dialogue could not be genuine. I can, however, engage him in dialogue about the possible justification for our opposing positions, about the likely consequences of such acts to himself and others, about the personal history of my own belief. I can share my reflections with him, and he may exert considerable influence on me by pointing out that I have not suffered the sort of experience that led him to his act. Clearly, time is required for such dialogue. Teacher and student must know each other well enough for trust to develop.

The caring teacher also wants students to have practice in caring. This suggests changes beyond the well-intended inclusion of community service in high school graduation requirements. Service, after all, can be rendered in either caring or noncaring ways. In a classroom dedicated to caring, students are encouraged to support each other; opportunities for peer interaction are provided, and the quality of that interaction is as important (to both teacher and students) as the academic outcomes. Small group work may enhance achievement in mathematics, for example, and can also provide caring occasions. The object is to develop a caring community through modeling, dialogue, and practice.

Although modeling, dialogue, practice, and confirmation are all important, the component I wish to emphasize here is confirmation. In caring or maternal thinking, we often use caring occasions to confirm the cared for. The idea here is to shape an acceptable child by assisting in the construction of his ethical ideal. He has a picture of a good self, and we, too, have such a picture. But as adults we have experience that enables us to envision and appreciate a great host of wonderful selves—people with all sorts of talents, projects, ethical strengths, and weaknesses kept courageously under control. As we come to understand what the child wants to be and what we can honestly approve in him, we know what to encourage. We know how to respond to his acts—both those we approve and those we disapprove. When he does something of which we disapprove, we can often impute a worthy motive for an otherwise unworthy act. Indeed, this is a central aspect of confirmation. "When we attribute the best possible motive consonant with reality to the cared-for, we confirm him; that is, we reveal to him an attainable image of himself that is lovelier than that manifested in his present acts. In an important sense, we embrace him as one with us in devotion to caring. In education, what we reveal to a student about himself as an ethical and intellectual being has the power to nurture the ethical ideal or to destroy it" (Noddings 1984, p. 193).

Confirmation is of such importance in moral education that we must ask about the settings in which it can effectively take place. Educators often come close to recognizing the significance of confirmation in a simplistic way. We talk about the importance of expectations, for example, and urge teachers to have high expectations for all their students. But, taken as a formula, this is an empty exhortation. If, without knowing a student—what he loves, strives for, fears, hopes—I merely expect him to do uniformly well in everything I present to him, I treat him like an unreflective animal. A high expectation can be a mark of respect, but so can a relatively low one. If a mathematics teacher knows, for example, that one of her students, Rose, is talented in art and wants more than anything to be an artist, the teacher may properly lower her expectations for Rose in math. Indeed, she and Rose may consciously work together to construct a mathematical experience for Rose that will honestly satisfy the institution, take as little of Rose's effort as possible, and preserve the teacher's integrity as a mathematics teacher. Teacher and student may chat about art, and the teacher may learn something. They will surely talk about the requirements for the art schools to which Rose intends to apply—their GPA demands, how much math they require, and the like. Teacher and student become partners in fostering the student's growth. The student accepts responsibility for both completion of the work negotiated and the mutually constructed decision to do just this much mathematics. This is illustrative of responsible self-affirmation. The picture painted here is so vastly different from the one pressed on teachers currently that it seems almost alien. To confirm in this relational fashion, teachers need a setting different from those we place them in today.

To be responsible participants in the construction of ethical ideals, teachers need more time with students than we currently allow them. If we cared deeply about fostering growth and shaping both acceptable and caring people, we could surely find ways to extend contact between teachers and students. There is no good reason why teachers should not stay with one group of students for three years rather than one in the elementary years, and this arrangement can be adapted to high school as well. A mathematics teacher might, for example, take on a group of students when they enter high school and guide them through their entire high school mathematics curriculum. The advantages in such a scheme are obvious and multiple: First, a setting may be established in which moral education is possible—teacher and students can develop a relation that makes confirmation possible. Second, academic and professional benefits may be realized—the teacher may enjoy the stimulation of a variety of mathematical subjects and avoid the deadly boredom of teaching five classes of Algebra I; the teacher may come to understand the whole math curriculum and not just a tiny part of it; the teacher takes on true responsibility for students' mathematical development, in contrast to the narrow accountability of teachers today; the teacher encounters relatively few new students each year and welcomes back many that she already knows well.

Are there disadvantages? Those usually mentioned are artifacts of the present system. Some people ask, for example, what would happen to students who are assigned to poor teachers for three or four years. One answer is that students should not have a demonstrably poor teacher for even one year, but a better answer is to follow out the implications of this fear. My suggestion is that students and teachers stay together by mutual consent and with the approval of parents. Ultimately, really poor teachers would be squeezed out in such a system, and all the fuss and feathers of detailed administrative evaluation would be cut considerably. Supportive and substantial supervision would be required instead, because teachers—now deeply and clearly responsible for a significant chunk of their students' growth—might well seek to foster their own growth and, thus, ensure a steady stream of satisfied clients.

Suggestions like the one above for extended contact—or like Sizer's alternative idea that teachers teach two subjects to 30 students rather than one subject to 60 (Sizer 1984)—are not simplistic, nor are they offered as panaceas. They would require imagination, perseverance, changes in training, and diligence to implement, but they can be accomplished. Indeed, these ideas have been used successfully and deserve wider trials. (I myself had this sort of experience in twelve years of teaching in grades 6–12.)

It sometimes seems to feminists and other radical thinkers that this society, including education as an institution, does not really want to solve its problems. There is too much at stake, too much to be lost by those already in positions of power, to risk genuine attempts at solution. What must be maintained, it seems, are the *problems,* and the more complex the better, for then all sorts of experts are required, and, as the problems proliferate (proliferation by definition is especially efficient), still more experts are needed. Helpers come to have an investment in the helping system and their own place in it rather than in the empowerment of their clients.[7]

I have discussed here just one major change that can be rather easily accomplished in establishing settings more conducive to caring and, thus, to moral education. Such a change would induce further changes, for, when we think from this perspective, everything we do in teaching comes under reevaluation. In the fifties, the nation moved toward larger high schools, in part because the influential Conant report persuaded us that only sufficiently large schools could supply the sophisticated academic programs that the nation wanted to make its first priority (Conant 1959). Now we might do well to suggest smaller schools that might allow us to embrace older priorities, newly critiqued and defined, and work toward an educational system proudly oriented toward the development of decent, caring, loved, and loving persons.

WHAT RESEARCH CAN CONTRIBUTE

If it is not already obvious, let me say explicitly that I think university educators and researchers are part of the problem. Our endless focus on narrow achievement goals, our obsession with sophisticated schemes of evaluation and measurement directed (naturally enough) at things that are relatively easy to measure, our reinforcement of the mad desire to be number one—to compete, to win awards, to acquire more and more of whatever is currently valued—in all these ways we contribute to the proliferation of problems and malaise.

Can researchers play a more constructive role? Consider some possibilities. First, by giving some attention to topics involving affective growth, character, social relations, sharing, and the pursuit of individual projects, researchers can give added legitimacy to educational goals in all these areas. A sign of our neglect is the almost total omission of such topics from the 987 pages of the third *Handbook of Research on Teaching* (Wittrock 1986). Second, researchers can purposefully seek out situations in which educators are trying to establish settings more conducive to moral growth and study these attempts at some length, over a broad range of goals, and with constructive appreciation. That last phrase, "with constructive appreciation," suggests a third way in which researchers might help to solve problems rather than aggravate them. In a recent article on fidelity, I argued:

> In educational research, fidelity to persons counsels us to choose our problems in such a way that the knowledge gained will promote individual growth and maintain the caring community. It is not clear that we are sufficiently concerned with either criterion at present. William Torbert, for example, has noted that educational research has been oddly uneducational and suggests that one reason for this may be the failure of researchers to engage in collaborative inquiry [see Torbert 1981]. There is a pragmatic side to this problem, of course, but from an ethical perspective, the difficulty may be identified as a failure to meet colleagues in genuine mutuality. Researchers have perhaps too often made *persons* (teachers and students) the objects of research. An alternative is to choose *problems* that interest and concern researchers, students, and teachers. [Noddings 1986, p. 506]

Here, again, feminists join thinkers like Torbert to endorse modes of research that are directed at the needs rather than the shortcomings and peculiarities of subjects. Dorothy Smith, a sociologist of knowledge, has called for a science *for* women rather than *about* women; "that is," she says, "a sociology which does not transform those it studies into objects but preserves in its analytic procedures the presence of the subject as actor and experiencer. Subject then is that knower whose grasp of the world may be enlarged by the work of the sociologist" (Smith 1981, p. 1).

Similarly, research *for* teaching would concern itself with the needs, views, and actual experience of teachers rather than with the outcomes produced through various instructional procedures. This is not to say that contrasting methods should not be studied, but, when they are studied, researchers should recognize that the commitment of teachers may significantly affect the results obtained through a given method. Research *for* teaching would not treat teachers as interchangeable parts in instructional procedures, but, rather, as professionals capable of making informed choices among proffered alternatives.

Research *for* teaching would address itself to the needs of teachers—much as pharmaceutical research addresses itself to the needs of practicing physicians. This suggests that research and development should become partners in education, as they have in industry. Instead of bemoaning the apparent fact that few teachers use small group methods, for example, researchers could ask teachers what they need to engage in such work comfortably. One answer to this might be materials. Researchers often assume that the answer is training, because this answer better fits their own preparation and research timetables. If materials are needed, however, the partnership of research and development becomes crucial.

Qualitative research may suppose that their methods are more compatible with research *for* teaching than the usual quantitative methods. Indeed, Margaret Mead said of fieldwork: "Anthropological research does not have subjects. We work with informants in an atmosphere of trust and mutual respect" (Mead 1969, p. 371).

But qualitative researchers, too, can forget that they are part of an educational enterprise that should support a caring community. Qualitative studies that portray teachers as stupid, callous, indifferent, ignorant, or dogmatic do little to improve the conditions of teaching or teachers. I am not arguing that no teachers are stupid, callous, indifferent, and so forth. Rather, I am arguing that teachers so described are sometimes betrayed by the very researchers to whom they have generously given access. What should we do when we come upon gross ignorance or incompetence? One of my colleagues argues strongly that it is our duty to expose incompetence. Would you keep silent if you observed child abuse? he asks. The answer to this is, of course, that we cannot remain silent about child abuse, and it is conceivable that some events we observe as researchers are so dangerous or worrisome that we simply must report them. But at that point, I would say, our research ends. We feel compelled to take up our duties as responsible citizens and to relinquish our quest for knowledge. So long as we seek knowledge in classrooms, we are necessarily dependent on the teachers and students who are there engaged in a constitutively ethical enterprise. To intrude on that, to betray a trust that lets us in, to rupture the possibility of developing a caring community, is to forget that we should be doing research *for* teaching.

Does this mean that we cannot report failures in the classrooms we study? Of course not. But just as we ask teachers to treat the success and failure of students with exquisite sensitivity, we should study teacher success and failure generously and report on it constructively. Teachers may be eager to explore their own failures if their successes are also acknowledged and if the failures are thoroughly explored to locate the preconditions and lacks responsible for them. Teachers, too, need confirmation.

CONCLUSION

I have suggested that moral education has long been and should continue to be a primary concern of educational institutions. To approach moral education from the perspective of caring, teachers, teacher-educators, students, and researchers need time to engage in modeling, dialogue, practice, and confirmation. This suggests that ways be explored to increase the contact between teachers and students and between researchers and teachers, so that collaborative inquiry may be maintained and so that relationships may develop through which all participants are supported in their quest for better ethical selves.

Notes

1. This is a question that was seriously asked by Carl Bereiter in 1973. See Bereiter 1973.
2. See the vivid and well-documented description of this attitude in Maguire 1978, pp. 424–29.
3. Bernard Williams (1985), e.g., argues that philosophy plays a limited role in the recreation of ethical life. Alasdair MacIntyre (1984), too, argues that morality and ethics

belong primarily to the domain of social experience and that philosophy must proceed from there.

4. Daniel C. Maguire (1978) has also described approaches to relational ethics.

5. For a fuller analysis of the roles of each, see Noddings 1984.

6. Paolo Freire (1970) describes as oppression any situation in which one person hinders another in "his pursuit of self-affirmation as a responsible person."

7. For a discussion of this unhappy result, see Freire 1970; see also Sartre 1949.

References

Bereiter, Carl. *Must We Educate?* Englewood Cliffs, N.J.: Prentice-Hall, 1973.

Bobbitt, Franklin. *What the Schools Teach and Might Teach*. Cleveland: Survey Committee of the Cleveland Foundation, 1915.

Boyer, Ernest L. *High School: A Report on Secondary Education in America*. New York: Harper & Row, 1983.

Carr, John W. "Introduction." In *Character Lessons,* by James Terry White. New York: Character Development League, 1909.

Conant, James B. *The American High School Today*. New York: McGraw-Hill, 1959.

———. *The Comprehensive High School*. New York: McGraw-Hill, 1967.

Dewey, John. *Experience and Education*. 1938. Reprint. New York: Collier, 1963.

Fletcher, Joseph. "The 'Right' to Live and the 'Right' to Die." In *Beneficent Euthanasia,* edited by Marvin Kohl. Buffalo, N.Y.: Prometheus, 1975.

Freire, Paolo. *Pedagogy of the Oppressed,* translated by Myra Bergman Ramos. New York: Herder & Herder, 1970.

Gann, L. H., and Peter Duignan. *The Hispanics in the United States: A History*. Boulder, Colo.: Westview, 1986.

———. "How Should the U.S. Deal with Multicultural Schoolchildren?" *Stanford University Campus Report,* March 4, 1987.

Gilligan, Carol. *In A Different Voice*. Cambridge, Mass.: Harvard University Press, 1982.

Kohlberg, Lawrence. *The Philosophy of Moral Development*. San Francisco: Harper & Row, 1981.

———. *The Psychology of Moral Development*. San Francisco: Harper & Row, 1984.

MacIntyre, Alasdair. *After Virtue,* 2d ed. Notre Dame, Ind.: University of Notre Dame Press, 1984.

Maguire, Daniel C. *The Moral Choice*. Garden City, N.J.: Doubleday, 1978.

Mayeroff, Milton. *On Caring*. New York: Harper & Row, 1971.

Mead, Margaret. "Research with Human Beings: A Model Derived from Anthropological Field Practice." *Daedalus* 98 (1969): 361–86.

A Nation Prepared: Teachers for the 21st Century. Report of the Task Force on Teaching as a Profession. New York: Carnegie Forum on Education and the Economy, 1986.

Noddings, Nel. *Caring: A Feminine Approach to Ethics and Moral Education*. Berkeley and Los Angeles: University of California Press, 1984.

———. "Fidelity in Teaching, Teacher Education, and Research for Teaching." *Harvard Educational Review* 56 (1986): 496–510.

Ruddick, Sara. "Maternal Thinking." In *Women and Values,* edited by Marilyn Pearsall. Belmont, Calif.: Wadsworth, 1986.

Satre, Jean-Paul. *What Is Literature?* translated by Bernard Frechtman. New York: Philosophical Library, 1949.

Sizer, Theodore R. *Horace's Compromise: The Dilemma of the American High School*. Boston: Houghton Mifflin, 1984.

Smith, Dorothy. "The Experienced World as Problematic: A Feminist Method." Sorokin Lecture no. 12. Saskatoon: University of Saskatchewan, 1981.

Tomorrow's Teachers: A Report of the Holmes Group. East Lansing, Mich.: The Holmes Group, 1986.

Torbert, William. "Why Educational Research Has Been So Uneducational: The Case for a New Model of Social Science Based on Collaborative Inquiry." In *Human Inquiry,* edited by Peter Reason and John Rowan. New York: Wiley, 1981.

Tyack, David, and Elizabeth Hansot. *Managers of Virtue.* New York: Basic, 1982.

Watson, Jean. *Nursing: Human Science and Human Care.* East Norwalk, Conn.: Appleton-Century-Crofts, 1985.

Williams, Bernard. *Ethics and the Limits of Philosophy.* Cambridge, Mass.: Harvard University Press, 1985.

Wittrock, Merlin C., ed. *Handbook of Research on Teaching.* New York: Macmillan, 1986.

12

BEYOND GENDER: EQUITY ISSUES FOR HOME ECONOMICS EDUCATION

Patricia J. Thompson

A major premise of feminism is that women have been defined as "the other" (de Beauvoir, 1952/1974). A corollary to this idea is that, in a society defined by men, women have been both invisible and voiceless. To the home economics professional—whether in education, business, government, or the home—such ideas have special poignancy. Home economics can be described as the "other" women's movement. To many, it is not even there. Home economics is an invisible part of the curriculum. Its practitioners are routinely denied the opportunity to speak "in their own voice." These existential problems are a challenge for home economics, a female-defined discipline never intended to be "for women only."

The field of home economics has been generally neglected within the literature focused on women, feminism, and education. During the ascendancy of the women's movement, some feminists saw home economics as "the enemy" (Cooper, 1972, p. 13). Home economics became a convenient scapegoat for the ills that had befallen women in their traditional roles.

In 1984, the same year that Gloria Steinem, a founder of *Ms.* magazine, celebrated her 50th birthday, home economics celebrated its 75th anniversary as a discipline with a professional organization. The American Home Economics Association was founded in 1909 as a result of 10 Lake Placid Conferences. Most feminists are not drawn to a detailed study of home economics and its history. However, it is as true for women as it is for others that those who are ignorant of their history will be condemned to repeat it.

Dorothy Storck (1985), a columnist for the *Philadelphia Inquirer,* mused on this odd state of affairs:

> I never took Home Ec in high school, but sometimes I'd pass the class and glance in at the sewing machines and nutrition charts and upturned girlish faces, and I'd dash to the hockey field, where, to my mind, freedom from housework lay.
>
> It never occurred to me that while I was fleeing the inequality of work in the home, I wasn't running toward much in the way of equal rights anywhere else. Nobody offered me a place on the boys' hockey team.

Home Ec in those days was Home ick. It was what you schemed to get out of at home. It was for girls who thumbed through *Bride* magazine instead of pre-law books.

I confess I still clung to that notion this week when I went to the Civic Center to interview Geraldine Ferraro, keynote speaker at the 76th national convention of the American Home Economics Association.

I was not prepared for the magnitude of the convention, for the range of the subjects and workshops, for the power of some of the speakers.

I was not prepared, once again, for the shifts that have taken place in a part of society that has been unexamined—by me—while I have been battling elsewhere. It may be feminists' destiny always to look back in wonder. We do seem to concentrate on the surges of discovery rather than the ensuing waves. (p. B-1)

Storck's commentary reveals the subtle ways in which gender stereotypes sometimes backfire. Storck raises important points that reach back over the past decades of the women's movement, women's education, and the changing field of home economics.

THE DILEMMA OF DOMESTICITY

Twenty years after the modern women's movement, a new generation of women continues to invest self-esteem and energy in the maintenance of households and families. Even the daughters of feminists express the wish to marry and to mother (Bolotin, 1982). What was once "the feminine mystique" has become today the "dilemma of domesticity." Women still embark on long-term commitments to bear and rear children. So compelling is this need that women in surprising numbers choose to become single parents rather than forego the domestic option. Is such commitment purely a product of sex role socialization, the result of collective stupidity, passivity, and oppression? Or is it, at least in part, something more?

Feminist scholars offer fresh insights into the dynamics of female social and intellectual development. Miller, in *Toward a New Psychology of Women* (1975), observes that society does not recognize most so-called women's work as "real activity" because it is usually associated with others' development rather than self-enhancement or self-employment (p. 53). She notes that a woman cannot use her own life activity to build an image of herself based on an authentic reflection of what she actually is and does. Miller says:

In the course of projecting into women's domain some of its most troublesome and problematic exigencies, male-led society may also have simultaneously, and unwittingly, delegated to women not humanity's "lowest needs" but its "highest necessities"—that is, the intense emotionally connected cooperation and creativity necessary for human life and growth. (pp. 25–26)

According to Gilligan (1977, 1979, 1982), girls and boys, women and men, pursue moral ends along different emotional and ethical vectors. Her work reveals the development of an "ethics of care" that motivates many women to remain connected, even when to do so leads to their physical or material disadvantage.

Elshtain (1982) delineates the public/private dichotomy and recognizes its challenge to feminists, saying that "the end point of the feminist argumentation . . .

requires that women, in the name of feminism, embrace the terms of public life that was created by men who had rejected or devalued the world of the traditionally 'feminine' with its 'softer' virtues" (p. 447). She says:

> I would never tell any woman who claims such work (i.e., homemaking) made her life fuller that she was wrong-headed. But I would also never tell a harassed, exploited woman worker that labor outside the home was her freedom, whether she wanted it or not. (1983, p. 253)

It is not fashionable today to ask the extent to which gender, intellect, interest, and knowledge are related and how they influence our perception of the "ideal" education for women as they do the "ideal" education for men. The assumption that gender generates intellectual dualism becomes untenable when we consider that males and females cross gender lines in aptitudes, interests, and occupations (Klein, 1985).

NEEDED: A NEW PARADIGM FOR WOMEN

Male-defined elitism assumes that male-designed educational priorities, curricula, values, and social rewards are also best for women. According to Rich (1979):

> The early feminists, the women intellectuals of the past, along with educated men, assumed that the intellectual structure as well as the contents of the education available to men was viable: that is, enduring, universal, a discipline civilizing to the mind and sensitizing to the spirit. Its claims for both humanism and objectivity went unquestioned. (p. 131)

The model proposed here is in its conceptual infancy, yet holds promise to break the grip of a "masculist" paradigm on female thought. The French *Annales* school attempted (among other things) to demasculinize history. *Annales* historians employ a metaphorical model with classical roots that has singular applicability for home economics (Thompson, 1985, 1986a, 1986b). It may also have relevance for feminists and women scholars in other disciplines.

In the *Annales* canon, the space of human action has a dual aspect that corresponds to the public and private spheres so familiar in contemporary feminist thought. The public space/sphere/world is visible and masculine. It is called "Hermean," after the messenger god Hermes, the Greek god of communication. By contrast, the private space/sphere/world is invisible and feminine. It is called "Hestian," after Hestia, the Greek goddess of hearth and home.

Unlike other gods and goddesses who received anthropomorphic characteristics, the symbol of Hestia was the hearth's living flame. So powerful was this symbol that burning coals from a public hearth were ritually taken from an old city state (polis) to the public hearth of a new one. Hestia's flame symbolized family connection, continuity, and the interdependence of the public and private spheres.

This invisible Hestian space is also the realm of everyday necessity that the ancient Greek male establishment devalued in favor of the life of the mind. This elitist dualism (as much as sexist gender dichotomies) has placed a mental straitjacket on subsequent Western thought and action. The Greeks assumed that slaves and women should perform the private sphere functions (i.e., "housework") demanded for day-to-day survival. This arrangement gave males—i.e., the free male citizens of the polis—the leisure to engage in the "intellectual work" demanded in the public world of the agora and the secluded groves of academe.

Behind this public facade lay the invisible, feminine Hestian space that is the life world of women as it exists historically and cross-culturally. Speaking phenomenologically, the Hermean world is concrete and manifest. By contrast, the Hestian world is immanent and latent, a world continually in the process of becoming.

The Hermean and Hestian domains are not mirror images of one another. They exist in *relation*. They are distinctive, yet complementary and interdependent. They are more amenable to systems thinking than to linear thinking. Males predominate in the valued Hermean sphere. Females predominate in the devalued Hestian sphere. Consequently, it has become privatized, feminized, and otherized.

The two systems form each other's boundaries, however. They exist simultaneously, each dependent on the other. In systems terms, they interface. Transactions (inputs and outputs) take place across their boundaries. The two spheres exist in dialectic relation—interdependent, interconnected, and interactive. To understand home economics requires a shift from a male-defined Hermean mind-set to a female-defined Hestian mind-set. This perceptual shift brings a holistic reality into focus and takes us beyond gender to more complex levels of social and intellectual organization.

Shifting the ground from gender-fixated discourse to one of the Hermean and Hestian domains permits syntheses of woman-centered knowledge from many disciplines and allows women to reconnect and to assert their primacy with respect to perennial human problems from a Hestian perspective. Rich (1979) spoke in a Hestian voice when she wrote:

> If we conceive of feminism as more than a frivolous label, if we conceive of it as an ethics, a methodology, a more complex way of thinking about, thus more responsibly acting upon, the conditions of human life, we need a self-knowledge which can only develop through a steady, passionate attention to *all* female experience. I cannot imagine a feminist evolution leading to radical change in the private/political realm of gender that is not rooted in the conviction that all women's lives are important; that the lives of men cannot be understood by burying the lives of women; and that to make visible the full meaning of women's experience, to reinterpret knowledge in terms of that experience, is now the most important task of thinking. (p. 213)

This would necessitate rethinking attitudes toward home economics.

THE BIRTH OF DOMESTIC SCIENCE

The idea of home economics (knowledge for the Hestian sphere) can be traced to antiquity in the Bible (Exod. 18:17–18), Book I of Aristotle's *Politics,* Xenophon's *Oekonomicus,* and Francis Bacon's "Salomon's House" in *The New Atlantis* (Costantakos, 1984). These works share the connecting thread of a Hestian focus on the practical matters of everyday life—what Miller (1975) calls humanity's highest necessities. Home economics education is the knowledge system organized to deal with such matters intelligently and effectively.

In the United States, the first glimmer of the domestic science idea appeared in the work of Benjamin Thompson (Count Rumford), a Tory physicist, chemist, and humanitarian who once appealed to King George III to establish a public institution for the application of science to the common purposes of life. Rumford turned a measure of his formidable talents to practical innovations for the household and to the scientific study of nutrition (Brown, 1979). Other scientists followed, but when such applied study was proposed at Harvard, the idea was rejected as unsuited to a liberal arts college. The Massachusetts Institute of Technology was then established to meet the need for a school of applied science.

Emma Willard proposed the retention of "housewifery" (i.e., Hestian knowledge) in women's higher education to provide the intellectual and esthetic training necessary to regulate the practical, everyday concerns of households (Ferrar, 1964, p. 4). In 1841, Catharine Beecher laid out the first comprehensive, systematically organized knowledge for the Hestian sphere in *A Treatise on Domestic Economy* (Beecher, 1841/1848). It included state-of-the-art information to be utilized in households. Beecher's plea was, in effect, that the comparable worth of the Hestian and Hermean spheres must be recognized. Historically, public education has been dominated by the Hermean paradigm. The Hestian paradigm persists in home economics education.

The nineteenth century domestic science movement grew, helped in large part by the establishment of the land grant colleges and universities in 1862. The Seneca Falls conference in 1869 called women to challenge male dominance in the Hermean sphere by spearheading the movement for women's suffrage. There were, in effect, two nineteenth century women's movements—one Hermean (the suffrage movement) and one Hestian (the home economics movement). The Hermean branch emphasized the ballot; the Hestian branch emphasized education, especially education grounded in the knowledge needs of women. Hilton (1972) points out that a comprehensive social and intellectual history of American women would have to take both movements into account.

A KNOWLEDGE SYSTEM—NOT A GENDER SYSTEM

Over a ten-year period (1899–1908), a number of women and some men, under the leadership of Ellen H. Swallow-Richards, a Vassar-educated chemist who was the Massachusetts Institute of Technology's first female instructor, met to define the focus of the domestic science movement for the twentieth century. They identified it as the family and the home, both Hestian institutions. After much discussion, in which they rejected the name *ecology*, they agreed on *home economics*. They were, in fact, wrestling with issues of Hestian education in an era when immigration, industrialization, and urbanization in the Hermean sphere were generating unprecedented pressures in the Hestian sphere.

As defined in the Lake Placid Conference *Proceedings* (1902), home economics (in its most comprehensive sense) was to be "the study of the laws, conditions, principles, and ideals which are concerned on the one hand with man's immediate physical environment and on the other hand with his nature as a social being." It was to be the special study of the relation between the two factors. Moreover, the founders characterized home economics as a "philosophical subject, i.e., a study of *relation*," while the academic subjects on which it depends were "empirical in their nature and concerned with *events* and *phenomena*." It is evident that the discipline was to be one of relation and connection. Home economics sought to "bind together into a consistent whole the pieces of knowledge at present unrelated" (emphasis in original, pp. 70–71).

Dean Sarah Louise Arnold of Simmons College made the following point in 1903 at the Fifth Lake Placid Conference:

> We have come upon an altogether new classification of knowledge, and, as we attempt to build a curriculum we discover that the extension of knowledge everywhere affects us too. We are part and parcel of all the rest. ... . Since we cannot compass all knowledge and include all subjects in our curriculum, is it not the part of wisdom for us to limit our subjects to certain essentials, certain fundamentals, and gather closely about these the related knowledge which science and art have made available for us? (*Proceedings,* 1903, p. 10)

From the start this discipline, in which women were the prime movers and most consistent supporters, focused on issues of knowledge rather than gender. While the early curricula in the schools focused on such then-essential household tasks as cooking and sewing, the tasks were sustained by knowledge of science, human relations, esthetics, and ethics. As a school subject, home economics aimed to provide the learning needed for "right living." By this was meant an ethically responsible life in the Hestian sphere to complement a similar quality of life in the Hermean sphere.

As the home economics curriculum developed, and as it has evolved for over a century, it shows programmatic regularities, a consistent pattern. Its subject matter is grouped around such core Hestian concerns as family relations, child development, shelter and home furnishings, food and nutrition, clothing and textiles, and the changing technologies and social institutions associated with their production, acquisition, maintenance, and consumption in households. In the secondary schools, this knowledge cluster and its subjects are most often found under the broad rubric "consumer/homemaking." In colleges and universities, departments of home economics, for political reasons (Hermean pressures) may go by other names, including "human ecology," "human development," and "family and consumer studies/sciences/resources."

THE FIRST WOMEN'S DISCIPLINE

Not surprisingly, a discipline defined by women will look different from one defined by men. According to Chafe (1972), in the nineteenth century:

> The curriculum of women's education underwent a striking change . . . reflecting a growing concern with preparing women for marriage and the home. The founders of most women's colleges had sought as much as possible to make them carbon copies of Harvard and Yale . . . and (Vassar), Mount Holyoke, Smith, Barnard, and Bryn Mawr all insisted that they offer the same courses as the best men's colleges. By the early twentieth century, however, the older view of female colleges came under increasing attack. Ethel Puffer Howe, a Radcliffe graduate and later head of the Smith Institute, urged women's colleges in 1913 to develop courses in domestic science, eugenics, hygiene, and the aesthetics of the home in order to train women for the domestic tasks which lay ahead. In a similar vein, an insurgent group at the 1923 convention of the American Collegiate Association condemned women's colleges for

not preparing women for the occupation of homemaking and child-rearing. (p. 101, citations omitted)

Vassar introduced a short-lived interdisciplinary School of Euthenics that focused on the development and care of the family and offered a series of courses: "husband and wife," "motherhood," and "the family as an economic unit" (Chafe, 1972, p. 103). Marion Talbot of the University of Chicago proposed a graduate program in "sanitary science" that evolved out of "domestic science" and that would later become home economics (Fish, 1985).

In the first quarter of the twentieth century, interest in family care and home economics expanded (Chafe, 1972, p. 104). In part as a result of federal financing under the Smith-Lever Act, and in part as a result of demand for teachers of cooking and hygiene in the public schools, this education area grew. Chafe describes the growing tension between Hermean and Hestian values in women's higher education:

> At a time when the sexual division of labor posed the primary obstacle to the advancement of economic equality, it appeared that the nation's colleges and universities were reinforcing the image of woman as wife and mother. (p. 104)

Home economics became a women's discipline, profession, and school subject by default. Although males and females share the same basic human needs, few men were attracted to work in the Hestian domain. So long as Hermean concerns are valued above Hestian, we can expect continued disequilibrium between the two spheres.

Over the past decades, minor gender shifts in home economics enrollment at the secondary and postsecondary levels have been noted. Data collection with respect to female and male enrollment has not been consistent, however, over time and at each educational level. Nevertheless, a slight rise in male enrollments might be interpreted as a positive trend. In 1985 Peggy S. Meszaros, associate dean in the College of Home Economics at Oklahoma State University, attributed an upturn in total degrees granted to men at the bachelor's, master's, and doctoral level from 2.0 percent in 1968–1969 to 4.6 percent in 1978–79 to four factors:

- program specialization trends
- more male role models among college home economics faculty
- increasing job opportunities
- a changing social ethic that allows both males and females more flexibility in career choices. ("Issues and Answers," 1985, p. 7)

In 1983 the figure had risen to 5.8 percent ("Colleges Take Home Economics," 1985).

VOCATIONAL EDUCATION MISNAMED

As the family shifted from a production to a consumption unit, needs that had traditionally been met in the privacy of the Hestian sphere could now be met through the service sector of the Hermean sphere. Initially, home economics was conceptualized as preparing women for work in the Hestian domain, i.e., for the vocation of homemaking. *Housewifery, housework,* and *homemaking* are all terms that have been used for this labor. As the field of economics became increasingly Hermean in character, it dropped out of its definition of work unpaid labor in the home—the Hestian domain.

Vocational education and home economics—both vocational and general—are devalued when a back-to-basics movement focuses on Hermean concerns at the expense of Hestian ones. We may ask, "Whose basics?" There is a Hermean assumption, going back to the early dualism in Greek thought, that the basis of the "good life" is purely intellectual. But people every day define the good life as one in which their ongoing basic needs are reasonably well met. Even when the slave, housewife, servant, and "labor saving devices" are replaced by service workers, much invisible work remains to be done in households.

The goal of a comfortable life with esthetic and ethical meaning is not reached by mastering the traditional disciplines alone. Personal life does not manage itself any more than does public life. Human beings must do the commonplace work of fixing fuses, detecting water leaks, changing linen or tires, and keeping up with things in general. Wires do not reconnect, linen or tires do not change themselves, chicken soup does not make itself, clothing and dishes do not rearrange themselves after being automatically washed, and children do not become civilized adults without parenting. Admittedly, repetitious tasks can become onerous. But they are ineluctable and important parts of being human. In sum, the Hestian world, where invisible connections are made day by day, makes up a person's whole life. Home economics education can make the difference in the quality of that life.

SEX BIAS AND STEREOTYPING

Mears and Haynes-Clements (1983) studied sex stereotyping and sex bias in educators' attitudes toward vocational home economics programs and found that principals', guidance counselors', and home economics teachers' perceptions of the sex-role characteristics of home economics students compared with their perceptions of non-home-economics students do not indicate sex bias. Their findings also suggest that both male and female home economics students are perceived as more expressive than non-home-economics students. This indicates that they are perceived as more helpful, kind, aware of others' feelings, understanding, and warm in their relationship to others. Traditionally, society has viewed such behavior as appropriate for females but not for males (p. 28).

Sex role research has supported the concept of androgyny and the importance of individuals (irrespective of sex) possessing both masculine and feminine characteristics. Mears and Haynes-Clements's findings do not support the stereotypic view that students in home economics programs receive feminized socialization. To the contrary, "the males in home economics were seen as equally instrumental by principals and guidance counselors and more instrumental by home economics teachers than were males who did not take home economics" (p. 28).

Thus by conventional standards of masculinity, males did not appear less masculine when they enrolled in home economics. From tacit knowledge, observing males in child care, foods, or clothing labs reveals that they undertake nontraditional assignments in typical male fashion, competing goodnaturedly and exhibiting satisfaction and pride in doing Hestian tasks. Males can praise one another for successful nonsexist achievements.

Mears and Haynes-Clements also found that females enrolled in home economics courses were perceived as more instrumental than those who did not take home economics. They, too, exhibited traits that were not viewed as feminine. While stereotypical perceptions of home economics would dictate that students in home economics courses would be high on expressive and low on instrumental characteristics, this does not appear to be the case. Despite this, the investigators found that females are more frequently encouraged to take home economics than males, and this *does* reflect bias in the guidance and counseling process (p. 29).

Clearly, home economics classrooms and laboratory settings offer a unique context in which to modify sex bias and sex stereotyping that needs further objective study. To the extent that shared work in the Hestian sphere is deemed as important as shared work in the Hermean sphere, home economics must be recognized for its potential to contribute to reduced gender role stereotyping of necessary everyday tasks. It also challenges the assumption that formal teaching is essential for success in the Hermean sphere but not for success in the Hestian sphere.

EQUITY AND GENDER

In the past, home economics was not included in the conceptual frameworks related to sex equity in society and education. It was seen as a special case. It is helpful to remember that equity in Greek, Roman, and English law was the law of special cases devised in a civilized spirit to assure fairness in treatment and to make up for "blind spots" or newly emerging circumstances not anticipated in either the written or the customary law. In this sense, equity in education demands a fair share for Hestian in relation to Hermean instruction. Addressing sex equity issues primarily in terms of the gender of the participants may be a conceptual trap into which feminists, women scholars, home economists, and male educational leaders collectively fall. Before the range of sex equity issues can be considered settled, we must ask about the equity involved when a women's field of endeavor such as home economics is made invisible—even as women have been made invisible (Hoye & Merrell, 1983).

A plea for nondiscrimination on the basis of gender alone is insufficient to make the equity case for home economics. The equity issue must be framed in the Hermean *and* the Hestian contexts of knowledge. Certain essential learnings are necessary for leading a satisfying human life, and they mandate Hestian educational imperatives for both sexes even as Hermean imperatives are mandated for both sexes. Title IX makes this option feasible through scheduling both sexes for co-educational work in home economics and industrial arts. In a review of the implications of feminist research for home economics education, Bovy (1984) urges home economics educators to accept a mandate for recommitment to sex equity (pp. 315–316). Wells calls for dialogue on women's equity and home economics (1984, p. 2).

Tittle (1985, p. 17) recognizes epistemological equality as a legitimate concern for educational research. Thus we are challenged to think of minds as well as bodies, ideas as well as statistics, to determine whether today's students are being exposed to a gender-balanced curriculum. Home economics represents a "textbook case" for epistemological equality—for balance between Hermean and Hestian knowledge.

Solutions for women's disadvantaged position have been sought through expanding educational opportunities and opening the doors to traditional male professions for so long closed to them. Opening the doors of previously male institutions extends a Hermean measure of valuation invented by men for men to women.

Data concerning gender equity today often measure women's achievements by the inroads they make into fields formerly dominated by men. What have we to say about the equity of an educational system that perpetuates male-defined values and masquerades them as benefits to women? How do we count as equitable a system that encourages women to explore traditional male occupations but continues to ridicule men who choose traditionally female occupations?

CONCLUSIONS

Myths and stereotypes are hard to dispel. It is also difficult for a Hestian discipline to confront the Hermean establishment and negotiate for equitable treatment. Patriarchy is alive and well in the academy.

Home economics does not promote homemaking as the only life option open for women. But home economists do make clear the potential danger of ignoring and distorting the homemaking imperatives of the Hestian domain. For those who advocate a single standard—a Hermean standard for both women and men—the Hestian world will continue to be devalued. Such devaluation is already exacting a heavy price and can be postulated as a contributing factor in a variety of societal ills; e.g., family breakups, mental and physical health problems, spouse and child abuse, neglect of the aging, homelessness, and a quality of life that is increasingly materialistic and pointless. Is that what we want for the future?

As science has brought invisible facets of the physical world to light, the social sciences and human sciences have helped to reveal invisible facets of woman's private world and man's public world. In one way or another, we are constantly returning to the touchstones of our human and material existence: family relations, child development, food and nutrition, shelter and home furnishings, and clothing and textiles. The new scholarship on women in traditionally male-defined disciplines makes new empirical evidence concerning these perennial problem areas in human life available every day. If new knowledge for the Hestian sphere is available, is it moral or ethical to exclude it from public education?

References

Beecher, C. E. (1848). *A treatise on domestic economy.* Rev. ed. New York: Harper & Brothers. (Original work published 1841).

Bolotin, S. (1982, October 17). Voices of the post-feminist generation. *The New York Times,* pp. 28–31, 103, 106–107, 114–116.

Bovy, B. (1984). Feminist research: Implications for home economics education. In P. J. Thompson (Ed.), *Knowledge, technology, and family change* 4th Yearbook, Teacher Education Section of the American Home Economics Association, pp. 293–316. Bloomington, IN: McKnight.

Brown, S. C. (1979). *Benjamin Thompson, Count Rumford.* Cambridge: MIT Press.

Chafe, W. H. (1972). *The American woman: Her changing social, economic, and political roles, 1920–1970.* New York: Oxford University Press.

Colleges take home economics beyond the home. (1985, June 27). *New York Times,* p. C–10.

Cooper, J. (1972, April). Home economics and the women's movement. *Forecast for home economics,* pp. F–11–13.

Costantakos, C. (1984). The home economics idea: An etymological odyssey. In P. J. Thompson (Ed.), *Knowledge, technology, and family change* 4th Yearbook, Teacher Education Section of the American Home Economics Association, pp. 176–194. Bloomington, IN: McKnight.

de Beauvoir, S. (1974). *The second sex.* Reprint. New York: Vintage Books. (Original work published 1952).

Elshtain, J. B. (1982, Fall). Feminism, family and the community. *Dissent, 29* (4), 442–449.

Elshtain, J. B. (1983, Summer). Feminism and family—The radical rhetoric puts the two on a collision course. *American Educator, 7,* 20–25.

Ferrar, B. M. (1964). *The history of home economics education in America and its implications for liberal education.* Lansing, Mich.: Michigan State University.

Fish, V. K. (1985). "More than love": Marion Talbot and her role in the founding of the University of Chicago. *International Journal of Women's Studies, 8* (3), 228–249.

Gilligan, C. (1977, November). In a different voice: Women's conceptions of self and morality. *Harvard Educational Review, 47,* 481–516.

Gilligan, C. (1979, November). Woman's place in man's life cycle. *Harvard Educational Review, 49,* 431–445.

Gilligan, C. (1982). *In a different voice: Psychological theory and women's development.* Cambridge: Harvard University Press.

Hilton, H. LeB. (1972, April). Now that women are liberated. *Journal of Home Economics, 64,* 3–5.

Hoye, S. and R. Merrell. (1983). *Home economics and the challenge of feminism.* Unpublished conjoint master's thesis. Herbert H. Lehman College, CUNY, The Bronx, N.Y.

Issues and answers. (1985, Winter). *Momentum,* pp. 2,7.

Klein, S. S. (1985). *Handbook for achieving sex equity in education.* Baltimore, Md.: Johns Hopkins University Press.

Mears, R. A. and L. Haynes-Clements. (1983). *Sex stereotyping and sex bias: A study of educators' attitudes toward vocational home economics programs.* Ruston, La.: Louisiana Tech University.

Miller, J. B. (1975). *Toward a new psychology of women.* Boston: Beacon.

Proceedings of the fourth Lake Placid conference on home economics, Lake Placid, N.Y. (1902, September 16–20). Washington, D.C.: American Home Economics Association.

Proceedings of the fifth Lake Placid conference on home economics. Lake Placid, N.Y. (1908, July 7–9). Washington, D.C.: American Home Economics Association.

Rich, A. (1979). *On lies, secrets, and silence: Selected prose 1966–1978.* New York: Norton.

Storck, D. (1985, June 27). The importance of home ec. *The Philadelphia Inquirer,* p. B–1.

Thompson, P. J. (1985, June). *Clio's stepdaughters: Reclaiming our heritage.* Paper presented at the annual meeting of the American Home Economics Association, Philadelphia, Pa.

Thompson, P. J. (1986a). Home economics and the Hestian mode. *Illinois Teacher of Home Economics, 29* (3), 87–91.

Thompson, P. J. (1986b, March/April). Myth for modern home economics empowerment: Making visible our Hestian world. *What's New in Home Economics, 19,* 10–11.

Tittle, C. K. (1985). Research on sex equity in education: An agenda for the divisions, SIGS, and AERA. *Educational Researcher, 14* (9), 10–18.

Wells, J. (1984, February). Women's equity and home economics: A call for dialogue. *What's New in Home Economics, 18,* 2.

13

DILEMMAS OF KNOWING: ETHICAL AND EPISTEMOLOGICAL DIMENSIONS OF TEACHERS' WORK AND DEVELOPMENT

Nona Lyons

When the philosopher Martha Nussbaum (1986) was exploring the implications of the single-focused value schemes of Antigone and Creon, Sophocles' protagonists, she turned to examine the style of *Antigone's* choral lyrics. Believing that the enigmatic style of the lyrics revealed the play's complexity, Nussbaum wanted to look at them in light of the play's larger themes. Nussbaum concludes that the lyrics not only point to an issue of interpretation, but also signal the play's assumptions about human learning and reflection. For, she asserts, the style in which matters of human choice are discussed—like the ethical choices in *Antigone*—is not likely to be neutral; it expresses a view of human understanding. Nussbaum identifies what is at work in the lyrics of *Antigone*:

> The lyrics both show us and engender in us a process of reflection and (self) discovery that works through a persistent attention to and (re)-interpretation of concrete words, images and incidents. We reflect on an incident not by subsuming it under a general rule, not by assimilating its features to the terms of an elegant scientific procedure, but by burrowing down into the depths of the particular, finding images and connections that will permit us to see it more truly, describe it more richly. (1986, p. 69)

In comparing this Sophoclean view of human learning with a Platonic view, one she finds more single-minded, Nussbaum likens the former to Heraclitus's image of a spider sitting in the middle of its web, able to feel and respond to any tug in any part of the complicated structure:

> It advances its understanding of life and of itself not by a Platonic movement from the particular to the universal, from the perceived world to a simpler, clearer world, but by hovering in thought and imagination around the enigmatic complexities of the seen particular (as we, if we are good readers of this style, hover around the

195

details of the text), seated in the middle of its web of connections, responsive to the pull of each separate thread. . . .

The image of learning expressed in this style, like the picture of reading required by it, stresses responsiveness and an attention to complexity; it discourages the search for the simple and, above all, for the reductive. It suggests that the world of practical choice, like the text, is articulated but never exhausted by reading; that reading must reflect and not obscure this fact, showing that the particular (or the text) remains there unexhausted, the final arbiter of the correctness of our vision; that correct choice (or good interpretation) is, first and foremost, a matter of keenness and flexibility of perception, rather than of conformity to a set of simplifying principles. (Nussbaum, 1986, p. 69)

Nussbaum presents a powerful and compelling image of human learning. It serves as an unexpected yet needed metaphor for revealing aspects of the complex nature of teachers' work. It is useful too in considering ways to interpret teachers' practical choices, especially the ethical conflicts they see and try to resolve in their professional lives. For as teachers hover in thought and imagination around the needs of their students, a body of subject matter knowledge, and the ways they endeavor to have their students encounter it, they hone a craft responsive to all elements on their horizon. They find in these activities what they call ethical dilemmas. This web of teachers' work can be observed through an examination of teachers' professional experiences and practical choices; like a text, they invite attention to their details, a starting place for understanding and interpretation.

This perception of teachers' dilemmas first emerged from a study of forty-six teachers, including twenty-nine secondary school teachers, who were asked in open-ended interviews to talk about the conflicts of their professional lives—to say how they dealt with them and if they found in them moral or ethical concerns (Lyons, Cutler, and Miller, 1986). The situations reported by teachers revealed several interconnected dimensions.

An experienced history teacher presented one succinct example:

When I first started as a teacher, I was quite a showman. I was a performer. I could hold ten balls in the air at once. The kids loved it. The parents loved it. I was considered a great teacher. The kids would look up at me and say, "God, I love this course." But they weren't doing history, they were watching the show. It was only after I had been teaching six or seven years that I began to realize that I wanted to [change]. If memory serves me it was a student . . . he shared that ball metaphor with me and he said to me, "You know, you're really wonderful and it's exciting but you have to show people how to do it. When are you going to teach us how to do it?" And that really forced me, it led me to try to do that. [But] I had to make a decision. I could say, "Go away, you bother me. Everybody likes me as I am." The kids had already dedicated the yearbook to me, teaching the old way. I had gotten all this publicity, fame, whatever, from doing it as a showman. . . . I had to make a decision.

But the history teacher acknowledged something more: that responding to his student created what he termed a "moral dilemma," specifically in determining if he should respond. In that acknowledgment he at once illuminated a set of issues embedded in teachers' work and development: the intricate interactions between a teacher's knowledge and values, assumptions about knowing, a craft, and relationships. As the teacher acts to respond to his dilemma, to help his students become historians, he implies other changes as well: changes in his own relationship with his students, in his approach to his discipline and, of necessity, in his teaching practices. Seeing that having students participate in class discussions makes them foils to the achievement of his lesson, the teacher sets in motion different approaches to learning, changes his assumptions about his students as knowers and learners. In this reorganization, he comes to a new way to conceive of himself as a teacher. As he says, he did not have to respond, nor did he have to change. Yet he describes himself today as a "person who tries to teach kids how they can do what I can do." As the teacher changes, his students as "historians" will ply a different set of tasks as knowers, shifting to a new way of learning. This situation suggests that practical choices, with ethical uncertainties, which can be part of teachers' everyday interactions, may, in turn, involve their growth and development as practitioners. Here ethical and epistemological issues—issues of knowers and ways of knowing—merge in the web of teachers' work.

Although researchers, educators, and scholars have argued that knowledge and values are important dimensions of teaching implicit in a teacher's sense of mission and critical to a conception of practice, there is a remarkable absence of references to knowledge and values in descriptions of teachers' lives or in their growth and learning (Britzman, 1988; Carnegie Task Force on Teaching as a Profession, 1986; Fenstermacher, 1986; Greene, 1978; 1986; Jackson, 1968, 1986; Lightfoot, 1983; McDonald, 1988; Noddings, 1986; Sarason, 1971; Schwab, 1964; Sizer, 1984). Following his discovery of the curious omission of content knowledge from most studies of teacher evaluation and assessment, Shulman (1986, 1987) argued convincingly for new research to describe teachers' knowledge. The knowledge bases and dimensions of teaching are only now being scrutinized and identified. Teachers' thinking was not even a topic in the 1973 state-of-the-art *Second Handbook of Research on Teaching*; it appeared for the first time in 1986 in the third *Handbook* (Clark and Peterson, 1986; see also Calderhead, 1987; Clandinin and Connelly, 1987; Eisner, 1985; Halkes and Olson, 1984; Shavelson and Stern, 1981). Similarly, in spite of some recognition of the significance of the value and ethical aspects of teaching, and even of their complexity, such significance has not often been investigated empirically from the teacher's point of view (Berlak and Berlak, 1981; Fenstermacher, 1986; Jackson, 1968, 1986; Lampert, 1985; Lortie, 1975; Sarason, 1971; Strike and Soltis, 1985; Tom, 1984; Waller, 1932/1961). Indeed, McDonald's (1988) recent examination of the new rhetoric of teacher voice argues that it is above all characterized not only by knowledge but also by the tacit sense of mission, referred to above, one that creates conflict for teachers. Yet exactly how conflicts about missions occur and reflect teachers' knowledge is not very well documented.

In this article I take up these issues to examine and describe how knowledge and ethical values are implicated in teachers' professional lives and to suggest how they may be part of the dynamics of teachers' professional development. In the first part, I use examples of ethical dilemmas teachers report to illustrate the diverse ways they may arise in teachers' experience. These examples indicate how values and ideas, teachers' subject knowledge, their craft, their relationships with students, and their conceptions of themselves and of their students as knowers may all be a part of these conflicts. Three case studies of teachers are presented in some detail and aspects of others discussed. A set of ideas emerging from these data is then examined and explored, especially the interaction between teachers' perspective on knowledge and knowing and students' way of knowing. This phenomenon, the relationship between students and teachers as knowers, is provisionally characterized as *nested knowing*; that is, students and teachers are considered to have nested, interacting epistemological perspectives. Finally, more speculatively, I outline some elements of the dynamics of teachers' professional change and development. I end with a discussion of the implications of this work for research, theory, and practice.

But to take up this agenda, it seems important to state that this project turned to research traditions not usually employed in the study of teachers and teaching: it joins research from the field of moral psychology with studies of people's natural epistemologies—their ways of knowing—and brings these to the current discussion of teachers' knowledge and the knowledge bases of teaching. Three bodies of research provide a context for this discussion.

LINKING RESEARCH ON TEACHING AND TEACHERS' KNOWLEDGE WITH RESEARCH ON ETHICS AND EPISTEMOLOGY

Research in moral psychology first connected peoples' ideas of self and relationships with ways they see and deal with practical, ethical conflict (Gilligan, 1977, 1982; Lyons, 1982, 1983. See also Gilligan, Ward, and Taylor, 1988). This research, with its open-ended interview design, seeks to capture an individual's own narrative and construction of experience; it provided the starting place and the method for the work reported here. In research interviews with a primary goal of exploring aspects of teachers' experiences revealed through conflict, teachers were asked about dilemmas they faced in their professional lives and whether these had moral or ethical components, about descriptions of themselves as teachers, and about whether and how they have changed over time (Lyons, Cutler and Miller, 1986). But an examination of teachers' situations of conflict—like the history teacher's experience described earlier—raised new questions, bringing into focus how teachers' views of knowledge and knowing might be part of their ethical choices and present in their changing practices.

Currently researchers are looking explicitly at teachers' knowledge (Calderhead, 1987; Connelly and Clandinin, 1985; Eisner, 1985; Elbaz, 1983; Feiman-Nemser, 1983; Grossman and Richert, 1988; Noddings, 1985; Shulman, 1986a, b, 1987; Stodolsky, 1988). Some, following Shulman's lead, are beginning to illuminate the depth of teacher content knowledge in the disciplines of history, English, math, and science (Gudmundsdottir, 1988; Smith and Neale, 1989; Wilson, Ball, Grossman and Roth, 1989; Wilson and Wineburg, 1988), to characterize teachers' pedagogical content knowledge (Smith and Neale, 1989; Wilson, Shulman, and Richert, 1987) and their knowledge in action, what Shulman calls "strategic" knowledge (Shulman, 1986b; see also Schön, 1983). Others seek to understand personal knowledge (Clandinin and Connelly, 1987) or to identify knowledge structures (Roehler, Duffy, Hermann, Conley, and Johnson, 1988). But the work reported here, while focusing on teachers' knowledge, needed a different perspective; it raised questions about the teachers' own stance toward knowledge, both within a discipline and toward the student as a knower. The emergence of these epistemological aspects of teachers' practical conflicts in the teacher interviews shifted attention to yet a third line of research, research in epistemology.

The work of Belenky, Clinchy, Goldberger, and Tarule (1986), like that of Perry (1970), explores people's ways of knowing and directly connects them to questions of value—to people's ethical ideas of good and bad, right and wrong. In addition, these researchers identify and describe different epistemological perspectives, suggesting that people can, over time, hold very different views of truth, authority, and knowledge as knowers, moving, for example, from the notion of one truth or one "right" way to the notion of the relativism of all knowledge, that is, that all knowledge is a human construction. It is this work—coupled with recent feminist views of different theories of knowledge (Bartlett, 1990)—which, I believe, provides a useful conceptual framework for interpreting the experiences of the teachers revealed in the interviews. This framework is outlined in detail below.

Here, in what follows, it is my purpose to present through interview data aspects of the ethical and epistemological dimensions of teachers' work and some of the detail of practitioners' reflective conversations with situations that may lead to change. This hovering in thought and imagination around teachers' thinking can, I believe, help to explain why a history teacher found in a response to a student an ethical dilemma, one that simultaneously made him reflective about his practice and determined to change (Geertz, 1973; Mishler, 1986; Schön, 1983).

ETHICAL AND EPISTEMOLOGICAL DIMENSIONS OF TEACHERS' PRACTICAL CONFLICTS

Chris Smith, an English teacher in his second year of teaching, articulated what he saw as characteristics of teachers' dilemmas. He paused as he speculated about a dilemma he faced, one not at first glance a likely example of conflict:

> I guess when I think of conflict, I think of an immediate situation where there's a head-on clash. But I think also of this kind of conflict that I think is a lot more like ones that classroom teachers face more frequently; which is a conflict spread out over time, that involves getting to know a student and establishing a relationship, a working relationship, and sort of being in a tenuous situation that by no means is going to succeed. There is no guarantee of success and that sort of requires day-in and day-out input and feedback on your part and also interaction and feedback [from the student], so that you can have at least the slightest hope of getting through the year successfully.

Describing what he termed a moral dilemma, Smith recounted a situation he faced as a new junior high school teacher with a student—a boy, "bright, but easily out of control." The problem was "how to deal with him and keep him directed . . . and, keep the relationship such that, what could easily deteriorate into [something] detrimental to you and to him and to the classroom in general, did not." Smith recognized that he could take a "real low course and allow him to sort of skate through and not learn and accomplish anything but not disturb you and not be a presence," yet he also believes "you can try and get him to do something and to work through the year so he passes." As Smith describes his struggle to find a way, he reveals how this situation is rooted in his own set of values and how it also relates to his ideas of practice.

"If your obligation as a teacher is not simply to contain children but to help them overcome weaknesses," then, he says, one must search for ways to reach

each one, "to find out what areas he could excel in and grow in, allowing him to bend certain assignments." But, he finds, there is not an instant solution. "So what you are dealing with is a situation that you have to try to live with and improve, with no guarantee of success or endpoint." And, as Smith discovered, there are days when the kid falls down, as when a substitute was in and "he did things that were crazy, ripping books and going toe to toe with the substitute," undermining everything that he had done for the entire year. In that situation, Smith sees:

> Your natural reaction is to say, "Yeah, I am going out of my way," and then you have the other feeling, which is to say, "he is a thirteen- or fourteen-year-old kid. He's slipped, but children slip all the time." So you've got two sides of the problem that don't really mesh very well and you as a teacher and an adult have to take up some of the slack and swallow some of the frustration and try to get on with it, you know.

What creates the dilemma for this teacher is his own expectations and sense of integrity; something, he says, that develops out of a perception of the environment, the work he does, and his sense of what kids' needs are nowadays. He sketches his hopes for this student:

> When he leaves here [I hope] that he doesn't perceive it as having been a wasted time. I want him to have a sense of having had a relationship with a teacher that meant something and a sense of trust in someone. I want him to believe that there are people who are willing to help him. He is in a way such a survivor, you know, but it is without outside assistance. . . . I want him to feel that there are other people he can work with . . . that he can trust people.

Smith describes how this dilemma goes to the question of his craft and ultimately to any notion of his change as a professional:

> Well you know, the . . . heart of the question is, am I able to cultivate new styles for dealing with students? In other words, was my working this situation out with him something that was really the result of who I am and what my style is, and did I choose it simply because of that? Or did I really consult the situation, to think what the best way would be and then, whether or not it went against the grain, took that?

In these responses it is evident that any given dilemma is likely to emerge in its particularity because of who the teacher is. As Smith states, in doing his job there is a sense of living up to "who you are: of yourself, your professionalism, your expertise, your values." Because this is so, standards held are not arbitrary but honed out of the teacher's own perceptions of the context of the school in its community, the lives of students, and their needs. Smith can ask himself if how he dealt with his conflict was really "a result of who I am or if I really did consult the situation," to think of what was the best way. Thus, linking the dilemma with his sense of self, his relationship with his student, and his pedagogical response, he asks if what he did was enough. Did he perhaps not pursue something he in fact saw and knew but needed to acknowledge in order to create an appropriate response to his student?

In his thinking, Chris Smith captures and articulates aspects of dilemmas other teachers have also described: dilemmas that come out of working relationships between people, like those between student and teacher, that are fed by the everyday interactions between them, that happen over time, and that have no real guarantee of success even though they require daily response and action. However resolved, the teacher lives with conflict and is faced with how and if "to take up the slack."

Another teacher, Caroline Brett, a high school history teacher, similarly points to her relationship with a student as the source of a conflict; but, for her, the dilemma is of a different kind. Having recently joined the faculty of a diverse urban high school after some six years of teaching in another school, Brett describes the shift as "tough, coming from a structured environment to one relatively structure free," Teaching a unit in her "World Cultures" class on South Africa and attempting to make sense out of a controversial issue, she finds that "as a Black American," she could not divorce herself from the situation of Black South Africans. Determined not "to give voice to White South Africa," she encounters several dilemmas:

> One is clearly, if a student expects to hear both sides, both sides of an issue, there's one side that is going to be left out and that's the White South African side. And secondly, it is hard to divorce myself as a Black American, as an African American, from the situation of Black South Africans. So that in trying to present all that, in the South African scenario, students may not quite understand the reasons behind the kind of presentation they are getting and some of them would want to question that and that would be okay. But they may not be happy with the answer, they just may not be happy with me.

This in fact proved difficult, because a student did counter her position. Brett presented her view "that Blacks in South Africa had been discriminated against unjustly by White South Africans and that no matter who you were within the White community, you still had privileges above and beyond those a Black South African could hope to have." A student then tried to raise an issue, suggesting that there might be exceptions to that, that there were other situations of unfairness and injustice, like what happened to the Jews. Wanting her students to focus on Black South Africans and their situation only, to see them in their own right and not in comparison with others in situations of oppression, Brett would not allow that comparison. She recognized her quandary. "My difficulty lay in identifying with Black South Africans and trying to help her see the degree of discrimination [only Blacks experienced]. But the student didn't feel comfortable with that response." For the teacher, that was difficult:

> It was difficult to know how to express my feelings in a moral way, in a way that did not seem disrespectful and mean and racist. I mean those things are immoral and I mean I took a big risk in responding the way I did . . . that was a kind of moral dilemma, . . . Do we as teachers try to couch our truthful responses, choose to give our kids the truth or do we choose to make it look nice and presentable and okay for them to hear? And to deal with? And I guess I come down on the hard core reality that isn't always nice. And that can have difficult consequences.

Seeing that the dilemma resides in the nature of the knowledge she wants her students to acquire, Brett continues:

> When you deal with controversial material, *that* can polarize people racially and politically and every other way. This kind of situation can be difficult because students, young people, don't necessarily want to admit to the badnesses of life. They don't necessarily want to see the evil, ugliness, especially they don't want to see it if the United States is involved. And . . . if it involves their families and themselves. But I have had to think about that a lot, and try to do some strategizing for this current year.

In her strategizing this teacher reveals how she has had to "look at places to remove myself from the argument at hand, and try to find ways of having the students themselves begin to identify with the ideas, the realities of a Black South African person. My aim is to educate my kids to certain realities."

Recognizing that it is impossible to remain on the fence in discussing South Africa, yet also believing that a good teacher ought to be able to present certain scenarios for students so that they can find ways to say what they think and feel, and to question, Brett acknowledges that she came to a new understanding about her own practice: "I tried to do better this year, with that curriculum, to look for ways that students could get closer to what it is they themselves feel and not reacting to what I felt."

Thus this teacher, reflecting on her practice, indicates the intricate ways her ethical concerns enter her teaching relationships, entangle her in a dilemma, and how she seeks to resolve it over time. Faced with something she cares about deeply—the plight of Black South Africans and her assessment of the pernicious nature of the White South African view, the teacher judges it wrong to voice that. The very knowledge Brett tries to impart is implicated, then, becoming a source of conflict and ultimately the center of her efforts to change her practice. What is again revealed is the way the individual and the context shape the particular nature of a dilemma.

Another teacher, Ramon Parks, who teaches philosophy in a small suburban high school, spoke similarly about how teaching controversial issues became an ethical dilemma. In his case the dilemma arose because the students *wanted* to know his opinion. For him the question became: "What is the context in which it is appropriate for me to express my opinion on sensitive issues—euthanasia, suicide, abortion—the kinds of things we are talking about?" Parks elaborates his ideas:

> They want to know my opinion and yet there is a danger in my mind of giving it too early because often the dialogue stops then. Now we know THE ANSWER, we can go on. Some kids don't do that, but a lot do. So I try to create an environment all year long whereby they are willing to question your opinions as another opinion, hopefully reasoned, but still an opinion. And then the conflict is reduced.

In the specific dilemma he encountered, Parks found himself considering whether or not to voice his opinion in a class discussion of a case of euthanasia, where a nurse with a terminally ill patient in a moment of crisis lets the patient die without calling for help. For the teacher, "The question is, 'Is the nurse right or wrong to do that?' And I felt if not right, at least I could understand what the nurse was doing, and I thought it was a rational decision for her to take, . . . and I thought that it was morally justifiable. . . . I am sure it is not legally justifiable." In that situation Parks saw that the students were not giving the situation the attention it deserved, nor were they treating it as "an open question." They saw it as a closed question, and so he ponders, "do I give my opinion and force it open, running the risk that twenty-two kids will change their vote because this is what the teacher thinks, which is not what I want?"

Although he wants his students to formulate positions and arguments, Parks admits the difficulty of that goal: "Kids tend to be very poor debaters. Their notion of debating is to say things louder and louder, rather than searching for some evidence . . . I would love to have them develop the whole range of opinions and arguments on their own—be able to expound the whole range before coming down someplace. Kids usually see things right away as either right or wrong, or [look for] instant answers and tend not to go much farther than that."

Embedded in Parks's situation, then, is a new element—the student's own view of the nature of knowledge. Here the teacher takes that into account as he struggles to determine just how he can voice his own views in class discussion, encourage the thinking of his students, and move them to new understandings about the nature of knowledge and how one knows.

In sum, these teachers reveal the ways their ethical values are implicated in their relationships with their students, found in their own approaches to their subject matter, and reflected in their own and their students' stances toward the nature of knowledge. While not all dilemmas teachers report have all of these dimensions, it is this particular set of elements—of self, relationships, craft, one's values and one's stance toward knowledge—that were revealed in this study. Before examining how these dimensions of dilemmas may also be involved in teachers' development, it is useful to look briefly at some related features of the dilemmas teachers reported in the original study, since these provide a context for those under discussion here.[1]

THE DILEMMAS OF TEACHING: THE WEB OF SELF, CRAFT, RELATIONSHIPS, VALUES, AND WAYS OF KNOWING

Teacher responses to questions about conflicts they faced in their professional lives revealed that 70 percent characterized their conflict as moral or ethical and a majority connected the dilemma either directly or indirectly to his or her sense of self (Lyons, Cutler, and Miller, 1986). As one women put it, "Well, you know, morality and everyday actions get pretty tied together when you're teaching. There are very few situations I've run into where there's a clear right way and a wrong way, or the shadings are very simple."

The majority of the dilemmas reported involved students, and surprisingly, only a few involved school administrators. Although Lortie (1975) reports that teachers complaints are predominantly about tasks, time use, or other adults, this research suggests the centrality of the student-teacher relationship. Teaching involves close human interactions. It is not surprising that teachers may experience their relationships to students as raising ethical issues. Piaget (1932/1965) asserts what my own research affirmed—that "Apart from our relations to others there can be no moral necessity" (p. 196). Morality resides in the relationship between people (Lyons, 1982, 1983, 1985, 1990).

This study supports the conclusion, too, that many of the dilemmas of teaching are not solvable and must simply be managed rather than resolved—a finding similar to that of Lampert (1985) and other researchers (Calderhead, 1987; Zeichner, Tabachnick, and Densmore, 1987). Fifty-two percent of the teachers said the dilemma was ongoing, and a majority indicated that their dilemma was likely to recur. The dilemmas, although broad-ranging and diverse, share certain features with teacher vignettes already discussed: these practical conflicts involve the self, usually include the teacher's relationships with students, and are considered ongoing or recurring. They demand deliberation, attention to detail, and new kinds of creative resolutions, ones that attend to all elements and people involved.[2]

What became salient in this analysis, however, were the various ways teachers' ideas about knowledge were part of their practical conflicts—as Caroline Brett, Ramon Parks, and others suggested. Their comments raise the questions of interpretation; that is, how to make sense of these issues of knowing. A current and growing body of work exploring people's epistemological perspectives from the individuals' own views provides a useful framework.

TEACHERS' PERSPECTIVES ON KNOWING:
A FRAMEWORK FOR INTERPRETATION

Many researchers interested in understanding how individuals understand the nature of knowledge and come to construct their own truths are guided by the work of William Perry and his study of college students (1970). During their undergraduate years, college students move, Perry argues, from a dualistic understanding of knowledge as either right or wrong to a position of relativism; that is, an understanding that all knowledge is constructed. In sketching these changes, which he outlines in nine positions, Perry suggests that a capacity for detachment and an ability to stand back from oneself in objectivity and to assess conflicting authorities and the relativism of one system of thought to another are necessary to achieve this epistemological revolution (p. 35). But when psychologists Mary Belenky, Blythe Clinchy, Nancy Goldberger, and Jill Tarule (1986) studied women's approaches to knowing—Perry's original work was derived largely from the study of college men—they discovered some differences.

First, although research revealed that women were able to act in detached objectivity, to see and respond to demands of external authorities, it also showed that women were especially concerned with understanding others' opinions, beliefs, and perspectives (Clinchy and Zimmerman, 1975). Essentially, women seemed to step into, not back from, situations, to see and respond to others in their own particular situations and contexts rather than to challenge them. To elaborate and verify these findings, Belenky and her colleagues expanded this research to a sample of one hundred and thirty-five women, including women in city colleges as well as rural mothers coping under difficult, sometimes oppressive situations. This work verified earlier findings (Clinchy and Zimmerman, 1975) of women's approaches to knowing and elaborated a theory to include five different epistemological perspectives. These categories range from "silence" and "received knowers," places where women deny or have no access to their own voices as they look to others as authorities, through a "subjectivist" belief that affirms their own deeply personal ideas; to a belief in reasoned, "procedural knowing," and, finally, to a conception, similar to Perry's, that all knowledge is contextual and constructed and that women are "constructivists," capable also of making theory.

Belenky and her colleagues found that the metaphor of "voice" captured accurately and most powerfully the way women came to understand themselves as knowers, especially in gaining or finding a voice. They also found links between women's ways of knowing, their ideas about themselves, and questions about value—about what is right and wrong, good and bad. Thus, in connecting these ideas of self, morality, and epistemology, Belenky and her colleagues expanded on what Carol Gilligan (1977, 1982) and my own work (Lyons, 1982, 1983) first suggested: that there are intricate connections between people's ideas of self, their ethical ideas, and their relationships to others.

This work in epistemology also suggests a way to begin to consider how to interpret the experiences of teachers. For example, this new research demonstrates that an individual—that is, a teacher or a student—can hold various stances toward knowledge and authority, truth and ways of knowing. The empirical mapping of these epistemological views is still underway. Belenky and her associates do not define a developmental progression, as Perry does, but their work clearly suggests changes in epistemological perspective. Further, they describe two different approaches to knowing used by "procedural knowers." One approach is more like traditionally known, objective, rule-seeking ways of evaluating, proving, and disproving truth. They label people using this approach "separate knowers" (similar to Bruner's (1985) "paradigmatic knowers"). A second approach seeks understanding and meaning from the individual's perspective. Belenky and her associates call users of this approach "connected knowers" (similar to Bruner's narrative knowers), people who look for connections between events, considering motives, intentions, and believability (Belenky et al., 1986; Bruner, 1985). While individuals can make use of both approaches or tend towards one over the other, each has its own logic. Thus, this work reminds us of three things: that individuals can hold various epistemological perspectives; that such perspectives may change over time; and, that within a given epistemological perspective, approaches to knowing may vary.

The teachers' views discussed here provide evidence of at least two kinds of views about knowledge: 1) the stance teachers hold towards knowledge in general, and in particular towards their individual subject discipline: 2) the stance teachers take towards their students as knowers, specifically in the way they believe their students construe knowledge. To elaborate these two views and to consider the question of how an epistemological perspective offers a useful interpretative framework for conceptualizing teacher's work and development, recall the case of Ramon Parks, the philosophy teacher. In talking about his conflict—of not knowing when to interject his own views into student discussion—he articulates a hope he has for his students, revealing his immediate and long-term goals for their development and how these connect with his and his students' ideas about knowing.

Parks wants his students to "develop a whole range of opinions and arguments on their own, either by having different people in the class do it, or individually by kids realizing that there are a range of responses that might be possible on a given question." To deal with this, and with his realization that kids would rather come down on some quick answer, he takes a "sort of devil's advocate role." And the reason he does this, he says, is "to get them to do what the course, philosophy, is all about, to think, reason, construe arguments . . . Not to change their minds, but to expose them to a methodology."

Parks also reveals how the situation in his class connects to his sense of values and how that in turn connects to a conception of knowing and knowledge:

> I suppose it is a moral issue in a sense that everyone is entitled to their own opinions, but I have never accepted the conclusion that is often drawn from that, that everyone's opinion is equally valid, which kids tend to do. They tend to slip into an easy relativism, "It's just an opinion." Well, some opinions are better than others and I believe that is an important value to me that kids realize that—that there are opinions that ought to be abandoned when persuaded to do so, and one ought to be open to that kind of persuasion.

He ponders a case:

> Kids will say, "Everybody on welfare's lazy" and even when presented with conflicting evidence, that 70 percent of [people on welfare] are children and all that kind of stuff, they maintain their opinion, and say, "Well, I am entitled to my opinion." And my point at that point is that—and I guess this is a strong moral issue, I would say "No, you're not, you are no longer entitled to your opinion . . . you can't hold an opinion in the face of contrary evidence." That's wrong and I think that is a moral dilemma.

Examining Parks's views more carefully, it is possible to tease apart several elements related to his conceptions and attitudes towards knowing—for himself and his students. A clear sense of his students' easy and precipitant conclusions suggests that he sees most of his students as dualistic thinkers, with some as multiplistic knowers, who accept all opinions since any opinion is as good as any other (Perry, 1970). He considers his role to be a teacher of procedures of knowing, of "methodology," and to move students to a new view of multiple perspectives of knowledge by having them create competing arguments of their own. But he also believes his responsibility includes teaching about the relativism of all knowledge grounded not in opinion but in different knowledge claims, some having greater validity than others.

In sum, Parks's views emphasize four things: 1) as a knower, he sees knowledge as relative, with different groundings for its validity; 2) he views students as knowers who have specific ways of knowing; 3) as a teacher, he makes explicit goals about students' epistemological development; for example, he wants to help his students move from a dualistic, "one-right answer" to a multiplistic understanding; and 4) as a teacher, he introduces specific procedures for knowing, ones he believes will promote or challenge students' epistemological development, like guiding students towards seeing that some perspectives may be more adequate than others.

Similarly, Caroline Brett's dilemma—whether to allow any opposing argument to that of Black South Africans—embodies implicit stances towards knowledge. But her dilemma reveals something more: her role in the presentation of knowledge is changing. In coming to see that there might be another way that her students could encounter controversial issues, she withdraws from an old stance— "removing myself from the argument at hand"—and works on creating a new one as she struggles to find ways her students can encounter "reality" and still appreciate controversial issues in their own terms. A dilemma "that arises out of what I am teaching in terms of how to deliver it to students" challenges Brett to see the problem as an intricate part of her position towards the knowledge she is teaching and the view of it she will allow discussed in class.

Brett's considerations resemble elements in Parks's thinking, but because her dilemma is leading her to change, she describes these elements as if in flux: 1) as a knower, she has her own perspective on the presentation of knowledge that, in this instance, is at the center of her conflict; 2) she assesses her students' stances towards knowing, but as she tries to respond to them and hold to her own goals in teaching, she changes; 3) as a teacher, she has goals for her students as knowers—that they take into account particular contexts and know the realities even if they are difficult to assimilate; and 4) as a knower and a teacher, she tries to find new ways to approach knowing and learning, not focusing on the nature of thinking or proofs needed for validity, but rather introducing the logic of contextuality to help herself and her students appreciate growing complexity.

Brett's particular dilemma "of what I am teaching and how I deliver it to students," of how to present knowledge "that would not be so hurtful versus a way that's close to the reality but perhaps could hurt" suggests a particular aspect of knowing. The teacher of a subject discipline is always at pains to determine just how that subject is to be "delivered." While a historian or a mathematician may worry about plying a discipline—of "doing" history or math, constructing new knowledge—the *teacher* of history or math has a different but related task. That task involves both the *presentation* of knowledge-of a subject or content-and a particular *kind* of knowledge construction. In a unique process, the teacher joins the students in encountering a body of data and in interpreting it, a co-joint activity constructing meaning and potentially new knowledge. These tasks involve special challenges that concern how to examine and approach knowledge, a view of one's discipline, an assessment of students, and interactions with students who, in turn, have unique views of knowledge and ways of knowing. Brett came away with a new puzzle in interacting with her questioning students; how to approach a truth she held dear in a way that students could grasp it in their own terms. In this case, the mutual interaction of students and teacher inspired in the teacher a new way of approaching knowing as well as new understandings and new knowledge.

But it seems important to suggest the difficulty of these epistemological achievements for students and teachers. Brett reveals the struggle of the teacher. Another teacher, a math teacher of fifteen years, Margaret Robinson, similarly engaged in the problem of connecting with students and their ways of knowing, illuminates the struggle of the student.

Working in a large urban high school as a special assistant to classroom teachers, Robinson encounters students who have grave difficulties learning math. Her task is to help them. But she sees the problem in a profoundly stark way: "how to help students to risk as learners, to ask questions, simply to raise a hand." Students, she believes, need help simply "knowing what they are knowing."

> I ask them, "Why didn't you ask this in class?" And they talk about the environment of a class, their reluctance. I even make contracts with kids that say, "If you are personally shy, which day of the week will you ask the question?" The kid could be a star, if [only] she'd say in class, "Ah, will you repeat that again, please?"
>
> But to address the fact that there is a fear and risk in learning . . . that risk as the learner, to ask the question, [to] raise the hand, is incredible.

Margaret Robinson tries in her work to reach a long-term objective: "I just want them to work up to their real, true questions." In the meantime, she seeks to help her students simply find a voice, to speak, echoing the struggles revealed by Belenky and her associates (Belenky et al., 1986), who depict the image of silent knowers. Robinson envisions the enormous potential achievement of a student who could at least say, "Ah, will you repeat that again, please?"

Implicitly or explicitly, then, epistemological and ethical dimensions exist in the social and intellectual relationships between teacher and student in everyday interactions. And in these situations, the teacher's self is intricately involved, as the English teacher Chris Smith suggested. Chris Smith's situation—whether he really "did consult the situation" and acknowledge what he knew of his student, his subject matter, and himself—as well as the experiences of the other teachers presented here, reveal elements of the dynamics of the epistemological interactions at work in teaching. A summary follows:

1. *Teacher's Stance Towards the Self as Knower.*

    Teacher holds implicit or explicit assumptions about knowledge and about her/his role in knowledge construction;

2. *Teacher's Stance Towards the Student as a Knower and Learner.*

    Teacher assesses student—implicitly or explicitly—as knower;

    Teacher identifies goals for students as knowers; employs specific procedures for knowing in teaching lessons; makes this assessment for the range of students in his or her classes;

    Teacher's assessment of student as knower is likely to include several epistemological perspectives. For example, from one of dualist, multiplist, relativist, and so on, of Perry's (1970) views, or "silence," received knower, subjectivist, proceduralist, or constructivist, of the Belenky et al. (1986) model of knowers.

3. *Teacher's Stance Towards Knowledge of a Discipline/Subject Matter in the Interactions of Learning:*

    Teacher's view of nature of subject matter knowledge similarly shapes the tasks of learning, interacting with assumptions about students as knowers and influencing a way of collaborating with students in knowledge construction, interpretation, or translation. (This stance may change over time, in part through the interactions of students and teachers.)

IMPLICATIONS: CONSIDERING TEACHER AND STUDENT CHANGE AND DEVELOPMENT—A MODEL AND OTHER SUGGESTIONS

The experiences of the teachers and students presented here make it possible to begin to sketch in a speculative way elements involved in teachers' professional change and development and several important implications for understanding aspects of students' development as well. Although more work is needed to test and refine these ideas, several concepts, dynamics, and implications may be identified.

The Concept of Nested Knowing

Implied in the interactions between teachers and students described previously is one phenomenon that needs to be examined in its own right; that is, the relationship between a teacher's views of knowing and his or her assessment of students as knowers, on the one hand, and students' own perspectives, on the other. It can be illustrated by the concept of nested epistemologies, or nested knowing, a characterization of the interdependence of students and teachers as knowers in learning. Like a set of dynamic objects that are interacting with one another, although each is distinct in its own right, students and teachers come together in a special relationship in learning, having a clear epistemological basis. While this conceptualization of nested knowing is a tentative one, in need of elaboration and verification, it is useful at this stage to mark an important domain. It holds implications educators need to understand. For example, a student or a teacher could be a dualistic knower, seeking or seeing one right answer; or hold a view of the multiplicity of all knowledge, or of the construction of all knowledge and of the individual as a constructor of knowledge—all in different configurations, having different outcomes.

In the data presented, for example, it is clear that Ramon Parks acted to respond to his students, given his assessment of their actual and developing approaches to knowing; that is, his assessment of their emerging epistemological capacities. Caroline Brett similarly assesses her students, but she reveals something else: how she came herself as a teacher to a new way of knowing through her interactions with her students. Thus, in learning, teachers and students influence and are influenced by each other's ways of knowing: they are nested knowers.

This analysis suggests Vygotsky's conception of the processes of development and of the social nature of learning (Vygotsky, 1978; also Williams, 1989). In Vygotsky's view, development occurs only in and through the social interactions between people like student and teacher. A special intersubjective learning relationship makes development possible. He posits, too, the idea of two aspects of student development: actual achievements and potential development—what he calls a zone of proximal development, that is, those emerging embryonic capacities of an individual. In the relationship between student and teacher in learning, a teacher needs to make some assessment of both a child's actual and potential capacities. It may be useful to consider a zone of proximal development as an emerging epistemological capacity. Defining and identifying students' different epistemological perspectives is one way to make concrete the idea of a zone of proximal development. Continuing research ought to make it possible to name and identify students' emerging epistemological capacities in a way that is useful to educators.

Similarly, the stance of the teacher toward knowledge and truth may be further examined in light of current feminist discussions about theories of knowledge. While it is not the purpose here to take these up in detail, they offer another interpretive lens for illuminating classroom activities of teachers. Positionality is one such epistemological theory or perspective that bears relation to the teacher's role. In this view, the positional knower conceives of truth as situated and partial. Truth is considered partial in that individual perspectives "that yield and judge truth are necessarily incomplete" (Bartlett, 1990, p. 881). Truth is "situated" because it emerges from particular involvements and relationships. Knowledge arises within social contexts and in multiple forms. Because this is so, the "key to increasing knowledge lies in the effort to extend one's limited perspective" (Bartlett, pp. 881–882). For a teacher like Caroline Brett, knowledge may be said to be positional. It emerges from her perspective and is elaborated through her relationships with her students, who similarly have partial perspectives. Similarly, Ramon Parks worked to expand his students' views. The goal teachers seek in their practice is a widening of their own and their students' perspectives.

This work is important in its theoretical implications, especially as it points to the dynamics at work in considering the interacting epistemologies of students and teachers. It keeps at bay a simplistic rendering or a reductionist categorization of either teachers' or students' epistemological perspectives as a nonlinear relationship emerges in the intersubjectivity of teachers and students as knowers and potential constructors of knowledge. Thus, the cases presented here offer glimpses of powerful interacting processes of teacher and student development, ones important to elaborate for theory and practice.

Elements of the Dynamics of a Model of Teacher Change

The interviews provided an opportunity for teachers to describe their own changing understandings of their practice. Several elements seem to interact in the dynamics of teachers' professional development:

the teacher's sense of self as a teacher, a practitioner;

a shifting conception of one's discipline and craft; that is, the teacher reconsiders a relationship to a discipline, especially how to present or consider a body of knowledge or discipline;

a realignment of one's relationships with students; that is, not only the teacher's way of interacting with students in learning, but a conception of the student as a knower and learner shifts;

the teacher's own conception of knowledge and knowing;

ethical and value concerns: situations of change may be experienced as having ethical dimensions, even though individuals may sometimes be unaware of them (Lyons, 1990).

This conception of teacher change—and by implication teacher professional development—thus involves a changing logic, one that touches self, craft, relationships, values, and ways of knowing.

While the cases presented here offer glimpses of the dynamics of teachers' change, they do not precisely explain what precipitates change and exactly how it comes about. That is a needed research agenda. This work offers a set of interconnected ideas that may facilitate and guide such a research task. Teacher change seems to involve a web of values and ideas, ways of knowing and interacting, and being in relationship with other knowers.[3]

Implications

Several implications follow from this research:

1. Teachers' work cannot be conceptualized primarily in terms of subject matter knowledge or defined solely by content and pedagogical knowledge. Although subject matter knowledge in teaching history, English, or any other discipline clearly matters, as does a teacher's repertoire of pedagogical knowledge strategies, teachers' work ought to be seen as comprising several interacting epistemological tasks, coming together in an encounter with knowledge in particular contexts and with specific students. The teacher's assessment of how to present subject matter is mediated by his or her understanding of students as knowers and is informed by his or her own stance towards a discipline and knowledge as well as consideration of the self as a knower. Research needs to continue to elaborate fully teachers' epistemological perspectives.

2. Teachers explicitly or implicitly, aware or unaware, interpret and assess students as knowers. This assessment enters into their consideration of long-term and day-to-day goals for student learning. Identifying students' different epistemological perspectives may provide one conceptual framework for teachers who want to analyze and name this aspect of students' approaches to learning as well as encourage students' emerging epistemological development.

3. Teachers and students are interdependent as knowers and learners. They have interconnected and interacting epistemological perspectives, what might be called nested epistemologies, each influencing the other in learning. This important interaction needs to be described so that the intersubjectivity of the student-teacher in learning may be outlined in its epistemological dimensions.

4. Teaching as an enterprise is likely to present teachers with practical ethical dilemmas. Given the characteristics of dilemmas identified here, prospective teachers ought to be alerted to these possibilities. Teacher education programs are likely to offer teachers—if anything—insights into the dilemmas of teaching associated with rights and fairness, of school and state regulations, contracts, student responsibilities and so on. Prospective teachers need to be able to consider as well the kinds of conflicts reported here: in teaching subject matter, in their learning relationships with students, and in the pedagogies they seek to explore and the knowledge they present.

5. Conceptualizing a model of teacher change needs to include several interlocking elements: self, craft, relationships, values, and ways of knowing. Epistemological and ethical issues are likely to be embedded in change. This view of teacher change may make it possible to evaluate and assess various efforts aimed at teachers' professional development. For example, short-term workshops and new wave pedagogies need to be assessed in light of the discussions presented here. Teachers themselves suggest that efforts to change their teaching practices can go on over several years. Professional development for teachers, like all developmental change, seems to be better understood as involving a changing logic, a new way of seeing and being in relationship with learners and learning.

6. Teachers themselves may want to be made aware of their own views about knowing, to characterize them and explore how they fit into their goals and

teaching strategies and materials. Teachers educated in the work of Perry (1970) and Belenky and her associates (1986), can use the idea of different epistemologies or ways of knowing in their own work. Teaching the ways of knowing ought to be part of teacher education programs.[4]

Research needs to meet the challenge of identifying systematically the epistemological perspectives not just of teachers but of students. My own work (1987) and that of Kitchener and King (King, Kitchener, and Wood, 1985) indicate that there may be as many diverse epistemological perspectives of high school students in a given class as there are learners. But few such systematic studies of high school students' epistemologies currently exist (Clinchy and Zimmerman, 1975; Maher and Dunn, 1984). Given the discoveries of work of Belenky and her colleagues (1986), this research with students seems clearly important. Similarly, given the discoveries of Belenky et al. through their focus on the experience of women, it is important to continue to pay attention to issues of gender as the mapping of approaches to knowing continues.

Finally, the outlining of the concept of nested knowing suggests that researchers need a new conception of method. The interactive, intersubjective nature of knowing of students and teachers presented here reveals the importance of finding ways that move beyond traditional psychological emphases and methods that focus on the individual. We need research that works with the interface between individuals like teachers and students. The student-teacher relationship, long acknowledged as critical to learning, is remarkably absent from systematic research studies. But as Hinde (1979) and Hartup and Rubin (1986) suggest, a needed psychology of the relationships between people is only now in its infancy. One critical task for the emerging science is the development of a methodology adequate to capturing the interactions between people. For the moment, as Hinde argues, it may be necessary to start simply with good descriptions (1979).

CONCLUSION

In her book _The Fragility of Goodness_, Martha Nussbaum (1986) elaborates a line of thinking about ethical conflict in human experience that highlights how individuals deal with life's contingencies, or what she calls "luck." Examining the works of Plato and Aristotle, and especially the tragedies of several Greek playwrights, including Aeschylus, Sophocles, and Euripides, Nussbaum shows that the idea of the good human life is dependent on things that human beings often do not control—not random, chance happenings, but all the things that are part of a human life that can just happen. Yet in the development of Greek ethical thought, especially through Plato, and later through the Kantian tradition, there emerged the idea that through reason, contingency in practical conflict could be contained. One could, for example, simplify the structure of one's value commitments, refusing to attach oneself to concerns that generated conflicting demands. In her efforts to recover this central dimension of Greek thought about contingency in human affairs, Nussbaum compellingly argues that because many of the valued constituents of a well-lived life are vulnerable to factors outside a person's control, there exists only the fragility of goodness.

These ideas do not play a central role either in current ethical theory or in the psychology of moral development. I suggest that the ethical dimensions of teachers' work presented here describe clearly the centrality of how contingency enters into our moral lives and is part of who we are as human beings and of our daily work. Although their dilemmas reflect social issues of a larger arena—Black South Africa, euthanasia—teachers encounter these in their particularity—with this class, a student who asks that question. And as the teachers like Caroline Brett disclosed, there are conflicting "goods" teachers struggle to enact, determined by who they are and how this historical moment intersects with their own life histories. What do I see? What do I know? Or believe? The complexities of what one knows requires a less confident and yet more particular wisdom. Nussbaum's work reminds us of the validity and complexity of these views, that moral goodness cannot be separate from the world of practice, and that no one can be secure from the vulnerability of ethical risk (also Arendt, 1986; Freire, 1970).

While more work will elaborate and verify the hypotheses presented here, Nussbaum's image of hovering in thought and imagination around complexities of the particular is a useful one, given the sometimes enigmatic complexities of teachers' lives and experiences. By attending to teachers' narratives, their words and experiences, we find a text that can be articulated but never exhausted, one that will remain there, the final arbiter of the correctness of our vision.

Notes

Preparation of this paper was made possible in part by grants from the Spencer Foundation, the Geraldine R. Dodge Foundation, and Miriam Dow. I am grateful for the criticism and counsel of Miriam Clasby, Blythe Clinchy, Don Freeman, Catherine Lacey, Namane Magau, Frinde Maher, Lee Shulman, Jill Tarule, and Robert Lyons, and for the generosity of the teachers who shared their lives and experiences in the research reported here.

1. The teacher interview data presented in this article were collected in two waves. In 1985, as part of the "Dilemmas of Teaching Project," 46 teachers (23F; 23M) from secondary and elementary schools in the Northeast were interviewed. In 1987, 20 teachers, including several previously interviewed in 1985, were interviewed as part of a Spencer Fellowship project, "Teaching: The Development of Mind, Craft, Self, and Relationships." All names of teachers presented here are fictitious.

2. In this article I refer to the dilemmas teachers report as "practical," "ethical" conflicts to distinguish them as real-life, specific, and particular kinds of human conflicts—that is, conflicts that have multiple perspectives and contradictions, and that are not easily dichotomized. Although I refer to these dilemmas and conflicts as "moral" or "ethical," I am deliberately avoiding a distinction between moral and nonmoral. The moral/nonmoral distinction is a heritage of Kantian philosophers, who make a sharp distinction between moral value and other kinds of value. Discussing these issues in light of early Greek dramatists and philosophers, Nussbaum (1986) argues:

The Greek texts make no such distinction. They begin from the general question: "How should we live?" and consider the claim of all human values to be constituent parts of the good life: they do not assume that there is any one group that has even a *prima facie* claim to be supreme. I believe that their approach is faithful to the way that our intuitive practical reasoning does in fact proceed, and that it recaptures aspects of our practical lives that tend to be obscured in works beginning from that distinction, however understood. (p. 5)

Similarly, I find that the term "practical conflict" better captures the kinds of dilemmas teachers report and the kind of deliberative reasoning they do as they seek to deal with them. These dilemmas cannot easily be dealt with by the choice of one principle over the other, but rather demand new kinds of integrations, where creative resolutions are sought (see Bartlett, 1990; Rorty, 1988). Since situations are unique, created out of the particularity of lives, situations, and circumstances, action to be taken is not a given, determined by the application of a single principle. Rather, action is determined by questioning, searching, and deliberating, and is dealt with by what one student of conflict negotiation called "creative integration" (Follett, 1924). Rules and laws—as Dewey (1932) suggests—are simply one set of useful guidelines.

3. This outline suggests some long-standing ideas about development. For example, Loevinger (1976) claims that development can only be considered as multidimensional. Teachers presented here suggest a similar configuration, one we need to understand more clearly.

4. I have been teaching the epistemological descriptions of both Perry (1970) and Belenky et al. (1986) to masters's level teachers in training, asking them to critique existing curriculum projects and texts to identify the underlying view of the student as a knower with such questions as, Is the student assumed to be a receiver of knowledge or a knowledge constructor? Similarly, it is possible to ask: What is the view of the teacher as a knower embedded in this lesson, text, or curriculum? Vallance (1985) has made a similar argument, suggesting that a conception of ways of knowing could be used as a perspective on practical curriculum choices, as are other systems of curriculum thought.

References

Arendt, H. (1986). The crisis in education. *Between past and future.* New York: Viking.

Bartlett, K. T. (1990). Feminist legal methods. *Harvard Law Review*, 103, 829–888.

Belenky, M., B. Clinchy, N. Goldberger and J. Tarule (1986). *Women's ways of knowing.* New York: Basic Books.

Berlak, A., and H. Berlak (1981). *Dilemmas of schooling: Teaching and social change.* New York: Methuen.

Britzman, D. (1988). On educating the educators. *Harvard Educational Review, 58*, 85–94.

Bruner, J. (1985). Narrative and paradigmatic modes of thought. *Learning and teaching the ways of knowing.* Chicago: University of Chicago Press.

Calderhead, J. (1987). *Exploring teachers' thinking.* London: Cassell Educational Limited.

Carnegie Task Force on Teaching as a Profession. (1986). A nation prepared: Teachers for the 21st century. Washington, D.C.: Carnegie Forum on Education and the Economy.

Clandinin, D. J., and F. M. Connelly (1988). Teachers' personal knowledge: What counts as 'personal' in studies of the personal. *Journal of Curriculum Studies, 19*, 487–500.

Clarke, C. M., and P. L. Peterson (1986). Teachers' thought processes. In M. C. Wittrock (Ed), *Handbook of research on teaching*, 3d ed. New York: Macmillan.

Clinchy, B., and C. Zimmerman (1975). *Cognitive development in college.* Unpublished manuscript, Wellesley College, Wellesley, Mass.

Connelly, F. M., and D. J. Clandinin (1985). Personal practical knowledge and the modes of knowing: Relevance for teaching and learning. In E. Eisner (Ed.), *Learning and teaching the ways of knowing.* Chicago: University of Chicago Press.

Dewey, J. (1932). Moral judgment and knowledge. In J. Dewey and J. H. Tufts, *Ethics.* New York: Henry Holt & Co.

Eisner, E. (1985). *Learning and teaching the ways of knowing. Eighty-fourth Yearbook of the National Society for the Study of Education.* Chicago: University of Chicago Press.

Elbaz, F. (1983). *Teacher thinking: A study of practical knowledge.* New York: Nichols.

Feiman-Nemser, S. (1983). Learning to teach. In L. S. Shulman and G. Sykes, (Eds.), *Handbook of teaching and policy.* New York: Longman.

Fenstermacher, G. (1986). Philosophy of research on teaching: Three aspects. In M. C. Wittrock, (Ed.) *Handbook of research on teaching.* 3d ed. New York: Macmillan.

Follett, M. P. (1924). *Creative experience.* New York: Longmans, Green.

Freire, P. (1970). *Pedagogy of the oppressed.* New York: Herder and Herder.

Geertz, C. (1973). *The interpretation of cultures: Selected essays.* New York: Basic Books.

Gilligan, C. (1977). In a different voice: Women's conceptions of self and morality. *Harvard Educational Review, 47,* 481–517.

———. (1982). *In a different voice: psychological theory and women's development.* Cambridge: Harvard University Press.

Gilligan, C., J. V. Ward, and J. M. Taylor with B. Bardige (Eds). (1988). *Mapping the moral domain: A contribution of women's thinking to psychological theory and education.* Cambridge: Harvard University Press.

Greene, M. (1978) Wide-awakeness and the Moral Life. In *Landscapes of learning.* New York: Teachers College Press.

———. (1986). Philosophy and teaching. In M. Wittrock, (Ed.), *Handbook of research on teaching.* 3d ed. New York: Macmillan

Grossman, P. L. and A. E. Richert (1988). Unacknowledged knowledge growth: A reexamination of the effects of teacher education. *Teaching and Teacher Education, 4,* 53–62.

Gudmundsdottir, S. (1988). *Knowledge use among experienced teachers.* Unpublished doctoral dissertation, School of Education, Stanford University.

Halkes, R., and J. K. Olson (1984). *Teacher thinking.* Lisse, The Netherlands: Swets & Zeitlinger.

Hartup, W., and Z. Rubin (Eds.). (1986). *Relationships and development.* Hillsdale, N.J.: Lawrence Erlbaum.

Hinde, R. A. (1979). *Towards understanding relationships.* London: Academic Press.

Jackson, P. W. (1968). *Life in classrooms.* New York: Holt, Rinehart & Winston.

———. (1986). *The practice of teaching.* New York: Teachers College Press.

King, P. M., K. S. Kitchener, and P. K. Wood (1985). *The development of intellect and character: A longitudinal-sequential study of intellectual and moral development in young adults.* New York: Praeger.

Lampert, M. (1985). How do teachers manage to teach? *Harvard Educational Review, 55,* 178–194.

Lightfoot, S. L. (1983). *The good high school.* New York: Basic Books.

Loevinger, J., with A. Blasi (1976). *Ego development.* San Francisco: Jossey-Bass.

Lortie, D. (1975). *Schoolteacher: A sociological study.* Chicago: University of Chicago Press.

Lyons, N. (1982). *Conceptions of self and morality and modes of moral choice.* Unpublished doctoral dissertation, Graduate School of Education, Harvard University.

———. (1983). Two perspectives: On self, relationships, and morality. *Harvard Educational Review, 53,* 125–145.

———. (1985). *Visions and competencies.* Paper presented at the American Educational Research Association Annual Meeting, Boston.

———. (1987). Ways of knowing, learning, and making moral choices. *Journal of Moral Education, 16,* 226–239.

———. (1990). Visions and competencies: Ethical and intellectual dimensions of decision-making and conflict negotiation. In J. Antler and S. Biklen (Eds.), *Changing education: Women as radicals and conservators.* Albany: SUNY Press.

Lyons, N., A. Cutler, and B. Miller (1986). *Dilemmas of teaching.* Unpublished manuscript, Graduate School of Education, Harvard University.

McDonald, J. (1988). The emergence of the teacher's voice: Implications for the new reform. *Teachers College Record, 89*, 471–486.

Maher, F., and K. Dunn (1984). *The practice of feminist teaching: A case study of interactions among curriculum, pedagogy, and female cognitive development.* Working Papers No. 144, Center for Research on Women, Wellesley College.

Mishler, E. (1986). *Research interviewing: Context and narrative.* Cambridge: Harvard University Press.

Noddings, N. (1985). Formal modes of knowing. In E. Eisner (Ed.), *Learning and teaching the ways of knowing.* Chicago: University of Chicago Press.

———. (1986). Fidelity in teaching, teacher education, and research for teaching. *Harvard Educational Review, 56*, 496–510.

Nussbaum, M. (1986). *The fragility of goodness.* New York: Cambridge University Press.

Perry, W. (1970). *Forms of intellectual and ethical development in the college years.* New York: Holt, Rinehart & Winston.

Roehler, L. R., G. R. Duffy, B. A. Herrmann, M. Conley, and J. Johnson (1988). Knowledge structures as evidence of the 'personal': Bridging the gap from thought to practice. *Journal of Curriculum Studies, 20*, 159–165.

Rorty, A. (1988). *Mind in action.* Boston: Beacon Press.

Sarason, S. (1971). *The culture of the school and the problem of change.* Boston: Allyn and Bacon.

Schön, D. (1983). *The reflective practitioner: How professionals think in action.* New York: Basic Books.

Schwab, J. (1964). The structures of the disciplines: Meanings and significances. In G. W. Ford and L. Pugno (Eds.), *The structure of knowledge and the curriculum.* Chicago: Rand McNally.

Shavelson, R. J., and P. Stern (1981). Research on teachers: Pedagogical thoughts, judgments, decisions, and behavior. *Review of Educational Research, 51*, 455–498.

Shulman, L. (1986a). Paradigms and research programs for the study of teaching. In M. C. Wittrock Ed.), *Handbook of research on teaching.* 3d ed. New York: Macmillan.

———. (1986b). Those who understand: A conception of teacher knowledge. *American Educator, 10*, 9–44.

———. (1987). Knowledge and teaching: Foundations of the new reform. *Harvard Educational Review, 57*, 1–22.

Sizer, T. (1984). *Horace's compromise: The dilemma of an American high school.* Boston: Houghton Mifflin.

Smith, D. C., and D. C. Neale (1989). The construction of subject matter knowledge in primary science teaching. *Teaching and Teacher Education, 1*, 1–20.

Stodolsky, S. S. (1988). *The subject matters.* Chicago: University of Chicago Press.

Strike, K. A., and J. F. Soltis (1985). *The ethics of teaching.* New York: Teachers College Press.

Tom. A. R. (1984). *Teaching as a moral craft.* New York: Longman.

Vallance, E. (1985). Ways of knowing and curricular conceptions: Implications for program planning. In E. Eisner (Ed.), *Learning and teaching the ways of knowing.* Chicago: University of Chicago Press.

Vygotsky. L. S. (1978). *Mind in society.* Cambridge: Harvard University Press.

Waller, W. (1932/1961). *The sociology of teaching.* New York: Russell & Russell.

Williams, M. (1989). Vygotsky's social theory of mind. *Harvard Educational Review, 59*, 108–125.

Wilson, S. W., D. L. Ball, P. L. Grossman, and K. Roth (1989). *Subject matter knowledge for teaching: Cross-disciplinary perspectives.* Symposium conducted at the American Educational Research Association Annual Meeting, San Francisco.

Wilson, S. M., L. S. Shulman, and A. E. Richert (1987). "150 different ways" of knowing: Representations of knowledge in teaching. In J. Calderhead (Ed.), *Exploring teachers' thinking.* London: Cassell Educational Limited.

Wilson, S. M. and S. S. Wineburg (1988). Peering at history through different lenses: The role of disciplinary perspectives in teaching history. *Teacher College Record, 89*, 525–539.

Zeichner, K. M., B. R. Tabachnick and K. Densmore (1987). Individual, instructional, and cultural influences on the development of teachers' craft knowledge. In J. Calderhead (Ed.), *Exploring teachers' thinking*. London: Cassell Educational Limited.

Part IV

Teaching and Pedagogy

14

TOWARD A TRANSFORMATIONAL THEORY OF TEACHING

Lynda Stone

In an elegant little volume introducing epistemology to undergraduates, W. V. Quine and J. S. Ulian describe knowledge as a web of belief.[1] Beliefs are tied together by a network of experience, cause, and justification. Some are easily changed through observation, some are almost impossible to change. These clusters contain explicit beliefs as well as strings of implicit beliefs that undergird them. Change of belief structures occurs through attention to clusters of them and the bringing to bear of evidence. If we want to reform teaching, says Gary Fenstermacher, we must work directly with beliefs about the meaning of the concept "teaching."[2] Beliefs necessarily connect ideas from research to new forms of practice and they include ideas of its purpose, passion and logic.

I want to begin construction of a new web of belief about teaching, to change how we think about it. To do this we need to uncover its belief structure. For instance, we need to make clear assumptions that tie theories of teaching and learning to understandings about cultural context and ethical implications. The present project looks not at beliefs about context or morality but at another significant foundation, inherent epistemological underpinnings. These require change if we believe the feminist assertion that one epistemology has defined how all persons come to understand the world. Traditionally, men have known, known in ways that are masculine, ways that are aspects of the world that comprise male experience. To consider gender bias as merely a political and ethical problem is to leave out the most significant element in its understanding, its epistemological character. The process of change, I believe, must be transformational. To see what this means, we must consider (1) theories of education, (2) an epistemological perspective, (3) a gender analysis, and (4) implications for transformation.

I. THEORIES OF EDUCATION

Beliefs about teaching are encapsulated within theories of education. In a recent commentary, Kieran Egan proposes that two fundamental views underlie all educational theories: the first he identifies as Platonic and the second as Rousseauean.[3] Egan writes that, for Platonists, attention is on the end of education. This end has always had something to do with objective forms, ideas, or essences that are there for our knowing. In practice, this is teaching for objectivity, for "accumulation and internalization of disciplines and their logics."[4] Acquiring knowledge means coming to understand the accumulated wisdom of the ages, systematized as abstract concepts of the disciplines. While seen by Rousseau as a complement to the first theory, the second has nevertheless had a distinct and often conflicting theoretical history. Within it, education is a process of facilitating the development of natural dispositions; here disciplinary knowledge must be made to conform to subjective experience. Even though Egan does not do so, for the sake of the present investigation, let me label the Platonic theory "objectivist," and that from Rousseau, "subjectivist." I turn now to two examples.[5] Both are well intentioned, articulated, and argued. Each one, I believe, is avowedly objective or subjective.

The objective model comes out of the writings of Margret Buchmann, Robert Floden, and John Schwille. For them, "education is taken to imply learning that recognizes students' rationality and enlarges the realm of their understanding."[6] Inherent is a particular definition and aim of rationality, one they take from Hegel:[7]

> The end of reason . . . is to banish natural simplicity . . . in which mind is absorbed. . . . The final purpose of education . . . is the hard struggle against pure subjectivity of feeling and . . . of inclination.[8]

Education is subjective when it is founded on sense perception and direct claims of knowing. In a process touted as down-to-earth and commonsensical, students learn primarily by living and doing. Cognitive and educational dangers are present: Immediate claims of knowing mask "anticipatory theories" with which all beliefs are impregnated[9] and further keep commonsense impervious to theoretical influence. What occurs in subjective education is a process where new information is fit merely to sometimes erroneous, old ideas—ideas then believed dogmatically.[10] Social and political consequences result. Limiting experience, leading to stunted imagination, in the larger sense leads to persons who rely on harmful egocentric and sociocentric patterns of thought and action.[11]

The opposite of subjective education is education for objectivity. Out of it comes meaningful, intellectual understanding. Like Egan's Platonic model, it emphasizes learning the concepts of the disciplines. This is valued particularly because disciplined concepts break with everyday beliefs. Through demonstration, coaching, imitation, and practice, the child masters abstract concepts as intellectual tasks, understanding them gradually and learning to modify and apply them to new situations. An ideal medium for objective learning is text. Texts come from all areas of systematic human learning, the arts as well as the sciences. An "objective stance" by the student is required toward text.[12] An objective stance, it must be understood, is not a total denial of connection to and value for subjective experience: all learning must in some ways tie new ideas to old beliefs, connections must and can be made between concepts from the disciplines and practical, instrumental life. Rather, in making connection "objectively," one begins outside of the localized world of oneself and one's group; in this way one learns to see beyond it to and from the perspectives of others.[13]

In a stance and language seemingly far different from their objectivist counter-parts, Madeleine Grumet and William Pinar advocate a theory of education that "honors both the historicity and agency of subjectivity."[14] Like Egan's model from Rousseau, it begins in the personal realm:

> I am experience . . . I am running a course . . . [the curriculum] . . . The rate at which I run, the quality of my running, my sensual-intellectual-emotional experience of moving bodily through space and time: all are my creations; they are my responsibilities.[15]

Drawing on the ideas of Merleau-Ponty, Grumet defines education as the idiosyncratic dialogue of each person moving toward and extending from her own physical, historical, and social environment.[16]

Education for subjectivity responds to an existing objectified form that is a distraction to and abstraction from humanizing education. What is missing "is the study of the student's point of view from the student's point of view"[17] and what results is intellectual dullness, emotional repression and lack of moral development. To change these educational results requires knowledge-of-self . . . as knower-of-the-world.[18] What must be understood is that there is no knowledge existing for its own sake; knowledge is humanly constructed. In subjective education what is undertaken is a logical, intellectual exploration that is neither naively introspective nor merely atavistic. At the end of the journey one comes to understand the paradoxical relationships of the world and learns to find foundational uncertainties attractive and live well with them.

Pinar has named his subjective method of teaching *currere*.[19] In it, students employ free association, autobiography, and hermeneutic response to text. Content from the disciplines receives attention as students reconstruct and reconceptualize their educational biographies. Currere is a four step process in which a person's past and future educational lives are described and juxtaposed to the educational present. A dialogical relationship is established between these stories and conceptual gestalts that capture their meaning. Interpretive lenses, particularly from literature, help substantiate the construction of knowledge.

II. AN EPISTEMOLOGICAL PERSPECTIVE

As our examples illustrate, objective and subjective theories of education imply strongly different conceptions of the roles of teacher and student and the stance each takes toward learning. Clearly, distinct belief structures underpin each theory; among these are ones concerning knowledge. To understand these, we can locate each theory as separate poles of what philosophers have called the subject-object debate. Richard Bernstein says that it is found in "almost every discipline and aspect of our lives."[20] He explains the dichotomy: "One position is objectivist, the foundational belief that "there is or must be some permanent, ahistorical matrix or framework to which we can ultimately appeal in determining the nature of rationality, knowledge, goodness or rightness."[21] Knowledge and the language we use to tell of it must be grounded or we become mired in skepticism. The second position is relativism, the assertion that the concepts we use about the world are related to specific theoretical views, historical times, and forms of culare related to specific theoretical views, historical times, and forms of cultural life. "For the relativist, there is no substantive, overarching framework or single metalanguage" that is not subject to temporal and cultural change.[22] Relativists argue that what objectivists take as fixed, necessary, and essential is only historically enduring. Objectivists argue that their opposites are locked in a paradox, an assertion of nonfoundationalism that is itself a founding claim.[23]

What philosophers describe as the subject-object debate I now want to call the metaphysical or grand framework. I do so to distinguish it from a corresponding stance within everyone's natural attitude, what I label the epistemic orientation.[24] Natural distinctions are made by persons between whether or not we crave "ultimate constraints." One side wishes for psychologically comforting anchors and the other delights in the tenuous. One orients toward that to be known and the other toward the knower, each believing in a separate origin of knowledge.

Making the distinction between the grand framework and epistemic orientation is educationally useful. This is because the more psychologized belief about the relation of knower to known figures strongly (yet often implicitly) in conceptions of teaching and learning. Taking this notion of epistemic orientation, we could now move to reform teaching beliefs. We could look at practice, identify the orientation of the teacher, and match up the two. Teachers could identify themselves as objective or subjective practitioners. But here I call for delay. To move too quickly to epistemic orientation leaves out consideration of the metaphysical framework that undergirds it and its relation to the epistemic orientation. Here we seek consistency between the two "levels" of belief, a consistency that is not simple.[25] But once again, to merely develop a correspondence of belief structures and practice leaves something more to which we must attend. This is the subject-object construct itself, the Enlightenment duality that has characterized modern intellectual thought. We ask: Why must we accept its formulation?

III. A GENDER ANALYSIS

To answer this question, I want now to turn to a gender analysis of the subject-object dualism. I use this lens because of my own membership in a feminized profession and because we know historically that gender bias has pervaded both the theorizing about and the actual practice of teaching.[26] There are three aspects of gender bias, writes philosopher of science Sandra Harding.[27] The first two are the social constructions of individual identity and division of labor, both manifested materially as well as in our belief systems.[28] The third is gender totemism or symbolism, the meanings of our belief systems and institutions. The most powerful gender totem is the epistemological dichotomy, the subject-object split just described. When we look at it through a feminist analysis, this is what we find: Traditionally, mind, the subject, has been associated with the male and nature, the object, with the female.[29] This means that what is real and certain is the female and what is irreal and uncertain is the male. That which is real poses a problem for the male, he does not know it and he must. To do this, he sets himself apart from the object of his inquiry and in so doing, objectifies the knowing process of which he is a part. As Evelyn Fox Keller says, there is a radical rejection of any commingling of subject and object.[30] In this act, mind thus assumes the active role of separating, not only as reason from emotion but also importantly from its own subjectivity. Only by ruling out subjectivity, so the masculinist-scientific mythology goes, can one objectively know.[31]

The epistemological dichotomy founds other ideological exemplifications. These come out of the one hegemonic order within which we live and within which gendered dualities are always asymmetrical. As Simone de Beauvior has so aptly defined women, she is always "other." She is always other in a hegemonic order that is hierarchical and patriarchal and built on control and domination. If we consider for one moment the following dualisms, we clearly recognize the power of gender symbolism: subjective-objective, passive-active, procreative-creative, reproduction-production, body-mind, emotion-cognition, nature-culture, private-public, submission-domination, other-person.[32] Within the system of ideological beliefs that we generally take for granted, the latter element of the pairing is more valuable than the former element. The first is feminine and the second is masculine, woman inferior to man.

IV. IMPLICATIONS FOR TRANSFORMATION

Given this gender analysis, we turn to implications for teaching reform and consideration of the two educational theories. The first point to make is that the exemplars presented are not antifeminist. I believe that the objectivists hold a liberal postition.[33] If, as must be implied, the objectivist side of the dichotomy is more culturally valued, then these well-meaning theorists advocate an educational model that provides a single and equal legitimacy for females and males. In contrast, subjectivists support a more radical view, the valuing of women's experience as equal in its own right[34] and perhaps as able to contribute something superior to the masculinist culture. My point, regardless of the extent to which these views are feminist, is to suggest that both are foundationally gender biased and therefore harmful because they have been theorized within the traditional epistemological dichotomy. Even as each attempts connection to the other side of the duality, the harm persists.[35] Importantly, within the dichotomy both male and female experience are stunted, although limited in different ways. Thus we turn to our question. If we do not wish to accept the Enlightenment split, what can we do?

To move beyond the subject-object split means to found a new epistemology and to establish a new belief structure for teaching. Here I have taken a first step by analyzing an existing structure and its bias.[36] Next we must transform the results of this and other similar studies. To my mind a transformational view is hopeful.[37] I see it as an altered metaphysical position, one located in the realm of possibility rather than actuality in order to dream about life as it might be. It aims for a world without inequality, without hierarchy, without power differentials—it aims for transformation.

An epistemological transformation is illustrative: Harding says that what we want is science (i.e., knowledge) that is "free of gender loyalties."[38] A transformed epistemology cannot be objectivist because such a position has publicly excluded or androgenized female experience. It cannot be subjectivist because this stance has imprisoned women within their own privatized, naive experience. It is not separating nor oppositional because within such a conception, female experience is afforded one inferior side.[39] Such biases, it is emphasized, also harm males. A transformed epistemology does recognize sexual difference and "reciprocal selves" and seeks the legitimacy of a wide range of ways of being. At its heart, it is a relational epistemology.

A relational epistemology is foundationally feminist and transformational. It is feminist in arguing that relation is basic. Along with educational philosophers Nel Noddings and Jane Roland Martin,[40] I am persuaded by Neo-Freudian accounts that attribute ontological relation to women because of their gendered upbringing. The idea is that men and women develop distinct forms of self. In this process, men must undergo a process of separating and distancing from a sexually different parent, their mother. Women, in contrast, remain in connected relation to her.[41] Relation is also transformational. This is because it can be understood as central to an alternative epistemological worldview, one that differs from that of dominant western males. In many other cultures, persons are defined as existing within, and therefore in harmony with, their worlds: the individual is *only* conceived as relative to others, as part of a communal social order.[42]

Much remains for us to do to unpack the notion of relation as an epistemological and an educational ideal. I emphasize the difficulty of this task given the scarcity of descriptive examples—given the founding hegemony. This paper has been a first step. I end it by suggesting a new strategy for a next phase, that is to take changes in belief and connect them to teaching practice. This strategy takes the form of a new educational construct. This is "pedagogical structuring," an idea that emerges only with a transformational turn to relational knowing. It is the understanding and working with educational elements that constitute the social, interactive, and connective construction of knowledge. We see these elements in our two initial educational theories and in a transformed view: context, teacher, individual student, other students, text and nontext, forms of experience that are instructional and noninstructional. Pedagogical structuring is defined as systemic, relational, and operational for all teaching-learning practice. It connects beliefs about how we know to teaching to know; it incorporates beliefs about culture and morality as well. Within it, the relational norm must be made explicit for the teacher as well as for the student. Clearly this is a part of the process of change, of altering the web of belief through insight and evidence. In seeking the ultimate reform of teaching practice, I have attempted to provide some justification for its change. I am mindful that this is an insufficient first move toward transformation. I know finally that the next steps, steps that connect beliefs to ideas about practice, are crucial ones. With this connection, I believe, comes the actual catalyst for teaching reform.

Notes

1. I use the web of belief as a metaphor, not necessarily accepting the behaviorist account of thinking that accompanies it in Quine's work. See W. V. Quine and J. S. Ulian, *The Web of Belief* (New York: Random House, 1970).

2. Gary D. Fenstermacher, "Philosophy of Research on Teaching: Three Aspects," in *Handbook of Research on Teaching*, ed. Merlin C. Witrock (New York: Macmillan, 1986), pp. 37–48.

3. Kieran Egan, "On Learning: A Response to Floden, Buchmann, and Schwille," *Teachers College Record* 88 (1987): 508–509.

4. Egan. p. 509.

5. Other examples of subjective and objective theories of education could easily have been selected for illustration. Of the first, I think generally of the work of Elliot Eisner or Jean Clandinin and Michael Connelly; for the second, writings of Thomas Green and Robin Barrow come to mind.

6. Robert E. Floden and Margret Buchmann, *The Trouble with Meaningfulness*, Institute for Research on Teaching, Occasional Paper No. 82 (East Lansing, Mich.: Michigan State University, 1984), p. 4.

7. These authors draw substantiation of their ideas from a wide range of scholarly writings that include analytic philosophy of education, sociology of knowledge, and cognitive psychology.

8. Georg Hegel, *Philosophy of Right* (London: Oxford University Press, 1952), cited in Margret Buchmann and John Schwille, "The Overcoming of Experience," *American Journal and Education 9* (1983): 46.

9. Buchmann and Schwille, p. 33.

10. See Floden and Buchmann, p. 8; Buchmann and Schwille, pp. 33–34.

11. Robert E. Floden, Margret Buchmann, and John S. Schwille, "Breaking with Everyday Experience," *Teachers College Record 88* (1987): 487.

12. Floden et al, p. 498.

13. Ibid., p. 487.

14. Madeleine R. Grumet, "The Politics of Personal Knowledge,: *Curriculum Inquiry 17* (1987): 319.

15. Much of the introduction to the teaching model of William F. Pinar and Madeleine R. Grumet comes in their text, *Toward a Poor Curriculum* (Dubuque, Iowa: Kendall/Hunt, 1976). See Preface, p. vii.

16. Madeleine R. Grumet, "Existential and Phenomenological Foundations," in *Toward a Poor Curriculum*, p. 32.

17. William F. Pinar, "Self and Others," in *Toward a Poor Curriculum*, p. 17.

18. Grumet, p. 35

19. See Pinar's chapter, "The Method," in *Toward a Poor Curriculum*, pp., 51–63.

20. Richard J. Bernstein, *Beyond Objectivism and Relativism: Science, Hermeneutics, and Praxis* (Philadelphia, Pa.: University of Pennsylvania Press, 1983), p. 1.

21. Ibid., p. 8.

22. Ibid.

23. Within Husserl's notion of the life-world is a grand thesis about the material existence of the world; this is the natural attitude. It seems to me that one horizon we have within the natural attitude is a naive perspective that psychologically favors realism or idealism. For the most helpful explanation of the life-world, see David Carr, "Husserl's Problematic Concept of the Life-World," in *Husserl: Expositions and Appraisals*, ed. Frederick A. Elliston and Peter McCormick (Notre Dame, Ind. University of Notre Dame Press, 1977), pp. 202–212.

24. Bernstein, p. 11.

25. For example, Kant and Husserl are subjectivist in the sense that they found knowing in mental structures and are objectivists in believing in the universality of their existing form and essential content.

26. Bias is clearly present in beliefs about teaching. The hegemony operates at both explicit and implicit levels of thought and in all aspects of our lives.

27. See the very important work by Sandra Harding, *The Science Question in Feminism* (Ithaca, N.Y.: Cornell University Press, 1986).

28. Educational feminists have written well about the first two categories. See, e.g., Maxine Greene, "The Lived World," in *Landscapes of Learning*, (New York: Teachers College Press, 1978), pp. 213–223; and Michael Apple, "Work, Gender and Teaching," *Teachers College Record 84* (1983): 612–628.

29. The roots of this tradition are found in the writings of Aristotle. See parts of two selections, "On the Generation of Animals" and "Politics," in *Philosophy of Women*, ed. Mary Briody Mahowald (Indianapolis, Ind.: Hackett, 1983), pp. 266–275.

30. Evelyn Fox Keller, "Gender and Science" in *Discovering Reality*, ed. Sandra Harding and Merrill B. Hintikka (Dordrecht, Holland: D. Reidel, 1983), p. 191.

31. Feminist philosophy of science has salience for this discussion because scientific knowing has traditionally been the exemplar of knowledge and its methods of inquiry the most legitimate. Its methods further have been adopted for research in the social sciences and in education.

32. Elsewhere I have presented an argument that defines women as non persons—incapable of human action. See Lynda Stone, *A Curriculum for Virginia Woolf*, paper presented before the College and University Faculty Assembly of the National Council for the Social Studies, New York, November 1986, revised as "The Relationship of Women to Curriculum," *Re–Visions 1* (1987): 7–9. For an important discussion of the relation of gendered dualities to sexuality, see Ruth Bleier, *Science and Gender* (New York: Pergamon Press, 1984), beginning p. 164.

33. See Alison Jaggar's excellent account of the historical development of a range of political feminist views of *Feminist Politics and Human Sexuality* (Totowa, N.J.: Powman and Allanheld, 1983).

34. Madeleine Grumet has written an eloquent series of feminist papers on educational topics. See particularly, "Conception, Contradiction, and Curriculum," *Journal of Curriculum Theorizing 3* (1981): 287–298; and "Pedagogy for Patriarchy: The Feminization of Teaching," *Interchange 12* (1981): 165–183.

35. Floden et al., p. 496; Grumet, "Foundations," p. 35.

36. Among these analyses must be ones that attend to class and racial/ethnic bias and the innerconnections of these with gender.

37. I take this term from my teacher, Nel Noddings, and Harding uses it also, p. 244.

38. Harding, p. 138.

39. Ibid., p. 148.

40. It seems to me that both Noddings and Martin accept relations as an ethical and not as an epistemological ideal. For their outstanding contributions to feminist educational thought, see Nel Noddings, *Caring* (Berkeley, Calif.: University of California Press, 1984): and Jane Roland Martin, *Reclaiming a Conversation* (New Haven Conn.: Yale University Press, 1985).

41. See Keller, beginning p. 192.

42. Harding warns of accepting too simply an alternative epistemology, particularly one of minority males in which minority females are then caught in a double bias. Harding, beginning p. 167. Finally, it has been suggested that references to "male" be deleted from "the dominant Western view." To do so would once again silence woman, would cover over her lack of participation in the epistemological construction, and would destroy the feminist project. However ameliorating such a step would be, justice and transformation cannot be served by it.

15

ONLY THE FITTEST OF THE FITTEST WILL SURVIVE: BLACK WOMEN AND EDUCATION

Barbara McKellar

People often ask me how I have managed to progress from the primary classroom to a post in the teacher education department at a London polytechnic. This question is pertinent when there is evidence of black underrepresentation in higher education. I would not find unreliable the informal survey of teacher education institutions carried out by the Anti-Racist Teacher Education Network (Table 1). This showed that I would be one of twenty-seven black teacher educators in England, Scotland, and Wales (0.6 per cent).

Further information would be needed to establish how many of these black teacher educators are women. The small percentage the survey revealed is indicative of the way in which both race and gender operate to prohibit the recruitment and career advancement of black women in the teaching profession. Since the teacher education sector has to recruit from the pool of qualified and experienced teachers, what is needed is an analysis of the career progress of black teachers, in order to explain the percentage of 0.6 in post. What follows is an account of this progress with special reference to the ways in which race, class, and gender relations have shaped the development of my career.

First, I shall discuss the structural position of black women in society with a view to interpreting how this position influences the development of identity and

TABLE 1 Number of Full-Time Staff in Teacher Education, with Number of Black Staff Shown in Parentheses

	Public Sector (including voluntary colleges)	University
England and Wales	2,150 (18)	1350 (8)
Scotland	709 (1)	17 (0)

Source: Anti-Racist Teacher Education Network (ARTEN) unpublished survey, 25 January 1988.

images. Second, I shall discuss the processes of schooling that have assisted in shaping my potential to benefit from higher education. Finally, I shall look at the issues that black women face in sustaining a career in the teaching profession.

BLACK WOMEN IN SOCIETY

Historical Background

The position of black women in society is structured by political and economic developments, both nationally and internationally. The past holds as much explanation for the experiences of black women today as the present social and political climate. The development of racial and gender superiority coincides with the rise of capitalism as a major means of production in Europe. Such developments have also defined the roles played by all women in society and dictated the nature of the relations that could exist both between gender groups and across racial groups. It would be unrealistic to discuss the processes by which roles are structured without reference to the historical factors, not least because the same terms of reference operate to structure the progress of black women in education in Britain today. The experiences that are enjoyed in education are a reflection of the relations that exist in society at large. I would go as far as to say that when I walk down any street those I meet would not necessarily know that I am a teacher educator but *would* know that I am black and female. Therefore, the cultures to which one belongs are only important insofar as society attaches significance to them.

Throughout the last two hundred years or more there has been a predominantly accepted image of black women, whereby they are portrayed as serving and/or servicing others. The subservient role played by black women was related primarily to the development of indentured societies in the Caribbean and in Central and North America. The role of black women in such societies is not dissimilar to one played by working-class women in Britain during a parallel historical period. But in the black diaspora, the women were invariably performing this role in all spheres of life without any of the social differentiation that would have been normal in the African societies from which they came. Such societies had the potential to allow a diversity of social and economic activity, but slavery introduced the limitations of domesticity wholesale to successive generations of black women.

Quite apart from the restrictive range of social and "economic" activity, the period of slavery marked the point at which gender segregation occurred amongst black people in slave societies. Thus the gender role reconstruction, as well as cutting men and women off from each other, removed from black women the privilege of being able to exercise the trading skills that had been part of their heritage. Although this is the case, entrepreneurial traits are still to be found in the cultural practices of modern Caribbean societies, where women are market holders and participate in international trade, mostly dealing with the American mainland: "Buying and selling, or higglering as it is called, is a common form of livelihood for women throughout Jamaica. . . . Higglers buy from the primary producers in the market at wholesale prices and retail them in villages nearby" (Clarke, 1979). This practice has expanded beyond the scale of fruit and vegetables to include all forms of commodity items. The shopfront or pavement site has been replaced by business enterprises that trade with the Americas, organized predominantly by females. So although slavery and capitalism have united to thwart the development of traditional economic patterns, despite the odds some things have managed to survive. The revival of African culture in the postindependence period has probably accelerated the trend of women adopting a higher profile within their communities.

Contemporary Forms of Oppression

The survival of traits related to the gender division of labor has occurred against a background of political struggle and extreme hardship, and the forms of oppression have assisted the construction of the particular kinds of gender relations that are to be found in black British communities. Because the norms of economic and political leadership were distinct from each other and attributable to separate gender groups in their previous culture both black women and black men are unable to assert themselves in the British context. This is because within British society women are not seen as the prime leaders in the field of business, and black men do not have access to the means of enfranchisement to the mainstream political spheres. The expectations of black people have been that they would fit into the existing patterns of gender differentiation, which are not in fact familiar to them. Moreover, when black women have become part of British society, they have been expected to assume the patterns of dependency experienced by white women, as well as to maintain continuity in the role assumed during the period of colonial rule. Colonialism had the effect of guaranteeing compatibility with the needs of industrial capitalism. Thus the possibility of fulfilling the cultural and social needs of black women is limited by the structural position of women in Britain per se. The degree to which British (white) women are second-class in status has been the source of discrimination for black women in particular and for minorities in general. One only has to refer to countries in Eastern Europe or to other moments in Britain's historical past to see how artificial is the allocation of gender roles. The existence of a correlation between power and economic activity, in addition to the conscription of women to the secondary labor market, has rendered women incapable of having access to equal status in society. The failure to meet the needs of black women is further worsened by the considerable gap in social and educational experience between the ethnic culture and the British one. When one then considers that for reproduction to occur, women must perform a dual role, it can be seen that black women have much with which to contend. That there has been social fragmentation in most parts of the black diaspora during the past cannot be disputed, and this has also meant that there was and is a greater need of urgency to stabilize the family base. The activities of many black women have this stabilization process as a prime concern.

Racism with Gender Groups

White male supremacy in international relations has been promoted via the development of patriarchal structures in European societies and via the extension of European power and influence in all parts of the world. This, in itself, has presented black men with an insuperable task in trying to regain a position of equality. In turn, the inferior position that black men hold makes more problematic the gender relations within black groups. In fact, the frame within which black women operate has to include favorable interactions with both of these groups, that is, a double source of dominant oppression. The resolution of conflicts that stem from male dominance has resulted in black women relying on their own resources. This is due in part to the fact that the dominant perspectives that influence the organizations and lobbying machinery within the women's liberation movement have not always recognized the racial dimensions of black women's experience. The birth of a movement called "Women against Racism and Fascism" sought to redress the balance. It has been suggested, however, that "the different strands of feminist and left politics were real impediments to thrashing out a common antiracist position" (Bourne, 1984, p. 9).

The inability to fuse the two perspectives that would address the issues related to black women's experience has been one of the major criticisms made by black women of the women's movement as a whole. Reasons suggested for this failure relate to the assumed differences that exist due to differences of race. When one considers that *race* is an artificial term, then many of the distinctions with regard to physical qualities, intellectual capacity, and the taboo subject of sexuality can be regarded as myth. Of the qualities referred to, it is often the physical and visual differences that are given prominence and then integrated via cultural and media representations to reproduce the ideologies that maintain the idea of significant difference. An example is the assumption that European standards in beauty are the ones by which to judge all others. Indeed the idea of racial superiority feeds assumptions about the qualitative distinctions that are mentioned above. For a long time there was assumed to be a scientific basis for the distinctions in academic achievement. The research of Mackintosh and Mascie-Taylor (Committee of Inquiry, 1985) suggests that IQ is not a reliable indicator of potential for academic achievement: "These findings tend to argue against those who would seek to provide a predominantly genetic explanation of ethnic differences in IQ" (p. 147). It is further explained that West Indian children do better in public examinations than IQ scores would indicate.

The other of the assumed differences, namely sexuality, is problematic because little has been written about sexuality and sexual relations, and what has been written has tended to remain in departments of higher education institutions and has not percolated to the world outside. It is unfortunate that this is the case, as stereotypes with regard to sexual prowess prevail to influence interracial interactions. Once again the period of slavery in the Caribbean has encouraged an image of black women as sex objects for the use of black and white men alike. It is unfortunate the current media portrayal adopts these stereotypes to keep alive the idea that black women are strippers and prostitutes (e.g., *Eastenders*, 27 March 1988).

Campaigning and political black women leading ordinary lives are rarely seen, so the predominant stereotype is perpetuated and used for referral by all. Consequently the intergender relations of the black community have tended to overemphasize the reproductive role that women perform. It shocks many people to find out, for instance, that I have no children. It is important, therefore, that the experiences of all women are related to the political processes that express resistance to oppression. Feminists of all varieties need to ask the question, "what does it feel like to be a black woman in British society?" Until this sensitivity is seen as crucial in policy development, the effect of feminist activity will always be only to liberate white females. There has been a change in consciousness with regard to women's issues and much of this has started to influence the processes of education. It is not apparent, however, that black female identity and social development have so far been included as high priorities in either resourcing or developing educational policy. It may be a major concern of teachers in inner-city areas where there are significant numbers of black pupils, but there needs to be full permeation of antiracist and antisexist perspectives in curriculum development, regardless of geographical location. Moreover, it would be common to find the cultural isolation I experienced in the 1950s and 1960s replicated today in the nonmetropolitan areas of Britain. Pupils in the all-white school need to develop antiracist and antisexist practices as much as, if not more than, pupils from multiracial schools. It was my experience that girls within my peer group were able to develop hostile patterns of behavior in a subtle way that often went undetected by the staff. The way in which pupils interact with each other has not always been a major concern of teachers, yet the implications for the development of racial attitudes in society are just as important as the transmission of values by the mass media.

Summary

Although this is a brief account of the factors that shape the structural position of black women in Britain, what is revealed is that multiple factors operate to ensure that gender-related experiences are racially differentiated. The relations between European people and those of "African origin" have been molded by the exploitative nature of colonialism. Society's institutions that are concerned with cultural reproduction—family, church, judiciary—have all played a part in sustaining these relations. Responses to the economic, political, social, and cultural forms of oppression that have resulted from the complex interaction of factors mentioned earlier have in turn confirmed the shape and form of the political platforms of resistance.

RACE, CLASS, AND GENDER IN SCHOOLING

Women, whether black or white, experience relations of sexual domination and exclusion and this, too, was central to their thinking about their lives inside and outside school. (Fuller, 1983, p. 170)

Unless their efforts to circumvent racial and sexual exclusion in employment are successful they are likely to find themselves in unskilled and semi-skilled jobs and being paid at even lower rates of pay than their male counterparts. (Fuller, 1983, p. 179).

It is dangerous to analyze racism or sexism in terms of individual achievement because, where it may be possible for small numbers of racial minorities or women to achieve success, often the structural position in society of both black people and women is not altered by such individual progress. Women are predominantly found in the lower paid sectors of employment. Together with sexual differentiation in employment, racism in employment and in education combine to produce a climate in which black girls perceive and experience the processes of schooling in an entirely different way. Evidence of racism in education can be seen in the fact that pupils from black and ethnic minority groups are rarely selected into higher education. Rather than examining all the issues simultaneously and thereby risking the creation of more generalizations, I shall look at the race and class dimensions briefly before considering the impact of gender on my school career.

Race and Class

My parents migrated to Britain from the Caribbean in the 1950s at a time when there was a positive recruitment policy for attracting workers from the Commonwealth. The flow of immigration in itself has "class" implications that, although never explicitly stated, were soon realized on arrival:

> After the war, which had killed off so many people, Britain was so desperate for workers to operate the factories, run hospitals and maintain transport and other services. In 1948 the Government passed a Nationality Act making all colonial and Commonwealth citizens British and actively recruited Black people. (IRR, 1986)

The hidden consequences of such recruitment practices had the effect of designating the housing class to which black people were assigned, while having repercussions for the life-styles of the first generation and the life chances of the second generation. Immediately prior to the arrival of significant numbers of racial minorities, there had been an extensive period of imperialism during which the foundations of prejudice and the ideologies that underpin discrimination were laid. Despite the positive view that many of the new arrivals had of their white "hosts," it rapidly became clear that at best they were ill-informed. A view of the world in which British is synonymous with best has permeated all aspects of culture and is transmitted via all institutions, for example, the family. On arrival at school, children bring with them the tacit knowledge and values that are enshrined in their preschool experiences. Similarly, the other institutions in society like the school absorb the prevailing culture of society to produce low expectations of black pupils by staff and other pupils alike.

Such low expectations assisted in influencing the cultural climate of the schools that I attended and in structuring the patterns of socialization into school as well as subsequently into British culture. Encoded in language and cultural practices are the predominant attitudes to "race." Teachers are educated and socialized to utilize this code, as they are a group that is drawn from a cross section of society. The mere fact of being successful in school is indicative of being able to conform to the social control mechanisms. Those who are not able to comply would not normally have a smooth career through school and would not achieve the necessary qualifications for entry to higher education.

Pupil-pupil interaction is often dismissed as being secondary to teacher-pupil relationships in the discussion of race relations in schools. Interactions with pupils, both in the classroom and the playground, can have a long-lasting effect on one's personal, emotional, and psychological development. The dynamics of social interactions in the case of minorities are numerically structured. The ratio of teachers to pupils is one: many, but the reverse is true for a peer group to a given child. Educational research reveals that teachers can only offer a small amount of individual time to each pupil in a day. Time spent with one's peer group is considerably longer. In my case there came a point when the negative attitudes of the teacher actually served to increase my determination and motivation. I began to carve out clear goals and ambitions. Instead of accepting the academic downfall signaled by failing the 11+, I sought avenues for achieving status, both in school and the world outside, as well as in the future that lay ahead of me. The swift results yielded by increased determination led to my transfer to grammar school after only a year. The consequence of this kind of thinking is that at an early age an awareness of one's overall position in society develops. Ideas emerge as to how to overcome obstacles and how long it takes to achieve one's goals: "Schooling and education provided an alternative and less undermining possibility in their search for greater freedom and control. Concentration on education as a way out was something which all the black girls whom I interviewed stressed" (Fuller, 1983, p. 172). Much of the research carried out by Fuller at a London comprehensive endorses my experience of receiving a British education.

Race and Gender

The brief account of the 'class' specificities of 'race' reveals that oppression has a double edge for those of an immigrant background. Black women experience two sorts of oppression that combine to shape the development of self-concept, as a direct result of being brought up in a racist and sexist culture. Recent attention has focused on the relative educational success of Afro-Caribbean girls in comparison to boys: "The average performance score obtained by girls was 17.7 compared to 13.7 for boys. In all ethnic groups, girls did better than boys" (ILEA, 1987, p. 7). It may be that this observation is accurate for areas outside the ILEA and relates to the differential treatment that each gender group receives, both in school and in society at large. At school the expectations of girls are that they will be quiet, docile, and diligent and adopt the values that are presented by female role models in school. The fact that these values are "middle-class" matches the aspirations held by black parents on behalf of their daughters.

During my education my father was an active source of encouragement, offering as much support as he was able to. More importantly, given that the links between the culture of the home and school may be weak, the link between the kinds of values that are fostered in black girls and those of the mainly male-orientated culture of the school are strong. It would seem that the female gender role constructed within black families displays features that are more often associated with the male gender role in British culture. Qualities such as independence, self-reliance, and a sense of responsibility for others are very much a part of the essential attributes associated with black females. Research has shown that the school cultures actually favor those who possess such traits, and it is the view of the writer that this attitude operates to encourage the success of black girls in certain spheres of school life. It would need a deeper analysis than can be offered here as to why this attitude does not contribute to the success of the black boys in school. It has been suggested that negative stereotypes exist with regard to their behavior (Tomlinson, 1983).

In theory I should have had a distinct advantage over my peers throughout my education, but my early periods of schooling were dogged by low expectations and these were exacerbated by the absence of black female models. There was nobody within school or in an equivalent status position elsewhere in society with whom to identify. I would suggest that experiences such as these serve to ensure that a lack of awareness of self-worth develops. The position with regard to the social mobility of black and other ethnic minorities is changing but there is still a long way to go.

Due consideration of the fact that immigration did not distribute the black population vertically within the class structure nor geographically suggests that a culturally pluralist educational climate is still of importance today, as it was when I started school in the mid-1950s. During my schooling I experienced racial harassment, mostly name calling. An experience of harassment that frequently occurred at grammar school related to name calling by a girl who was not even in my class but who was in my year group. Throughout most of the period of secondary school I combed my hair in about twenty plaits and consequently I had many partings. It became fashionable for the girl and her clique to call me "streets." I was thick skinned, but initially this remark hurt not least because others laughed and thereby condoned it. There were many other pranks that yielded nicknames, but these I would put down to high spirits and immaturity. The personal nature of being called "streets" could not even be offset by having somebody with whom to share this. I find it sad that the incidence of racial harassment has increased not decreased:

> The Commission of Racial Equality's two latest reports—the one alleging widespread racial harassment in schools, the other detailing the shortage of ethnic minority teachers—came just as the all-party consensus which greeted the Swann report three years ago shows ominous signs of cracking (*Guardian*, 5 April 1988, p. 21).

The reports indicate that the ethos is not changing, nor are the black personnel with motivation to change the position being recruited. Currently, the cultural climate is marked by a range of regressive political moves that have encouraged the collapse of consensus on issues of cultural pluralism. One such political development is the introduction of the Education Reform Act, which does not appear to encourage the trends that had been initiated at grass roots level related to multicultural education. In fact, aspects of the reform have encouraged the expression of negative racial attitudes, as illustrated by the case of the (white) Dewsbury parents' group who, in refusing places for their children at a nearby school with mostly Asian pupils, theoretically were taking up their rights under the new arrangements for open enrollment.

Personal Testimony

Rather than listing the catalogue of negative encounters that took place, I shall elicit what I did to combat the effects of stereotyping. The area of pupil-pupil interactions was made more favorable by my development of competencies displaying high prowess. I was able to accomplish peer group approval via athletics. It was possible in this area to have clear-cut results that were associated with my own innate skills, both physical and psychological. It is useful to point out, however, that towards the end of my school career there were clashes with the PE teacher, who did not accept my case that there would be times when academic work, such as summer public examinations, would take priority over practices and training. Nevertheless, athletics was an area where I could establish my worth. Doing this is important for all children as it is in this way that being the butt of scorn from one's peer group is avoided. However, it applies even more to a black child who may acquire unfortunate labels even more easily.

The reputation one develops throughout schooling has more to do with evidence of academic ability than the level of involvement in extramural activities, important though this may be. It is important to achieve academic consistency in order that achievements are not questioned. This may involve investing more time and effort across a range of subjects. It is worthy of note that the "work twice as hard" theory applies to both black and female pupils. Those children who make additional effort are off-setting the disadvantage of an inadequate educational provision themselves. The educational system is actually making additional requirements of such pupils. The responsibility of schools should primarily be that of facilitating the educational attainment of all pupils, of whatever race, gender, or class. As well as burning the midnight oil, I developed other strategies, for example, analyzing what my areas of strength were and applying them in other contexts. I found I was able to boost my confidence by previewing what I perceived as the next likely obstacle to achieving my aims. An example of this would be asking pupils in the year above me in school a range of questions about the procedures necessary to gain work experience, at the time when I was considering career choice. Eventually I was able to pass high status subjects and enter teacher training.

BLACK WOMEN IN THE TEACHING PROFESSION

The experiences of being black and a woman overlap with being a black teacher and with being a woman teacher. What follows may not depart significantly from what is already known about either of these but may serve to highlight the concerns of both.

Teacher Education, Ideology, and Gender

The efforts of racism are that some doors open and others remain firmly closed, due to the lower position held by racial minority groups. One such door that has remained closed for many black school leavers is the one by which entry is gained to higher education institutions. The divisions that exist in society between different social strata are engineered via the way that higher education institutions devise the criteria that select and recruit. One effect of restricted entry procedures is that for those with overseas qualifications, or without the full complement of qualifications, access is barred.

"Access" courses have been developed for those who may have or may not have had a British education and not achieved success because of reasons outlined earlier or due to disruptions to their schooling. It is significant that Access courses that were set up specifically to attract mature students who have not been able to make use of the education system are now attracting younger applicants, the majority of whom have been educated here (mostly from primary school onwards). Research I conducted for an M.A. dissertation revealed that a third were fully educated here, with many others arriving during the secondary period of schooling. Often the primary reason for taking an Access course is to satisfy vocational needs. It would appear that schools fall short of satisfying this need to the extent that Access is now a popular alternative. The expansion of the number and range of such provisions reflect the increase in demand.

For those with the correct qualifications, the race to qualify only begins on deciding to opt for higher education. The first stage of choosing an appropriate institution is an important one. When I applied to college, I read as much available literature as I could and once again listened to the impressions that those who had already been interviewed had of those colleges and the courses for which they had applied. The main guiding principle that I adopted was that the college should above all be situated in or near a city with a cosmopolitan population. The idea of living in total cultural isolation for three years seemed unbearable. Eventually the decision to move from London to a city in the East Midlands was a correct one. No sooner had I been exposed to the "middle-class" environment of the college campus than I found myself gravitating towards the schools in the city nearby. I did this in order that I could more easily identify with the pupils whom I taught. It became clear, too, that I could make specific contributions in such social and cultural areas because of the perspectives I could bring to the classroom and because of my ability to empathize with pupils. A black family who lived next door to my digs in my second year was a good cultural anchor.

The ethos of many teacher education institutions is so elitist, with terms of reference that are middle-class, that only the fittest of the fittest can survive. The advance preparation strategies that I utilized in order to jump all the "hurdles" during school needed to be reemployed during training. I attended a campus-style college in my late teens and so there was no escape at the end of the day by way of a home to go to. The predominantly middle-class students flew in from distant places laden with exotic souvenirs and revealed the social background from which they had come on the first day. Such experiences serve to highlight that teachers are on the "official" side of the desk representing the establishment. The realization soon dawns that as a black teacher participating in the management of the education system, one is likely to be operating against the interests of the community from which one came. The responsibilities of being a teacher, coupled with the negative experiences black people have of school, tend to limit the appeal of teaching as a career. The same arguments can be applied to other professions: witness the low recruitment rates for black and ethnic minority groups to the police force.

Teaching on the one hand, carries high status within Caribbean cultures and so there is a pull, particularly for women. On the other hand, boys' negative experience of the school system may discourage entry by them into the teaching profession. Another feature of being a member of the teaching profession is that in many ways black teachers have, of necessity, to be bicultural at school and to prioritize developing a British cultural perspective during college and subsequently during their teaching career if advancement is the aim. The period of adolescence has often signaled a reassertion of ethnicity for many black male youths. Thus the secondary forces that operate to engender success are minimized. I would go as far as to say that at college the norms of ethnic cultures do not apply and could potentially be a source of clash. Black teachers need to develop a professional identity that while accommodating British values, relates to the social status of black people in society after they qualify.

Role of the Black Teacher

The education system, having been founded by men for men, has tended not to reflect positively the contributions of women or black people. When any teacher presents or introduces a curriculum to the class that reflects this exclusionary perspective, it is clear that they are colluding with the system. The development of initiatives that respond to bias in the curriculum and to the management of pupils assists in establishing that black pupils can make a positive contribution in schools and can also improve the educational climate of the school. It is clear that the current processes of education overburden those black pupils who are keen to succeed, and so it is essential that black teachers play their part in alleviating the burden. More significant than developing innovative practice in one's classroom is the permeation of such innovations throughout the school via curriculum leadership. In order to do this, it is necessary to be a part of the process of forming structures or organizations that will articulate the necessary issues and lobby for change. To tackle the form and content of the education process in one's own classroom is adequate when one first starts teaching, but it is not enough in the long term for the black teacher. It is a part of the role of the black teacher to think of the wider concerns of education; the positions of groups in society; the differential rates of achievement of pupils; the way schools induct pupils into different roles in society. It could be argued that all teachers need to have an overview of the processes of education, but because black women teachers are most likely to be able to understand the issues involved in throwing off oppression it becomes a part of their lot. One criticism that I would level at teachers is that the time has come for them to be involved in the development of noneducational issues in the wider community instead of confining themselves to what is traditionally seen as relevant to school. Initiatives like Industry-links are to be welcomed in encouraging a greater development of broader educational perspectives.

In my case I taught lower juniors but tried to develop links with the infant department and also worked in local youth clubs that assisted in the development of a longitudinal perspective of children with whom I worked. Where the organization of schooling fragments the experience of children, it is an important part of the politicization of the black teacher to develop a wide perspective on educational issues. One cannot form part of the discussion on the outcomes of schooling if one does not know what happens beyond the age of 10–11 in the educational system.

Promotion and the Black Teacher

It is often reported that black teachers are in the lower grades, on temporary contracts, in posts designated as Teacher above Authorized Numbers, or Section 11 (Ranger, 1988). There is some evidence to suggest that black teachers may be employed as a last resort when there is nobody else to fill a post and there is a danger that classes might be sent home. An experienced black London teacher has shared this problem since starting her career in 1970: "she has done well at interview and then not got the job. One school told her that she was very good but we don't have many blacks here" (*Guardian*, 5 April 1988, p. 21). This teacher's experience can be seen to occur for reasons previously mentioned. She taught a subject that relates to a vocational field that is regarded as women's work. Ninety percent of employees in secretarial work are women. The low status that such work confers on those women involved no doubt contributes to being perceived as inferior. Added to being black, opportunities for advancement are few.

My teaching career was marked by my entering an expanding field in which opportunities were available vertically as well as horizontally. Primary education is also regarded as women's work, but the position I held as a language teacher involved having detailed discussions with all teachers about the curriculum they taught and the progress of their children in much the same way as the headteacher would do. The key to success is being farsighted, especially in analyzing the nature of the promotional levers. Career-minded teachers who do not ask questions about the educational developments on the horizon and how they can be a part of them are going to find the progress of their career stifled.

Career advancement is also based on the level of qualifications one has, both academic and professional. No doubt the lengthy process of qualifying may deter many from working to pursue other qualifications, but it is important to see teaching and learning as inextricably linked, as well as essential to one's own professional development. There is a wealth of courses from which to choose: teachers' center courses, DES short and long courses, higher degrees, etc. I started with the first of these in my probationary year and progressed from a diploma to a masters degree within ten years. In the intervening years (between taking the diploma and masters degree) I tended to "top-up" with short courses within the local authority for which I worked. Quite apart from the knowledge gained, being involved in such courses allows contact with other teachers whose experience of teaching is as valuable as (if not more than) the course curriculum. In this way one can keep up with changing educational trends. Gaining extra qualifications alone is not sufficient from my observations. Having a good relationship with those in senior positions assists in ensuring that your professional needs are known. The possibility of communicating curriculum needs to those in a policy-making position, as well as the curriculum consequences of educational change for minority groups in schools, ought to be the aim of the black teacher.

CONCLUSION

The introduction of perspectives that put women, black people, and other ethnic minorities on the agenda of the school's curriculum has increasingly become important. The success of black people in education is structured by external influences in society and extends the range of what counts as valued knowledge. The path of social mobility needs to be unblocked, and education is one way of achieving this. Black women have a central role in the process, not least due to their role within the family and the wider community. Their role in education will continue to be an important one insofar as they can assist in ensuring that the extra effort that black people make is honored by the school system. Racial and sexual differentiations have assisted in producing the position whereby black women are carrying the torch.

References

Bourne, J. (1984) *Towards an Anti-Racist Feminism*. London: Institute of Race Relations.

Clarke, E. (1979) *My Mother Who Fathered Me: A Study of the Family in Three Selected Communities in Jamaica*. London: Allen and Unwin.

Committee of Inquiry Into the Education of Children from Ethnic Minority Groups (1985) *Education for All* (The Swann Report). London: HMSO.

Fuller, M. (1983) "Qualified Criticism, Critical Qualifications," in L. Barton and S. Walker (Eds.), *Race, Class, and Education*. London: Croom Helm.

Inner London Education Authority (1987) *Ethnic Background and Examination Results 1985 and 1986*. London: ILEA.

Ranger, C. (1988) *Ethnic Minority School Teachers: A Survey in Eight Local Education Authorities*. London: Commission for Racial Equality.

Tomlinson, S. (1983) *Ethnic Minorities in British Schools*. London: Heinemann.

orists who use gender as a key analytic category and seem reasonably familiar with feminist discourse (Sears, 1983; Pinar, 1981, 1983; Pinar and Johnson, 1980; Taubman, 1981). There is the work of Connell et al. in Australia where, after a year's fieldwork, the research team of academics and classroom teachers came to the unexpected realization that the interaction of gender and class is central to understanding what happens in schools (1982, p. 73). Both class and gender were recognized as structures of power that involve control of some over others and the ability of the controllers to organize social life to their own advantage. Class and gender "abrade, inflame, amplify, twist, negate, dampen and complicate one another. In short, they interact vigorously . . . with significant consequences for schooling" (p. 182). But the norm among "neo-Marxist curricularists" (Schubert et al., 1984) is a lack of awareness regarding gender issues, including the wealth of academic scholarship that has developed over the last fifteen years.

Feminism provides a golden opportunity for Marxists to do their part in what Aronowitz calls "the long process by which society learns to make the self-criticism needed to save itself" (1981, p. 53). Grasping the implications for social transformation of women's struggle for self-determination requires an end to the sexism and economism inherent in the refusal to see cultural resistance and revolutionary struggle outside of the "workerism" that permeates the male neo-Marxists search for revolutionary actors (Rowbotham, 1981, p. 32; Lather, 1984).

Heidi Hartmann (1981) has termed the relationship of feminism and Marxism an "unhappy marriage": Whether orthodox, neo- or "post-Althusserean,"[3] Marxists cannot see women's experiences and capacities as a motor force in history. So, as in patriarchal marriage, two become one and that one is the husband. Gender considerations become secondary, if acknowledged at all. Class is the ultimate contradiction. To see women's subordination as a central rather than a peripheral feature of society would require a probing of "the epistemological contradictions of using gender analysis as an appendage to an androcentric theoretical perspective" (Tabakin and Densmore, 1985, p. 13). It is, of course, much easier to ignore the whole issue, especially in terms of the philosophically fundamental dimensions of the feminist challenge. The "and women, of course" phenomenon allows male Marxist scholars to feel they have addressed gender issues—without ever asking how a field of inquiry must be reconstructed "if it is genuinely to include women's lives, experiences, work, aspirations" (Martin, 1986).

Habermas has termed feminism a new ideological offensive (1981). As such, it is, I argue, the contemporary social movement taking fullest advantage of the profound crisis of established paradigms in intellectual thought. The charge of feminist scholars is to document the specificity of how gender inequality permeates intellectual frameworks and to generate empowering alternatives. The challenge of such work to neo-Marxist sociology of education is no less than this: to bring women to the center of our transformative aspirations is an opportunity to address the "black holes"[4] that have stymied a Marxist praxis relevant to the conditions of life under advanced monopoly capitalism.

ISSUES OF PRAXIS

My argument in this section is that if we want to understand and change the work lives of teachers, issues of gender are central. What follows is a sketch of what opens up both theoretically and strategically when we bring gender to the center of our efforts to understand the nature of teacher work. After an overview of the way gender has shaped the social relations of teaching, three problematic areas of Marxism will be touched upon: the public/private split, the failure to come to grips with subjectivity, and the reductionism that still typifies so much of contemporary Marxism and stymies the sustaining of systematic opposition.

Gender and the Shaping of Public School Teaching

The central claim of materialist-feminism[5] is that gender specific forms of oppression are not reducible to the demands of capitalism. There is an interactive reciprocity and interweaving of the needs of patriarchy and capital that must be taken into account in understanding the work lives of teachers. How has gender shaped the nature of teacher work?

To see the family as a "greedy institution for women" (Coser and Rokoff, 1974, p. 545) is to understand that the conditions of maintaining capitalism via the gender system require an analysis of the reproduction of mothering by women both inside and outside the home (Chodorow, 1978: Dinnerstein, 1976; Sokoloff, 1980). Problematizing the feminization of the teaching role provides an exemplary illustration of the way women's labor in the "helping professions" becomes "motherwork": the reproduction of classed, raced, and gendered workers.

Sara Lightfoot writes: "mothers and teachers are also involved in an alien task. Both are required to raise children in the service of a dominant group whose values and goals they do not determine. . . . to socialize their children to conform to a society that belongs to men" (1978, p. 70). Teaching has come to be formulated as an extension of women's role in the family: to accept male leadership as "natural" and to provide services that reproduce males for jobs and careers, females for wives and mothers and a reserve labor force. Margaret Adams (1971) calls this "the compassion trap": Women feed their skills into social programs they have rarely designed that, while ripe with contradictions, are "fundamentally geared to the maintenance of society's status quo in all its destructive, exploitative aspects" (p. 562).

Women's subordination has been built into the very dynamics of the teaching role. This is not to deny that classroom teachers exert a form of power over their students. But Jean Baker Miller's (1976) distinction between relationships of temporary and permanent inequality is helpful here. Women are dominant in relations of temporary inequality such as parent and teacher, where adult power is used to foster development and eventually removes the initial disparity; they are submissive in permanently unequal relations where power is used both to cement dominant/subordinate dynamics and to rationalize the need for continued inequality (pointed out in Gilligan, 1982, p. 168).

Teachers stand at the juncture of nurturing and sending out, preparing children to go from the private to the public world. To the degree women teachers serve as transmitters of cultural norms rather than cultural transformers, they, like mothers, find themselves caught in the contradiction of perpetuating their own oppression. With training for docility,[6] teaching becomes an extension of women's maternal role as capitalism's "soft cops" (Wasserman, 1974), serving the dual function of both presenting the capitalist-patriarchy's human face and providing social and political containment (Rowbotham, 1973, p. 91).

As "the secular arm of the church" (Howe, 1976, p. 85), dedicated to sacrifice and service, disempowered by the "normal school mentality" fostered by their education (Mattingly, 1975), crowded into an occupation full of structural disincentives, and oversocialized to be "good girls," women teachers have focused on responsive concern for students and worries about job performance at the cost of developing a more critical stance toward their cultural task of passing on a received heritage. The structure of the public schools has grown up around women's subordination. Little wonder, then, that the possibilities for nurturing Giroux's "oppositional teacher" (1983) or Zaret's "the teacher as transition agent" (1975) are directly linked to empowering women.

The Public/Private Split

The public/private split that is the foundation of the capitalist-patriarchy has relegated women's sphere to the periphery of social thought, the realm of the "natural" and hence unchangeable, the biological. Materialist-feminist analysis grows out of the primary female experience with reproduction and reproduction expanded to include nurturing, caretaking, and socializing work—"shadow work" that does not get counted in either the gross national product (Illich, 1982, p. 45) or Marxist theories of the motor forces of history (Jaggar, 1983). The materialist-feminist analysis insists that the forces and relations of reproduction be recognized to be as central as production in the social fabric (O'Brien, 1981; Ferguson, 1979; Bridenthal, 1976; Kuhn and Wolpe, 1979). Materialist-feminist theory posits that reproduction stands in dialectical relationship to production as the material base of history; they are, in effect, warp and woof of the social fabric.

Mary O'Brien (1981) argues that to continue dismissing change in the reproductive sector as being of no historical consequence is rooted in a biologism that contradicts Marxism's essential postulate of the dialectical relationship between nature and culture. Other major shifts in social consciousness have been rooted in the public realm. With feminism, "the private realm is where the new action is" (p. 189), as women undertake "a conscious struggle to transform a social reality that in turn will transform consciousness" (p. 208).

Coming to Grips With Subjectivity

Rosalind Coward (1983) argues that just as the great debate of nineteenth century social theory, the relationship between nature and culture, was moved forward by focusing on sexual relations, the position of women holds great hope for theoretical advances in the late twentieth-century quest to understand the relationship between consciousness and social structure. The focus on false consciousness, hegemony, and ideology that characterizes contemporary Marxist thought is rooted in the hidden nature of exploitation under advanced monopoly capitalism (Jaggar, 1983, p. 215); this results in a society where "the very *fact* of domination has to be proven to most Americans" (Giroux, 1981). Because as women, we live intimately with our patriarchal oppressors, we have been especially subjected to layers of myths about our own nature and that of the society in which we live. Studying "the extent to which gender is a world-view-structuring experience" (Hartsock,

1983, p. 231) can hence shed much light on the processes of both ideological mystification and coming to critical consciousness.

Western women presently find themselves in an extremely contradictory position. Widespread access to birth control gives women broad-based reproductive control for the first time in history. Aspirations are geometrically advancing in a no-growth era; most women put in "double days" in a culture that in practice cares little for children (Grubb & Lazerson, 1982). Some women experience double and triple oppression due to race, class, and sexual preference; many are part of the feminization of poverty. All receive double messages from our culture with schizophrenic regularity. Women are, collectively, prime candidates for ideological demystification, the probing of contradictions to find out why our ways of looking at the world do not seem to be working in our favor (Eisenstein, 1982).

"Feminism is the first theory to emerge from those whose interest it affirms" (MacKinnon, 1982, p. 543). It is rooted in a deep respect for experience-based knowledge. It is best summarized in the phrase "the personal is political"—a radical extension of the scope of politics that transcends the public/private split. Feminism is premised on an intimate knowledge of the multifaceted and contradictory elements of consciousness and the deeply structured patterns of inequality reinforced through dominant meanings and practices. As we extend the question of consent from the public to the private realm, we find that "because women's consensus shows more signs of erosion than working-class consensus, it is a more promising field for research and political praxis" (O'Brien, 1984, p. 58).

Transcending Reductionism

What a materialist-feminism refuses is to reduce Marxism solely to an analysis of capital; it insists that historical materialism can shed much light on the oppression of women and that Marxism would benefit from a focus on the interactive reciprocity and interweaving of the needs of patriarchy and capital. Perhaps most importantly, feminism argues the need for Marxism to recognize that revolutionary constituencies shift with historical circumstances. To the degree women's struggle is made invisible by economistic reductionism, Marxism loses touch with the potential that feminism offers for social transformation.

The relationship between the theoretical analysis and political strategies is a long-standing concern within Marxism. Whitty argues that change efforts in the schools must be linked to broader oppositional movements (1985, p. 24). To continue to disallow gender in our analysis of teacher work is to not tap into the potential that feminism offers for bringing about change in our schools. As Zaret wrote in 1975: "For women who are teachers, the starting point is you in your own situation" (p. 47). Until the rebirth of feminism, women had no access to oppositional ideologies that encouraged them to question the gender status quo. Making gender problematic opens one up to the layers of shaping forces and myths in our society with great implications for one's conception of the teaching role. Let us look, for example, at some of the contradictions in the lives of women teachers that a gender analysis illuminates.

- As women teachers, we are simultaneously assumed to place home and family above career and to be dedicated "professionals," which often means "a kind of occupational subservience (Dreeben, 1970, p. 34; see Darling-Hammond, 1985).

- The "paradox of conformity" (Zaret, 1975, p. 46) makes us complicitors in our own oppression to the extent that we maintain the status quo.

- As women teachers, we are simultaneously in positions of power and power-lessness. Like motherhood, teaching is "responsibility without power" (Rich, 1976). Women's subordination has been built into the very dynamics of the teaching role. Lightfoot writes of the cultural perceptions of the teacher as woman and as child (1978, p. 64). Yet we expect teachers to perform miracles, to overcome our society's most intransigent problems.

- As both teachers and mothers, we daily witness the rhetoric of America as a child-centered society versus the reality of our culture's devaluation of the care and raising of children.

- As married women teachers, we live daily the contradiction of needing the home as a refuge from the alienating dimensions of teaching versus the alien-ating reality of our double day (Sokoloff, 1980, p. 210; see Pogrebin, 1983, regarding how little household work American men do).

It is the central contention of this paper that taping the estrangement and sense of relative deprivation that feminism engenders in women is a key to transforming the occupation of public school teaching.

Conclusion

Given the androcentrism of Marxist theory, feminism benefits from exposure to this powerful, well-developed body of social theory that continues to dominate revolutionary discourse so long as feminists remain aware of the need to subvert the intellectual ground under our feet. We need to be sure we do not become "good wives" of a Marxist patriarch. What neo-Marxist sociology of education needs right now is a way to transcend its theoreticism, its lack of praxis, its malaise rooted in its long-standing lament regarding "the continuing absence of a move-ment capable of advancing alternatives" (Genovese, 1967, p. 102).

Given the intimate connection of public school teaching with the social role of women, the continued invisibility of gender in neo-Marxist analysis of public school teaching greatly limits its usefulness in restructuring the work lives of teach-ers. To the extent male neo-Marxists continue to ignore the forces and relations of patriarchy and to marginalize women as historical protagonists in their theory and strategy building, they are as much a part of the problem as of the solution.

Notes

1. Gender as a social construction is a key assumption of all strands of feminism. Feminism argues that what gender is, what men and women are, and what types of relations they have are not so much the products of biological "givens" as of social and cultural forces. Symbolic and ideological dimensions of culture play especially important roles in cre-ating, reproducing, and transforming gender. See S. Ortner and H. Whitehead (Eds.), *Sexual Meanings: The Cultural Construction of Gender and Sexuality*. New York: Cam-bridge University Press, 1981.

2. Barrett (1980) and Coward (1983) discuss the analytic problems with the concept of patriarchy in feminist work.

3. In a continuing profusion of "kinds of Marxism," Mary O'Brien defines post-Althusserean Marxism as "attempts to re-socialize the substructural/superstructural model . . . which is problematic in any case" (1984, p. 45).

4. I first heard Jim Sears use this term at the Fifth Curriculum Theorizing Conference, Dayton, 1984.

5. I now call myself a "materialist-feminist," thanks largely to French social theorist, Christine Delphy (1984), but I have also, finally, grasped the essence of the "new French feminists" (Marks and de Courtivon, 1980): that I am a constantly moving subjectivity. To be a materialist means to understand social reality as arising in the lived experiences of concrete individuals under particular historical conditions.

6. For a feminist critique of teacher education, see Lather, "Gender and the Shaping of Public School Teaching: Do Good Girls Make Good Teachers?"; paper presented at the National Women's Studies Association annual meeting, New Brunswick, New Jersey, 1984. See, also, Ava McCall, "Learning to Teach: The Empowering Quality of Nurturance"; paper presented at the Curriculum Theorizing Conference, Dayton, 1986.

References

Adams, M. (1971). The compassion trap. In V. Gornick and B. Moran (Eds.), *Woman in a sexist society: studies in power and powerlessness*. New York: Basic Books.

Apple, M. (1982). Reproduction and contradiction in education: an introduction. In M. Apple (Ed.), *Cultural and economic reproduction in education: Essays on class, ideology and the state*. Boston: Routledge and Kegan Paul.

———. (1983a). Curricular form and the logic of technical control. In M. Apple and L. Weis (Eds.), *Ideology and practice in schooling*, (pp. 143–166). Philadelphia: Temple University Press.

———. (1983b). Work, gender, and teaching. *Teacher's College Record, 84*(3), 611–628.

———. (1985). Teaching and "women's work": A comparative historical and ideological analysis. *Teacher's College Record, 86*(3), 455–473 .

Apple M. and L. Weis (Eds.). (1983). *Ideology and practice in schooling*. Philadelphia: Temple University Press.

Aronowitz, S. (1981). *The crisis in historical materialism: Class, politics, and culture in marxist theory*. New York: Praeger.

Barrett, M. (1980). *Women's oppression today: Problems in marxist-feminist analysis*. London: Verso.

Barton, L., R. Meighan, and S. Walker (Eds.). (1981). *Schooling, ideology, and the curriculum*. Barcombe, England: Falmer Press.

Bridenthal, R. (1976). The dialectics of production and reproduction in history. *Radical America, 10*, 3–11.

Chodorow, N. *The reproduction of mothering: Psychoanalysis and the socialization of gender*. Berkeley: University of California Press.

Clarricoates, K. (1981). The experience of patriarchal schooling. *Interchange, 12*(23), 185–204.

Connell, R. W., D. J. Ashenden, S. Kessler, and G. W. Dowsett (1982). *Making the difference: schools, families, and social division*. Sydney: George Allen and Unwin.

Coser, R. and G. Rokoff (1971). Women in the occupational world: Social disruption and conflict. *Social Problems, 18*, 535–554.

Coward, R. (1983). *Patriarchal precedents: Sexuality and social relations*. Boston: Routledge and Kegan Paul.

Dale, R., G. Esland, and M. MacDonald (Eds.). (1981). *Education and the state.* Vol. 2. Barcombe, England: Falmer Press.

Darling-Hammond, L. (1985). Valuing teachers: The making of a profession. *Teacher's College Record, 87*(2), 205–218.

Delphy, C. (1984). *Close to home: A materialist analysis of women's oppression.* Amherst: University of Massachusetts Press.

Dinnerstein, D. (1976). *The mermaid and the minotaur: Sexual arrangements and the human malaise.* New York: Harper Colophon.

Dreeban, R. (1970). *The nature of teacher work: Schools and the work of teachers.* Glenview, Ill.: Scott-Foresman.

Eisenstein, Z. (Ed.). (1979). *Capitalist patriarchy and the case for socialist-feminism.* London: Monthly Review Press.

Eisenstein, Z. (1982). The sexual politics of the new right: Understanding the "crisis of liberalism" for the 1980s. *Signs 7*(3), 567–588.

Ferguson, A. (1979). Women as a new revolutionary class. In P. Walker (Ed.), *Between labor and class.* Boston: South End Press.

Flax, J. (1980). Mother-daughter relationships. In H. Eisenstein and A. Jardine (Eds.), *The future of difference* (pp. 20–40). Boston: G. K. Hall.

Fox Keller, E. (1985). *Reflections on gender and science.* New Haven, Conn.: Yale University Press.

Freire, P. (1973). *Pedagogy of the oppressed.* New York: Seabury Press.

Genovese, E. (1967). On Antonio Gramsci. *Studies on the left, 7*(1–2), 83–107.

Gilligan, C. (1982). *In a different voice.* Cambridge: Harvard University Press.

Giroux, H. (1981). *Ideology, culture, and the process of schooling.* Philadelphia: Temple University Press.

———. (1983). *Theory and resistance in education.* New York: J. F. Bergin.

Gray, E. D. (1982). *Patriarchy as a conceptual trap.* Wellesley, Mass.: Roundtable Press.

Grubb, W. and M. Lazerson (1982). *Broken promises: How Americans fail their children.* New York: Basic Books.

Grumet, M. (1981). Pedagogy for patriarchy: The feminization of teaching. *Interchange 12*(2–3), 165–184.

Habermas, J. (1981). New social movements. *Telos 49*, 33–38.

Hartmann, H. (1981). The unhappy marriage of marxism and feminism: Towards a more progressive union. In L. Sargent (Ed.), *Women and revolution* (pp. 1–41). Boston: South End Press.

Hartsock, N. (1983). *Money, sex, and power: Toward a feminist historical materialism.* Boston: Northwestern University Press.

Howe, F. (1981). Feminist scholarship—the extent of the revolution. In *Liberal education and the new scholarship on women: Issues and constraints in institutional change* (A report of the Wingspread Conference, October 22–24; pp. 5–21). Washington, D.C.: Association of American Colleges.

Illich, I. (1982). *Gender.* New York: Pantheon Books.

Jaggar, A. (1983). *Feminist politics and human nature.* Totowa, N.J.: Rowman and Allanheld.

Kuhn, A. and A. M. Wolpe (Eds.). (1978). *Feminism and materialism: Women and modes of production.* Boston: Routledge and Kegan Paul.

Lather, P. (1984). Critical theory, curricular transformation, and feminist mainstreaming. *Journal of Education, 166*(1), 49–62.

Lightfoot, S. L. (1978). *Worlds apart: Relationships between families and schools.* New York: Basic Books.

Macdonald, M. (1981). Schooling and the reproduction of class and gender relations. In R. Dale et al. (Eds.), *Education and the state: Politics, patriarchy, and practice.* Vol. 2 (pp. 159–178). Barcombe: Open University Press.

MacKinnon, C. (1982). Feminism, marxism, method, and the state: An agenda for theory. *Signs* 7(3), 515–544.

Mahony P. (1985). *Schools for boys? Co-education reassessed.* London: Hutchinson.

Marks, E. and I. de Courtivon (Eds.). (1980). *New french feminisms.* Amherst, Mass.: University of Massachusetts Press.

Martin, J. (1986). Questioning the question. (Review of S. Harding, *The Science Question in Feminism,* 1986.) *Women's Review of Books* 4(3), 17–18.

Mattingly, P. (1975). *The classless profession: American schoolmen in the nineteenth century.* New York: University Press.

Mazza, K. (1983, April). *Feminist perspectives and the reconceptualization of the disciplines.* Paper presented at the meeting of the American Educational Research Association, Montreal, Canada.

McRobbie, A. (1980). Settling accounts with subcultures. *Screen Education* 34, 37–39.

Miller, J. (1986). *Toward a new psychology of women.* Boston: Beacon Press.

O'Brien, M. (1981). *The politics of reproduction.* Boston: Routledge and Kegan Paul.

———. (1984). The commatization of women: Patriarchal fetishism in the sociology of education. *Interchange 15*(2), 43–60.

Pinar, W. (1981). Gender, sexuality, and curriculum studies: The beginning of the debate. *McGill Journal of Education 16*(3), 305–316.

———. (1983). Curriculum as gender text: Notes on reproduction, resistance, and male-male relations. *Journal of Curriculum Theorizing 5*, 26–52.

———. and L. Johnson (1980). Aspects of gender analysis in recent feminist psychological thought and their implications for curriculum. *Journal of Education 162*(4), 113–126.

Pogrebin, L. C. (1983). *Family politics: love and power on an intimate frontier.* New York: McGraw-Hill.

Rich, A. (1976). *Of woman born: motherhood as experience and institution.* New York: Bantam Books.

Rowbotham, S. (1973). *Woman's consciousness, man's world.* Middlesex, England: Penguin Books.

Rowbotham, S., L. Segal, and H. Wainwright (1981). *Beyond the fragments: Feminism and the making of socialism.* Boston: Alyson.

Sargent, L. (Ed.). (1981). *Women and revolution: A discussion of the unhappy marriage of marxism and feminism.* Boston: South End Press.

Schubert, W., G. Willis, and E. Short (1984). Curriculum theorizing: An emergent form of curriculum study in the U.S. *Curriculum Perspectives 4*(1), 69–74.

Sears, J. (1983, June). *Sex equity: An ethnographic account of meaning-making in teacher education.* Paper presented at the meeting of the National Women's Studies Association, Columbus, Ohio.

Smith, D. (1979). A sociology for women. In J. Sherman and E. Beck (Eds.), *The prism of sex: Essays on the sociology of knowledge* (pp. 135–188). Madison, Wis.: University of Wisconsin Press.

Sokoloff, N. (1980). *Between money and love: The dialectics of women's home and market work.* New York: Praeger.

Tabakin, G. and K. Densmore (1985, April). *Teacher professionalization and gender analysis.* Paper presented at the meeting of the American Educational Research Association, Chicago, Ill.

Taubman, P. (1981). Gender and curriculum: discourse and the politics of sexuality. *Journal of Curriculum Theorizing.*

Walker, S. and L. Barton (1983). *Gender, class, and education.* New York: Falmer Press.

Wasserman, M. (1974). *Demystifying school.* New York: Praeger.

Whitty, G. (1985, April). *Curriculum theory, research, and politics: A rapprochement.* Paper presented at the meeting of the American Educational Research Association, Chicago, Ill.

Zaret, E. (1975). Women/school/society. In J. Macdonald and E. Zaret (Eds.), *Schools in search of meaning.* Washington D.C.: Association for Supervision and Curriculum Development.

17

TEACHING WOMEN

Jo Anne Pagano

Teaching is an art form. I shall not argue for that claim since there can be no disagreement if one accepts certain paradigmatic propositions, as Wittgenstein called them, and there can be no argument if one does not. The artistic medium of the teacher is the narrative; her teaching is a narrative enactment. When we teach, we tell stories. We tell stories about our disciplines, about the place of these disciplines in the structure of human knowledge. We tell stories about knowledge, about what it is to be a human knower, about how knowledge is made, claimed, and legitimated. The stories that we tell are stories built on other stories; they work to forge continuity between our stories and those of others, to confirm community among ourselves and others, and to initiate others into our communities. In educational theory we tell stories of teaching, stories that at once reveal, constitute, and confirm the values that give significance to pedagogical acts. These are stories in which we represent those whom we teach in their relationship to ourselves and in which we define the nuances of the relationship, identity, power, and authority of individuals in their relationship to a community and its knowledge.

I am interested in those stories of teaching that tell us that its practice is an art and that the curriculum is an art form. Finally, I am interested in stories about women as teachers, hence in stories about the relationship between women and art and between women and the practice of the art of teaching. In particular, I am interested in the art of women teaching women.

The business of women teaching has always been thought problematic in the modern age. Henry Barnard is not the only one among our nineteenth-century fathers to have concerned himself with the injurious effects of hard intellectual work on women's fragile psyches and with the yet more deleterious effect of their precious wombs. But the continuing problem for women teachers is authority. During the nineteenth century one of the chief arguments against permitting women to teach in the secondary schools was that their small size and fragile emotional constitution would prevent their exercising authority over the "big boys." According to this point of view, the business of education is something like a football skirmish and the exercise of authority amounts to subduing the other's body. The question of authority and what it consists of, who can legitimately exercise it, whether it is possible for a female teacher to exercise authority or be an authority, continues to figure as a prominent theme in discussions of women teaching. It recurs with some considerable frequency in contemporary feminist writing. Susan Stanford Friedman, for example, suggests that authority, at least as authority is usually conceived, is a contradiction in the feminist classroom.[1] The apparent contradictions between such activities as testing, evaluating, grading, and syllabus control and the nurturing and empowering aims of feminist pedagogy are regularly adduced as issues of authority and its vicissitudes. Others have written about the ways in which women professors are disdained by their students: if they behave toward their students as their male colleagues do, they are seen as bitches or as trying too hard; if they attempt to teach from a feminist perspective, they are seen as lightweight. Either of these student perceptions undermines the teacher's authority. But in contemporary mainstream writing on problems of teaching, issues of authority are conceived within the bounds of considerations of management and control and are read as gender neutral. Such writing ignores what all women teachers know. But the exercise of authority has even wider ramifications for feminist teachers.

Authority in all of its meanings refers to some sort of power or right. When teaching is considered to be the enactment of narrative, *authority* refers to the power to represent reality, to signify, and to command compliance with one's acts of signification. Even in this context, though, authority eludes women, or at least makes us uncomfortable. Reading feminist philosophy and literary criticism leads us to suspect that our discomfort may have something to do with women's peculiar relationship to language and to art. Women exercise powers or rights to represent reality only as surrogates for men. Only by proxy have we the right to command, to enforce obedience to the father's law. Still, it is doubtful that we ever do it well. Part of the reason is that women are either not represented in the father's law or we are represented as lack or deficiency.[2]

The question of authority is complicated for women when we relate *authority* to *author*. The first meaning for *author* given in the *Oxford English Dictionary* has to do with making something grow or with the person who originates or gives existence to something. The author is an artist, or perhaps a mother. But according to the *OED*, the author is the father who begets. Our author is an artist, a father who begets. An author represents. Art represents. Teaching and art may be seen as cognate activities in that both are acts of representation. To become a human who knows is to become one who knows the world through a language in which the author, he who holds the power (the authority) to represent, is a father. Just as women's relationship to authority in the social world has always been perplexing, so has the relationship of women to language and writing—to art. This is something that the literature on the art of teaching ignores, either because it has never occurred to writers on the topic that it matters or because, if called on it, such writers would likely deny that gender ought to make a difference. The truly talented, the story goes, never think of themselves as "women artists" or "women teachers." What are the consequences of this neglect for women teaching and for all of us, men and women, teaching women?

If we choose to consider teaching an art, then we must understand it to be also a gendered art. The narratives of pedagogy and criticisms of the art of teaching have neglected this. Even if women are treated elsewhere in educational discourse, when the discussion turns to the art of teaching, women largely disappear. Gilbert Highet, for example, makes it quite clear that artistry in teaching is to be reserved for teaching boys and that the teacher-artist is a man even if she happens to be female. More recently, Louis Rubin enumerates several characteristics of artistry in teaching, none of which acknowledges differences in male and female art.[3] A 1982 publication of the Harvard-Danforth Center for Teaching and Learning, *The Art and the Craft of Teaching*, assumes that art is art is art.[4] Eisner's work in curriculum criticism, while acknowledging the complexities of judgement and interpretation, also neglects the role of gender in both art and interpretation. That Charlotte Brontë did not write Thomas Hardy's novels nor did Thomas Hardy write Charlotte Brontë's has as much to do with gender as with anything else. The neglect is a curious, but not a mysterious, one.

I will argue that the educational stories we tell and our readings of those stories are, among other things, gendered, even when they appear to be universal and gender neutral. In thinking about teaching women, about the art of women teaching, and about women teaching women, we need to learn to undertake gendered readings. If stories about education are gendered, then our interpretations and criticisms of those stories must also be gendered. Jonathan Culler argues that texts, or our experiences of texts, change substantially when women read as women—something, he notes, women have not done until recently. What does it mean to read as a woman?

Feminist theory in education provides us with examples of what it means to read as a woman. Feminist studies of teaching have helped us attune our ears to the conversations and the subtexts beneath the surface of the foregrounded text. They have urged us to enlarge the space of pedagogical discourse and to insist on the gendered nature of pedagogical experience. Nel Noddings has brought us to an awareness of the liberatory and humane possibilities of an education that honors a feminist ethic.[5] Like Carol Gilligan, she has tried to rescue morality from the abstract and to situate moral discourse in the realm of personal relations. Jane Roland Martin, in entering the conversation of educational theory, has made us take women seriously, not as surrogate men, but as gendered creatures owning a specifically genderized knowledge. She has rendered untenable any universal appeal of the Peters ideal or the Hirst model of liberal education.[6] In Madeleine Grumet's work we read explicitly the maternal subtext in the background of women's teaching.[7] All of this has required that we take women students and ourselves seriously in a way that we have not done before. When educational discourse is enlarged to include women, then what we choose to observe, the stories that we tell, and the principles that guide our action all undergo significant changes.

A STORY

Somewhere I read (I have it written down in a notebook), "Man is a creature of passion who must live out that passion in the world." It was in one of my more undisciplined moments that I wrote that sentence, so I have no idea whose was the fiery mind in which it was forged. Nietzsche's perhaps, or Sartre's. Likely some romantic perched on the end of this thought in one of those moments of soaring far above the quotidian mercantile concerns and conversations of utilitarians and other philistines. Perhaps it was Freud in one of his more desolately biological moments.

"Man is a creature of passion who must live out that passion in the world." This sentence beings one of those stories meant to tell us how one ought to live, how one ought to live because one has no choice—one *must* live out one's passion in the world. This story is one of those about being human—one of those about being a human artist. We might read it as a description of a world that exists only as an object of passion—of my passion. Then it might be read as the beginning of one of those stories about knowledge that began to appear during the eighteenth century, as well as about art. Then its teller is a skeptic. The source of that passion is another matter. Libido perhaps. Libido transformed, but libido nonetheless. Or it might be the beginning of a story about failure, about the failure of human knowledge to constitute a meaningful life. It may be intended as a charm to protect the teller from despair over the inadequacies of human knowledge by making a virtue of necessity. Perhaps it is an invocation against what Stanley Cavell has called "the wisdom of skepticism"—the knowledge that we can never know the Other as we know ourselves.[8]

Of course, it might not be the *beginning* of a story at all. It might be the ending. It might be the end of a story that opens with Descartes's "discovery" that everything but "I" can be doubted. It might be the end of a spiritual saga that spans the distance from the radical skepticism of Hume to the radical indifference of Nietzsche to the apparent elimination of desire in twentieth-century analytic philosophy. It might be the old familiar conclusion in postmodern literature that the story is only about itself but that desire for an object, a subject matter of the story, is unslakeable. In any case, it *is* a story about *man*, about *man's* impulse to art and about his relation to knowledge. It is a story deeply embedded in a peculiarly male anxiety. But it is a story that we have all heard and learned to repeat in the course of our educations.

As I write, I find myself getting away from myself. The assertion distracts, and yet that creature of passion who has no choice but to live out his passion in the world exerts a fatal fascination. In some ways I know him better than I know myself. Of course, I have had a great deal more experience with him than I have had with myself. His is the voice of the great Western bourgeois tradition; his is the voice that sets the pitch for mine. I am his creation; he is the professor of desire. And what does he profess, this secular Jonathan Edwards of a professor? What does he desire? I ask these questions because he has been my teacher. As his student, I strove to satisfy his desire; as a teacher, I have taken his desire for my own.

When I was in college, I took a course in mythology. It was taught by a woman in a soft green sweater with a mothhole near the wrist of the right sleeve. She wore glasses. On the first day of class she sat on the desk. The rest of the semester, she joined us in a circle. There were only six of us; the red-haired girl was smartest. She always found her way out of the labyrinth first and stood on the magic stones of literature in the brilliant sunlight of definition, waiting for the rest of us to stagger out of the darkness and into language. In our struggle through the maze, we recapitulated the literary project, a project that begins with the birth of the hero and ends with his journey away from his mother, away from his desire for his mother to a state of perfect knowledge and grace. This journey too leads me away from myself. What do these stories have to do with the art of women teaching, or with the art of women teaching women?

"The art of teaching" is a subject with a venerable history. Scarcely anyone claiming to be educated has been silent on the matter. It is necessarily part of the discussion of the status and future of culture—real culture, that is, as opposed to mass culture. As a reader moves through the books and essays on this subject, she must infer one of three things: the art of teaching women is no different from the art of teaching men; women teaching are not engaged in art; the teaching of women requires little art. This is not to say that the professors have been silent on the education of women. Because we women are particularly charged with guardianship of culture (though not its production), the education of women has been of especial interest, along with the subject of women's teaching. Women do not beget culture; they mind it—both in the sense of tending and in the sense of obeying. The "art of teaching" and the "education of women" seem to be two very different, and unrelated, topics. The education of women is the education of those who are represented, but not of those who represent; it is the education of those who mind, but not of those who create culture.

Gender is one of the fundamental categories according to which we organize our experience of ourselves and others. A prominent theme in women's writing, both as art and about art, is and always has been that gender makes a difference in the production of art. Feminist scholars in all of the arts argue that indeed gender makes a difference. E. Anne Kaplan argues that filmmaking may be inseparable from male voyeurism—scopophilia, the need to see without being seen.[9] Virginia Woolf over and over again notes the ways in which a woman's sensibility differs from that of a man. Sandra Gilbert and Susan Gubar explore the images peculiar to the female imagination.[10] Feminist literary critics in general question the standards of literary production and taste. The stories women tell are very different from the stories men tell. Their difference has been sufficient to consign those stories to the realm of the sentimental or the minor. When these stories are judged to be sentimental or minor, they are judged to be so against the apparently neutral universal standards imposed by the totalizing tendencies of patriarchal discourse. If they are read instead as presenting vital alternative visions to those that ground patriarchal storytelling, our assessment of them changes. Feminist rereadings of the domestic literature that was, until recently, dismissed by literary critics as inconsequential and sentimental argue that that literature in fact is to be identified with human concerns unlike the gentlemanly and heroic concerns that define the canon.[11] If gender makes a difference in art, it must then make a difference in the practice of the art of teaching as well. But the literature on the art of teaching suggests that the teacher is sexless, that artistic teaching is simply artistic teaching, is gender neutral. Of course this view is compatible with the dominant conception of the artist in our culture.

Artistry demands an attitude, a way of being in the world. The artist in modern Western culture is precisely that man who is a creature of passion and who must live out that passion in the world, a passion psychoanalytic theory tells us is a passion to possess the absent and unpossessable mother—she-who-is-presumed-to-know, the source of life and the truth of his paternity. *His* passions, and the anxieties associated with them, are very different from those of the women artist. In his work he transforms the raw stuff of his passion into an image of the world crafted in the likeness of his own beautiful soul. He becomes his own substitute for the absent and forbidden mother. His passion is the foundation of our culture; through it he represents to us the deepest values and anxieties of our communities.

He is the solitary one, the man who stands outside of traditions and social structures. Lonely and disdained, with a sensibility so finely drawn that he must loathe the mess and fuss of everyday life, the talk that neither inspires nor enlightens, he spends himself only in his work—the endless creation and recreation of the woman suitable to protect his genius. Something inevitably goes wrong, though, and he makes a shrew or a whore. Few are so fortunate as Pygmalion who, Susan Gubar argues, embodies myths of male primacy, myths that enable the male to evade "the humiliation, shared by many men, of acknowledging that it is *he* who is really created out of and from the *female* body." Gubar argues that "such myths, securing for the male that creative power which makes women fearsome to him, acts to limit women's options for self-expression to the medium of their own bodies and faces."[12] What is involved in the art of teaching for such men? What have women to do with such art? When we find ourselves represented, we are either exemplars of virtue or objects of derision and fear. We are either above the world, and so worthy to be its guardians, or we are the source of all evil in the world.

Women are the objects out of which art is made. And the art that women have made has often represented just that state. If we cannot become artists, we can, as Gubar asserts, turn ourselves into objects of art. She reminds us of Woolf's Mrs. Ramsey and of Wharton's Lily Bart. Indeed, many have interpreted the situation of the woman in fiction as that of an artist without a medium. Questions of art are pertinent to questions of women's education because what art has made of women, education has made of us. Reading Rachel Brownstein, the female reader is recalled to her own history as a student, as a reader who finds and forms herself in literature.[13] We are affected in our deepest selves by the images and representations of those women in literature and art who stand for us qua women. It is important to us, then, that one easily spends four years in college classrooms meeting mostly harlots, courtesans, fishwives, and bourgeois consumers who in the act of consumption consume themselves along with their husbands, children and best friends. I teach a course, a "core" course at our university, in which we meet an astonishing number of women for sale, along with a violent and threatening Mother Nature who must be brought to her knees and in the words of one of the scientists in our curriculum, "forced to unveil herself."[14] When we find ourselves, we find ourselves hated and feared—unless of course we are to die tragically young either for our foolishness or our extreme goodness. Simultaneously as we find our identities as knowers, we find ourselves Other to ourselves, knowing ourselves and the world as the fathers do. Their desires and their anxieties become our own. At what cost to ourselves and to men?

ANOTHER STORY

Teaching women: It's neither an easy thing to do or to be. It's still less an easy thing to talk or write about when the language of teaching excludes, as it does, women's experience. In *The Small Room*, by May Sarton,[15] Harriet Summerson asks Lucy Winters, "Was there ever a life more riddled with self-doubt than that of a female professor?" "No," I said on first reading those words, "there never was. But why did no one ever notice it before?"

Lucy Winters has just taken a position in the English department of a small, elite women's liberal arts college, somewhere—anywhere—in New England. Appleton is every small northeastern liberal arts college, a place of personalities and political conflicts and a place of dedication to a certain notion of educational excellence. The fundamental proposition of the ideology of excellence that defines college life asserts that the price of excellence is exquisite pain and loneliness. The scholar, like than artist, is a solitary figure.

Lucy has just completed a Ph.D. in American literature at Harvard and ended an engagement. She is not sure that she wants to teach, is not sure that she will be a good teacher. In truth, she pursued an advanced degree only in order to be with her fiancé while he was in medical school. Her professional doubts and her personal sadness intertwine. They become equally important to her work as a teacher and in particular, I think, because she is a teacher of young women. Lucy's story of private failure is precipitated into that of her public commitment and anxiety by her discovery of a case of student plagiarism. The act of plagiarism threatens to unravel the bonds of community so carefully and precariously protected by the fractious faculty that prides itself on its members' distinguishing idiosyncrasies. The student is the favorite of a senior professor, one of a handful of respected scholars in medieval history. Carryl Cope is middle-aged, fiercely brilliant, totally immersed in her work, and dedicated to nurturing genius in those rare cases when it is to be found in a student. She is the professor of desire. Professor Cope has spent four years inspiriting and inspiring Jane Seaman with her own brilliance and ambition. Like Pygmalion molding his wax woman, Professor Cope has tried to create a wax student in her own image and has tried then to instill in that image her own life and passion. The art she has produced is a half-formed and oddly shaped thing, crippled in its spirit, a solitary one, suffering the fire of her brilliance without warmth or comfort. Jane's is a brilliance cracked and dimmed by anger and scorn. Speaking to Jane about a paper the student has written for her seminar, Lucy says:

> It was a straight A paper. . . . But I found it disturbing. I'm sure it gave you great pleasure to tell off so many clever people and prove yourself, to yourself, a match for them. . . .
>
> Your intelligence is, if you will, an angel. You are putting it to poor work for an angel. Really, that paper was full of hatred and self-hatred, hatred of the intellect, hatred of all those critics who can prove themselves superior to the artist they analyse because they can analyse him.[16]

Jane's anger and scorn congeal in her reading and diffuse throughout her writing, becoming finally the distinguishing mark of her identity. Consumed by hatred and self-hatred, she sabotages that which she believes to be all that legitimates any claim of hers on the attention or affection of others, in particular the attention and affection of Carryl Cope—her reputation as a brilliant student. Without the brilliant heat of her angry intelligence, what is Jane? How is she to be represented for others?

Lucy discovers the plagiarism quite by accident as a result of her rummaging in the library looking for something that might give her a new slant on teaching *The Iliad* to her first-year students. Jane Seaman's brilliant analysis of *The Iliad* for a forthcoming issue of a college journal turns out to have been stolen from "an obscure and forgotten essay" by Simone Weil. Everything that we know about living in an academic community demands that Lucy report her discovery. Like the messenger of Greek tragedy, Lucy's news sets in motion the machinery of justice and principle, a machinery that threatens to destroy the community it is meant to preserve.

Putting one's own name to another's work may be the gravest crime known to the academic community. It is interesting that in a culture in which the appropriation of the labor of others is the rule rather than the exception, only works of the creative mind retain any claim to individuality and to the right of the producer to control those works. Only through works of the intellect does one live out one's passion in the world. In a sense this view represents a sentimentalization of the life of the mind, a sentimentalization charted across the degradation of the body.

The English department at Cornell University distributes to students (or did in 1982) the following statement on plagiarism:

> Since one of the principal aims of a college education is the development of intellectual honesty, it is obvious that plagiarism is a particularly serious offense and the punishment for it is commensurately severe. What a penalized student suffers can never really be known by anyone but himself; what the student who plagiarizes and "gets away with it" suffers is less public and probably less acute, but the corruptness of his act, the disloyalty and baseness it entails, must inevitably leave an ineradicable mark upon him as well as on the institution of which he is privileged to be a member."[17]

Neil Hertz calls this document an extravagant teaching. Analyzing the above statement, he is intrigued by the imagined private consequences speculated on in the statement and by the fact that they are pure fantasy. People do get away with it, and we are probably safe in assuming that some of them do not suffer and that they may in future years have no memory of the act, much less an "ineradicable mark." Hertz invites us to imagine the following scenario:

> You have either found yourself caught up in the process or listened as some colleague eagerly recited the details of his own involvement. There is first the moment of suspicion, reading along in a student's paper; then the verification of the hunch, the tracking down of the theft, most exhilarating when it involves a search through the library stacks, then the moment of "confrontation" when the accusation is made and it is no longer the student's paper but this face which is read for signs of guilt, moral anguish, contrition, whatever.[18]

According to Hertz, the motivation for this extravagance is a projection, a projection of the professor's anxiety about his own originality stemming from "the self-division implicit in all linguistic activity." The word, we think, is an expression of the soul. But in words we deceive, and we betray. The anxiety, says Hertz, is "about the kind of 'writing' involved in teaching—the inscription of a culture's heritage on the minds of its young." A student's plagiarizing relieves our anxiety because it stands over against and demonstrates, by the fact of institutional violation, the integrity between one's own words and one's self, a binding of the self and its signs.[19] My words are my own; they are an expression of my soul. But where did these come from? Are they really my own? Do they really express my soul?

The binding of self to signs assures a continuity in the stories that maintain our institutions. Our stories are representations of individual identity and of the connection of individuals to communities. The entire network of human relationships is threatened when the word, that representation of identity, turns out to belong to another. But these stories, these stories of selves and institutions are male stories signifying the child's successful individuation from its mother. In all cases the child is, however genderless the story makes him appear, a male child still yearning after the story that binds him to the mother.

Man is a creature of passion who must live out that passion in the world. The object of passion, the object of desire, is integrity, integrity in the sense of being undivided, attached—attached to one's life and to one's words. The primal source of this desire for integrity, though, is the infant's powerlessness, his dependence on, his helpless *need* for, the often absent and frustrating mother. The mother represents not only frustrated attachment, but a creative power that the child must wrest from her in order to free himself of his need, in order to become individuated and autonomous. As the child becomes a man, though, integrity can be asserted only through the name of the father, the father's word and the father's law. And always this integrity must be demonstrated by individualness, by separateness, and, in the academic world, by creative originality that denies its genesis in the primal passions. The passionate life of the mind may turn out to have a great deal to do with the mind's displacement of passion onto the cultural heritage and its institutions.

Finally, the integrity of Appleton College is threatened not so much by the breaking of the law as by the recognition of the possibility that the law is inadequate to the task of insuring the integrity that is wanted. Unlike the messenger in Greek tragedy, who is not responsible for his message, Lucy knows that she in fact made a choice, the choice that started the machinery of the law. She wishes that she had not; she wishes that someone else would take responsibility; she shares none of the exhilaration of Hertz's Professor Sherlock. Other members of the community wish that the theft had not been discovered. Somehow the law of integrity seems, in this case, to require a violation of morality and a violation of all that one thought one was up to in the act of educating. The very definition of education is called into question. Finally, each member of the Appleton community is forced to come face to face with the way in which she is implicated in Jane's act because of the way in which she is implicated in the institution and its laws. Was there ever a life more riddled with self-doubt than that of the female college professor?

Lucy Winters is a teacher in spite of herself. She has come to Appleton only to escape the world she had inhabited with her fiancé. We learn that he ended the relationship and that his doing so had something to do with their being unable to speak to one another. Lucy describes their difficulty as rooted in the fact that she is a woman and he a man, that he thinks clearly and rationally, while she thinks sloppily and intuitively. His is a clean world and an ordered one, while hers is a clutter of irrelevant details hanging out of half-closed drawers, a world in which memories and sensations come tumbling out of jammed cupboards. Lucy is not sure that John's way is not superior—a tidy house with a place for everything and everything in its place, a house in which one can find one's way blindfolded or blind. How often has blindness figured in our cultural heritage?

Standing at her office window after having refused a student the emotional response that student was after, Lucy pleads with herself for a world in which all of the irrelevant details and distracting memories and sensations can be neatly pasted in scrapbooks and stacked at the back of the closet shelf. "I want to be free to teach my students in peace," she thought. "I want to be free to do that unself-consciously, without all this personal stuff."[20] And yet she thinks:

> But had one any right to protect oneself? What had she been protecting? A relationship that could not be maintained as fruitful if it lapsed into personalities? And what was teaching all about anyway? If one did not believe one was teaching people how to live, how to experience, giving them the means to ripen, then what did one believe? Was it knowledge that concerned her primarily? And would knowledge alone bring them to appreciate Thoreau?[21]

That education is about teaching people how to live and giving them the means to ripen is in fact exactly what one believes when one talks about the art of teaching. But this is not how art is represented in the patriarchal condition. Over and over again, the faculty of Appleton speak the same words. Jane's act forces us to wonder whether this art can be practiced in the small rooms of professors' offices or in the small room of the life of the mind. What Jane wanted from Professor Cope was the sort of love and approval that confirm the Other. Jane received books and higher expectations along with the sense that not she, but some power not honestly her own, was the basis of her value in the professor's eyes. Just as women are represented but do not represent themselves in the patriarchal tradition, Jane does not exist in herself, in her own voice. She is the object of her professor's desire, a desire that demands that she relinquish her own.

Women students are not unique in wanting something more from us than our passionate intellects lived out in our works of creative genius, our inscriptions of ourselves on the world. Male students are as likely to make the same demands. Women professors, for whatever reasons, are likely to feel the pull of those demands in ways than men are not. Perhaps it has something to do with women's self-doubt, a self-doubt that is very different from that of Hertz's professor.

Professor Sherlock doubts his own authorship, his own integrity, because he must doubt everything, because his inscription of himself, the living out of his passion in the world, is an inscription of desire and fear. A number of psychoanalytic theorists, following the work of Lacan, argue that subject-object relations, the very constitution of human subjectivity, and hence the constitution of that which subjectivity intends through its participation in human institutions, is rooted in patriarchal anxiety, an anxiety grounded in the conflict attending separation from the mother and in the male's uncertainty that his wife's offspring are indeed the flower of his seed. It is said that the male's inscriptions in culture and its laws are invocations permitting males to make the inference of paternity and to gain control of the threatening power of female generativity. The structures of their language and knowledge are saturated with the unconscious conflicts attending their exile from the all-powerful, phallic mother—the one-presumed-to-know. But she is not permitted to know, or at least not permitted to claim her knowledge, for the only available modes of representation are those that insure, by inference, male creativity, generativity, and legitimacy. The sense of an I and a you emerges at the same moment as does language, as does the power to represent, to make present to consciousness the absent mother.

Psychoanalytic theory teaches us that becoming a woman is an exceedingly difficult psychosexual task.[22] Achieving womanhood—or perhaps more appropriately, a female social identity—requires that we maintain identification with our mother even as we repudiate our primary love for her. Hers is the world that we must leave in order to individuate ourselves from her, even as hers is the world that our futures have in store for us. But because we are like our mothers physically, our turn from the mother to the father is a turning from ourselves. Social arrangements in the modern West require of the mother that she deliver both male and female children to the world of the fathers, to the world of public authority and civic power. But in that world male and female children are delivered to different locations. The male child's destination places him in direct alignment with the structure of authority and power. Although she enters the world of her brothers and fathers, the female's situation is problematic in a way that theirs cannot be. For she carries around inside her the Other whom the laws of the father require her to relinquish and leave behind—even to repudiate. The language in which she learns to represent herself and to maintain in presence the originary human relationship with her mother is the language of the father, a language that denies the power of the creative mother.

In some ways the relationship of the female teacher to her students recapitulates the mother-child relationship. Her duty is to wean the student from dependence on her, from preoccupation with his or her own subjectivity, to a mastery of the objective rules of the disciplines and to an independent place in the disciplinary order. She represents a disciplinary canon and an institutional text from which she is excluded, within which she must treat herself as Other to herself.

Was there ever a creature so riddled with self-doubt as the female professor? No. There never was. But hers is a different sort of anxiety, different both from that of the mother who relinquishes part of herself and from that of the male teacher, a compounded anxiety born of her continued identification with the mother and her exile in the language and knowledge that is our cultural heritage inscribed in our fathers' passions and texts, while yet she remains the Other of those passions and texts. She is simultaneously the object of art and the surrogate artist who creates, through the medium of the fathers' passions and texts, the female student. The male teacher, like the father, serves directly and unproblematically as the representative from the abstract world of order, method, beauty, justice, etc. He is "the reader," "the scientist," "the philosopher," "the lover," "the artist," the "he" whose voice we mimic.

Our institutional and disciplinary stories are compensatory, as Freud taught us in *Civilization and Its Discontents*. They are salve from the narcissistic wound. But they are male medicine. The wounds that men and women suffer are different. The male child loses the Other; the female loses herself as well. The shift from pre-Oedipal to Oedipal reality for the male requires that he substitute a like object for the original lost object. Female existence for him becomes a matter of infinite, but fairly simple, substitution of like objects. That shift for the female requires of her a total and entire repudiation of the original object, a moment of identification with the father—complicity in scorn for the lost object, and a shift of object to one totally unlike the original. Male art is a simple representation, a reenactment of the original loss attended either by scorn or exaltation of the new object. What have women to do with such stories? In these stories our silence and our authorial illegitimacy are encoded.

Jane's crime is plagiarism. In a way, it's the perfect female crime, much more suitable than poisoning, even when the poison is conveyed to its victim in a lovely red apple. Academic women commonly express the theme of imposture when talking about professional anxieties. Insofar as we speak in our work the language of the exile, are we not all of us plagiarists? We project ourselves into the world through the language that we speak, by obeying the narrative conventions of storytelling. But women's inscription in language is in the character of an inaccessible or despised Other, always beyond reach. Our words are expressions of our souls. Our words replace the original symbiotic wordless connection to the mother, making other connections with other speakers. When women speak, though, we speak in the compensatory language of the fathers, a language that stands in for male separation and male creative anxiety. The language both compensates the male for his loss by making a virtue of necessity in his loss of the mother—keeping her eternally lost, keeping woman eternally lost to herself.

Psychologists and other moralists will tell us that Jane's act is a response to pressure. They may tell us that she fears success or that she suffers from a peculiarly female self-defeating personality disorder. Her plagiarism then is read as a cry for the help she cannot ask for, a plea to be caught. But for what crime? Her only crime up until her claiming of the Weil essay as her own had been academic brilliance. If we are willing to be playful about our most sacred intellectual prejudices, we might argue that in fact Jane's act can be seen as an attempt toward a radical reenactment of what it means to be a woman in the academy and as a protest against exile. That she chose to steal the work of Simone Weil, she whose philosophy is one of radical nearness, of connectedness to its object, is in itself provocative. Simone Weil's work, both in life and in text, contests patriarchal authority. Patriarchal authority is legitimate only because it appeals to something beyond, indeed minimizes the demand for the threat of intimacy; a philosophy of radical nearness acknowledges both demand and threat.

The question becomes one of possibility. If art and language by their nature exclude women, are born of the male's need for and fear of female otherness, then what can we say regarding a feminist practice of the art of teaching? It would seem an impossible achievement.

In "Femininity," Freud announced his discovery of the persistent importance of pre-Oedipal development in women's lives. For Freud the pre-Oedipal moment is the "dark continent" of the female psyche, buried as was the Minoan civilization behind the Cretan and as inaccessible to the hungry eyes of man. The Minoan civilization is a figure for women's pre-Oedipal relationship to their mothers, a relationship that persists even through the achievement of post-Oedipal heterosexuality. "What do women want?" Freud asked.[23]

Freud hits a note of desperation in that question. As he acknowledges his ignorance of the dynamic of female desire, he recognizes that contrary to his own earlier view, male and female development are not symmetrical. In this moment, female development becomes infinitely complicated. Any understanding of the achievement of femininity resists all attempts to assimilate understanding of the feminine to the masculine dynamic. All of Freud's narrative ploys and habits of reason fail him at this moment.

The evidentiary base for Freud's theories of human development was literature. Freud himself never got so far as recognizing that that literature was written by men. His self-analysis, his treatment of his patients all devolved on his interpretations of literature and an analysis of present cases that proceeded principally through modes of analogy and assimilation. His reading of the literature that makes up our patriarchal heritage is subtle, perspicacious, and plausible. However, when we consider his one notable failure, his treatment of Dora, we encounter failure of the strategies of analogy and assimilation, recognition of which permeates the later "Femininity."

Dora is often read as a detective story. But it can also be read as a contest for narrative control. It can also be read as a story about the ways in which men passed women around among themselves—Dora's father first handing her over to Herr K. in payment for Herr K.'s indulgence of his wife's affair with Dora's father, and the father's then handing Dora over to the doctor who is to persuade her that there is no affair and that Herr K. never tried to seduce her. Although Freud believes Dora's account of events, he denies the authority of her interpretation. Freud takes on the role of the teacher here. His task is to teach the reluctant student to read the deeper thread of her narrative, which he read as her repressed attraction for Herr K. and her homosexual desire for his wife. Freud's insistence that Dora's illness masks her sexual desire for her father and is exacerbated by her repressed desire for Herr K. may in fact be read as Freud's story. It is curious that it should never have occurred to Freud that the sexual advances of a forty-year-old man would surely be *sexually* unwelcome to a fourteen-year-old girl. Forty is old to fourteen. Old and ugly. But Freud was forty-six and himself a sufferer of hysteric disorders. Freud read Dora's transference, but not his own, as he later admitted. He also neglected Dora's mother and what may have been the key to Dora's relationship with Frau K. She says of Frau K.'s children: "I was like a mother to them." According to Freud's own lights, Dora must become like her mother. But Dora's relationship to her mother is ambivalent, so Frau K. stands in for an idealized mother in Dora's negotiation of female identity. Freud had not yet discovered the Minoan civilization, the subtext of Dora's story.

When Freud refuses to permit Dora her story, she terminates analysis, giving him two weeks' notice—"like a governess or a servant," he says. She inverts the master-servant relationship, the male-female relationship. She refuses to play. A year later she returns to Freud for one meeting only to tell him that she has insisted on claiming her knowledge. She has forced her story, the story of her father's affair and Herr K.'s attempted seduction of her, on the adults who have persisted in denying it. Dora's anger wins. Yet Dora is the victim. The knowledge she insists on is the knowledge of her own victimization, a knowledge that imprisons her. She marries unhappily and suffers from a variety of hysterical and physical complaints until her death. Freud failed as a teacher in this case. He failed because Dora would not and could not take his story as her own. And the pre-Oedipal subtext of her own story remained buried beneath the ruins of patriarchal authority.[24]

Elizabeth Abel's reading of *Mrs. Dalloway* corrects Freud's mistakes with Dora. Using the development of Clarissa Dalloway as an example, Abel excavates a Minoan subtext in women's novels. She argues that while courtship or romance plots may dominate the narrative in women's novels, an effort at excavation uncovers a subtext of mother-daughter relations—a subtext "that both predates and coexists with the heterosexual orientation" that appears as the central element of the plot. Development in the female novel, Abel argues, proceeds from "an emotionally pre-Oedipal female-centered natural world to the heterosexual male world. . . . But the textual locus of this development . . . is a buried *subtext* that endures through the domestic and romantic plots of the foreground. In contemporary feminist fiction, the maternal plot is likely to be more insistently inscribed."[25] In contemporary women's fiction the foregrounded plot is equally likely to have to do with professional and economic success as with romantic and domestic arrangements, but even so these foregrounded plots continue to be countered by the maternal theme.

Jane's story recapitulates the female dilemma in making the transition from pre-Oedipal to Oedipal reality in a patriarchal world. And hers is a story complicated by her having been raised by rejecting and self-centered parents. She compensates for her familial loss by her self-invented brilliance. She masters the language of the fathers; she moves easily in the public world. But she fears that she is a fraud, and she resents that her legitimacy inheres in her adopting another's story—Carryl Cope's story of the price of brilliance. And Jane is angry. Rather than choose silence or confrontation, though, she exaggerates what she thinks of as her fraud by undertaking to do explicitly that which she has always suspected herself of doing. In response to Lucy's accusation that Jane has chosen to throw Carryl Cope to the wolves, Jane says: "What a sell for her! The infant prodigy turns out to be a fake!"[26] And Carryl says at another time, "Where did I go wrong? What happened? Am I crazy to think that for Jane Seaman to behave as a thief is a personal attack; that, consciously or not, it is an attack on me?" To which Lucy responds:

> Jane said it was like taking jumps on a horse with the bars set higher and higher. My guess is that at some point she went into panic. Possibly she realized without really knowing it that something was being left out; perhaps she wanted something of you quite desperately that you could not afford to give. It's not that she was right, only that she was stuffing herself with the wrong food and suffering from malnutrition, if you like.[27]

The story of Jane's plagiarism is on the surface a story of the relationship between institutions and individual responsibility, a story of the tension between authority and caring. It is complicated, though, by a mother-daughter subtext. The tensions in the foregrounded plot are fairly standard in novels about education. But rather than the novel being about individual development—Jane does not mature in the ordinary sense—it is a novel about the adjustment of others in the institution to a criminal act by one of its members, about their complicity in the act. Appleton is a patriarchal institution, and the tragedies that its members live are the sacrifices demanded by patriarchy—the price of genius or of excellence. Jane is caught in the story of the price of excellence, but it is not her story. The story of the price of excellence is the story that Lucy and her colleagues must rewrite if they are to teach young women and if they are to achieve their own voices in the institution.

Carryl Cope is a surrogate patriarch. She embodies the authority of institutions and disciplines, and it is she through whom that authority is passed on. She has never married, nor will she, having chosen to love another woman rather than men. Jane Seaman (semen) is as close as Carryl will ever come to having a child of her own; Professor Cope is Pygmalion, but her creation goes wrong, will never come to life and satisfy her desire. Carryl's friend says of her, "Carryl is like a man, of course. . . . I think Carryl saw in that girl, the image of herself when she was young."[28]

Jane's rebellion, like Dora's, is a struggle for the word. But her rebellion is also a peculiarly female one, one turned against herself, one that insures her expulsion from the institution against which she rebels. Jane's theft of another's words reveals her anomalous position within the institution, an institution that demands of women that they enact the father's stories, that they take those stories as their own.

Lucy learns in the course of the novel to attend to the subtext of women's lives and to foreground the subtext of her own. Only when she is able to do so is she able to commit herself to teaching. Lucy manages to avoid what another character describes as the poison of "this atmosphere of self-mutilation"[29] and is able in the end to assert her own need for both profession and belonging and to say, "If I stay, it will be for love."[30] And so does Carryl, but only through a special act of attention in which she comes to understand the sense in which, as she says, "Teaching women is a special kind of challenge. Most of the cards are stacked against one."[31]

If we would make our institutions more humane places for women (and consequently for men as well), we must learn to attend to the maternal subtexts in women's lives. We must fashion stories in which the word ceases to function only as a mark of loneliness and separation, pregnant with the possibility of betrayal. Excellence is too dear if its price is the pain of separation and the fear that one's identity is a pose. If the word, our stories, are to grant us the power to forge relationships rather than to compensate for the loss of the originary maternal relationship, we must find new forms and a new language.

The female artist manqué, having no medium of her own, makes of herself a work of art within the silent spaces allotted to her. She becomes her mother, and, as work of art, she makes of herself an object of aesthetic and erotic desire. For this reason women's art will always be personal, having a nearness to the self denied in the fathers' stories, but understood as the subtext and source of anxiety of those stories. The male artist creates in order to produce and control the Other; the female artist creates herself. Women's stories of the art of teaching, like Lucy Winters's, must produce, as they acknowledge, this difference.

A DIFFERENT STORY

"Call me (not Ishmael) Mary Beton, Mary Seton, Mary Carmichael, or by any name you please—it is not a matter of any importance." In order to talk about women and fiction, Virginia Woolf found herself obliged to invent a new literary form and to reexamine the literature we have.[32] *A Room of One's Own* is an essay. But it is an essay with a fictional narrator—Mary Beton, Mary Seton, Mary Carmichael. Essays do not ordinarily have fictive narrators, nor do their authors take their names to be of little importance. But then the narrator of this essay, a narrator who at its opening has been refused admission to the library at Oxbridge on account of her gender, wonders whether it isn't perhaps worse to be locked in than to be locked out. This is also a narrator who remarks of all those women writers who used the names of men, "Anonymity runs in their blood. The desire to be veiled still possesses them. They are not even now as concerned about the health of their fame as men are, and, speaking generally, will pass a tombstone or a signpost without feeling an irresistible desire to cut their names on it, as Alf, Bert or Chas. must do in obedience to their instinct."[33]

The fictive narrator of *A Room of One's Own* is all women. She is the subject, the I, the writer of this essay, as she is its subject (object) that she announces as "W" or woman. Susan Gubar has argued that all women writers have been simultaneously the subject and the object of their art, denied the distance from the object safeguarded to their brothers, those creators of well-wrought urns. Virginia Woolf uses the denial of access to the library as a figure for her being denied access to the essay form, to the structures of language and knowledge of Professor Sherlock and his colleagues. To try to speak through the essay would be plagiarism. In speaking for Carryl Cope, in the idiom of excellence that threads through the discourse of Appleton, Jane Seaman committed plagiarism. Virginia Woolf creates a fictive narrator and uses time and space novelistically in this essay in order to get us to think about the form itself. Woolf's ambition is to feminize the essay, to make it congenial to women's voices, by adopting the conventions of the genre that has been most congenial to women's lives—the novel.

The fictive narrator of this novelistic essay hints that she might have written a proper essay, but as she was chasing a fugitive thought on the nature of art through her mind while walking rapidly across a grass plot,

> instantly, a man's figure rose to intercept me. Nor did I at first understand that the gesticulations of a curious-looking object, in a cut-away coat and evening shirt were aimed at me. His face expressed horror and indignation. Instinct rather than reason came to my help; he was a beadle: I was a woman. This was turf; there was the path. Only the Fellows and Scholars are allowed here; the gravel is the place for me.[34]

The beadle intervenes. The forces of the male world that excludes women intervene. What in the male world has stopped the female essayist? It is the male's total appropriation of both form and content. But the small room of the essay, with its confining attention to facts and to truth and to grand conclusions, is itself a fiction, a fiction in which men have created women only in relation to men, as they have in their poems and plays and novels. *A Room of One's Own* is, above all, a new form and one that contains a new sort of truth, one that creates a new sort of relationship between the author and her life and her work.

The relationship between the author and her work, as it has always been between women writers and their work, is a personal one. Mary Beton, Mary Seton, Mary Carmichael rejects the old artistic molds and forms because these molds and forms distort our understanding of women, of men, and of art. Suppose, she says, all we knew of the male world we had learned from the female domestic novel. Suppose that all men knew of themselves they had learned from the ways that women have seen men in their relationship to women. And yet that is precisely how we women have come to know ourselves through the art in which we are represented, through the language in which we represent ourselves. It is precisely this art that we teach when we practice the art of teaching. In teaching women, we lead them into exile, giving them up to the forms and languages of the fathers. The forms and languages of the arts we employ frighten us with their contradictory appeals to integrity and their insistence on solitariness and division. Was their ever a creature more riddled with self-doubt?

Those who talk about the art of teaching often engage in, or urge the rest of us to engage in, an analysis of the art of teaching analogous to analyses of other art forms. Those forms and their analyses, however, leave out the experience of women teaching women and avoid our gendered modes of making art. To confront the classroom as a text or other object of art requires us to understand women as object of art and to posit a woman reader of that art. Such a reader might ask, "What is so dreadful about plagiarism? What has been stolen or violated?"

Man is a creature of passion who must live out that passion in the world. What is the passion about and what is the source of the despair that reverberates through his insistence? That it is a cry of despair as well as an assertion, I have no doubt. I am certain that, knowing the history of my own relationship with that creature of passion, at the moment I inscribed that cry into my notebook it was as a treasured confession from a lover, the artist who alone possesses the creative power to animate me. He was my teacher.

In Guber's reading of the male creative myth, his desire is for the power to create the one who must love and totally comprehend him, a power of creation that the male artist usurps from woman. She who in her own corporealness is opaque must be made transparent. Her transparency is achieved by the artist's conception of her as empty. Gubar brings to us the words of male artists describing woman as a blank page, a page waiting to receive the writer's imprint. The male appropriation of the female body as the object of art results perforce in an aesthetic of distance. The object, however fashioned as a mirror of the artist's ideal, remains irredeemably, intractably Other. His passion and his despair are unabated. In response, Gubar tells us, women have taken themselves as texts, their bodies as objects out of which to create art. Necessarily, then, a woman's art is a personal one, one that collapses distance since her art is made from her body—her body as object of art. Rather than creating an idealized or despised Other, the female artist creates herself.[36] But still her language is the language of the fathers, and the stories that she tells follow their narrative conventions.

When we practice the art of teaching, we engage in the art of telling and embellishing stories we have read. We teach our students to read. We now suspect that reading and telling stories are gendered acts. Elaine Showalter argues that the hypothesis of a woman reader substantially changes our experience of a text and, by implication, our teaching of it. First, such reading requires us to investigate the ways in which our understanding of the cultural heritage and its institutions and laws serve male interests. Second, our experience changes because we come to see just how vehemently our subjectivity is denied, and we become aware of what many have called our "divided consciousness."[36] Our divided consciousness is the product of our always experiencing ourselves through the eyes of others. In novels by such female writers as Doris Lessing and in accounts given by women in psychotherapy, women frequently report the experience of standing outside themselves, watching and monitoring themselves. The woman who comes to know herself through male literature and art comes to know herself as Other to herself. How, then, does she teach legitimately and artistically? On what world does she impress her passion? The art of teaching as a woman, like the art of reading as a woman, leads us to search for a female aesthetic.

Showalter traces the development of women's work in literature through three historically distinct phases: the feminine phase in which women tried to equal the achievements of male culture and "internalized its assumptions about female nature"; the feminist phase, which involved a protest against the postures of "femininity," a protest involving the depiction of the wrongs of women; and the female phase, which begins with such writers as Virginia Woolf—a rejection of both imitation and protest, both coming to be seen as forms of dependency. To paraphrase Showalter, our entry into the female phase involves our refusal to be the Annie Halls of our disciplines, walking around in men's clothes. But it does not require us to relinquish or deny what is useful in our disciplines.

Like our art, our education denies us access to female experience. That such is the case has been amply demonstrated in research on women and education. Our education either disvalues experiences and qualities that psychologists have taught us to associate with the female, ignores them, or reshapes them. It is an education that requires of us all that we look on the world from the distance safeguarded by the Law. It is an education that denies the personal and one that denies the body—the body about which we women learn to become so acutely self-conscious. It is an education that denies the knowledge that we are limited in what we can know and one that succeeds in that denial because of its effacing of the personal. The privileging of the visible over the invisible, inference over intuition, is a consequence of the forever to be frustrated passion to claim with certainty the elusive object of desire—the knowledge of the one presumed to know.

According to Luce Irigaray, in the end the male project requires an unspoken denial of gendered difference. This denial of difference, she says, amounts to a denial of the legitimacy of woman's experience of herself, her only legitimate way of knowing her place in the world being through men's experience of her. The women's project, as psychoanalyst, as teacher, as artist, says Irigaray, is to reclaim women's experience by producing difference, by insisting on differing. She urges us to have a fling with the philosophers by challenging all of their systems and ideas.[37] What is so awful about plagiarism?

In the spirit of Irigaray, it seems to me that we should reexamine what we take for granted about educational life. Why is plagiarism considered a more heinous act than nearly any other a student may commit at the university? At Appleton, plagiarism meant expulsion. Of course, it is true that universities are centers of intellectual work, that our work as professors is to help students achieve their full intellectual capacity and to teach them to think and write honestly. I am not condoning plagiarism. Rather, I am trying first to explore the possibility that a female student's plagiarism may have psychological and political dimensions not previously considered. Second, I mean to remind us that university preparation, at least according to most catalogues of liberal arts colleges and universities, is usually declared by professors and administrators to embody aims in addition to those having to do with the life of the mind. I should like us to ask ourselves why we do not punish other student transgressions of the aims and values of our institutions so drastically as plagiarism.

Disrespect of self and others, disregard for the future of the planet, failure to take social and political responsibility, moral apathy, spiritual enslavement to fashion or anything else—such things as these seem to me subversive of educational goals, for it seems to me that a sense of respect and regard ought to be a primary educational goal. In fact, if we look at any college catalogue description of the liberal arts project, we find enumerated such cares as I have listed. And yet the structure of our institutions, the laws, the regulations and the regularities, the form and the content of our teaching places those cares beneath what we may take as a concern to safeguard private property. For knowledge has come to be a sort of property, just as women are, and plagiarism is an infringement on private property rights. But more important than the status of knowledge as private property, I think, is our expectation that knowledge do more than it can. Suppose that Jane's plagiarism is a denial of property relations and an assertion of the limits of patriarchal knowledge. We academics tend naively to suppose that to know the good is to do it. We suppose that the truth will set us free. And knowledge, we hope, will heal the narcissistic wound, will assure us our integrity. It is for this reason that we confront plagiarism with such horror. But when our knowing is an act of splitting, then it becomes unclear what plagiarism is. At Appleton, the language and knowledge contained in the narratives of the values and commitments of the community for whom that language and knowledge served as the single mode of discourse is undermined finally by the exclusion of women from those narratives—by inattention to the maternal subtexts of the stories of what teachers and students are like. The cards are stacked against us because of what is foregrounded in our narratives and what is denied, split off, but what nonetheless complicates the foregrounded story.

Women's art denies that splitting, as should women's teaching. The primary task of women teaching women (and men) is to enact a language and an art in which we can all converse as ourselves and in which the intellectual and emotional in each of us remain in conversation. The image of the polis of the mind that haunts Western philosophy, an image in which one part of the mind—the rational, defined in terms of one kind of truth and one kind of process that controls discourse—must be replaced by an image of a democratic mind in which all mental processes and all of one's history are in conversation. Elizabeth Young-Bruehl has pointed out in this regard Freud's caution: If those secondary mental processes associated with what we commonly call thinking are detached from primary unconscious processes, the result is psychological disturbance. And yet our educational practice depends on such detachment, a detachment that I have argued is particularly injurious to women, although it harms men as well. Young-Bruehl urges us to conceive of ourselves as thinkers whose mental processes (primary and secondary) are in conversation with themselves and with others. It is in such conversation that we defy the project of subordination and repression and move toward achieving the liberatory project of education.[38] We may say that practicing the art of teaching involves us in the art of conversation, to the subtleties and intricacies of which women novelists are well attuned.

We do not plead for a rejection of the rational or the inferential. Nor do we mean to devalorize the experience of that creature of passion, our brother. Rather, we plead for a conception of art and education that opens the door to other rooms, rooms that are larger. In these larger rooms, the solitary singer might find a choir, the lonely teller of tales, that ancient mariner, an audience and a cast of characters on whose solidity and integrity he may depend. Such a conception would not deny difference, nor would it insist on unity. Such a conception would not deny the personal, would not deny the body. It would enable us to bring ourselves to our art and our education, both for ourselves and for each other.

CONCLUSION

Contemporary philosophy, social science, and literary theory have accustomed most of us to perceive authority and authorship as these are judged and achieved or conferred through our institutions as products of human interest and to understand that human interest is socially and historically conditioned—that knowledge itself is institutional. We have been comfortable for some time now with texts that have no stable meanings, with the shift of authority from the text to the interpretation of the text; we have learned to inhabit a world in which knowledge claims are judged according to standards of truthfulness rather than of truth; we live with the suspicion that social research constitutes, in an important sense, its phenomena. Accelerating technological changes and national and international political events inscribe the world as a text of shifting meanings, constructing a scene of interpretation in which the only certainty is the indeterminacy of the text. Authority becomes displaced from text to reader, calling into question the very notion of authorship.

The art of teaching, conceived as the art of conversation, as the construction of narrative, has to be rethought in the present scene of interpretation. "Was there ever a life more riddled with self-doubt than that of a woman teacher?" What is it that she doubts? The dominant forms of knowledge, privileged ways of knowing and thinking and speaking, Freud teaches us, all are oriented to the male experience of separation from the mother. This is also the foundation of all art. Knowledge, high-status knowledge—that is, objective inferential (indeterminate), and principle-based knowledge—mirrors the inferential (indeterminate) nature of knowledge of paternity. Like the father who knows his son, the scientist and the priest come to their knowledge through inferences about causes and their effects. What women know is a dangerous knowledge and one that threatens the fathers' order; it is a knowledge that must be refused admission to that order. To know ourselves as women is to know our knowledge as illegitimate—outside the father's order. Wittgenstein once said that it is the purpose of philosophy to prevent the bewitchment of the sense by language. The work of certain psychoanalytic feminist theorists persuades us that language itself is the instrument of patriarchal domination, in that it must devalorize women's experience and knowledge. "If I stay, it will be for love," Lucy says. How far from that creature of passion, our artist brother whose indeterminate texts are those from which we have taken the significance of our own lives. Through his art, his passion and his private self are projected onto the public world. But what of *her* art?

We know that women have traditionally been excluded from public authority—that is from access to public language used for public purposes. We know with what horror the brothers and fathers and husbands of nineteenth-century feminists and abolitionists greeted their public speech making even when they supported their causes. We know, with some exceptions, of course, that when women have not been excluded from authorship, their work has been disvalued. Those of us whom Virginia Woolf referred to as "educated men's daughters" indeed had no public value. Woolf thought that when women gained access to public institutions, when we were no longer locked out and forbidden entrance to the library at Oxbridge, when we gained 500 pounds a year and rooms of our own, we would find our voices. But admission to the library may be a mixed blessing alienating us from our own experience, drowning our voices in those of our educated fathers, trapping us in an indeterminate universe in which we ourselves are all too determinate, created in the father's stories. The female professor is simultaneously locked in and locked out. Excellence costs her a good deal more than the romantic loneliness exacted from her male colleagues. It requires something still more of her—silence. She is a women who certifies male knowledge and is constructed as an object of that knowledge.

Being locked out can have its advantages. Being locked out, Woolf was able to reconstruct the project of fiction, to find new forms for it, and to endow it with new concerns as she continued her search for the woman's sentence, the language that will admit what women know by virtue of their otherness.

The story of the art of teaching, when it is practiced by women and when it is practiced in the teaching of women, must begin by producing difference, by acknowledging what women know. Either we are locked out or we are plagiarists. The stories that we tell are not our own. The impulse to the art of women teaching and the art of teaching women begins in that recognition. The impulse is triggered by the recognition of our public standing, our excellence as scholars and teachers, exacts from us a different sort of pain, the pain of personal self-effacement.

I have argued that the practice of the art of teaching presents women teachers with difficulties that inhere in women's peculiar relationship to art in general. Supposing that the teacher is a woman, I have tried to explore the possibilities of teaching as a woman rather than as a surrogate patriarch.

In his summary of feminist theory in literature, Jonathan Culler locates three moments. In the first moment, criticism is thematic, appeals to the reader's experience, and argues a continuity between her experience of texts and her experience in the social world. In that moment, the critic defines gender identity as critical and that which privileges the reader's interpretation. The second moment is one of irony, in which the woman reader understands that she has not been reading as a woman, that the interpretive problem lies in her having been led, against her intentions, to identify with male interests. It is in this moment of awareness that difference is enacted and the condition of being a woman created even as it is already given in experience. At this moment, the presumed gender neutrality of male knowledge and male art is challenged and a reading produced that is intended to correct for male defenses and distortions. The reading produced demonstrates how male interests have coopted the rational. The third moment is the most difficult to achieve, for it is here that the feminist reader examines ways in which her own notions of the work are tied to, and even complicit with, the males. These moments, of course, overlap in the actual experience, the residue of the first moment being present in the second, and so on. The task here is to explore alternatives to methods, assumptions, and goals that have served to preserve male authority. But, says Culler,

> It is not a question of rejecting the rational in favor of the irrational, of concentrating on metonymical relations to the exclusion of the metaphorical, or on the signifier to the exclusion of the signified, but of attempting to develop critical modes in which the concepts that are the products of male authority are inscribed within a larger textual system.[39]

Inscribing the act of plagiarism within a textual system larger than that of institutional expectation and sanction, a textual system in which gender serves as a fundamental organizing principle and women's relationship to the production of art and knowledge is understood as different from that of men, brings us to a moment in which we must rethink what it means for women to practice the art of teaching and what it means for all of us who teach women.

Notes

I should like to express my appreciation to Jane L. Pinchin for her reading of Virginia Woolf, a reading that influenced many of the ideas in this essay. For their judicious and constructive criticisms of an earlier draft of this essay and for their encouragement, I am grateful to Nel Noddings and two anonymous reviewers of *Educational Theory*. To Madeleine R. Grumet, whose good talk, generous yet demanding criticism, and whose own writing have taught me much that found its way into this essay, I affirm the importance of those conversations.

1. Susan Stanford Friedman, "Authority in the Feminist Classroom: A Contradiction in Terms?" In *Gendered Subjects*, ed. Margo Culley and Catherine Portuges (London: Routledge & Kegan Paul, 1985), 203–8.

2. For a full account of women's peculiar relationship to the authority of language, see Jacques Lacan, *Feminine Sexuality*, ed. Juliet Mitchell and Jacqueline Rose (New York: Norton, 1985); Jane Gallop's reading of the relationship between Lacan and Luce Irigaray in *The Daughter's Seduction* (Ithaca, N.Y.: Cornell University Press, 1982); and Luce Irigaray, *The Sex Which Is Not One* (Ithaca, N.Y.: Cornell University Press, 1985).

3. Louis Rubin, *Artistry in Teaching* (New York: Random House, 1985).

4. Margaret Morganroth Gullette, ed., *The Art and Craft of Teaching*, distributed for the Harvard-Danforth Center for Teaching and Learning, Faculty of Arts and Sciences (Cambridge: Harvard University Press, 1984).

5. Nel Noddings, *Caring: A Feminine Approach to Ethics and Moral Education* (Berkeley: University of California Press, 1984).

6. Jane Roland Martin, *Reclaiming a Conversation: The Ideal of the Educated Woman* (New Haven, Conn.: Yale University Press, 1985), "The Ideal of the Educated Person," *Educational Theory* 31, no. 2 (Spring 1981), and "Bringing Women into Educational Thought," *Educational Theory* 34, no. 4 (Fall 1984).

7. Madeleine R. Grumet, "Conception, Contradiction, and Curriculum," *Journal of Curriculum Theorizing* 7 (Winter 1981); "My Face Is Thine Eye, Thine in Mine Appears: The Look of Parenting and Pedagogy," *Phenomenology + Pedagogy* 1, no. 1 (Winter 1983); *Bitter Milk* (Amherst: University of Massachusetts Press, 1988).

8. Stanley Cavell, *The Claim of Reason* (New York: Oxford University Press, 1979).

9. E. Anne Kaplan, *Women and Film* (New York: Methuen, 1983).

10. Sandra M. Gilbert and Susan Gubar, *The Madwoman in the Attic: The Woman Writer and the Nineteenth-Century Literary Imagination* (New Haven, Conn.: Yale University Press, 1979).

11. Lillian Robinson, "Treason Our Text: Feminist Challenges to the Literary Canon," and Jane P. Tompkins, "Sentimental Power: *Uncle Tom's Cabin* and the Politics of Literary History," in *Feminists Criticism: Essays on Women, Literature, and Theory*, ed. Elaine Showalter (New York: Pantheon Books, 1985).

12. Susan Gubar, " 'The Blank Page' and the Issues of Female Creativity," in *Feminist Criticism*, 292.

13. Rachel M. Brownstein, *Becoming a Heroine* (New York: Penguin Books, 1984).

14. Claude Bernard, *An Introduction to the Study of Experimental Medicine* (New York: Dover, 1957).

15. May Sarton, *The Small Room* (New York: Norton, 1961), 29.

16. Ibid., 163.

17. Neil Hertz, Two Extravagant Teachings," in *The Pedagogical Imperative: Teaching as a Literary Genre*, ed., Barbara Johnson (New Haven, Conn.: Yale University, Yale French Studies no. 63, 1982), 60, quoting from "A Writer's Responsibilities," which was in turn excerpted from Harold C. Martin, *The Logic and Rhetoric of Exposition* (New York: Holt, 1958).

18. Ibid., 61, 62.

19. Ibid., 63.

20. Sarton, *The Small Room*, 200.

21. Ibid., 201.

22. It should be understood that I am not making biological or universal claims in my use of psychological theory. With Simone de Beauvoir and others, I am assuming that gender is made within our relational experiences of same- and difference-sexed others and that our ways of making gender emerge from a social, political, and economic complex, which is in turn influenced by our ways of making gender and by our relational experiences of gender.

23. Sigmund Freud, "Femininity," in *New Introductory Lectures on Psychoanalysis* (Hamondsworth, England: Penguin, 1933).

24. Sigmund Freud, *Dora: An Analysis of a Case of Hysteria* (New York: Macmillan, 1963). See also the essays on this case collected in *In Dora's Case: Freud, Hysteria, Feminism*, ed., Charles Bernheimer and Claire Kahane (London: Virago Press, 1985).

25. Elizabeth Abel, "Narrative Structure(s) and Female Development: The Case of *Mrs. Dalloway*," in *The Voyage In: Fictions of Female Development*, ed. Elizabeth Abel, Marianne Hirsch, and Elizabeth Langland (Hanover, N.H.: University Press of New England, 1983).

26. Sarton, *The Small Room*, 102.

27. Ibid., 125, 126.

28. Ibid., 204.

29. Ibid., 234.

30. Ibid., 249.

31. Ibid., 237.

32. Virginia Woolf, *A Room of One's Own* (New York: Harcourt Brace Jovanovich, 1929). Much of the use I shall make of Woolf's essay I owe to a lecture given in a Colgate University course, entitled "Interdisciplinary Perspectives on Women," by Professor Jane Pinchin.

33. Woolf, *A Room of One's Own*, 52.

34. Ibid., 6.

35. Gubar, " 'The Blank Page' and Issues of Female Creativity."

36. Elaine Showalter, "Toward a Feminist Poetics," in *Feminist Criticism*.

37. See Luce Irigaray, *This Sex Which Is Not One* and *Speculum of the Other Woman* (Ithaca, N.Y.: Cornell University Press, 1986).

38. Elizabeth Young-Bruehl, "The Education of Women as Philosophers," *Signs* 12, no. 2 (Winter 1987): 207–21.

39. Jonathan Culler, *On Deconstruction* (Ithaca, N.Y.: Cornell University Press, 1982), 61.

PART V

Diversity and Multiculturalism

18

SCHOOLING AND RADICALISATION: LIFE HISTORIES OF NEW ZEALAND FEMINIST TEACHERS

Sue Middleton

INTRODUCTION

Sociologists of education have become increasingly concerned with the school as a site of social and cultural reproduction. Rejecting the liberal view that schools are agents of social mobility and human emancipation, many sociologists have focused their analyses on how schooling constructs and reproduces the social relations of class, racism, and gender in the wider, capitalist society. In this, they have failed to account for the emergence of radicals (including sociologists) in educational settings. Sociologists have neglected to study the educational experiences of those who become radical critics of education, of radical teachers.

Since the resurgence of feminism as a mass social movement in the early 1970s, schooling has been viewed as a site of gender struggle. Many of today's feminist teachers, however, attended schools in the 1950s and early 1960s—a time when curricular provisions rested on firm, and largely unquestioned, assumptions of differentiated gender-roles. Despite the conservative intentions of the policymakers, many women of the post–World War II generation resisted the dominant ideology of patriarchal femininity that characterized the overt selection and social organisation of school knowledge. As feminist teachers, such women have come to view schooling as a means of working towards equity in gender relations. The paper is drawn from a wider study of feminist teachers who were born and educated in New Zealand in the years immediately following World War II (Middleton, 1985c). It analyses the school experiences of two of the women studied and explores the part played by these experiences in their adoption, as adults, of a radical analysis of the social world.

The method used is life history analysis, which focuses on what Mills and others have referred to as "biography, history and social structure" (Mills, 1976; Laing, 1971; Plummer, 1983; Sedgwick, 1983). A life history approach can help the researcher to analyse both the lives of individuals and the social context of their experience, relating "the personal troubles of milieu and the public issues of social structure" (Mills, 1975, p. 14). People are seen not as mere passive victims of their socialization, but as creative strategists who devise means of dealing with, resisting, and resolving the contradictions they experience. The first part of this paper analyzes contradictions in expectations for the New Zealand educated 'postwar woman' through studying the ideas expressed by policymakers in curriculum documents. The second part presents two case studies. These focus on the strategies these women developed in their school years to deal with the contradictions of femininity and their experiences of marginality and to trace the relevance of these to the beginnings of their political radicalisation.

CONTRADICTIONS IN THE POSTWAR WOMAN'S EDUCATION: THE COMPULSORY CORE CURRICULUM, WOMEN'S WORK, AND THE POLITICS OF FEMALE SEXUALITY

In New Zealand, as elsewhere in the 'western' world, the years that followed World War II were a time of increased access to secondary schooling. During the war, the Thomas Commission produced the blueprint for postwar secondary education (Department of Education, 1944, 1959 edition). The Labour government's prescription for postwar education, as outlined in the Thomas Report (1944, 1959 edition), was both liberal and meritocratic. Schooling was conceptualised as "reconstructionist" (Codd, 1985) as a bastion against the resurgence of fascism. A core curriculum was recommended for all pupils in the first three years of secondary school "as an aid to growth and as a general preparation for life in a modern democratic community" (Dept. of Education, 1959 edition, p. 6). Schools would produce adults able to take their place in a liberal democracy as "workers, neighbours, homemakers and citizens" (p. 5)—the only limit to their aspirations was to be the (then largely uncriticised) notion of 'merit' or 'ability'. All pupils were to take social studies, mathematics, English, general science, music, art, and crafts.

However, a feminist reading of the Thomas Report and other key policy documents of the time (Middleton, 1986) shows that expectations for the postwar woman were contradictory. The role expected of married women after the war was a domestic one: they would leave their wartime jobs and devote themselves to domestic life (Cook, 1985). This would ensure the rehabilitation of military men, a growing population of stable, psychologically well-adjusted children and a 'booming,' growing economy. Women who failed to live up to the ideal of domestic femininity were regarded as 'poorly adjusted' and in need of the curative powers of contemporary medical psychological science (Ehrenreich and English, 1979; Friedan, 1963). The postwar woman was to experience in her schooling a set of cultural practices that were based on the assumptions of both a liberal ideology of equality and meritocracy and, at the same time, an ideology of domestic femininity. A woman's true role economically was as biological and social reproducer of the work force (Marx, 1976 edition). The patriarchal nuclear family, with the husband as breadwinner, was seen as essential to the maintenance of social cohesion and public morality. Schooling was to reproduce a gendered labour force. Certain jobs, such as teaching and nursing, were seen as suitable work for girls, but only as a "short adventure between school and marriage" (Watson, 1966, p. 159), or, as in the teacher shortage of the 1950s and 1960s, when their labour was seen as necessary as patriotic service in a (peacetime) national emergency (Department of Education, 1962, p. 585). Their 'true calling' however, was domestic and, to ensure that girls were adequately prepared, a stiff dose of compulsory domestic science was included in the core curriculum:

> An intelligent parent would wish a daughter to have, in addition, the knowledge, skill and taste required to manage a home well and make it a pleasant place to live in. (Department of Education, 1959 edition, p. 7)

The Thomas Report also made specific recommendations on sex education (Middleton, 1986). Control of female sexuality was a central theme in wartime and postwar planning. According to Foucault (1980a), sexuality has acquired a

> specific significance in modern times because it concerns characteristics that are at the intersection between the discipline of the body and the control of the population. (Giddens, 1982, p. 219)

Concern with a threatened drop in the birthrate had been expressed before and during the war: control of sexuality became a central political issue. It was also seen as necessary to maintain the social order and prevent 'delinquency'. These concerns were evident in the Thomas Report and other sex education documents (Middleton, 1986). At secondary school, children were to learn the 'facts of reproduction' as preparation for marriage and family life. These were to be taught as a part of the General Science curriculum: in Foucault's terms, sex was treated as a 'medical' issue, reduced to "lessons in biology and in the anatomy and physiology of the reproductive system" (Department of Education, 1959 edition, p. 54). Sex education materials of the time show that they were premised on the sexual 'double standard'—men had uncontrollable urges, which virtuous women, who did not have such urges, must curb for them (Middleton, 1986). Learning to be 'attractive' was very much the overt and covert curriculum for girls (Taylor, 1984). One was supposed to learn to attract males, but one was not supposed to give in to their sexual advances—only delinquents did this. Girls in academic streams who were to train for the professions were expected to delay sexual activity,[1] including marriage, until after they had finished their training. Teacher trainees who married while training lost their studentships. Overt sexuality and intellectuality/professionality were socially constructed as contradictory.

The educational expectations for women and girls in postwar New Zealand, then, were contradictory. On the one hand, girls were promised equality of opportunity on the liberal/meritocratic model—the chance to pursue study and a career, to attain personal and professional autonomy. On the other hand, they were expected upon marriage to become economically and emotionally dependent. Liberalism and femininity were contradictory. In terms of expression of their sexuality, girls were expected to be 'attractive' but not to 'give in'. Academic study and a professional career were antithetical to full expression of their sexuality.

The recommendations in the Thomas Report were adopted and made policy in the Education (Postprimary Instruction) Regulations of 1945. Its implementation was made difficult, however, because of the sudden vast increase in the pupil population and the drastic shortage of teachers. Providing enough classrooms and teachers became the Education Department's main priority (McLaren, 1974;

Whitehead, 1974). Secondary schools were organised as multilateral comprehensives that streamed their pupils on the basis of courses (combinations of optional subjects) taken, e.g., academic or professional streams (foreign languages), commercial and homecraft streams (Department of Education, 1962; Harker, 1975; Whitehead, 1974). By means of two case studies, I shall show how these streaming practices, based on hierarchies of knowledge, reproduced the contradictions between the expectations of liberalism and femininity and also the sexual double standard. Within the schools, the girls devised strategies to resist and resolve these contradictions (Findlay, 1973; Frame, 1983).

Feminist scholars such as Bartky (1977), Eisenstein (1982), and Mitchell (1973) have argued that women's experiences of widespread social contradictions in the postwar years generated the second wave of feminism. Mitchell (1973) has argued that this resurgence of feminism as a mass social movement was largely stimulated by 'educated' women. Increased access to education gave women access to ideas with which to articulate their discontent and to the credentials that would give access to both economic and professional independence and to positions of power from which to effect change. According to Mitchell (1973, p. 38),

> The belief in the rightness and possibility of equality that women share has enabled them to feel 'cheated' and hence has acted as a precondition of their initial protest . . . It offered a mystifying emancipation and participating in an ideology of equality, and the sense of something wrong that is more acute than when women share in the openly dominative structure of feudal, semifeudal or early capitalist societies.

Not all women of the postwar era who experienced contradictions became feminists, however. Conducive social conditions are a necessary, but not a sufficient, explanation for why some women became feminists while others did not. Furthermore, at the time these women were at school, the 1950s and 1960s, specifically feminist ideas were not yet widely accessible to help them articulate their personal experiences of contradictions as wider social issues.

Other radical theories, however, were available. New Zealanders were deeply embroiled in internal conflicts over the Vietnam War and rugby tours with South Africa—issues of racism and imperialism were widely debated in the popular media. Many school students of the time came from families that did not have a tradition of secondary and higher education—rural children and working-class children had increased access to education (Nash, 1981; NZCER, 1965: Watson, 1966). As the first in their families to have access to secondary education, academic courses, and/or professional training, their experience was often one of 'marginality'. Bourdieu (1971a, p. 179) commented that it was often the "marginal intellectual" in academic settings who was most likely to develop a radical critique of education:

> the attacks against academic orthodoxy come from the intellectuals situated on the fringes of the university system who are prone to dispute its legitimacy, thereby providing that they acknowledge its jurisdiction sufficiently for not approving them.

> Experiencing contrasting expectations as to how he or she should live, the subject becomes aware of the essentially artificial and socially constructed nature of social life, how potentially fragile are the realities that people make for themselves.

The experience of not belonging can be fraught with tension—it is not pleasant, particularly if the group to which one is 'the stranger' is the dominant group. The experience of marginality (as working class, Black, etc.) is radicalising when it is understood theoretically as a manifestation of the unequal power relations in society: for example, a working-class student who interprets her sense of alienation in the top stream as a consequence of bourgeois hegemony rather than her own 'ignorance', a Maori who views the clustering of Maori children in low streams as a product of institutionalised racism rather than because 'Maoris are dumb or lazy.' By means of two case studies, I shall argue that women who become (liberal or socialist or radical) feminists in postwar New Zealand have had personal experiences of contradictions and/or marginality, have had access to feminist and other radical ideas that helped them to perceive the contradictions and sense of marginality they experienced as *social* phenomena (rather than mere personal inadequacies) and have apprehended both the desirability and the possibility of change in their own lives and in the lives of other women. In feminist terms, the personal becomes political.

THE SCHOOL EXPERIENCES OF FEMINISTS:
AN ORAL HISTORY APPROACH

Oral histories enable the researcher to focus on both individual agency and the power relations of the wider society and the limitations these impose on personal choice. How individuals interpret and analyse their experience becomes the focus of study. The social world is seen, as Schutz (1970, p. 11) expressed it, in terms of "the specific meaning and relevance structure for the human beings living, thinking and acting within it." People's interpretations and explanations of biographical and/or historical events and influences, rather than the events and influences themselves, are being studied—in this case the women's *feminist* perspectives on their lives. Foucault has called such as approach "writing a history of the present" (Foucault, 1979, 1980a; Sheridan, 1980).

Twelve women were selected on the basis of their espoused theoretical perspective:[2] liberal or equal rights feminists, radical feminists (including lesbian separatists), Marxist/socialist feminists, and Maori feminists were chosen.[3] The directions pursued in the interviews were how they had reached their present theoretical positions and how these influenced their practice as educators. The analysis of the women's lives was developed through a process of feedback and reinterviewing[4]— it should be viewed as a collective product, a result of collaboration between researcher and researched.[5] Small portions of two of the case studies will be discussed here. The first is Marjorie, a Pakeha (New Zealand European) woman,[6] who has, as an adult, become a socialist feminist educator who is highly involved in antiracist teaching.[7] The second is Tahuri, a Maori woman who has been involved in radical Maori, as well as feminist, groups. The material selected for this discussion has been severely limited by issues of confidentiality. The studies will be restricted here to the women's school days and will focus on two central themes: the process of becoming 'educationally successful'[8] and the process of beginning to develop a radical political consciousness.

(1) Marjorie: a socialist feminist against racism

Marjorie described her parents as middle class, although her father had come from a working-class family. It is important to analyse the influence of both of her parents on Marjorie's educational motivation and achievements. In this study, Bourdieu's model is useful. According to Bourdieu, within the family, children acquire the linguistic competencies, tastes, habits of mind, and dispositions ("habitus") of their parents' class/cultural group. Whereas the children of landed aristocracy or wealthy parents may inherit property or capital, the children of professional and other middle-class families may "inherit cultural capital"—that particular "habitus" that is characteristic of the ruling or professional classes and is validated in the academic streams of schools:

> Those whose 'culture' (in the ethnologists' sense) is the academic culture conveyed by the school have a system of categories of perception, language, thought and appreciation that sets them apart from those whose only training has been through their work and their social contacts with people of their own kind. (Bourdieu, 1971b, p. 200)

Life histories can provide the kind of information needed for a sociological analysis of the subtle influences significant others such as parents, teachers, and grandparents, may have on a child's aspirations, expectations, achievements, and perspectives. Previous studies of children's school success have not taken the mother's influence sufficiently into consideration, but have focused on establishing statistical correlations between father's occupation and pupil's school achievement.[9] As Madeleine MacDonald/Arnot has expressed it, sociologists should place greater emphasis on "the operation of the sexual division of labour in the creation of the nature of cultural capital" (MacDonald, 1979/80, p. 151).

Marjorie was the daughter of British immigrants, although she herself was born in New Zealand. She described her mother as being of upper-middle-class origins, although she had been brought up in an orphanage until family members were able to support her through a boarding school, thus "she did not go to school with the children from the village."

Marjorie described her father as having had working-class origins, although his parents had had middle-class aspirations. Successful at school, he had become an accountant. His parents' working-class origins had left him with a fear of entrepreneurial risk taking and an obsession with security. She described her father's parents as,

> incredibly right-wing . . . even though they were poor they bought the capitalist myth. If you work hard, you can make it. . . . The only future for a young man is in the office and that's where you get your pension. You don't want to go working for yourself because that's the road to ruin. You don't get anywhere. So that's why he came into office work.

In this, Marjorie's father exemplified the values described by Willis (1977) and others as characteristic of educationally successful working-class boys ('Ear 'oles' in Willis's terminology). Rachel Sharp (1980, pp. 112–113) has described these values as "petit-bourgeois ideology," with its accompanying themes of ontological anxiety, exaggerated commitment to individualistic competitiveness and its conceptualisation of social hierarchies as open, natural and just . . . such people (arguably) mistakenly look to education as the key to their social improvement.

As Bernstein (1975) pointed out, this fraction of the middle class is highly dependent on the education system for the reproduction or improvement of its class position: without property or real capital to pass on to their children, petit bourgeois parents rely on schools to turn the 'symbolic property' (Bernstein, 1975), or cultural capital (Bourdieu, 1971a, b, 1976) handed on in the family into school credentials.[10] Marjorie saw her father as very "upward aspiring" and saw his aspirations for social class mobility as one of the reasons he had married her mother: educated in a private school, she had the habitus of the English middle-class lady. From her father, Marjorie acquired high academic aspirations:

I was very much pushed into the academic thing and the leadership thing. I was really encouraged in that by my teachers and my parents.

From her mother, Marjorie learned the mannerisms and language of the cultivated middle-class Englishwoman, a habitus that was foreign to the culture of the small New Zealand country town in which she spent her primary school years:

I had to speak 'properly' . . . I wasn't allowed to have a 'Kiwi' accent. I was brought up as an English child in New Zealand. I was brought up to despise and dislike the New Zealand bush, the New Zealand accent, all those kinds of things. I was 'different.' I always felt different from everybody else because I was English, I wasn't a New Zealander.

Marjorie described her childhood as characterised by two related experiences of marginality:

I had these two things that were separating me—the thing of being English and not New Zealand, even though I was born here, and being 'bright.' Those two things really pushed me apart from people when I was a child in a small New Zealand town.

During her primary school years, Marjorie turned her cultural marginality as English and middle class to her own advantage. Confident of her cultural superiority to 'the locals,'

I used to tell my friends that I went to boarding school in England. It was just a bullshit story that I used to make up. And I used to get more stories from Billy Bunter comics because we used to get the English comics. That made me feel very different and separate from people.

Marjorie also experienced marginality as a "bright girl" and her strategies of resistance to the contradictions of femininity are worthy of detailed analysis. As a child, Marjorie had sensed that her father despised women. Accordingly, she developed an identity as a tomboy as a strategy of resistance to the dominant ideology and culture of femininity:

I was always called a tomboy and I was very proud of that. I didn't like being a girl. I hated girls, I despised girls utterly and completely and that only changed recently when I became a feminist. I took on the beliefs of the society around me and identified with the men. As a child I was very much a tomboy. I used to climb trees and fight and do all those kinds of things and really act brash and smart to be accepted by the local community boys.

While being a tomboy was acceptable in childhood, at puberty and early adolescence, the early secondary school years, girls came under increasing pressure to become feminine and heterosexually aware. Marjorie spent her third form year in the top stream at her local coeducational high school. Here, her desire to be "one of the boys" worked out to her disadvantage academically. Femininity and intellectuality were socially constructed as contradictory—in order to be accepted by the "superior sex," Marjorie "played dumb":

I subsided, really, in puberty . . . I got friendly with some boys and really wanted to be accepted by them and liked by them and discovered really quickly that if you're bright with boys, and brighter than them, they don't like you. So I immediately became dumb . . . I used to sit up the back of the classroom and just flirt.

After her third form year, Marjorie's family moved to a larger town, where she attended the local state girls' school. Because of her poor reports from her previous school, she was going to be put in a lower stream. Her mother forcefully intervened:

My mother went down there and on the strength of my results I wasn't going to be put in the top class. My mother wasn't having that, thank you very much, so she went down to the school and said, "Put my daughter in the top class." So they said, "all right," because my mother was the sort of person who if she wanted something, she would get it. And they took me aside and said, "OK, you'll be here on sufferance, deary. If you don't shape up, you ship out."

Marjorie did well academically, attributing her success at least partly to the single-sex nature of the school:

I had no boys there to flirt with, so I pulled my finger out and worked very hard, and of course did very well in that top class.

Her attitude to boys and sexuality changed from her "flirting" days in the third form. She became part of a virginal subculture of "swots," whose major concerns were academic success. Boys and sex were not amongst their interests. She described her top-stream peers:

They were all pretty much the same as me—involved in their work. We were always above those boys. We thought they were greasy little grotty pimply creatures and couldn't stand them basically.

Overt heterosexuality was viewed as incompatible with intellectuality. In those days before contraceptive knowledge and technology were widely available to teenagers, this attitude protected these girls from early pregnancies or involvement that would have distracted them from their career ambitions. Sexuality was for the nonintellectuals. Speaking of the girls in the lower streams, Marjorie commented on the typifications constructed of them by top-stream girls. She noted that it was the habitus of the lower-stream girls that gave the impression that they were more sexually active as a group than their more academic counterparts:

> I don't actually know that they were all sexually active. I always had the impression that they were, because they had all these love bites . . . they used to talk, they used to make more crude jokes and it was just a stereotype we had of them. . . . As the top stream we never had anything to do with the rest of the school. We were totally into ourselves, just self-sufficient and arrogant and kept to ourselves.

During this time, however, Marjorie was under pressure to conform to more conventionally feminine adolescent concerns. For example, she described her style of dress as a deliberate strategy of resistance of the image of femininity to which she was expected to conform:

> My mother kept telling me that I could be quite attractive if I'd only dress better. But it was because of this whole thing that I rejected creativity, I rejected beauty right from the beginning. So I quite deliberately dressed in a sloppy and casual way, in an antifeminine manner. I always did, and I always have, and I continue to. My mother tried desperately to buy me pretty dresses and things, but it never worked.

In her senior year at Girls' College, Marjorie specialized in science subjects, viewing this as an aspect of her rejection of the dominant attitudes towards femininity:

> I was very good at science and I was very good at math and I got prizes in math. I just like it. I had a logical kind of bent and in fact that was always considered to be my downfall—that I wasn't emotional, attractive, and creative. I was logical and cold and unattractive.

Marjorie became interested in the political issues of the day while still at secondary school. Her interest in becoming a scientist was partly motivated by this concern: as a soil scientist, she was going to "clean up Vietnam." Her early views on world events, however, reflected her parents' conservatism, in particular her father's "petit bourgeois" views of the social order as "open, natural and just" (Sharp, 1980, pp. 112–113). At first, she supported American intervention in Vietnam, supported New Zealand's involvement in this war, and National Party policies in general:

> I scrutineered for the National Party in the elections. My parents were National Party supporters and so I was too, automatically. I just took on their beliefs.

Confident and assertive, Marjorie took on leadership positions in the school and the church, where she "ran the Anglican Bible class." When she was made Head Prefect, Marjorie conformed to the conservative and authoritarian style favored in school and the wider society:

> I'd be like a policewoman. I used to encourage uniform checks. I did the bloody teachers' work for them. I got a prize for leadership that year. I was an up-and-coming right wing young leader.

Marjorie had, largely out of curiosity, begun taking part in protest marches against the Vietnam war. Her stand on political issues began to shift when she became increasingly aware of the sheer horror, and atrocities of that war and began to question the justification for New Zealand and American perpetuation of these. Her conversion to a more radical view occurred at a gut level—an identification with the women and children affected. She began to question her father's analysis:

> At that stage I had glimmerings of feelings about maybe my father isn't really right about this. It was an emotional thing. I just couldn't bear the pictures of the starving children and the napalm and the women—that started to get to me in an emotional way.

As Arlie Hochschild has pointed out (1975), sociological explanations must deal with feeling and emotion as well as rationality in the social world.

When she first attended university, Marjorie intended to use her scientific training in what she, like contemporary feminist scientists (Fox-Keller, 1982), viewed as a female way (cleaning up the world), enrolled in a very specialized male-dominated course that she hoped would further this end. She was horrified, however, by the sexism of the lecturers and the students and was very critical of the course content, which seemed removed from human concerns. Although she was gaining top grades, she felt so alienated from the course—its content and its people—that she dropped out to enroll in an ordinary program:

> The students were male and they were boorish and I couldn't stand them. . . . I was developing, without realising it, a feminist consciousness, because I was top of my class and I was also incredibly critical of the course I was taking.

Marjorie, then, experienced marginality in three aspects of her education, that she describes as "the strands of my beginnings, which led me to where I am now." First, her social class background had both working-class and upper-middle-class influences, giving her both a petit bourgeois drive to achieve and an upper-middle-class sense of superiority. Her sensitivity to class differences later led her to a sophisticated study of Marxist theories of education when she encountered these in the course of tertiary study. Second, her parents' British origins, and her mother's attitudes towards New Zealanders alienated her from the country of her birth. She was later to become involved with white women against racism groups concerned with shaking off the British colonial mentality and seeking a national identity rooted in Maori sovereignty.[11] Third, as a bright girl with an interest in science, she rejected the dominant image of femininity. Her cultural capital was sufficient to enable her to theorise her sense of marginality in terms of class, nationality, and gender when she had access to radical ideas (Marxism, Maori sovereignty, and feminism) that enabled her to translate these personal experiences into broader social issues.

(2) Tahuri: a radical Maori feminist

Tahuri's career was marked by outstanding academic success and an involvement with radical Maori, as well as feminist, groups. Tahuri was brought up by adoptive parents who were working-class in the Pakeha (European) sense. Her whakapapa (orally transmitted genealogy), however, traced a lineage of scholars in both Maori and Pakeha traditions: "My Maori ancestry is rich with scholars in the Maori tradition. My Pakeha ancestry is just as strong." Although her adoptive parents were not 'educated,' other relatives passed on knowledge that would be regarded as cultural capital at school:

> My auntie used to hang around the house a lot. . . . She was delightful, she was a teacher and she had some pretty radical ideas—one of her ideas was to have any kid, any Maori kid that seemed bright and receptive, reading as soon as the kid could pick up a book . . . I don't come from a bookish environment at all, there weren't books around, but when Auntie would come, and she was my babysitter a lot of the time, she would bring books. By age four I was reading.

Tahuri was a sickly child, spending time in the hospital. This alienated her from her peers, who preferred outdoor, physical pursuits to indoor ones. By the time she started primary school, Tahuri described herself as "always buried somewhere between the pages."

Because of domestic upheavals in her adoptive family, Tahuri experienced a number of changes of school, living in turn in several towns with different relatives. Some of her relatives were Catholics and one convent school experience was particularly significant to Tahuri in developing her awareness of racism and imperialism as well as providing her with examples of strong women to emulate in her own life. She identified several themes in the curriculum of this school that had a major influence on her political awareness—apartheid in South Africa, British imperialism in Ireland, and studies of women saints and war heroines:

> I'll tell you about the curriculum. Just thinking back—I was ten, eleven, twelve years old and I was introduced during those years to issues like apartheid, racism, the Ku-Klux-Klan, Nazi Germany, to strong, extraordinary women who flew aeroplanes and fought against spies and blew them up, wore shining armour and rode horses—those nuns, they were the daughters of the IRA.

The nuns provided Tahuri with strong female role models through both the stories they told and their personal examples. Tahuri described some of the heroines she had heard about in the classroom:

> We were told things like the story of Violet Szabo, who was the woman who got the Military Cross, and how she was a war hero and they made a movie about her called *Carve Her Name with Pride* and how she was so wonderful and fantastic. We were read reams about Joan of Arc and how she was a warrior and that is really good for a woman to be. We were told about the heroines of the French Resistance. We were given amazingly dynamic models of what women could do as well as men.

Tahuri was impressed with the physical strength, intellectuality, and independence of some of the nuns and cited two examples:

> She coached the boys in football—in her habit. The huge nun, who was six feet tall—she was huge—in this great long black swaddling medieval garb that she sort of hitched between her legs. She'd get the back skirt, hitch it between her legs and tuck

it into her belt. They had these masses of black leather wide belts with chains and beads and God knows what and she'd rope it all around her waist. She'd have big thick stockings and these great big boots and she'd pick up the football and off she'd go. And no man could better her. This was her image. Such power. God, I loved that woman. My other mentor was much more sedate and certainly very much a lady of leisure. One looked at her and immediately thought of illuminated medieval manuscripts and church embroidery—the much more orthodox image of the nun. As models for me they were brilliant. Not only in their life-style but also in their ideas, in their celebration and reinforcement of things.

As a Maori in this particular school, Tahuri felt proud of her cultural identity. She described this convent primary school as "a true multicultural school," noting that Maoris there were in the majority. The school also had a substantial immigrant population, and cultural diversity was regarded as a strength, a learning resource for the pupils. Positive in her identity as a Maori, Tahuri was horrified by stories told her at school of racism overseas, stating that they had been taught

> gut-level things. We were told about the Ku-Klux-Klan and about the slaves. . . . I can remember when Verwoed got in and we had to pray for the black babies and the nuns actually weeping about apartheid and what was happening in South Africa.

In addition to the horrors of racism, she was told about the evils of imperialism and the heroism of those who stood up against oppression in Ireland and in the civil rights movement in the United States. Sometimes this touched the class at a very personal level: "one of the boys, who was very Irish, came to school one day in tears and we learned that his uncle had been shot."

It was hardly surprising, then, that as a university student Tahuri would become involved with radical Maori groups. At primary school, however, she had not connected the issues of racism and imperialism she knew about in overseas contexts with the situation of Maoris in New Zealand. This was to come in her secondary school years. She acknowledged her debt to these nuns for helping to prepare the ground for this later insight insofar as they had introduced topics

> like the IRA, like the French Resistance, like the civil rights movement. Admittedly, it was never given a New Zealand context, but I suppose that would have been much too subversive. But the seeds were sown. God, I do owe them that. I really do.

At secondary school, Tahuri had shattering experiences of racism—on both institutional and personal levels. Here, her enculturation as a Maori was viewed as inappropriate by other pupils and by teachers and the devaluation of her culture was made explicit. In a provincial girls' school that streamed pupils at least partly on the basis of test results, Tahuri was prevented from taking Maori language:

> To get into the Maori language classes you had to be in the general stream, which meant second or third-class intellect. Certainly not remedial, or vocational or technical, but definitely not top-stream, and because I was top-stream I had to be fed a diet of French and Latin. And there was no way they were going to let me do Maori, no way at all.

Tahuri's adoptive mother, who had been severely punished at school and had such an aversion to schools that she had never been near any of Tahuri's previous schools, attempted to intervene. Whereas Marjorie's mother, as outlined in the previous case study, had successfully intervened in the school's streaming practices, Tahuri's mother was treated as ignorant. Maori knowledge was not cultural capital in the eyes of the school. She was told:

> There's no way this girl can do Maori. She has to be in the top third form and you should feel very pleased that we are putting her in the top third form because that's where she belongs.

The relative status in this school of Maori culture and the habitus of the Pakeha middle class exemplify Bourdieu's (1971a, p. 175) notion of a "hierarchy of cultural works":

> The structure of the intellectual field maintains a relation of interdependence with one of the basic structures of the cultural field, that of cultural works, established in a hierarchy according to their degree of legitimacy. One may observe that in a given society at a given moment in time not all cultural signs . . . are equal in dignity and value.

Tahuri was the only Maori in "3 Professional A," which she described as

> the most elitist, most exalted third form in the school which included the daughters of the town's professional and business elite. The high school teachers' kids, the doctors' kids, the lawyers' kids, the accountants' kids, the boss of the supermarket's kids, the research scientists' kids.

In order to be 'any good' in the eyes of the school, Tahuri had to deny her Maoriness, which she refused to do. She teamed up with the few other outcasts in the top stream. Part of their resistance was an exaggerated display of sexuality—assuming the trappings of 'tartiness.' As an example of this form of resistance, Tahuri described mufti day at Girls' High:

> 3 Professional A would turn up in the little twinsets and pearls, and beautifully cut skirts and neat shoes with discreet heels and they'd be carbon copies of their mothers. You know, with a little bit of lipstick, and maybe earrings, and terribly prissy. And I'd wear things like black pants and black shirt—in those days they had those things called jerkins, that sort of V-neck, sleeveless tunic. When I wore my black pants and black shirt with jerkin I thought I looked real smooth. And I used to Brylcream, coconut oil, my hair and get it all like Elvis. And that's how we used to go to school.

Pakeha women in my study, such as Marjorie, mentioned the stigmatising of 'non-academic' girls in low steams as promiscuous. In Tahuri's school, the association of sexual promiscuity with lack of intellect was further exacerbated by racism. Maori girls were concentrated in the lower streams and seen by some of the academic girls as more sexually promiscuous. Tahuri described the headmistress of the provincial school as racist, and her account of the practice of streaming suggests strongly that it reflected and reproduced the social class structure of the wider community:

> It was just so dreadful that we were in the class, degrading its quality like that. Meanwhile, down in 3 Vocational, 3 Reform, and 3 Commercial B, there were all

the tarts. All the tarts like us. At Girl's High the lower forms were brown. And so there was not only the class-sexuality dimension but there was also the class-sexuality-race. They were brown sluts, bags.

In this school, racism was evident not only on an institutional level, but also in the attitudes of individuals. Tahuri perceived the attitudes of her top-stream peers as overtly racist. For example, she described her experience of a class fund-raising project:

We had a lunchtime cake-stall. Each kid had to say what they were going to bring and some brought things like coconut ice, cream sponges, this and that. And I got up and said "I'll bring a rawene bread." "Ugh, what's that." And I said, "Maori bread." "We don't want that on our stall." And that's what they said and I can still see them rising out of their desks in mortification that their pristine little white stall with its goddamn gingham table cloth was going to be contaminated by this ethnic presence.

Tahuri and the two other 'deviants' in the class became involved in 'delinquent' activities such as running away from home, breaking the rules of the school, shoplifting, stealing from lockers, truanting. For this, she was expelled. Despite her unhappiness, however, she had continued to maintain high standards in her academic work.

After her expulsion, Tahuri was accepted as a pupil at a local coeducational high school. At this school, her Maoriness was viewed in a positive light—as appropriately academic cultural capital. This time she shared her top-stream class with other Maori pupils. Her academic career "just took off" and she proceeded from high academic honours at school to a highly successful university career. Here she became involved with Maori radical student groups, and when the women's liberation movement began in the early 1970s, she became active in this. The seeds of her awareness of racism and imperialism had been sown in her school years. The academic cultural capital from her whanau group (extended family) had enabled Tahuri to transcend the setbacks and disruptions in her nuclear family and first secondary school experiences.

CONCLUSIONS

The education system of the postwar period in New Zealand constructed and reproduced in both its stated curricular policies and its everyday cultural practices within schools a gendered intellectuality that embodied contradictions in the dominant ideology of femininity. While the official educational ideology of the postwar years was premised on the liberal value of equality of opportunity to compete for positions in the social hierarchy, femininity was socially constructed as subordination. The stratification of knowledge (hidden curriculum) brought about within schools by postwar curriculum policies created a hierarchy of youth cultures whose attitudes to sexuality and intellectuality/professionality were influenced by the contradictory sets of expectations they experienced in their families, schools, and wider social networks.

During their childhood years, the women studied had felt ambivalent about growing up female. Marjorie developed strategies of resistance to the dominant

Pakeha construction of femininity by becoming a tomboy: "I didn't like being a girl. I despised girls." She refused to wear pretty dresses and instead "quite deliberately dressed in a sloppy and casual way." Tahuri, frequently sick and in the hospital, was unable to join in the boisterous outdoor activities of her whanau group and instead became a reader, "always buried somewhere between the pages," a habit that alienated her from her Maori peer group.[12]

The women's secondary school experiences lend support to Foucault's (1980a, p. 28) analysis of sexuality in these institutions:

> On the whole one can have the impression that sex was hardly spoken of at all in these institutions. But one only has to glance at the architectural layout, the rules of discipline, and their whole internal organization: the question of sex was a constant preoccupation. . . . What one might call the internal discourse of the institution . . . was based largely on this assumption that this sexuality existed, that it was precocious, active, and ever present.

While the intention of overt curriculum policies were to confine sex to a few lessons in general science, the life histories show clearly that, in the hidden curriculum of schools, sexuality was indeed "precocious, active, and ever present." The interwoven cultural practices in the home and the school reproduced a gendered, racist intellectuality based on the 'double standard' of female sexual morality. 'Low-stream,' and particularly low-stream Maori, girls, were typified as more sexually active and less intelligent than their 'top-stream' peers. Overtly sexual academic girls were treated as deviant. Sexuality and intellectuality were socially constructed as contradictory.

Both Marjorie and Tahuri engaged in brief periods of deviance in dealing with this contradiction. At first, Marjorie adopted the strategy of becoming ultra-feminine in order to be accepted to males who were, she believed, the superior sex: "if you're brighter than them they don't like you. So I immediately became dumb," Tahuri, "the only Maori in the top stream," assumed the trappings of "tartiness" characteristic of the nonacademic rebels in the bottom streams: "down in 3 Vocational, 3 Reform, and 3 Commercial B, there were all the tarts like us." Her expression of rebellion against the "most elitist third form in the school" with their "little twinsets and pearls" was to dress in an antifeminine way: "I wore my black pants and black shirt with jerkin . . . I used to coconut oil my hair and get it all like Elvis." The habitus of the top-stream, Pakeha middle-class girls—what the school valued as cultural capital—was a denial of the value of Maori culture: "because I was top stream, I had to be fed a diet of French and Latin. And there was no way they were going to let me do Maori, no way at all." In Mitchell's (1973, p. 28) terms, both women had a "sense of something wrong." At this stage of their lives, however, their strategies of resistance were contributing to almost certain school failure. Rather than being well-reasoned strategies for social change, they were merely what Giroux (1983, p. 225) termed "faint bursts of misplaced opposition that eventually incorporate the very logic they struggle against."

How, then were these two women able to move from "faint bursts of misplaced opposition" to clearly articulated theories of human oppression and strategies aimed at bringing about educational, and broader social, change? How were they able to theorize these personal experiences of victimisation, discrimination, contradictions, and marginality?

In the cases of these two particular women, both were given a second chance through a change of school. In Marjorie's case, this involved a shift to a single-sex school "where there were no boys to flirt with." In Tahuri's case, the shift was to a coeducational school that was multicultural in the sense that her Maoriness was valued as academic cultural capital (bicultural capital). Both women could have repeated their cycles of deviance at their new schools. Both, however, were strongly academically motivated and had sufficient cultural capital to believe in their abilities. Marjorie had a father who had transcended his working-class origins to achieve upward social mobility through education (he had become an accountant) and her mother had the confidence of the private-school-educated, upper-middle-class Englishwoman who believed herself superior to mere New Zealanders. Tahuri had strong male and female role models in her extended family, past and present scholars in both Maori and Pakeha traditions. Her adoptive parents were not "educated" ("I don't come from a bookish environment"), but she was exposed to strong female intellectuals through her other relatives and at school: "Violet Szabo, who was a war hero . . . Joan of Arc, who was a warrior . . . the heroines of the French Resistance. We were given amazingly dynamic models of what women could do as well as men." Strong images from her school days remained with her, for example, "this huge nun . . . she'd have big thick stockings and these big boots and she'd pick up the football and off she'd go. And no man could better her."

At the time these women were at school, feminist ideas were not widely accessible to help them articulate their "sense of something wrong" in terms of their experiences of the contradictions of femininity. The second wave of feminism did not crash across the bookstalls, newspapers, and television sets of the 'western' world until the 1970s.[13] Ideas about racism, imperialism, and pacifism were available, however, in particular, the anti-Vietnam war protests, and protest against sporting contacts with South Africa. Feminist scholars such as Juliet Mitchell (1973) have noted that many women who became active in the second wave of feminism had had previous involvements in the peace and civil rights movements. The strong Maori, and overseas Black, role models Tahuri encountered during her school years had given her a sense of both the desirability and possibility of change towards Maori self-determination and equality. She described, as particularly formative, the knowledge she had been given in school of "the IRA, the French Resistance, and the civil rights movement."

In their senior years at school, both women experienced outstanding academic success. Tahuri was able to turn her considerable literary skills to focus on issues that concerned her. Marjorie's choice of science was a strategy for dealing with the contradictions of femininity: "I had a logical kind of bent . . . I wasn't emotional, attractive, and creative. I was logical and cold and unattractive." Embracing intellectuality, she rejected sexuality—for those in her virginal subculture of top-stream intellectuals, boys were merely "greasy little grotty pimply creatures." However, in other ways, her love of science and her motivation for studying it was characteristically female—a nurturant concern with "cleaning up the world." Her feminist attitude to science was stimulated by her negative experiences with the sexism and boorishness of male students and lecturers at the university level, the abstractness of the course, and its remoteness from human problems, such as the environmental devastations of war. While Marjorie had come to view change in the lives of women and oppressed people as desirable, education was going to help her make this possible. Despite the conservatism of her parents and teachers, Marjorie was converted to an identification with the oppressed when her study of the Vietnam War made her aware of the human suffering perpetuated by American policies and New Zealand's involvement: it was "an emotional thing. I just couldn't bear the pictures of the starving children and the women." Both Tahuri and Marjorie, then, had come into contact with ideas that helped them to articulate their personal experiences of marginality and contradictions as social issues. They perceived change as desirable and education as a means to make it possible. Their resistance became more clearly articulated. The life history approach, then can help educational theorists "to understand how subordinate groups embody and express a combination of reactionary and progressive ideologies, ideologies that both underlie the structure of social domination and contain the logic necessary to overcome it" (Giroux, 1983, p. 225).

This analysis has some important implications for pedagogy. Despite the dominant attitude towards subordinate, domestic femininity evidenced in the curriculum policies and cultural practices of schooling at the time, large numbers of women rejected this ideology and became feminists. Their schooling and higher education had played an important part in this. Individual teachers had given them access to radical ideas through their handling of the curriculum and their personal examples. Schooling had also provided access to the credentials that would gain them access to higher education and to positions of power in the social hierarchy from which they could work for change. These women's experiences and analyses of them suggest that teaching should be viewed, in Giroux's terms, as "an intensely personal affair" (1982, p. 158). Teaching must help students to link "biography, history, and social structure" (Mills, 1976 edition). In schools,

> students must be given the opportunity to use and interpret their own experiences in a manner that reveals how the latter have been shaped and influenced by the dominant culture. Subjective awareness becomes the first step in transforming those experiences (Giroux, 1982, p. 124).

Notes

1. Used here in the sense of being a (heterosexual) 'non-virgin.' The term sexual activity is problematic—discussed by Diorio (1984).

2. Without betraying confidentiality, I cannot be too specific about how any woman was chosen. The only way that women's theoretical perspectives could be ascertained was if they had espoused them in pubic situations, e.g., if they had written them down (e.g., in publications, conference, or seminar presentations), if they had spoken about them at feminist gatherings, or if the woman were known to me personally. I included women who described their thinking as influenced by Marxism/socialism, radical feminism, lesbian separatism, Maori radicalism and liberalism. I also included women who did not fit my initial categories—"anarchist" feminist, for example. The theoretical categories upon which I based my choice of women should be regarded as a typology, a set of "ideal typifications" (Berger & Luckman, 1971): real individuals draw their theories from many different sources and their perspectives are eclectic.

3. There have been a number of reviews of theoretical tendencies in the 'Western' women's movement, e.g., Banks (1981); Eisenstein (1981); Jaggar (1977); Jaggar and Struhl

(1978); Sayers (1981). For a New Zealand study, see Bunkle (1979/80). The analysis I developed is outlined in Middleton (1984b, c).

4. More details of my methodology are given in Middleton (1984a) (1987 copies available from the author).

5. Collaborative research has been strongly advocated by feminists. See the various papers in Bowles and Klein (1983); Keohane et al. (1982); Roberts (1981). Also Stanley and Wise (1979, 1983).

6. Not her real name. The choice of material to be discussed has been confined to the women's own school years (childhood and adolescence) and has been limited by ethical considerations of confidentiality. In a country the size of New Zealand, with a population of three million people, it is difficult to preserve the confidentiality of one's informants: to reveal somebody as Maori, a lesbian, and a kindergarten teacher would immediately identify her. My study contains much personal, e.g., sexual material. For this reason, the wider study uses different names for different parts of the women's lives, e.g., the chapter an childhood and adult careers, the chapter on sexuality. For this reason the study has lost some of its methodological and theoretical strength and, ironically, perpetuates the contradiction between sexuality and intellectuality—inevitably since researchers and research are part of the culture they are studying (e.g., see Oakley, 1981).

7. Without risking confidentiality, I cannot reveal her adult profession. When I chose the women, I wanted a diverse range of teaching experiences. Of the twelve, three had taught in preschools, seven in primary schools, two in secondary schools, one in a special school, three had worked for adult community education services, two had done some part-time teaching in technical institutes, and seven had done some tutoring at the university level.

8. As educators, all twelve had ultimately been successful in terms of the formal education system. Not all had proceeded straight from successful school careers, however; seven had been recruited to teaching as school leavers during the recruitment drives of the 1960s, four had left school after fifth form and had resumed their education as adults. Two had been expelled from schools; some became pregnant in their teens.

9. E.g., Harker (1975); Elley and Irving (1976); Watson (1966). The invisibility of women (e.g., housewives) in stratification studies is critiqued by Delphy (1981); Gray (1981); Oakley (1974); Irving and Elley (1977).

10. In the case of girls, school success may be seen as an aspect of "family marital strategies" aimed at class endogamy or social mobility (Bourdieu and Boltansky, 1971; Connell, et al., 1982; Tilly, 1979). For a case study, see Middleton (1985a).

11. Donna Awatere's articles (1982a, b, c) stimulated a great deal of debate in the feminist community.

12. According to Rose Pere (1983), the stereotype of passive femininity characteristic of sex stereotypes identified amongst Pakehas was not true of Maori girls. Girls and boys played the same games and were of equal status.

13. Germaine Greer's visit to New Zealand in 1972 received great publicity. An early second wave publication was Kedgley and Cederman (1972). Broadsheet magazine was established in 1972. Useful histories are in the tenth birthday issue of Broadsheet (July/August 1982); Bunkle (1979/80); Dann 1986).

References

Awatere, D. (1982/3). Maori sovereignty, in three parts. *Broadsheet*, June 1982, pp. 38–40; October 1982, pp. 24–29; February 1983, pp. 12–19.

Banks, O. (1981). *Faces of Feminism* (Oxford:Martin Robinson).

Bartky, S. (1977). Towards a phenomenology of feminist consciousness. In M. Veiterling-Braggin (Ed.), *Feminism and Philosophy* (Tottowa: Littlefield Adams).

Berger, P. and T. Luckmann (1971). *The Social Construction of Reality* (London: Penguin).

Bernstein, B. (1975). Class and pedagogies; visible and invisible. In B. Bernstein, *Class, Codes, Control*, 3 (London: Routledge & Kegan Paul).

Bourdieu, P. (1971a). Intellectual field and creative project. In M. F. D. Young (Ed), *Knowledge and Control* (London: Collier Macmillan).

———. (1971b). Systems of education and systems of thought. In M. F. D. Young (Ed.) *Knowledge and Control*.

———. (1976). The school as a conservative force: scholastic and cultural inequalities. In R. Dale et al. *Schooling and Capitalism: a sociological reader* (London: Open University Press).

Bourdieu, P. and L. Boltansky (1971). Changes in social structure and changes in the demand for education. In M. S. Archer, and S. Giner (Eds.), *Contemporary Europe* (London: Weidenfield & Nicholson).

Bowles, G. and R. D. Klein (Eds.). (1983). *Theories of Women's Studies* (London: Routledge & Kegan Paul).

Bunkle, P. (1979–80). A history of the women's movement, in five parts in five consecutive issues of *Broadsheet*: September 1979a, pp. 24–28; October 1979b, pp. 26–28; November 1979c, pp. 26–28; December 1979d, pp. 28–32; January/February 1980, pp. 30–35.

Codd, J. (1985). Images of schooling and the discourse of the state. In J. Codd, R. Harker and R. Nash (Eds.), *Political Issues in New Zealand Education* (Palmerston North: Dunmore).

Connell, R. W., D. J. Ashendon, S. Kessler, and G. Dowsett (1981). *Making the Difference* (Sydney: Allen & Unwin).

Cook, H. (1985). The contradictions of post-war reconstruction: the aspirations and realities of a post-war generation of wives and mothers. In NZ Women's Studies Association. *Conference Papers '84*, pp. 46–53 (Auckland: NZWSA).

Dann, C. (1986). *Up from Under* (Wellington: Allen & Unwin/Port Nicholson).

Delphy, C. (1981). Women in stratification studies. In H. Roberts (Ed.), *Doing Feminist Research* (London: Routledge & Kegan Paul).

Department of Education (1944, 1959 edition). *The Post-primary School Curriculum* (Thomas Report) (Wellington: Government Printer).

———. (1962). *Report of the Commission on Education in New Zealand* (Currie Report) (Wellington: Government Printer).

Department of Health (1955). *Sex and the Adolescent Girl* (Wellington: Government Printer).

Diorio, J. A. (1984) Contraception, copulation domination, and the theoretical barrenness of sex education literature. Paper presented to the Sixth Conference of the NZ Association for Research in Education, Knox College, Otago University, Dunedin, November.

Ehrenreich, B. and D. English (1979). *For Her Own Good* (New York: Doubleday).

Ebbett, E. (1984). *When the Boys were Away: NZ women in World War Two* (Wellington: Reed).

Eisenstein, Z. (1981). *The Radical Future of Liberal Feminism* (New York: Longman).

———. (1982). The sexual politics of the new right: understanding the "crisis of liberalism" for the 1980s. In N. Keohane et al., (Eds.). (1982). *Feminist Theory: a critique of ideology* (Chicago: Harvester).

Elley, W. B. and J. E. Irving (1972). A socio-economic index for New Zealand based on levels of education and income from the 1966 census, *New Zealand Journal of Educational Studies*, 7, pp. 153–167.

Findlay, M. (1974). *Tooth and Nail: the story of a daughter of the depression* (Wellington: Reed).

Foucault, M. (1979). In S. M. Morris, and P. Patton, *Power, Truth, Strategy* (Sydney: Feral Publications).

———. (1980a). *A History of Sexuality*, 1 (New York: Vintage).

———. (1980b). *Power-knowledge* (New York: Pantheon).

Fox-Keller, E. (1982). Feminism and science. In N. Keohane et al. (Eds.) *Feminist Theory: a critique of ideology* (Chicago: Harvester).

Frame, J. (1983). *The Is-land* (Auckland: Hutchinson).

Friedan, B. (1963). *The Feminine Mystique* (London: Penguin).

Giddens, A. (1982). *Profiles and Critiques in Social Theory* (London: Macmillan).

Giroux, H. (1982). *Ideology, Culture, and the Process of Schooling* (Philadelphia: Temple).

———. (1983). *Theory and Resistance in Education* (Massachusetts: Bergin & Garvey).

Gray, A. (1981). Women and class: a question of assignation. *New Zealand Journal of Educational Studies* 16, pp. 37–42.

Harker, R. (1975). Streaming and social class. In P. D. K. Ramsay (Ed.). *Family and School in New Zealand Society* (Auckland: Pitman).

Hochschild, A. R. (1975). The sociology of feeling and emotion: selected possibilities. In M. Millman. and R. Kanter (Eds). *Another Voice* (New York: Doubleday).

Irving, J. and W. B. Elley (1977). A socioeconomic index for the female labour force in New Zealand. *New Zealand Journal of Educational Studies* 12, pp. 154–163.

Jaggar, A. (1977). Political philosophies of women's liberation. In M. Vetterling-Braggin (Ed.), *Feminism and Philosophy* (Tottowa: Littlefield Adams).

Jaggar, A. and P. Struhl (1978) (Eds.). *Feminist Frameworks* (New York: McGraw Hill).

Kedgley, S. and S. Cederman (Eds.) (1972). *Sexist Society* (Wellington: Alister Taylor).

Laing, R. D. (1971). *The Politics of the Family* (London: Penguin).

MacDonald, M. (1979/80). Cultural Reproduction: the pedagogy of sexuality, *Screen Education*, Autumn/Winter, pp. 141–153.

McLaren, I. (1974). *Education for a Small Democracy: New Zealand* (London: Routledge & Kegan Paul).

Marx, K. (1867, 1976 edition). *Capital*. Vol. 1 (London: Penguin).

Middleton, S. (1984a). On being a feminist educationist doing research on being a feminist educationist: life-history analysis as consciousness-raising. *New Zealand Cultural Studies Working Group Journal* 8, pp. 29–37.

———. (1984b). The sociology of women's education as a field of academic study. In *Discourse 5*, November pp. 42–62. Reprinted in M. Arnot and G. Weiner (Eds.).*Gender and the Politics of Schooling* (London: Routledge).

———. (1984c). Towards a sociology of women's education in New Zealand: perspectives and directions. In P. D. K. Ramsay (Ed.) *Family, School, and Community* (Sydney, Allen & Unwin).

———. (1985a). Family strategies of cultural reproduction: case studies in the schooling of girls. In J. Codd et al., (Eds.). *Political Issues in New Zealand Education* (Palmerston North: Dunmore). Reprinted in G. Weiner, and M. Arnot (Eds.) *Researching Gender and Education: new lines of inquiry* (London: Hutchinson).

———. (1985b). Feminism and education in post-war New Zealand: an oral history perspective. Paper presented at the Westhill Conference, Birmingham, January 1987. Also published in R. Openshaw, and D. McKenzie (Eds.). (1987). *Reinterpreting the Educational Past* (Wellington: NZ Council for Educational Research).

———. (1985c). *Feminism and education in Post-war New Zealand: a sociological analysis*. (D. Phil. Thesis, University of Waikato).

———. (1986). Workers and homemakers: contradictions in the education of the New Zealand post-war woman. *New Zealand Journal of Educational Studies*, 21, pp. 13–28.

Mills. C. Wright (1959, 1975 edition). *The Sociological Imagination* (London : Penguin).

Mitchell, J. (1973). *Women's Estate* (London: Penguin).

Nash, R. (1981). The New Zealand district high schools: a study in the selective function of rural education. *New Zealand Journal of Educational Studies* 16, pp. 150–160.

New Zealand Council for Educational Research (1965). Data Summary 6/65.

Oakley, A. (1974). *The Sociology of Housework* (Oxford: Martin Robinson).

———. (1981). Interviewing women: a contradiction in terms. In H. Roberts (Ed.), *Doing Feminist Research* (London: Routledge & Kegan Paul).

Pere, R. (1983). *Ako: concepts and learning in the Maori tradition* (Hamilton: University of Waikato, Department of Sociology Monograph).

Plummer, K. (1983). *Documents of Life* (London: Allen & Unwin).

Roberts H. (Ed.). (1981). *Doing Feminist Research* (London: Routledge & Kegan Paul).

Sayers, J. (1982). *Biological Politics* (London: Tavistock).

Schutz, A. (1944). The stranger: an essay in social psychology. *American Journal of Sociology* 49, pp. 499–507.

———. (1970). Concept and theory formation in the social sciences. In D. Emmett and A. MacIntyre (Eds.), *Sociological Theory and Philosophical Analysis* (Basingstoke: Macmillan).

Sedgwick. C. (1983). *The Life History: a method with issues, troubles and a future*, 2d ed. (Christchurch: Department of Sociology Monograph, University of Canterbury).

Sharp. R. (1980). *Knowledge, Ideology, and the Process of Schooling* (London: Routledge & Kegan Paul).

Sheridan. A. (1980). *Michel Foucault: the will to truth* (London: Tavistock).

Stanley, I. and S. Wise (1979). Feminist research, feminist consciousness, and experiences of sexism. *Women's Studies International Quarterly* 2. pp. 359–374.

Stanley, I. and S. Wise. (1983). *Breaking Out: feminist consciousness and feminist research* (London: Routledge & Kegan Paul).

Taylor, S. (1984). Reproduction and contradiction in schooling: the case of commercial studies. *British Journal of Sociology of Education* 5, pp. 3–18.

Tilly, I. (1979). Individual lives and family strategies in the French proletariat. *Journal of Family History*, Summer, pp. 137–140.

Watson, J. (1966). Marriages of women teachers. *New Zealand Journal of Educational Studies* 1, pp. 149–161.

Whitehead, I. (1974). The Thomas Report: a study in educational reform. *New Zealand Journal of Educational Studies* 9, pp. 52–64.

Willis, P. (1977). *Learning to Labour* (Westmead: Saxon House).

Young, M. F. D. (Ed.). (1971). *Knowledge and Control* (London: Collier Macmillan).

19

WHY DOESN'T THIS FEEL EMPOWERING? WORKING THROUGH THE REPRESSIVE MYTHS OF CRITICAL PEDAGOGY

Elizabeth Ellsworth

In the spring of 1988, the University of Wisconsin-Madison was the focal point of a community-wide crisis provoked by the increased visibility of racist acts and structures on campus and within the Madison community. During the preceding year, the FIJI fraternity had been suspended for portraying racially demeaning stereotypes at a "Fiji Island party," including a 15-foot-high cutout of a "Fiji native," a dark-skinned caricature with a bone through its nose. On December 1, 1987, the Minority Affairs Steering Committee released a report, initiated and researched by students, documenting the university's failure to address institutional racism and the experiences of marginalization of students of color on campus. The report called for the appointment of a person of color to the position of vice chancellor of economic minority affairs/affirmative action; effective strategies to recruit and retain students, faculty and staff of color, establishment of a multicultural center; implementation of a mandatory six-credit ethnic studies requirement; revamping racial and sexual harassment grievance procedures; and initiation of a cultural and racial orientation program for all students. The release of the report and the university's responses to it and to additional incidents such as the FIJI fraternity party have become the focus of ongoing campus and community-wide debates, demonstrations, and organizing efforts.

In January, 1988, partly in response to this situation, I facilitated a special topics course at UW-Madison called "Media and Anti-Racist Pedagogies," Curriculum and Instruction 607, known as C&I 607. In this article, I will offer an interpretation of C&I 607's interventions against campus racism and traditional educational forms at the university. I will then use that interpretation to support a critique of current discourses on critical pedagogy.[1] The literature on critical pedagogy represents attempts by educational researchers to theorize and operationalize pedagogical challenges to oppressive social formations. While the attempts I am concerned with here share fundamental assumptions and goals, their different emphases are reflected in the variety of labels given to them, such as "critical pedagogy," "pedagogy of critique and possibility," "pedagogy of student voice," "pedagogy of empowerment," "radical pedagogy," "pedagogy for radical democracy," and "pedagogy of possibility."[2]

I want to argue, on the basis of my interpretation of C&I 607, that key assumptions, goals, and pedagogical practices fundamental to the literature on critical pedagogy—namely, "empowerment," "student voice," "dialogue," and even the term "critical"—are repressive myths that perpetuate relations of domination. By this I mean that when participants in our class attempted to put into practice prescriptions offered in the literature concerning empowerment, student voice, and dialogue, we produced results that were not only unhelpful, but actually exacerbated the very conditions we were trying to work against, including Eurocentrism, racism, sexism, classism, and "banking education." To the extent that our efforts to put discourses of critical pedagogy into practice led us to reproduce relations of domination in our classroom, these discourses were "working through" us in repressive ways, and had themselves become vehicles of repression. To the extent that we disengaged ourselves from those aspects and moved in another direction, we "worked through" and out of the literature's highly abstract language ("myths") of who we should be and what should be happening in our classroom, and into classroom practices that were context specific and seemed to be much more responsive to our own understandings of our social identities and situations.

This article concludes by addressing the implications of the classroom practices we constructed in response to racism in the university's curriculum, pedagogy, and everyday life. Specifically, it challenges educational scholars who situate themselves within the field of critical pedagogy to come to grips with the fundamental issues this work has raised—especially the question, What diversity do we silence in the name of "liberatory" pedagogy?

PEDAGOGY AND POLITICAL INTERVENTIONS ON CAMPUS

The nation-wide eruption in 1987–1988 of racist violence in communities and on campuses, including the University of Wisconsin-Madison, pervaded the context in which Curriculum and Instruction 607, "Media and Anti-Racist Pedagogies," was planned and facilitated. The increased visibility of racism in Madison was also partly due to the UW Minority Student Coalition's successful documentation of the UW system's resistance to and its failure to address monoculturalism in the curriculum, to recruit and retain students and professors of color, and to alleviate the campus culture's insensitivity or hostility to cultural and racial diversity.

At the time that I began to construct a description of C&I 607, students of color had documented the extent of their racial harrassment and alienation on campus. Donna Shalala, the newly appointed, feminist chancellor of UW-Madison, had invited faculty and campus groups to take their own initiatives against racism on campus. I had just served on a university committee investigating an incident of racial harassment against one of my students. I wanted to design a course in media and pedagogy that would not only work to clarify the structures of institutional racism underlying university practices and its culture in spring 1988, but that would also use that understanding to plan and carry out a political intervention within that formation. This class would not debate whether racist structures and practices were operating at the university; rather, it would investigate *how* they operated, with what effects and contradictions—and where they were vulnerable to political opposition. The course concluded with public interventions on campus, which I will describe later. For my purposes here, the most important interruption of existing power relations within the university consisted of transforming business-as-usual—that is, prevailing social relations—in a university classroom.

Before the spring of 1988, I had used the language of critical pedagogy in course descriptions and with students. For example, syllabi in the video production for education courses stated that goals of the courses included the production of "socially responsible" videotapes, the fostering of "critical production" practices and "critical reception and analysis" of educational videotapes. Syllabi in the media criticism courses stated that we would focus on "critical media use and analysis in the classroom" and the potential of media in "critical education." Students often asked what was meant by critical—critical of what, from what position, to what end?—and I referred them to answers provided in the literature. For example, critical pedagogy supported classroom analysis and rejection of oppression, injustice, inequality, silencing of marginalized voices, and authoritarian social structures.[3] Its critique was launched from the position of the radical educator who recognizes and helps students to recognize and name injustice, who empowers students to act against their own and others' oppressions (including oppressive school structures), who criticizes and transforms her or his own understanding in response to the understanding of students.[4] The goal of critical pedagogy was a critical democracy, individual freedom, social justice, and social change—a revitalized public sphere characterized by citizens capable of confronting public issues critically through ongoing forms of public debate and social action.[5] Students would be empowered by social identities that affirmed their race, class, and gender positions and provided the basis for moral deliberation and social action.[6]

The classroom practices of critical educators may in fact engage with actual, historically specific struggles, such as those between students of color and university administrators. But the overwhelming majority of academic articles appearing in major educational journals, although apparently based on actual practices, rarely locate theoretical constructs within them. In my review of the literature I found, instead, that educational researchers who invoke concepts of critical pedagogy consistently strip discussions of classroom practices of historical context and political position. What remains are the definitions cited above, which operate at a high level of abstraction. I found this language more appropriate (yet hardly more helpful) for philosophical debates about the highly problematic concepts of freedom, justice, democracy, and "universal" values than for thinking through and planning classroom practices to support the political agenda of C&I 607.

Given the explicit antiracist agenda of the course, I realized that even naming C&I 607 raised complex issues. To describe the course as "Media and Critical Pedagogy" or "Media, Racism, and Critical Pedagogy," for example, would be to hide the politics of the course, making them invisible to the very students I was trying to attract and work with—namely, students committed or open to working against racism. I wanted to avoid colluding with many academic writers in the widespread use of code words such as "critical," which hide the actual political agendas I assume such writers share with me—namely, antiracism, antisexism, antielitism, antiheterosexism, antiableism, anticlassism, and anti-neoconservatism.

I say "assume" because, while the literature on critical pedagogy charges the teacher with helping students to "identify and choose between sufficiently articulated and reasonably distinct moral positions,"[7] it offers only the most abstract, decontextualized criteria for choosing one position over others, criteria such as "reconstructive action"[8] or "radical democracy and social justice."[9] To reject the term "critical pedagogy" and name the course "Media and Anti-Racist Pedagogies" was to assert that students and faculty at UW-Madison in the spring of 1988 were faced with ethical dilemmas that called for political action. While a variety of "moral assessments" and political positions existed about the situation on campus, this course would attempt to construct a classroom practice that would act *on the side* of antiracism. I wanted to be accountable for naming the political agenda behind this particular course's critical pedagogy.

Thinking through the ways in which our class's activities could be understood as political was important, because while the literature states implicitly or explicitly that critical pedagogy is political, there have been no sustained research attempts to explore whether or how the practices it prescribes actually alter specific power relations outside or inside schools. Further, when educational researchers advocating critical pedagogy fail to provide a clear statement of their political agendas, the effect is to hide the fact that as critical pedagogues, they are in fact seeking to appropriate public resources (classrooms, school supplies, teacher/professor salaries, academic requirements and degrees) to further various "progressive" political agendas that they believe to be for the public good—and therefore deserving of public resources. But however good the reasons for choosing the strategy of subverting repressive school structures from within, it has necessitated the use of code words such as "critical," "social change," "revitalized public sphere," and a posture of invisibility. As a result, the critical education movement has failed to develop a clear articulation of the need for its existence, its goals, priorities, risks, or potential. As Liston and Zeichner argue, debate within the critical education movement itself over what constitutes a radical or critical pedagogy is sorely needed.[10]

By prescribing moral deliberation, engagement in the full range of views present, and critical reflection, the literature on critical pedagogy implies that students and teachers can and should engage each other in the classroom as fully rational subjects. According to Valerie Walkerdine, schools have participated in producing "self-regulating" individuals by developing in students capacities for engaging in rational argument. Rational argument has operated in ways that set up as its opposite an irrational Other, which has been understood historically as the province of women and other exotic Others. In schools, rational deliberation, reflection, and consideration of all viewpoints has become a vehicle for regulating conflict and the power to speak, for transforming "conflict into rational argument by means of universalized capacities for language and reason."[11] But students and professor entered C&I 607 with investments of privilege and struggle already made in favor of some ethical and political positions concerning racism and against other positions. The context in which this course was developed highlighted that fact. The demands that the Minority Student Coalition delivered to the administration were not written in the spirit of engaging in rationalist, analytical debates with those holding other positions. In a racist society and its institutions, such debate has not and cannot be public or democratic in the sense of including the voices of all affected parties and affording them equal weight and legitimacy. Nor can such debate be free of conscious and unconscious concealment of interests or assertion of interests that some participants hold as nonnegotiable no matter what arguments are presented.

As Barbara Christian has written, "what I write and how I write is done in order to save my own life. And I mean that literally. For me literature is a way of knowing that I am not hallucinating, that whatever I feel/know *is*."[12] Christian is an African-American woman writing about the literature of Afro-American women, but her words are relevant to the issues raised by the context of C&I 607. I understood the words written by the Minority Student Coalition and spoken by other students/professors of difference[13] on campus to have a similar function as a reality check for survival. It is inappropriate to respond to such words by subjecting them to rationalist debates about their validity. Words spoken for survival come already validated in a radically different arena of proof and carry no option of luxury of choice. (This is not to say, however, that the positions of students of color, or of any other group, were to be taken up unproblematically—an issue I will address below.)

I drafted a syllabus and circulated it for suggestions and revisions to students I knew to be involved in the Minority Student Coalition and to colleagues who shared my concerns. The goal of "Media and Anti-Racist Pedagogies," as stated in the revised syllabus, was to define, organize, carry out, and analyze an educational initiative on campus that would win semiotic space for the marginalized discourses of students against racism. Campus activists were defining these discourses and making them available to other groups, including the class, through documents, demonstrations, discussions, and press conferences.

The syllabus also listed the following assumptions underlying the course:

1. Students who want to acquire knowledge of existing educational media theory and criticism for the purpose of guiding their own educational practice can best do so in a learning situation that interrelates theory with concrete attempts at using media for education.

2. Current situations of racial and sexual harassment and elitism on campus and in the curriculum demand meaningful responses from both students and faculty, and responses can be designed in a way that accomplishes both academic and political goals.

3. Often, the term "critical education" has been used to imply, but also to hide, positions and goals of antiracism, anticlassism, and so forth. Defining this course as one that explores the possibility of using media to construct antiracist pedagogies asserts that these are legitimate and imperative goals for educators.

4. What counts as an appropriate use of media for an antiracist pedagogy cannot be specified outside of the contexts of actual educational situations; therefore student work on this issue should be connected to concrete initiatives in actual situations.

5. Any antiracist pedagogy must be defined through an awareness of the ways in which oppressive structures are the result of *intersections* between racist, classist, sexist, ablest, and other oppressive dynamics.

6. Everyone who has grown up in a racist culture has to work at unlearning racism—we will make mistakes in this class, but they will be made in the context of our struggle to come to grips with racism.

Naming the political agenda of the course, to the extent that I did, seemed relatively easy. I was in the fourth year of a tenure-track position in my department and felt that I had "permission" from colleagues to pursue the line of research and practice out of which this course had clearly grown. The administration's response to the crisis on campus gave further "permission" for attempts to alleviate racism in the institution. However, the directions in which I should proceed became less clear once the class was underway. As I began to live out and interpret the consequences of how discourses of "critical reflection," "empowerment," "student voice," and "dialogue" had influenced my conceptualization of the goals of the course and my ability to make sense of my experiences in the class, I found myself struggling against (struggling to unlearn) key assumptions and assertions of current literature on critical pedagogy and straining to recognize, name, and come to grips with crucial issues of classroom practice that critical pedagogy cannot or will not address.

FROM CRITICAL RATIONALISM TO THE POLITICS OF PARTIAL NARRATIVES

The students enrolled in "Media and Anti-Racist Pedagogies" included Asian American, Chicano/a, Jewish, Puerto Rican, and Anglo-European men and women from the United States; and Asian, African, Icelandic, and Canadian international students. It was evident after the first class meeting that all of us agreed, but with different understandings and agendas, that racism was a problem on campus that required political action. The effects of the diverse social positions and political ideologies of the students enrolled, my own position and experiences as a woman and a feminist, and the effects of the course's context on the form and content of our early class discussions quickly threw the rationalist assumptions underlying critical pedagogy into question.

These rationalist assumptions have led to the following goals: the teaching of analytic and critical skills for judging the truth and merit of propositions, and the interrogation and selective appropriation of potentially transformative moments in the dominant culture.[14] As long as educators define pedagogy against oppressive formations in these ways, the role of the critical pedagogue will be to guarantee that the foundation for classroom interaction is reason. In other words, the critical pedagogue is one who enforces the rules of reason in the classroom—"a series of rules of thought that any ideal rational person might adopt if his/her purpose was to achieve propositions of universal validity."[15] Under these conditions, and given the coded nature of the political agenda of critical pedagogy, only one "political" gesture appears to be available to the critical pedagogue. S/he can ensure that students are given the chance to arrive logically at the "universally valid proposition" underlying the discourse of critical pedagogy—namely, that all people have a right to freedom from oppression guaranteed by the democratic social contract and that in the classroom, this proposition be given equal time vis-à-vis other "sufficiently articulated and reasonably distinct moral postions."[16]

Yet educators who have constructed classroom practices dependent upon analytical critical judgment can no longer regard the enforcement of rationalism as a self-evident political act against relations of domination. Literary criticism, cultural studies, poststructuralism, feminist studies, comparative studies, and media studies have by now amassed overwhelming evidence of the extent to which the

305

myths of the ideal rational person and the "universality" of propositions have been oppressive to those who are not European, white, male, middle class, Christian, able-bodied, thin, and heterosexual.[17] Writings by many literary and cultural critics, both women of color and White women who are concerned with explaining the intersections and interactions among relations of racism, colonialism, sexism, and so forth, are now employing, either implicitly or explicitly, concepts and analytical methods that could be called feminist poststructuralism.[18] While poststructuralism, like rationalism, is a tool that can be used to dominate, it has also facilitated a devastating critique of the violence of rationalism against its Others. It has demonstrated that as a discursive practice, rationalism's regulated and systematic use of elements of language constitutes rational competence "as a series of exclusions—of women, people of color, of nature as a historical agent, of the true value of art."[19] In contrast, poststructuralist thought is not bound to reason, but "to discourse, literally narratives about the world that are admittedly *partial*. Indeed, one of the crucial features of discourse, is the intimate tie between knowledge and interest, the latter being understood as a 'standpoint' from which to grasp 'reality.' "[20]

The literature on critical pedagogy implies that the claims made by documents, demonstrations, press conferences, and classroom discussions of students of color and white students against racism could rightfully be taken up in the classroom and subjected to rational deliberation over their truth in light of competing claims. But this would force students to subject themselves to the logics of rationalism and scientism that have been predicated on and made possible through the exclusion of socially constructed irrational Others—women, people of color, nature, aesthetics. As Audre Lorde writes, "The master's tools will never dismantle the master's house,"[21] and to call on students of color to justify and explicate their claims in terms of the master's tools—tools such as rationalism, fashioned precisely to perpetuate their exclusion—colludes with the oppressor in keeping "the oppressed occupied with the master's concerns."[22] As Barbara Christian describes it:

> the literature of people who are not in power has always been in danger of extinction or cooptation, not because we do not theorize, but because what we can even imagine, far less who we can reach, is constantly limited by societal structures. For me, literary criticism is promotion as well as understanding, a response to the writer to whom there is often no response, to folk who need the writing as much as they need anything. I know, from literary history, that writing disappears unless there is a response to it. Because I write about writers who are now writing, I hope to help ensure that their tradition has continuity and survives.[23]

In contrast to the enforcement of rational deliberation, but like Christian's promotion and response, my role in C&I 607 would be to interrupt institutional limits on how much time and energy students of color, White students, and professors against racism could spend on elaborating their positions and playing them out to the point where internal contradictions and effects on the positions of other social groups could become evident and subject to self-analysis.

With Barbara Christian, I saw the necessity to take the voices of students and professors of difference at their word—as "valid"—but not without response.[24] Students' and my own narratives about experiences of racism, ableism, elitism, fat oppression, sexism, anti-Semitism, heterosexism, and so on are partial—partial in the sense that they are unfinished, imperfect, limited; and partial in the sense that they project the interests of "one side" over others. Because those voices are partial and partisan, they must be made problematic, but not because they have broken the rules of thought of the ideal rational person by grounding their knowledge in immediate emotional, social, and psychic experiences of oppression,[25] or are somehow lacking or too narrowly circumscribed.[26] Rather, they must be critiqued because they hold implications for other social movements and their struggles for self-definition. This assertion carries important implications for the "goal" of classroom practices against oppressive formations, which I will address later.

Have We Got a Theory for You![27]

As educators who claim to be dedicated to ending oppression, critical pedagogues have acknowledged the socially constructed and legitimated authority that teachers/professors hold over students.[28] Yet theorists of critical pedagogy have failed to launch any meaningful analysis of, or program for, reformulating the instutitonalized power imbalances between themselves and their students, or of the essentially paternalistic project of education itself. In the absence of such an analysis and program, their efforts are limited to trying to transform negative effects of power imbalances within the classroom into positive ones. Strategies such as student empowerment and dialogue give the illusion of equality while in fact leaving the authoritarian nature of the teacher/student relationship intact.

"Empowerment" is a key concept in this approach, which treats the symptoms but leaves the disease unnamed and untouched. Critical pedagogies employing this strategy prescribe various theoretical and practical means for sharing, giving, or redistributing power to students. For example, some authors challenge teachers to reject the vision of education as inculcation of students by the more powerful teacher. In its place, they urge teachers to accept the possibility of education through "reflective examination" of the plurality of moral positions before the presumably rational teacher and students.[29] Here, the goal is to give students the analytical skills they need to make them as free, rational, and objective as teachers supposedly are to choose positions on their objective merits. I have already argued that in a classroom in which "empowerment" is made dependent on rationalism, those perspectives that would question the political interests (sexism, racism, colonialism, for example) expressed and guaranteed by rationalism would be rejected as "irrational" (biased, partial).

A second strategy is to make the teacher more like the student by redefining the teacher as learner of the student's reality and knowledge. For example, in their discussion of the politics of dialogic teaching and epistemology, Shor and Freire suggest that "the teacher selecting the objects of study knows them *better* than the students as the course begins, but the teacher *re-learns* the objects through studying them with their students."[30] The literature explores only one reason for expecting the teacher to "re-learn" an object of study thorugh the student's less adequate understanding and that is to enable the teacher to devise more effective strategies for bringing the student "up" to the teacher's level of understanding. Giroux, for example, argues for a pedagogy that "is attentive to the histories, dreams, and experiences that . . . students bring to school. It is only by beginning with these subjective forms that critical educators can develop a language and set of practices"[31] that can successfully mediate differences between student understandings and teacher understandings in "pedagogically progressive" ways.[32] In this example, Giroux leaves the implied superiority of the teacher's understanding and the undefined "progressiveness" of this type of pedagogy unproblematized and untheoritized.

A third strategy is to acknowledge the "directiveness"[33] or "authoritarianism"[34] of education as inevitable and to judge particular power imbalances between teacher and student to be tolerable or intolerable depending upon "towards what and with whom [they are] directive."[35] "Acceptable" imbalances are those in which authority serves "common human interests by sharing information, promoting open and informed discussion, and maintaining itself only through the respect and trust of those who grant the authority."[36] In such cases, authority becomes "emancipatory authority," a kind of teaching in which teachers would make explicit and available for rationalist debate "the political and moral referents for authority they assume in teaching particular forms of knowledge, in taking stands against forms of oppression, and in treating students as if they ought also to be concerned about social justice and political action."[37] Here, the question of "empowerment for what" becomes the final arbiter of a teacher's use or misuse of authority.

But critical pedagogues consistently answer the question of "empowerment for what?" in ahistorical and depoliticized abstractions. These include empowerment for "human betterment,"[38] for expanding the "the range of possible social identities people may become,"[39] and "making one's self present as part of a moral and political project that links production of meaning to the possibility for human agency, democratic community, and transformative social action."[40] As a result, student empowerment has been defined in the broadest possible humanist terms and becomes a "capacity to act effectively" in a way that fails to challenge any identifiable social or political position, institution, or group.

The contortions of logic and rhetoric that characterize these attempts to define "empowerment" testify to the failure of critical educators to come to terms with the essentially paternalistic project of traditional education. "Emancipatory authority"[41] is one such contortion, for it implies the presence of, or potential for, an emancipated teacher. Indeed, it asserts that teachers "can link knowledge to power by bringing to light and teaching the subjugated histories, experiences, stories, and accounts of those who suffer and struggle."[42] Yet I cannot unproblematically bring subjugated knowledges to light when I am not free of my own learned racism, fat oppression, classism, ableism, or sexism. No teacher is free of these learned and internalized oppressions. Nor are accounts of one group's suffering and struggle immune from reproducing narratives oppressive to another's—the racism of the women's movement in the United States is one example.

As I argued above, "emancipatory authority" also implies, according to Shor and Freire, a teacher who knows the object of study . . . better . . . than do the students. Yet I did not understand racism better than my students did, especially those students of color coming into class after six months (or more) of campus activism and whole lives of experience and struggle against racism—nor could I ever hope to. My experiences with and access to multiple and sophisticated strategies for interpreting and interrupting sexism (in White middle-class contexts) do not provide me with a ready-made analysis of or language for understanding my own implications in racist structures. My understanding and experience of racism will always be constrained by my white skin and middle-class privilege. Indeed, it is impossible for anyone to be free from these oppressive formations at this historical moment. Furthermore, while I had the institutional power and authority in the classroom to enforce "reflective examination" of the plurality of moral and political positions before us in a way that supposedly gave my own assessments equal weight with those of students, in fact my institutional role as professor would always weight my statements different from those of students.

Given my own history of white-skin, middle-class, able-bodied, thin privilege and my institutionally granted power, it made more sense to see my task as one of redefining "critical pedagogy" so that it did not need utopian moments of "democracy," "equality," "justice," or "emancipated" teachers—moments that are unattainable (and ultimately undesirable, because they are always predicated on the interests of those who are in the position to define utopian projects). A preferable goal seemed to be to become capable of a sustained encounter with currently oppressive formations and power relations that refuse to be theorized away or fully transcended in a utopian resolution—and to enter into the encounter in a way that owned up to my own implications in those formations and was capable of changing my own relation to and investments in those formations.

THE REPRESSIVE MYTH OF THE SILENT OTHER

At first glance, the concept of "student voice" seemed to offer a pedagogical strategy in this direction. This concept has become highly visible and influential in current discussions of curriculum and teaching, as evidenced by its appearance in the titles of numerous presentations at the 1989 American Educational Research Association convention. Within current discourses on teaching, it functions to efface the contradiction between the emancipatory project of critical pedagogy and the hierarchical relation between teachers and students. In other words, it is a strategy for negotiating between the directiveness of dominant educational relationships and the political commitment to make students autonomous of those relationships (how does a teacher "make" students autonomous without directing them?). The discourse on student voice sees the student as "empowered" when the teacher "helps" students to express their subjugated knowledges.[43] The targets of this strategy are students from disadvantaged and subordinated social class, racial, ethnic, and gender groups—or alienated middle-class students without access to skills of critical analysis, whose voices have been silenced or distorted by oppressive cultural and educational formations. By speaking, in their "authentic voices," students are seen to make themselves visible and define themselves as authors of their own world. Such definition presumably gives students an identity and political position from which to act as agents of social change.[44] Thus, while it is true that the teacher is directive, the student's own daily life experiences of oppression chart her/his path toward self-definition and agency. The task of the critical educator thus becomes "finding ways of working with students that enable the full expression of multiple 'voices' engaged in dialogic encounter,"[45] encouraging students of different race, class, and gender positions to speak in self-affirming ways about their experiences and how they have been mediated by their own social positions and those of others.

309

Within feminist discourses seeking to provide both a place and power for women to speak, "voice" and "speech" have become commonplace as metaphors for women's feminist self-definitions—but with meanings and effects quite different from those implied by discourses of critical pedagogy. Within feminist movements, women's voices and speech are conceptualized in terms of self-definitions that are oppositional to those definitions of women constructed by others, usually to serve interests and contexts that subordinate women to men. But while critical educators acknowledge the existence of unequal power relations in classrooms, they have made no systematic examination of the barriers that this imbalance throws up to the kind of student expression and dialogue they prescribe.

The concept of critical pedagogy assumes a commitment on the part of the professor/teacher toward ending the student's oppression. Yet the literature offers no sustained attempt to problematize this stance and confront the likelihood that the professor brings to social movements (including critical pedagogy) interests of her or his own race, class, ethnicity, gender, and other positions. S/he does not play the role of disinterested mediator on the side of the oppressed group.[46] As an Anglo, middle-class professor in C&I 607, I could not unproblematically "help" a student of color to find her/his authentic voice as a student of color. I could not unproblematically "affiliate" with the social groups my students represent and interpret their experience to them. In fact, I brought to the classroom privileges and interests that were put at risk in fundamental ways by the demands and defiances of student voices. I brought a social subjectivity that has been constructed in such a way that I have not and can never participate unproblematically in the collective process of self-definition, naming of oppression, and struggles for visibility in the face of marginalization engaged in by students whose class, race, gender, and other positions I do not share. Critical pedagogues are always implicated in the very structures they are trying to change.

Although the literature recognizes that teachers have much to learn from their students' experiences, it does not address the ways in which there are things that I as professor could *never know* about the experiences, oppressions, and understandings of other participants in the class. This situation makes it impossible for any single voice in the classroom—including that of the professor—to assume the position of center or origin of knowledge or authority, of having privileged access to authentic experience or appropriate language. A recognition, contrary to all Western ways of knowing and speaking, that all knowings are partial, that there are fundamental things each of us cannot know—a situation alleviated only in part by the pooling of partial, socially constructed knowledges in classrooms—demands a fundamental retheorizing of "education" and "pedagogy," an issue I will begin to address below.

When educational researchers writing about critical pedagogy fail to examine the implications of the gendered, raced, and classed teacher and student for the theory of critical pedagogy, they reproduce, by default, the category of generic "critical teacher"—a specific form of the generic human that underlies classical liberal thought. Like the generic human, the generic critical teacher is not, of course, generic at all. Rather, the term defines a discursive category predicated on the current mythical norm, namely: young, White, Christian, middle-class, heterosexual, able-bodied, thin, rational man. Gender, race, class, and other differences become only variations on or additions to the generic human—"underneath, we are all the same."[47] But voices of students and professors of difference solicited by critical pedagogy are not additions to that norm, but oppositional challenges that require a dismantling of the mythical norm and its uses as well as alternatives to it. There has been no consideration of how voices of, for example, White women, students of color, disabled students, White men against masculinist culture, and fat students will necessarily be constructed in opposition to the teacher/institution when they try to change the power imbalances they inhabit in their daily lives, including their lives in schools.

Critical pedagogues speak of student voices as "sharing" their experiences and understandings of oppression with other students and with the teacher in the interest of "expanding the possibilities of what it is to be human."[48] Yet White women, women of color, men of color, White men against masculinist culture, fat people, gay men and lesbians, people with disabilities, and Jews do not speak of the oppressive formations that condition their lives in the spirit of "sharing." Rather, the speech of oppositional groups is a "talking back," a "defiant speech"[49] that is constructed within communities of resistance and is a condition of survival.

In C&I 607, the defiant speech of students and professor of difference constituted fundamental challenges to and rejections of the voices of some classmates and often of the professor. For example, it became clear very quickly that in order to name her experience of racism, a Chicana student had to define her voice in part through opposition to—and rejection of—definitions of "Chicana" assumed or taken for granted by other student/professor voices in the classroom. And in the context of protests by students of color against racism on campus, her voice had to be constructed in opposition to the institutional racism of the university's curriculum and policies—which were represented in part by my discourses and actions as Anglo-American, middle-class woman professor. Unless we found a way to respond to such challenges, our academic and political work against racism would be blocked. This alone is a reason for finding ways to express and engage with student voices, one that distances itself from the abstract, philosophical reasons implied by the literature on critical pedagogy when it fails to contextualize its projects. Furthermore, grounding the expression of and engagement with student voices in the need to construct contextualized political strategies rejects both the voyeuristic relation that the literature reproduces when the voice of the professor is not problematized, and the instrumental role critical pedagogy plays when student voice is used to inform more effective teaching strategies.

The lessons learned from feminist struggles to make a difference through defiant speech offer both useful critiques of the assumptions of critical pedagogy and starting points for moving beyond its repressive myths.[50] Within feminist movements, self-defining feminist voices have been understood as constructed collectively in the context of a larger feminist movement or women's marginalized subcultures. Feminist voices are made possible by the interactions among women within and across race, class, and other differences that divide them. These voices have never been solely or even primarily the result of the pedagogical interaction between an individual student and a teacher. Yet discourses of the pedagogy of empowerment consistently position students as individuals with only the most abstract of relations to concrete contexts of struggle. In their writing about critical pedagogy, educational researchers consistently place teachers/professors at the center of the consciousness-raising activity. For example, McLaren describes alienated middle-class youth in this way:

These students do not recognize their own self-representation and suppression by the dominant society, and in our vitiated learning environments they are not provided with the requisite theoretical constructs to help them understand why they feel as badly as they do. Because teachers lack a critical pedagogy, these students are not provided with the ability to think critically, a skill that would enable them to better understand why their lives have been reduced to feelings of meaningless, randomness, and alienation.[51]

In contrast, many students came into "Media and Anti-Racist Pedagogies" with oppositional voices already formulated within various antiracism and other movements. These movements had not necessarily relied on intellectuals/teachers to interpret their goals and programs to themselves or to others.

Current writing by many feminists working from antiracism and feminist poststructuralist perspectives recognize that any individual woman's politicized voice will be partial, multiple, and contradictory.[52] The literature on critical pedagogy also recognizes the possibility that each student will be capable of identifying a multiplicity of authentic voices in her/himself. But it does not confront the ways in which any individual student's voice is already a "teeth gritting" and often contradictory intersection of voices constituted by gender, race, class, ability, ethnicity, sexual orientation, or ideology. Nor does it engage with the fact that the particularities of historical context, personal biography, and subjectivities split between the conscious and unconscious will necessarily render each expression of student voice partial and predicated on the absence and marginalization of alternative voices. It is impossible to speak from all voices at once, or from any one, without the traces of the others being present and interruptive. Thus the very term "student voice" is highly problematic. Pluralizing the concept as "voices" implies correction through addition. This loses sight of the contradictory and partial nature of all voices.

In C&I 607, for example, participants expressed much pain, confusion, and difficulty in speaking because of the ways in which discussions called up their multiple and contradictory social positionings. Women found it difficult to prioritize expressions of racial privilege and oppression when such prioritizing threatened to perpetuate their gender oppression. Among international students, both those who were of color and those who were White found it difficult to join their voices with those of U.S. students of color when it meant a subordination of their oppression as people living under U.S. imperialist policies and as students for whom English was a second language. Asian American women found it difficult to join their voices with other students of color when it meant subordinating their specific oppressions as Asian Americans. I found it difficult to speak as a White woman about gender oppression when I occupied positions of institutional power relative to all students in the class, men and women, but positions of gender oppression relative to students who were White men, and in different terms, relative to students who were men of color.

Finally, the argument that women's speech and voice have not been and should not be constructed primarily for the purpose of communicating women's experiences to men is commonplace within feminist movements. This position takes the purposes of such speech to be survival, expansion of women's own understandings of their oppression and strength, sharing common experiences among women, building solidarity among women, and political strategizing. Many feminists have pointed to the necessity for men to "do their own work" at unlearning sexism and male privilege, rather than looking to women for the answers. I am similarly suspicious of the desire of the mostly White, middle-class men who write the literature on critical pedagogy to elicit "full expression" of student voices. Such a relation between teacher/student becomes voyeuristic when the voice of the pedagogue himself goes unexamined.

Furthermore, the assumption present in the literature that silence in front of a teacher or professor indicates "lost voice," "voicelessness," or lack of social identity from which to act as a social agent betrays deep and unacceptable gender, race, and class biases. It is worth quoting bell hooks at length about the fiction of the silence of subordinated groups:

> Within feminist circles silence is often seen as the sexist defined "right speech of womanhood"—the sign of woman's submission to patriarchal authority. This emphasis on women's silence may be an accurate remembering of what has taken place in the households of women from WASP backgrounds in the United States but in Black communities (and in other diverse ethnic communities) women have not been silent. Their voices can be heard. Certainly for Black women our struggle has not been to emerge from silence to speech but to change the nature and direction of our speech. To make a speech that compels listeners, one that is heard. . . . Dialogue, the sharing of speech and recognition, took place not between mother and child or mother and male authority figure, but with other Black women. I can remember watching, fascinated, as our mother talked with her mother, sisters, and women friends. The intimacy and intensity of their speech—the satisfaciton they received from talking to one another, the pleasure, the joy. It was in this world of woman speech, loud talk, angry words, women with tongues sharp, tender sweet tongues, touching our world with their words, that I made speech my birthright—and the right to voice, to authorship, a privilege I would not be denied. It was in that world and because of it that I came to dream of writing, to write.[53]

White women, men and women of color, impoverished people, people with disabilities, gays and lesbians are not silenced in the sense implied by the literature on critical pedagogy. They just are not talking in their authentic voices, or they are declining/refusing to talk at all to critical educators who have been unable to acknowledge the presence of knowledges that are challenging and most likely inaccessible to their own social positions. What they/we say, to whom, in what context, depending on the energy they/we have for the struggle on a particular day, is the result of conscious and unconscious assessments of the power relations and safety of the situation.

As I understand it at the moment, what got said—and how—in our class was the product of highly complex strategizing for the visibility that speech gives without giving up the safety of silence. More than that, it was a highly complex negotiation of the politics of knowing and being known. Things were left unsaid, or they were encoded, on the basis of speakers' conscious and unconscious assessments of the risks and costs of disclosing their understandings of themselves and of others. To what extent had students occupying socially constructed positions of privilege at a particular moment risked being known by students occupying socially constructed positions of subordination at the same moment? To what extent had students in those positions of privilege relinquished the security and privilege of being the knower?[54]

As long as the literature on critical pedagogy fails to come to grips with issues of trust, risk and the operations of fear and desire around such issues of identity and politics in the classroom, their rationalistic tools will continue to fail to loosen deep-seated, self-interested investments in unjust relations of, for example, gender, ethnicity, and sexual orientation.[55] These investments are shared by both teachers and students, yet the literature on critical pedagogy has ignored its own implications for the young, White, Christian, middle-class, heterosexual, ablebodied man/pedagogue that it assumes. Against such ignoring, Mohanty argues that to desire to ignore is not cognitive, but performative. It is the incapacity or refusal "to acknowledge one's own implication in the information."[56] "[Learning] involves a necessary implication in the radical alterity of the unknown, in the desire(s) not to know, in the process of this unresolvable dialectic."[57]

FROM DIALOGUE TO WORKING TOGETHER ACROSS DIFFERENCES

Because student voice has been defined as "the measures by which students and teacher participate in dialogue,"[58] the foregoing critique has serious consequences for the concept of "dialogue" as it has been articulated in the literature on critical pedagogy. Dialogue has been defined as a fundamental imperative of critical pedagogy and the basis of the democratic education that insures a democratic state. Through dialogue, a classroom can be made into a public sphere, a locus of citizenship in which:

> students and teachers can engage in a process of deliberation and discussion aimed at advancing the public welfare in accordance with fundamental moral judgments and principles. . . . School and classroom practices should, in some manner, be organized around forms of learning which serve to prepare students for responsible roles as transformative intellectuals, as community members, and as critically active citizens outside of schools.[59]

Dialogue is offered as a pedagogical strategy for constructing these learning conditions and consists of ground rules for classroom interaction using language. These rules include the assumptions that all members have equal opportunity to speak, all members respect other members' rights to speak and feel safe to speak, and all ideas are tolerated and subjected to rational critical assessment against fundamental judgments and moral principles. According to Henry Giroux, in order for dialogue to be possible, classroom participants must exhibit "trust, sharing, and commitment to improving the quality of human life."[60] While the specific form and means of social change and organization are open to debate, there must be agreement around the goals of dialogue: "all voices and their differences become unified both in their efforts to identify and recall moments of human suffering and in their attempts to overcome conditions that perpetuate such suffering."[61]

However, for the reasons outlined above—the students' and professor's asymmetrical positions of difference and privilege—dialogue in this sense was both impossible and undesirable in C&I 607. In fact, the unity of efforts and values unproblematically assumed by Giroux was not only impossible but potentially repressive as well. Giroux's formula for dialogue requires and assumes a classroom of participants unified on the side of the subordinated against the subordinators, sharing and trusting in an "us-ness" against "them-ness." This formula fails to confront dynamics of subordination present among classroom participants and within classroom participants in the form of multiple and contradictory subject positions. Such a conception of dialogue invokes the "all too easy polemic that opposes victims to perpetrator," in which a condition for collective purpose among victims is the desire for home, for synchrony, for sameness.[62] Biddy Martin and Chandra Mohanty call for creating new forms of collective struggle based on and enforcing a harmony of interests. They envision collective struggle that starts from an acknowledgement that "unity"—interpersonal, personal, and political— is necessarily fragmentary, unstable, not given, but chosen and struggled for—but not on the basis of sameness.[63]

But despite early rejections of fundamental tenets of dialogue, including the usually unquestioned emancipatory potentials of rational deliberation and unity, we remained in the grip of other repressive fictions of classroom dialogue for most of the semester. I expected that we would be able to ensure all members a safe place to speak, equal opportunity to speak, and equal power in influencing decisionmaking—and as a result, it would become clear what had to be done and why. It was only at the end of the semester that I and the students recognized that we had given this myth the power to divert our attention and classroom practices away from what we needed to be doing. Acting as if our classroom were a safe space in which democratic dialogue was possible and happening did not make it so. If we were to respond to our context and the social identities of the people in our classroom in ways that did not reproduce the oppressive formations we were trying to work against, we needed classroom practices that confronted the power dynamics inside and outside of our classroom that made democratic dialogue impossible. During the last two weeks of the semester, we reflected in class on our group's process—how we spoke to and/or silenced each other across our differences, how we divided labor, made decisions, and treated each other as visible and/or invisible. As students had been doing with each other all along, I began to have informal conversations with one or two students at a time who were extremely committed on personal, political, and academic levels to breaking through the barriers we had encountered and understanding what had happened during the semester. These reflections and discussions led me to the following conclusions.

Our classroom was not in fact a safe space for students to speak out or talk back about their experiences of oppression both inside and outside of the classroom. In our class, these included experiences of being gay, lesbian, fat, women of color working with men of color, White women working with men of color, men of color working with White women and men.[64] Things were not being said for a number of reasons. These included fear of being misunderstood and/or disclosing too much and becoming too vulnerable; memories of bad experiences in other contexts of speaking out; resentment that other oppressions (sexism, heterosexism, fat oppression, classism, anti-Semitism) were being marginalized in the name of addressing racism—and guilt for feeling such resentment—confusion about levels of trust and commitment surrounding those who were allies to another group's struggles; resentment by some students of color for feeling that they were expected to disclose "more" and once against take the burden of doing the pedagogic work of educating White students/professor about the consequences of White middle-class privilege; and resentment by White students for feeling that they had to prove they were not the enemy.

Dialogue in its conventional sense is impossible in the culture at large because at this historical moment, power relations between raced, classed, and gendered students and teachers are unjust. The injustice of these relations and the way in which those injustices distort communication cannot be overcome in a classroom, no matter how committed the teacher and students are to "overcoming conditions that perpetuate suffering." Conventional notions of dialogue and democracy assume rationalized, individualized subjects capable of agreeing on universalizable "fundamental moral principles" and "quality of human life" that become self-evident when subjects cease to be self-interested and particularistic about group rights. Yet social agents are not capable of being fully rational and disinterested, and they are subjects split between the conscious and unconscious and among multiple social positionings. Fundamental moral and political principles are not absolute and universalizable, waiting to be discovered by the disinterested researcher/teacher; they are "established intersubjectively by subjects capable of interpretation and reflection."[65] Educational researchers attempting to construct meaningful discourses about the politics of classroom practices must begin to theorize the consequences for education on the ways in which knowledge, power, and desire are mutually implicated in each other's formations and deployments.

By the end of the semester, participants in the class agreed that commitment to rational discussion about racism in a classroom setting was not enough to make that setting a safe space for speaking out and talking back. We agreed that a safer space required high levels of trust and personal commitment to individuals in the class, gained in part through social interactions outside of class—potlucks, field trips, participation in rallies and other gatherings. Opportunities to know the motivations, histories, and stakes of individuals in the class should have been planned early in the semester.[66] Furthermore, White students/professor should have shared the burden of educating themselves about the consequences of their white-skin privilege, and to facilitate this, the curriculum should have included significant amounts of literature, films, and videos by people of color and White people against racism—so that the students of color involved in the class would not always be looked to as "experts" in racism or the situation on the campus.

Because all the voices within the classroom are not and cannot carry equal legitimacy, safety, and power in dialogue at this historical moment, there are times when the inequalities must be named and addressed by constructing alternative ground rules for communication. By the end of the semester, participants in C&I 607 began to recognize that some social groups represented in the class had had consistently more speaking time than others. Women, international students for whom English was a second language, and mixed groups sharing ideological and political languages and perspectives began to have very significant interactions outside of class. Informal, overlapping affinity groups formed and met unofficially for the purpose of articulating and refining positions based on shared oppressions, ideological analyses, or interests. They shared grievances about the dynamics of the larger group and performed reality checks for each other. Because they were unofficial groups constituted on the spot in response to specific needs or simply as a result of casual encounters outside the classroom, alliances could be shaped and reshaped as strategies in context.

The fact that affinity groups did form within the larger group should not be seen as a failure to construct a unity of voices and goals—a possibility unproblematically assumed and worked for in critical pedagogy. Rather, affinity groups were necessary for working against the way current historical configurations of oppressions were reproduced in the class. They provided some participants with safer home bases from which they gained support, important understandings, and a language for entering the larger classroom interactions each week. Once we acknowledged the existence, necessity, and value of these affinity groups, we began to see our tasks not as one of building democratic dialogue between free and equal individuals, but of building a coalition among the multiple, shifting, intersecting, and sometimes contradictory groups carrying unequal weights of legitimacy within the culture and the classroom. Halfway through the semester, students renamed the class Coalition 607.

At the end of the semester, we began to suspect that it would have been appropriate for the large group to experiment with forms of communication other than dialogue. These could have brought the existence and results of affinity group interactions to bear more directly on the larger group's understandings and practices. For example, it seemed that we needed times when one affinity group (women of color, women and men of color, feminists, White men against masculinist culture, White women, gays, lesbians) could "speak out" and "talk back" about their experience of Coalition 607's group process or their experience of racial, gender, or other injustice on the campus, while the rest of the class listened without interruption. This would have acknowledged that we were not interacting in class dialogue solely as individuals, but as members of larger social groups, with whom we shared common and also differing experiences of oppression, a language for naming, fighting, and surviving that oppression, and a shared sensibility and style. The differences among the affinity groups that composed the class made communication within the class a form of cross-cultural or cross-subcultural exchange rather than the free, rational, democratic exchange between equal invividuals implied in critical pedagogy literature.

But I want to emphasize that this does not mean that discourses of students of difference were taken up and supported unconditionally by themselves and their allies. There had been intense consciousness-raising on the UW-Madison campus between African American students, Asian American students, Latino/a, Chicano/a students, Native American students, and men and women of color about the different forms racism had taken across the campus, depending on ethnicity and gender—and how no single group's analysis could be adopted to cover all other students of color.

Early in the semester, it became clear to some in Coalition 607 that some of the antiracism discourses heard on campus were structured by highly problematic gender politics, and White women and women of color could not adopt those discourses as their own without undercutting their own struggles against sexism on campus and in their communities. We began to define coalition-building not only in terms of what we shared—a commitment to work against racism—but in terms of what we did not share—gender, sexual orientation, ethnicity, and other differences. These positions gave us different stakes in, experiences of, and perspectives on, racism. These differences meant that each strategy we considered for fighting racism on campus had to be interrogated for the implications it held for struggles against sexism, ableism, elitism, fat oppression, and so forth.

We agreed to a final arbiter of the acceptability of demands/narratives by students of color and our class's actions on campus. Proposals would be judged in light of our answers to this question: to what extent do our political strategies and alternative narratives about social difference succeed in alleviating campus racism, while at the same time managing *not to undercut* the efforts of other social groups to win self-definition?

A PEDAGOGY OF THE UNKNOWABLE

Like the individual students themselves, each affinity group possessed only partial narratives of its oppressions—partial in that they were self-interested and predicated on the exclusion of the voices of others—and partial in the sense that the meaning of an invidual's or group's experience is never self-evident or complete. No one affinity group could ever "know" the experiences and knowledges of other affinity groups or the social positions that were not their own. Nor can social subjects who are split between the conscious and unconscious and cut across by multiple, intersecting, and contradictory subject positions ever fully "know" their own experiences. As a whole, Coalition 607 could never know with certainty whether the actions it planned to take on campus would undercut the struggle of other social groups, or even that of its own affinity groups. But this situation was not a failure; it was not something to overcome. Realizing that there are partial narratives that some social groups or cultures have and others can never know, but that are necessary to human survival, is a condition to embrace and use as an opportunity to build a kind of social and educational interdependency that recognizes differences as "different strengths" and as "forces for change."[67] In the words of Audre Lorde, "Difference must be not merely tolerated, but seen as a fund of necessary polarities between which our creativity can spark like a dialectic. Only then does the necessity for interdependency become unthreatening."[68]

In the end, Coalition 607 participants made an initial gesture toward acting out the implications of the unknowable and the social, educational, and political interdependency that it necessitates. The educational interventions against racism that we carried out on campus were put forth as Coalition 607's statement about its members' provisional, partial understanding of racial oppression on the UW-Madison campus at the moment of its actions. These statements were not offered with the invitation for audiences to participate in dialogue, but as a speaking out from semiotic spaces temporarily and problematically controlled by Coalition 607's students. First, we took actions on campus by interrupting business-as-usual (that is, social relations of racism, sexism, classism, Eurocentrism as usual) in the public spaces of the library mall and administrative offices. (The mall is a frequent site for campus protests, rallies, and graffiti, and was chosen for this reason.) These interruptions consisted of three events.

At noon on April 28, 1988, a street theater performance on the library mall, "Meet on the Street," presented an ironic history of university attempts to coopt and defuse the demands of students of color from the 1950s through the 1980s. The affinity group that produced this event invited members of the university and Madison communities who were not in the class to participate. That night, after dark, "Scrawl on the Mall" used overhead and movie projectors to project towering images, text, and spontaneously written "graffiti" on the white walls of the main campus library. Class members and passersby drew and wrote on transparencies for the purpose of deconstructing, defacing, and transforming racist discourses and giving voice to perspectives and demands of students of color and

White students against racism. For example, students projected onto the library a page from the administration's official response to the Minority Student Coalition demands, and edited it to reveal how it failed to meet those demands. Throughout the semester, a third group of students interrupted business-as-usual in the offices of the student newspaper and university administrators by writing articles and holding interviews that challenged the university's and the newspaper's response to the demands by students of color.

These three events disrupted power relations, however temporarily, within the contexts in which they occurred. Students of color and white students against racism opened up semiotic space for discourses normally marginalized and silenced within the everyday uses of the library mall and administrators' offices. They appropriated means of discourse production—overhead projectors, microphones, language, images, newspaper articles—and controlled, however problematically, the terms in which students of color and racism on campus would be defined and represented within the specific times and spaces of the events. They made available to other members of the university community, with unpredictable and uncontrollable effects, discourses of antiracism that might otherwise have remained unavailable, distorted, more easily dismissed, or seemingly irrelevant. Thus students engaged in the political work of changing material conditions within a public space, allowing them to make visible and assert the legitimacy of their own definitions, in their own terms, of racism and antiracism on the UW campus.

Each of the three actions was defined by different affinity groups according to differing priorities, languages of understanding and analysis, and levels of comfort with various kinds of public action. They were "unified" through their activity of mutual critique, support, and participation, as each group worked through, as much as possible, ways in which the others supported or undercut its own understandings and objectives. Each affinity group brought its proposal for action to the whole class to check out in what ways that action might affect the other groups' self-definitions, priorities, and plans for action. Each group asked the others for various types of labor and support to implement its proposed action. During these planning discussions, we concluded that the results of our interventions would be unpredictable and uncontrollable, and dependent upon the subject positions and changing historical contexts of our audiences on the mall and in administrative offices. Ultimately, our interventions and the process by which we arrived at them had to make sense—both rationally and emotionally—to *us*, however problematically we understand "making sense" to be a political action. Our actions had to make sense as interested interpretations and constant rewritings of ourselves in relation to shifting interpersonal and political contexts. Our interpretations had to be based on attention to history, to concrete experiences of oppression, and to subjugated knowledges.[69]

CONCLUSION

For me, what has become more frightening than the unknown or unknowable are social, political, and educational projects that predicate and legitimate their actions on the kind of knowing that underlies current definitions of critical pedagogy. In this sense, current understandings and uses of "critical," "empowerment," "student voice," and "dialogue" are only surface manifestations of deeper contradictions involving pedagogies, both traditional and critical. The kind of knowing I am referring to is that in which objects, nature, and "Others" are seen to be known or ultimately knowable, in the sense of being "defined, delineated, captured, understood, explained, and diagnosed" at a level of determination never accorded to the "knower" herself or himself.[70]

The experience of Coalition 607 has left me wanting to think through the implications of confronting unknowability. What would it mean to recognize not only that a multiplicity of knowledges are present in the classroom as a result of the way difference has been used to structure social relations inside and outside the classroom, but that these knowledges are contradictory, partial, and irreducible? They cannot be made to "make sense"—they cannot be known, in terms of the single master discourse of an educational project's curriculum or theoretical framework, even that of critical pedagogy. What kinds of classroom practice are made possible and impossible when one affinity group within the class has lived out and arrived at a currently useful "knowledge" about a particular oppressive formation on campus, but the professor and some of the other students can never know or understand that knowledge in the same way? What practice is called for when even the combination of all partial knowledges in a classroom results in yet another partial knowing, defined by structuring absences that mark the "terror and loathing of any difference?"[71] What kinds of interdependencies between groups and individuals inside and outside of the classroom would recognize that every social, political, or educational project the class takes up locally will already, at the moment of its definition, lack knowledges necessary to answer broader questions of human survival and social justice? What kind of educational project could redefine "knowing" so that it no longer describes the activities of those in power "who started to speak, to speak alone and for everyone else, on behalf of everyone else?"[72] What kind of educational project would redefine the silence of the unknowable, freeing it from "the male-defined context of Absence, Lack, and Fear," and make of that silence "a language of its own" that changes the nature and direction of speech itself?[73]

Whatever form it takes in the various, changing, locally specific instances of classroom practices, I understand a classroom practice of the unknowable right now to be one that would support students/professor in the never-ending "moving about" Trinh Minh-ha describes:

> After all, she is this Inappropriate/d Other who moves about with always at least two/four gestures: that of affirming "I am like you" while pointing insistently to the difference; and that of reminding "I am different" while unsettling every definition of otherness arrived at.[74]

In relation to education, I see this moving about as a strategy that affirms "you know me/I know you" while pointing insistently to the interested partialness of those knowings and constantly reminding us that "you can't know me/I can't know you," while unsettling every definition of knowing arrived at. Classroom practices that facilitate such moving about would support the kind of contextually, politically, and historically situated identity politics called for by Alcoff, hooks, and others.[75] That is, one in which identity is seen as "nonessentialized and emergent from a historical experience"[76] as a necessary stage in a process, a starting point—not an ending point. Identity in this sense becomes a vehicle for multiplying and making more complex the subject positions possible, visible, and legitimate at any given historical moment, requiring disruptive changes in the way social technologies of gender, race, ability, and so on define "Otherness" and use it as a vehicle for subordination.

Gayatri Spivak calls the search for a coherent narrative "counterproductive" and asserts that what is needed is "persistent critique"[77] of received narratives and a priori lines of attack. Similarly, unlike postliberal or post-Marxist movements predicated on repressive unities, Minh-ha's moving about refuses to reduce profoundly heterogeneous networks of power/desire/interest to any one a priori, coherent narrative. It refuses to know and resist oppression from any a priori line of attack, such as race, class, or gender solidarity.

But participants in Coalition 607 did not simply unsettle every definition of knowing, assert the absence of a priori solidarities, or replace political action (in the sense defined at the beginning of this article) with textual critique. Rather, we struggled, as S.P. Mohanty would have us do, to "develop a sense of the profound *contextuality* of meanings [and oppressive knowledges] in their play and their ideological effects."[78]

Our classroom was the site of dispersed, shifting, and contradictory contexts of knowing that coalesced differently in different moments of student/professor speech, action, and emotion. This situation meant that individuals and affinity groups constantly had to change strategies and priorities of resistance against oppressive ways of knowing and being known. The antagonist became power itself as it was deployed within our classroom—oppressive ways of knowing and oppressive knowledges.

This position, informed by poststructuralism and feminism, leaves no one off the hook, including critical pedagogues. We cannot act as if our membership in or alliance with an oppressive group exempts us from the need to confront the "grey areas which we all have in us."[79] As Trinh Minh-ha reminds us, "There are no social positions exempt from becoming oppressive to others . . . any group—any position—can move into the oppressor role,"[80] depending upon specific historical contexts and situation. Or as Mary Gentile puts it, "everyone is someone else's 'Other.' "[81]

Various groups struggling for self-definition in the United States have identified the mythical norm deployed for the purpose of setting the standard of humanness against which Others are defined and assigned privilege and limitations. At this moment in history, that norm is young, white, heterosexual, Christian, able-bodied, thin, middle-class, English-speaking, and male. Yet, as Gentile argues, no individual embodies, in the essentialist sense, this mythical norm.[82] Even individuals who most closely approximate it experience a dissonance. As someone who embodies some but not all of the current mythical norm's socially constructed characteristics, my colleague Albert Selvin wrote in response to the first draft of this article: "I too have to fight to differentiate myself from a position defined for me—whose terms are imposed on me—which limits and can destroy me—which does destroy many White men or turns them into helpless agents. . . . I as a White man/boy was not allowed—by my family, by society to be anything *but* cut off from the earth and the body. That condition is not/was not an essential component or implication of my maleness."[83]

To assert multiple perspectives in this way is not to draw attention away from the distinctive realities and effects of the oppression of any particular group. It is not to excuse or relativize oppression by simply claiming, "we are all oppressed." Rather, it is to clarify oppression by preventing "oppressive simplifications,"[84] and insisting that oppression be understood and struggled against contextually. For example, the politics of appearance in relation to the mythical norm played a major role in our classroom. Upon first sight, group members tended to draw alliances and assumed shared commitments because of the social positions we presumed others to occupy (radical, heterosexual, antiracist person of color, and so on). But not only were these assumptions often wrong, at times they denied ideological and personal commitments to various struggles by people who appeared outwardly to fit the mythical norm.

The terms in which I can and will assert and unsettle "difference" and unlearn my positions of privilege in future classroom practices are wholly dependent on the Others/others whose presence—with their concrete experiences of privileges and oppressions, and subjugated or oppressive knowledge—I am responding to and acting with in any given classroom. My moving about between the positions of privileged speaking subject and Inappropriate/d Other cannot be predicted, prescribed, or understood beforehand by any theoretical framework or methodological practice. It is in this sense that a practice grounded in the unknowable is profoundly contextual (historical) and interdependent (social). This reformulation of pedagogy and knowledge removes the critical pedagogue from two key discursive positions s/he has constructed for her/himself in the literature—namely, origin of what can be known and origin of what should be done. What remains for me is the challenge of constructing classroom practices that engage with the discursive and material spaces that such a removal opens up. I am trying to unsettle received definitions of pedagogy by multiplying the ways in which I am able to act on and in the university both as the Inappropriate/d Other and as the privileged speaking/making subject trying to unlearn that privilege.

This semester, in a follow-up to Coalition 607, Curriculum and Instruction 800 is planning, producing, and "making sense" of a day-long film and video event against oppressive knowledges and ways of knowing in the curriculum, pedagogy, and everyday life at UW-Madison. This time we are not focusing on any one formation (race *or* class *or* gender *or* ableism). Rather, we are engaging with each other and working against oppressive social formations on campus in ways that try to "find a commonality in the experience of difference without compromising its distinctive realities and effects."[86]

Right now, the classroom practice that seems most capable of accomplishing this is one that facilitates a kind of communication across differences that is best represented by this statement: "If you can talk to me in ways that show you understand that your knowledge of me, the world, and 'the Right thing to do' will always be partial, interested, and potentially oppressive to others, and if I can do the same, then we can work together on shaping and reshaping alliances for constructing circumstances in which students of difference can thrive."

Notes

This article is a revised vesion of a paper preseneted at the Tenth Conderence on Curriculum Theory and Classroom Practice, Bergamo Conference Center, Dayton, Ohio, October 26–

29, 1988. It was part of a symposium entitled "Reframing the Empirical Feminist, Neo-Marxist, and Post-structuralist Challenges to Research in Education." I want to thank Mimi Orner, Ph.D. candidate and teaching assistant in the Department of Curriculum and Instruction, UW-Madison, for her insights and hours of conversations about the meanings of C&I 607. They have formed the backbone of this article.

1. By "critique" I do not mean a systematic analysis of the specific articles of individual authors' positions that make up this literature, for the purpose of articulating a theory of critical pedagogy capable of being evaluated for its internal consistency, elegance, powers of prediction, and so on. Rather, I have chosen to ground the following critique in my interpretation of my experiences in C&I 607. That is, I have attempted to place key discourses in the literature on critical pedagogy *in relation* to my interpretation of my experience in C&I 607—by asking which interpretations and "sense making" do those discourses facilitate, which do they silence and marginalize, and what interests do they appear to serve?

2. By "the literature on critical pedagogy," I mean those articles in major educational journals and special editions devoted to critical pedagogy. For the purpose of this article, I systematically reviewed more than thirty articles appearing in journals such as *Harvard Educational Review, Curriculum Inquiry, Educational Theory, Teachers College Record, Journal of Curriculum Theorizing,* and *Journal of Curriculum Studies* between 1984 and 1988. The purpose of this review was to identify key and repeated claims, assumptions, goals, and pedagogical practices that currently set the terms of debate within this literature. "Critical pedagogy" should not be confused with "feminist pedagogy," which constitutes a separate body of literature with its own goals and assumptions.

3. Some of the more representative writing on this point can be found in Michelle Fine, "Silencing in the Public Schools," *Language Arts,* 64 (1987), 157–174; Henry A. Giroux, "Radical Pedagogy and the Politics of Student Voice," *Interchange 17* (1986), 48–69; and Roger Simon, "Empowerment as a Pedagogy of Possibility," *Language Arts 64* (1987), 370–382.

4. See Henry A. Giroux and Peter McLaren, "Teacher Education and the Politics of Engagement: The Case of Democratic Schooling," *Harvard Educational Review 56* (1986), 213–238; and Ira Shor and Paulo Freire, "What is the 'Dialogical Method' of Teaching?" *Journal of Education 969* (1987), 11–31.

5. Shor and Freire, "What is the 'Dialogical Method?' " and Henry A. Giroux, "Literacy and the Pedagogy of Voice and Political Empowerment," *Educational Theory 38* (1988), 61–75.

6. Daniel P. Liston and Kenneth M. Zeichner, "Critical Pedagogy and Teacher Education," *Journal of Education 169* (1987), 117-137.

7. Liston and Zeichner, "Critical Pedagogy," p. 120.

8. Liston and Zeichner, "Critical Pedagogy," p. 127.

9. Giroux, "Literacy and the Pedagogy of Voice," p. 75.

10. Liston and Zeichner, "Critical Pedagogy," p. 128.

11. Valerie Walkerdine, "On the Regulation of Speaking and Silence: Subjectivity, Class, and Gender in Contemporary Schooling," in *Language, Gender, and Childhood,* ed. Carolyn Steedman, Cathy Urwin, and Valerie Walkerdine (London: Routledge and Kegan Paul, 1985), p. 205.

12. Barbara Christian, "The Race for Theory," *Cultural Critique 6* (Spring, 1987), 51–63.

13. By the end of the semester, many of us began to understand ourselves as inhabiting intersections of multiple, contradictory, overlapping social positions not reducible either to race, or class, or gender and so on . Depending upon the moment and the context, the degree to which any one of us "differs" from the mythical norm (see conclusion) varies along multiple axes, and so do the consequences. I began using the terms "students of difference," "professor of difference," to refer to social positionings in relation to the mythical norm (based on ability, size, color, sexual preference, gender, ethnicity, and so on). This reminded us of the necessity to construct how, within specific situations, particular socially constructed differences from the mythical norm (such as color) get taken up as vehicles for institutions such as the university to act out and legitimate oppressive formations of power. This enabled us to open up our analysis of racism on campus for the purpose of tracing its relations to institutional sexism, ableism, elitism, anti-Semitism, and other oppressive formations.

14. Giroux and McLaren, "Teacher Education and the Politics of Engagement," p. 229.

15. Stanley Aronowitz, "Postmodernism and Politics," *Social Text 18* (Winter, 1987/88), 99–115.

16. Liston and Zeichner, "Critical Pedagogy," p. 120.

17. For an excellent theoretical discussion and demonstration of the explanatory power of this approach, see Julian Henriques, Wendy Hollway, Cathy Urwin, Couze Venn, and Valerie Walkerdine, *Changing the Subject: Psychology, Social Regulation, and Subjectivity* (New York: Methuen, 1984); Gloria Anzaldua, *Borderlands/La Frontera: The New Mestiza* (San Francisco: Spinsters/Aunt Lute, 1987); Theresa de Lauretis, ed., *Feminist Studies/ Critical Studies* (Bloomington: Indiana University Press, 1986); Hal Foster, ed., *Discussions in Contemporary Culture* (Seattle: Bay Press, 1987); Chris Weedon, *Feminist Practice and Poststructuralist Theory* (New York: Basil Blackwell, 1987).

18. Weedon, *Feminist Practice and Poststructuralist Theory.*

19. Aronowitz, "Postmodernism and Politics," p. 103.

20. Ibid.

21. Audre Lorde, *Sister Outsider* (New York: Crossing Press, 1984), p. 112.

22. Lorde, *Sister Outsider*, p. 112.

23. Christian, "The Race for Theory," p. 63.

24. For a discussion of the thesis of the "epistemic privilege of the oppressed," see Uma Narayan, "Working Together Across Difference: Some Considerations on Emotions and Political Practice," *Hypatia 3* (Summer, 1988), 31–47.

25. For an excellent discussion of the relation of the concept of "experience" to feminism, essentialism, and political action, see Linda Alcoff, "Cultural Feminism versus Post-Structuralism: The Identity Crisis in Feminist Theory," *Signs 13* (Spring, 1988), 405–437.

26. Narayan, "Working Together Across Difference," pp. 31–47.

27. This subtitle is borrowed from Maria C. Lugones and Elizabeth V. Spelman's critique of imperialistic, ethnocentric, and disrespectful tendencies in White feminists' theorizing about women's oppression, "Have We Got a Theory for You! Feminist Theory, Cultural Imperialism, and the Demand for 'The Women's Voice,' " *Women's Studies International Forum* (1983), 573–581.

28. Nicholas C. Burbules, "A Theory of Power in Education," *Educational Theory 36* (Spring, 1986), 95–114; Giroux and McLaren, "Teacher Education and the Politics of Engagement," pp. 224–227.

29. Liston and Zeichner, "Critical Pedagogy and Teacher Education," p. 120.

30. Shor and Freire, "What is the 'Dialogical Method' of Teaching?," p. 14.

31. Giroux, "Radical Pedagogy," p. 64.

32. Ibid., p. 66.

33. Shor and Freire, "What is the 'Dialogical Method' of Teaching?" p. 22.

34. Burbules, "A Theory of Power in Education"; and Giroux and McLaren, "Teacher Education and the Politics of Engagement," pp. 224–227.

35. Shor and Freire, "What is the 'Dialogical Method' of Teaching?," p. 23.

36. Burbules, "A Theory of Power in Education," p. 108.

37. Giroux and McLaren, "Teacher Education and the Politics of Engagement," p. 226.

38. Walter C. Parker, "Justice, Social Studies, and the Subjectivity/Structure Problem," *Theory and Research in Social Education 14* (Fall, 1986), p. 227.

39. Simon, "Empowerment as a Pedagogy of Possibility," p. 372.

40. Giroux, "Literacy and the Pedagogy of Voice," pp. 68–69.

41. Giroux and McLaren, "Teacher Education and the Politics of Engagement," p. 225.

42. Ibid., p. 227.

43. Shor and Freire, "What is the 'Dialogical Method' of Teaching?" p. 30; Liston and Zeichner, "Critical Pedagogy," p. 122.

44. Simon, "Empowerment as a Pedagogy of Possibility," p. 80.

45. Ibid., p. 375.

46. Aronowitz, "Postmodernism and Politics," p. 111.

47. Alcoff, "Cultural Feminism versus Post-Structuralism," p. 420.

48. Simon, "Empowerment as a Pedagogy of Possibility."

49. bell hooks, "Talking Back," *Discourse 8* (Fall/Winter, 1986/87), 123–128.

50. bell hooks, *Talking Back: Thinking Feminist, Thinking Black* (Boston: South End Press, 1989).

51. Peter McLaren, *Life in Schools* (New York: Longman, 1989).

52. Alcoff, "Cultural Feminism versus Post-Structuralism"; Anzaldua, *Borderlands/La Frontera*; de Lauretis, *Feminist Studies/Critical Studies*; hooks, *Talking Back*; Trihn T. Minh-ha, *Woman, Native, Other* (Bloomington: Indiana University Press, 1989); Weedon, *Feminist Practice and Poststructuralist Theory*.

53. hooks, "Talking Back," p. 124.

54. Susan Hardy Aiken, Karen Anderson, Myra Dinerstein, Judy Lensink, and Patricia MacCorquodale, "Trying Transformations: Curriculum Integration and the Problem of Resistance," *Signs 12* (Winter, 1987), 225–275.

55. Aiken et al., "Trying Transformations," p. 263.

56. Shoshana Felman, "Psychoanalysis and Education: Teaching Terminable and Interminable," *Yale French Studies 63* (1982), 21–44.

57. S. P. Mohanty, "Radical Teaching, Radical Theory: The Ambiguous Politics of Meaning," in *Theory in the Classroom*, ed. Cary Nelson (Urbana: University of Illinois Press, 1986), p. 155.

58. Giroux and McLaren, "Teacher Education and the Politics of Engagement," p. 235.

59. Ibid., p. 237.

60. Giroux, "Literacy and the Pedagogy of Voice," p. 72.

61. Ibid.

62. Biddy Martin and Chandra Talpade Mohanty, "Feminist Politics: What's Home Got to Do with It?" in *Feminist Studies/Critical Studies*, ed. Theresa de Lauretis (Bloomington: Indiana University Press, 1986), pp. 208–209.

63. Martin and Mohanty, "Feminist Politics," p. 208.

64. Discussions with students after the semester ended and comments from students and colleagues on the draft of this article have led me to realize the extent to which some international students and Jews in the class felt unable or not safe to speak about experiences of oppression inside and outside of the class related to those identities. Anti-Semitism, economic and cultural imperialism, and the rituals of exclusion of international students on campus were rarely named and never fully elaborated in the class. The classroom practices that reproduced these particular oppressive silences in C&I 607 must be made the focus of sustained critique in the follow-up course, C&I 800, "Race, Class, Gender, and the Construction of Knowledge in Educational Media."

65. John W. Murphy, "Computerization, Postmodern Epistemology, and Reading in the Post-modern Era," *Educational Theory* 38 (Spring, 1988), 175–182.

66. Lugones and Spelman assert that the only acceptable motivation for following Others into their worlds is friendship. Self-interest is not enough, because "the task at hand for you is one of extraordinary difficulty. It requires that you be willing to devote a great part of your life to it and that you be willing to suffer alienation and self-disruption . . . whatever the benefits you may accrue from such a journey, they cannot be concrete enough for you at this time and they are not worth your while" ("Have We Got a Theory for You," p. 576). Theoretical or political "obligation" is inappropriate, because it puts Whites/Anglos "in a morally self-righteous position" and makes people of color vehicles of redemption for those in power (p. 581). Friendship, as an appropriate and acceptable "condition" under which people become allies in struggles that are not their own, names my own experience and has been met with enthusiasm by students.

67. Lorde, *Sister Outsider*, p. 112.

68. *Ibid.*, p. 112.

69. Martin and Mohanty, "Feminist Politics," p. 210.

70. Alcoff, "Cultural Feminism versus Post-Structuralism," p. 406.

71. Lorde, *Sister Outsider*, p. 113.

72. Trinh T. Minh-ha, "Introduction," *Discourse 8* (Fall/Winter, 1986/87), p. 7.

73. Ibid., p. 8.

74. Ibid., p. 9.

75. Alcoff, "Cultural Feminism versus Post-Structuralism"; bell hooks, "The Politics of Radical Black Subjectivity," *Zeta Magazine* (April, 1989), 52–55.

76. hooks, "The Politics of Radical Black Subjectivity," p. 54.

77. Gayatri Chakravorty Spivak, "Can the Subaltern Speak?" in *Marxism and the Interpretation of Culture*, ed. Cary Nelson and Lawrence Grossberg (Urbana: University of Illinois Press, 1988), p. 272.

78. S. P. Mohanty, "Radical Teaching, Radical Theory," p. 169.

79. Minh-ha, "Introduction," p. 6.

80. A. Selvin, personal correspondence (October 24, 1988).

81. Mary Gentile, *Film Feminisms: Theory and Practice* (Westport, Conn.: Greenwood Press, 1985), p. 7.

82. Gentile, *Film Feminisms*, p. 7.

83. A. Selvin, personal correspondence.

84. Gentile, *Film Feminisms*, p. 7.

20

"WHY DO WE HAVE TO READ ABOUT GIRLS LIVING IN AUSTRALIA AND LONDON?"

REFLECTIONS FROM A WOMANIST THEORIST ON CRITICAL EDUCATION[1]

Dianne Smith

INTRODUCTION

During the 1990 fall semester I taught Education 548 Curriculum Study, and sixty graduate students were enrolled. I planned the syllabus to reflect a multiplicity of voices (or discourses) that resonate such critical issues as race, class, gender, sexuality, etc. Two texts included were Angela McRobbie's, "Working Class Girls and the Culture of Femininity" and S. Kessler et al.'s "Gender Relations in Secondary Schooling." McRobbie's piece is based on "work carried out in a Birmingham [England] youth club over a period of six months . . . prompted by a recognition that throughout a range of disciplines dealing broadly with youth, there was a whole dimension missing, namely girls."[2] Kessler et al.'s essay points to a need to "renew the campaign for resources for countersexist educational work"[3] and to interrogate research on "gender relations in Australian secondary schools." This essay "proposes a line of theoretical analysis that bears on some of the dilemmas of current practices,"[4] i.e., the discourse of gender and education has been guided by the concept of sex roles.

As we began to engage the two texts in class, Thomasena[5] asked me the following question: "Why do we have to read about girls living in Australia and London?" Thomasena suggested to me that the discussion of gender and education in these "other" parts of the world was not relevant to "us United States citizens." I believe that it is important to note that I felt some hostility spew from the mouth of this unknowing myopicist.

As I reflect on this encounter with Thomasena, I am reminded of an Ernst Bloch quote: "What begins with us stirs with us and is never still. Ever and again it steps back to see what lies ahead; for its questioning also allows doubt . . . when conventional and supposedly lucid explanations no longer suffice . . . when question-ing—even if it has already been allayed—reappears, once more unsettled, new questions occur in new material of the very answers themselves."[6] I draw from Bloch's text in order to illuminate the stirring within me to engage an unsettled question: "Why do we have to read about girls living in Australia and London?" I surmise that a new question, which stems from the preceding question, is "What constitutes reflective, critical thinking about the world?"

In order to construct new meanings relevant to critical education and reflective thinking, I will disguise this narrative essay in the form of a letter to Thomasena. In this letter I will critically respond to Thomasena's question while simultaneously suggesting that one must begin with local struggles as the site of confrontation with power, outside and beyond all global instances such as parties and classes.[7] That is to say that as reflective intellectuals/practitioners we must grapple with the social construction of "relations of power which permeate, characterize and constitute the social body,"[8] which most often lead to a myopic view rather than a world view.

A LETTER TO THOMASENA: REFLECTIONS ON POWER AND TRUTH

Dear Thomasena:

I write this letter to you as a response to your question "Why do we have to read about girls living in Australia and London?" and it becomes a forum for illuminating my premise that one must critically interrogate discursive practices that inform power and truth. In so doing, one begins to understand that "each society has its regime of truth, its 'general politics' of truth: that is, the types of discourse which it accepts and makes function as true."[9] And this leads one to confront these local struggles that bring about myopicism.

Thomasena, please indulge me as I present a rather lengthy Michel Foucault quote, for I believe that it is most relevant at this particular textual juncture.

> Truth is centered on the form of scientific discourse and the institutions which pro-duce it; it is subject to constant economic and political incitement (the demand for truth, as much for economic production as for political power); it is the object, under diverse forms, of immense diffusion and consumption (circulating through appara-tuses of education and information whose extent is relatively broad in the social body, notwithstanding certain strict limitations); it is produced and transmitted un-der the control, dominant if not exclusive, of a few great political and economic apparatuses (university, army, writing, media); lastly, it is the issue of a whole po-litical debate and social confrontation (ideological struggles).[10]

I present his theoretical discourse regarding power and regimes of truth to suggest that through educational apparatuses such as schooling, curricula, textbooks, masternarratives, media and technology, etc., we have come to believe that one worldview is legitimate.

This is to suggest that the acceptance of such legitimacy disempowers one to examine the ways in which knowledge, or truth, misinforms or misrepresents social reality. For example, S. Kessler et al. argue that "There is abundant evidence that inequality between women and men is a very general feature of Western educational systems" and "One must break down the stereotyped expectations and redefine the accepted boundaries of women's and men's roles."[11] Angela McRobbie's research looks at the culture of working class girls, and the responses of the girls were "typified by an ultimate if not wholesale endorsement of the traditional female role and of femininity, simply because to the girls these seemed to be perfectly *natural*."[12] While their discourses resonate particular voices in Sydney, Australia, and London, England, I have developed a discourse that suggests that a group of African American women teachers are fearful to report suspected and/or known cases of child abuse because of patriarchal power relations within the environs of public schools.[13]

Thomasena, I contend that this is a clear indication that patriarchal power relations are not exclusive. We experience this social and political phenomenon throughout the world, and it becomes imperative that we examine and critique our social worlds to understand what has happened in the past, what is happening in the present,[14] not only in our own space but in other world spaces. In so doing we will come to understand the connections of the local struggles and the global struggles, and it is my belief that such an understanding leads to the recognition of the multiplicity of voices speaking and creating in this world space.

In essence, my challenge to you is this: Critically interrogate those general politics of a society that create and accept regimes of truth. Just as Zora Neale Hurston wrote against stereotypes of her day and gave us new ways of thinking and being,[15] you must give increasing thought and energy to the subjects of power and truth. And while reflecting on local struggles in order to connect them with global struggles, please be cognizant that self-determination must be a dominant factor in personal liberation. For "truth isn't outside power, or lacking power . . . truth isn't the reward of free spirits, the child of protracted solitude . . . Truth is a thing of this world: it is produced only by virtue of multiple forms of constraint."[16]

As I conclude this section of my letter, Thomasena, my reflections have caused me to rethink my assumption that you were a hostile, unknowing myopicist. Rather, I suggest that the mystification of power and regimes of truth have cast you (and others) in a sea of fear, which leads one to immobilization. And I must say that your questioning has moved me to consider the conflicts and/or tensions embedded within this curricular choice of literature for this course. I find that I am struggling with this question: "Why do we have to read about girls living in Australia and London?" In essence, I will act womanish and engage in outrageous, audacious, and courageous behavior[17] and say to you, "I agree with you." Hence, I will speak to these conflictual moments in the section that follows.

DIANNE AND THOMASENA: A WOMANIST CRITIQUE OF CONFLICTS AND TENSIONS

Thomasena, as you know, one of my favorite lines in this class is "We live lives that are filled with conflicts, tensions and contradictions." And I must state that reading about white adolescent females living in London and Australia creates some conflictual moments for me. My passion for black women and our families moves me to say that we need to read about women such as Maya Angelou and Linda Brent who have depicted positive images of black women in their writings. Linda Brent defines herself as a revolutionary seeking the freedom of herself and her bound sisters in the South during the era of overt bondage, and Maya Angelou defines the women in her life as proud, intelligent, and resourceful.

I say this to suggest that since the larger society chooses to construct us as symbols for unwed mothers, welfare queens, whores, and pathological matriarchs, it remains the responsibility of black women to deconstruct those images and redefine our "selves" through speech and/or the recall of dangerous memories. As bell hooks writes:

> For us, true speaking is not solely an expression of creative power, it is an act of resistance, a political gesture that challenges politics of domination that would render us nameless and voiceless. As such it is a courageous act—as it represents a threat. To those who wield oppressive power, that which is threatening must necessarily be wiped out, annihilated, silenced.[18]

And such political gesturing can be found in the enslaved woman's narrative or speech. These women speak out against the ownership of their bodies, souls, and minds; they speak out against the disintegration of their families; and they speak out against the mutilations and killings that were as much a part of the system as the tyrannical rapes of the women.

For example, Linda Brent states in her autobiography that it would have been more pleasant for her to remain silent about her experiences as a slave girl. She breaks her silence, however, in order to become "named" and "voiced." As she pursues the theme of resistance to the slave system and the slaveholder's sexual exploitation, she projects to the reader her feelings about the oppression:

> What does *he* know of the half-starved wretches toiling from dawn till dark on the plantations? of mothers shrieking for their children, torn from their arms by slave traders? of young girls dragged down into moral filth? of pools of blood around the whipping post? of hounds trained to tear human flesh? of men screwed into cotton gins to die? The slaveholder showed him none of these things, and the slaves dared not tell of them if he had asked them.[19]

In addition, enslaved women not only raised the issue of the hatred and maltreatment they experienced from the male slaveholder, they included in their writings the hatred and maltreatment they suffered at the hands of the white women, namely the wives of these men. A prime example of such acts is etched in Harriet E. Wilson's *Our Nig*. According to Ann Allen Shockley, Harriet E. Wilson's autobiography is masked in fiction and spins a tragic tale of social, racial, and economic dehumanization. The autobiography shows a different kind of black bondage in the North at a time when abolitionists were violently attacking slavery in the South, and it exposes white women who were committing the sins of the patriarchs, as well as those of southern mistresses, in their relationships with black women.[20]

While I have attempted to present these womanists creating counterhegemonic discourses of resistance, I must claim that I have not begun to touch the surface of the many black women who have written or told of their lived experiences as oppressed women. For such writings did not stop after the Emancipation Proclamation, just as oppression did not stop. Black women continue to write and speak about their lived experiences, whether in personal journals, diaries, or published work such as novels. Consequently, Thomasena, the contradiction is that the voices of black women must be heard in order to counter racism, patriarchy, classism, heterosexism, etc.; and these voices must not be overshadowed by the privileged voices of white women. The voices of white women living in the United States, London and Australia, however, must tell their stories about patriarchy, heterosexism, classism, etc. In essence, we can share our stories through multiple voices in order to understand oppression. Such a revolutionary act can create a stir that challenges domination and transforms society to that which can be.

In summary, the mere fact that women speak becomes a form of resistance or oppression to the existing assumptions as we know them to be. As bell hooks notes, talkin' back is no mere gesture of empty words,[21] it is the expression of our movement from object to subject—the transformed, liberated voice. This is why we must read about girls living in London and Australia; it is a transformational, curricular act. And what follows is a discourse of possibility embedded within pedagogy and curriculum.

A Discourse of Possibility: Transformation through Pedagogy and Curriculum

Thomasena, I have tried to create a liberating, transforming text that imbues passion within human beings. I have sought to take you to another dimension in talking about reflective thinking about the world; for, it is my hope that you might rethink the ways in which knowledge, power, and truth are constructed. My goal is to advocate a political project that is committed to the notion of hope and emancipation to be achieved through self-and social empowerment. An artery through which this might flow is curriculum theory and pedagogy. I will not offer traditional curricular recipes, or steps, for you to follow, for a discourse of possibility goes beyond the traditional curricular "how to's."

> Henry Giroux and Stanley Aronowitz theorize that with respect to the discourse of possibility, we are proposing that the study of curriculum be informed by a language that acknowledges curriculum as the introduction, preparation and legitimation for particular forms of social life. Underlying such a political project would be a fundamental commitment to the notions of hope and emancipation. Curriculum theory as a form of cultural politics would be linked to the goals of self-and social empowerment. Moreover, as an expression of specific forms of knowledge, values, and skills, it would take as its object the task of educating students to become active and critical citizens, capable of intellectual skills and willing to exercise the forms of civic courage needed to struggle for a self-determined, thoughtful, and meaningful life.[22]

Thus, I suggest to you that curriculum theory and pedagogy as forms of cultural politics become a political project committed to hope and social change. By this I mean that we as transformative intellectuals can be silent no more about curricular exclusivity and myopicism. In essence, we begin to understand "Why do we have to read about girls living in Australia and London?" or "What constitutes reflective thinking about the world?"

You see, Roger Simon posits:

> An education that empowers from possibility must raise questions of how we can work for the re-construction of social imagination in the service of human freedom

. . . The project of possibility requires an education rooted in a view of human freedom as the understanding of necessity and the transformation of necessity. . . . Beyond its emphasis on deconstruction of dominant knowledge forms and social identities, a project of possibility requires practices that do not simply advocate possibility
but also enable it.[23]

Consequently, a discourse of possibility empowers one to mobilize her fear and
confusion; instead of being silent, thereby denying the fruitfulness of a worldview
of living and understanding, we must take risks for self and curricular transformation. That is, as teachers or agents of curricular practice, we must name those
structures that indirectly, or directly, cause us to doubt our power and control
over our lives and our beliefs. For such a task, Thomasena, does "not mean de-
bunking existing forms of schooling and educational theory; it means reworking
them, contesting the terrains on which they develop, and appropriating from them
whatever radical potentialities they might contain."[24]

In order to concretize the proposed discourse of possibility, I suggest that practicing teachers form reading groups or support groups, develop newsletters, and
seek university courses that address curriculum theory as a form of cultural politics
and courses that engage local struggles (race, class, gender, etc.) and link these to
global struggles. For example, one could use storytelling or testifying to give political value and meaning to the lives of girls and women, and link this local
struggle with a global struggle by illuminating the fact that South African women
are employing narrative as a means toward freedom.

A second example is for teachers to form a critical reading group that speaks
to how power and knowledge are socially constructed and legitimated through
the education process. Reading about girls living in a small midwestern town and
girls living in a working class neighborhood in London, England, informs themes
of sexist oppression and mechanisms for change.

Participating in courses, reading groups, or support groups empowers us to
name our fears in a broader, critical form. This is a sign that we are doing transformational work—our dream is bonding with reality. A discourse of possibility
enhances our vision to know, or assert, that society is both exploitative and oppressive, but it is also capable of being changed, and in the process of transformation there is a constant struggle between our capacity to think critically about
the power of hegemonic ideology and the material constraints that act upon us.[25]

Thomasena, I close my letter to you with this: To live in a world which is not
yet attained, we must engage in a language of critique that contributes to the
establishment of a just and compassionate community within which a discourse
of possibility becomes the guiding principle for a new social order. A language of
critique meshes with a language of possibility, that creates a passion for that which
can be. In order to do this we must constantly raise new questions for critique.
Come join me in accepting the risk that such work will be trivialized or romanticized in rhetoric. In order to create liberation and abolish myopicism, we must
create a shift in paradigms while talking, listening, and hearing in a new way.

Your former teacher,
Dianne Smith.

Notes

1. The original title of this chapter is entitled " 'Why Do We Have to Read About Girls
   Living in London and Australia?' Reflections on Global Education, Power and Truth,"

presented at the annual meeting of the American Educational Studies Association, Kansas City, 1991.

2. Angela McRobbie, "Working Class Girls and the Culture of Femininity," 96.

3. S. Kessler et al., "Gender Relations in Secondary Schooling," 34.

4. Ibid.

5. This woman's name has been changed for confidentiality.

6. Ernst Bloch, *A Philosophy of the Future* (New York: Herder and Herder, 1970), 11.

7. Michel Foucault, *Power and Knowledge*, edited by Colin Gordon and translated by Colin Gordon, Leo Marshall, John Mepham, and Kate Soper (New York: Pantheon Books, 1977), 125.

8. Ibid., 93.

9. Ibid., 131.

10. Ibid., 131–132.

11. S. Kessler et al., 34.

12. Angela McRobbie, 96–97.

13. Dianne Smith, *A Social and Political Construction of Child Abuse: A Study of AfraAmerican Women Teachers* (Ph.D. dissertation, Miami University [Ohio], 1990).

14. Kathleen Weiler, *Women Teaching for Change* (South Hadley, Mass.: Bergin and Garvey, 1989), 90.

15. See Zora Neale Hurston, *Their Eyes Were Watching God* (Philadelphia: J. B. Lippincott, 1937; reprint 1965).

16. Michel Foucault, 131.

17. Alice Walker, *In Search of Our Mothers' Gardens: Womanist Prose* (San Diego: Harcourt Brace Jovanovich, 1983), xi. Alice Walker defines womanish to involve such behavior.

18. bell hooks, *Talking Back* (Boston: South End Press, 1989), 8.

19. Linda Brent, *Incidents in the Life of a Slave Girl: Written by Herself* (Boston: Thayer and Eldridge, 1861), xiii.

20. Ann Allen Shockley, *Afro-American Women Writers 1746–1933: An Anthology and Critical Guide* (New York: Meridan Books, 1988), 86.

21. See bell hooks, *Talking Back*.

22. Stanley Aronowitz and Henry Giroux, *Education Under Siege* (South Hadley, Mass.: Bergin and Garvey, 1985), 141.

23. Roger Simon, "For a Pedagogy of Possibility," *Critical Pedagogy Networker* 1 (1988): 2.

24. Stanley Aronowitz and Henry Giroux, 160.

25. Kathleen Weiler, 5 and 74.

References

Angelou, Maya. *I Know Why the Caged Bird Sings*. New York: Random House, 1969.

Aronowitz, Stanley and Henry Giroux. *Education Under Siege*. South Hadley, Mass.: Bergin and Garvey, 1985.

Bloch, Ernst. *A Philosophy of the Future*. New York: Herder and Herder, 1970.

Brent, Linda [Harriet Jacobs]. *Incidents in the Life of a Slave Girl: Written by Herself*. Boston: Thayer and Eldridge, 1861.

Foucault, Michel. *Power and Knowledge*. Translated by Colin Gordon, Leo Marshall, John Mepham, and Kate Soper. New York: Pantheon Books, 1977.

hooks, bell. *Talking Back*. Boston: South End Press, 1989.

Hurston, Zora Neale. *Their Eyes Were Watching God*. Philadelphia: J. B. Lippincott, 1937, reprinted in 1965.

Kessler, S., D. J. Ashenden, R. W. Connell, and G. W. Dowsett. "Gender Relations in Secondary Schooling." *Sociology of Education* 58 (1985): 34–48.

McRobbie, Angela. "Working Class Girls and the Culture of Femininity." In *Women Take Issue*, ed. Women's Studies Group, 96–108. London: Hutchison, 1981.

Shockley, Ann Allen. *Afro-American Women Writers 1746–1933: An Anthology and Critical Guide*. New York: Meridan Books, 1988.

Simon, Roger. "For a Pedagogy of Possibility." *Critical Pedagogy Networker* 1 (1988): 1–4.

Smith, Dianne. "African American Women Teachers and Sexual Abuse." In *African American Women in (White) Academe*, ed. Joy James and Ruth Farmer. New York: Routledge, [in print, 1993].

———. *A Social and Political Construction of Child Abuse: A Study of AfraAmerican Women Teachers*. Ph.D. dissertation, Miami University [Ohio], 1990.

Walker, Alice. *In Search of Our Mothers' Gardens: Womanist Prose*. San Diego: Harcourt Brace Jovanovich, 1983.

Weiler, Kathleen. *Women Teaching for Change*. South Hadley, Mass.: Bergin and Garvey, 1989.

Wilson, Harriet E. *Our Nig or Sketches from the Life of a Free Black, in a Two-Story White House North. Showing that Slavery's Shadows Fall Even There*. Boston: George Rand and Avery, 1859. Reprinted New York: Random House, 1963.

21

DYSCONSCIOUS RACISM: IDEOLOGY, IDENTITY, AND THE MISEDUCATION OF TEACHERS

Joyce E. King

They had for more than a century before been regarded as . . . so far inferior . . . that the negro might justly and lawfully be reduced to slavery for his benefit. . . . This opinion was at that time fixed and universal in the civilized portion of the white race. It was regarded as an axiom in morals as well as in politics, which no one thought of disputing . . . and men in every grade and position in society daily and habitually acted upon it . . . without doubting for a moment the correctness of this opinion. (*Dred Scott v. Sanford,* 1857)

Racism can mean culturally sanctioned beliefs which, regardless of the intentions involved, defend the advantages whites have because of the subordinated positions of racial minorities. (Wellman, 1977, p. xviii)

The goal of critical consciousness is an ethical and not a legal judgement about the social order. (Heaney, 1984, p. 116)

CELEBRATING DIVERSITY

The new watchwords in education, "celebrating diversity," imply the democratic ethic that all students, regardless of their sociocultural backgrounds, should be educated equitably. What this ethic means in practice, particularly for teachers with little personal experience of diversity and limited understanding of inequity, is problematic. At the elite private Jesuit university where I teach, most of my students (most of whom come from relatively privileged, monocultural backgrounds) are anxious about being able to deal with all the diversity in the classroom. Not surprisingly, given recent neoconservative ideological interpretations of the problem of diversity, many of my students also believe that affirming cultural difference is tantamount to racial separatism, that diversity threatens national unity, or that social inequity originates with sociocultural deficits and not with unequal outcomes that are inherent in our socially stratified society. With respect to this society's changing demographics and the inevitable "browning" of America, many of my students foresee a diminution of their own identity, status, and security. Moreover, regardless of their conscious intentions, certain culturally sanctioned beliefs my students hold about inequity and why it persists, especially for African Americans, take White norms and privilege as givens.

The findings presented herein will show what these beliefs and responses have to do with what I call "dysconscious racism" to denote the limited and distorted understandings my students have about inequity and cultural diversity—understandings that make it difficult for them to act in favor of truly equitable education. This article presents a qualitative analysis of dysconscious racism as reflected in the responses of my teacher education students to an open-ended question I posed at the beginning of one of my classes during the fall 1986 academic quarter to assess student knowledge and understanding of social inequity. Content analysis of their short essay responses will show how their thinking reflects internalized ideologies that both justify the racial status quo and devalue cultural diversity. Following the analysis of their responses and discussion of the findings, I will describe the teaching approach I use to counteract the cognitively limited and distorted thinking that dysconscious racism represents. The concluding discussion will focus on the need to make social reconstructionist liberatory teaching an option for teacher education students like mine who often begin their professional preparation without having ever considered the need for fundamental social changes (see also Ginsburg, 1988; and Ginsburg and Newman, 1985).

Critical, transformative teachers must develop a pedagogy of social action and advocacy that really celebrates *diversity*, not just random holidays, isolated cultural artifacts, or "festivals and food" (Ayers, 1988). If dysconscious racism keeps such a commitment beyond the imagination of students like mine, teacher educators need forms of pedagogy and counterknowledge that challenge students' internalized ideologies and subjective identities (Giroux and McLaren, 1988). Prospective teachers need both an intellectual understanding of schooling and inequity as well as self-reflective, transformative emotional growth experiences. With these objectives in mind, I teach my graduate-level Social Foundations of Education course in the social reconstructionist tradition of critical, transformative, liberatory education for social change (see Gordon, 1985; Freire, 1971; Giroux and McLaren, 1986; Heaney, 1984; Shor, 1980; Searle, 1975; Sleeter and Grant, 1988). In contrast to a pedagogy for the oppressed, this course explores the dynamics of a liberatory pedagogy for the elite. It is designed to provide such teacher education students with a context in which to consider alternative conceptions of themselves and society. The course challenges students' taken-for-granted ideological positions and identities and their unquestioned acceptance of cultural belief systems that undergird racial inequity.

Thus, the course and the teaching methods I use transcend conventional social and multicultural Foundations of Education course approaches by directly addressing societal oppression and student knowledge and beliefs about inequity and diversity. By focusing on ways that schooling, including their own miseducation, contributes to unequal educational outcomes that reinforce societal inequity and oppression, students broaden their knowledge of how society works. I offer this analysis of dysconscious racism and reflections on the way I teach to further the theoretical and practical development of a liberatory praxis that will enable teacher education students to examine what they know and believe about society, about diverse others, and about their own actions.

DISCOVERING DYSCONSCIOUS RACISM

Dysconsciousness is an uncritical habit of mind (including perceptions, attitudes, assumptions, and beliefs) that justifies inequity and exploitation by accepting the existing order of things as given. If, as Heaney (1984) suggests, critical consciousness "involves an ethical judgement" about the social order, dysconsciousness accepts it uncritically. This lack of critical judgment against society reflects an absence of what Cox (1974) refers to as "social ethics;" it involves a subjective identification with an ideological viewpoint that admits no fundamentally alternative vision of society.[1]

Dysconscious racism is a form of racism that tacitly accepts dominant White norms and privileges. It is not the *absence* of consciousness (that is, not unconsciousness) but an *impaired* consciousness or distorted way of thinking about race as compared to, for example, critical consciousness. Uncritical ways of thinking about racial inequity accept certain culturally sanctioned assumptions, myths, and beliefs that justify the social and economic advantages white people have as a result of subordinating diverse others (Wellman, 1977). Any serious challenge to the status quo that calls this racial privilege into question inevitably challenges the self-identity of white people who have internalized these ideological justifications. The reactions of my students to information I have presented about societal inequity have led me to conceptualize dysconscious racism as one form that racism takes in this post–civil rights era of intellectual conservatism.

Most of my students begin my Social Foundations course with limited knowledge and understanding of societal inequity. Not only are they often unaware of their own ideological perspectives (or of the range of alternatives they have not consciously considered), most are also unaware of how their own subjective identities reflect an uncritical identification with the existing social order. Moreover, they have difficulty explaining "liberal" and "conservative" standpoints on contemporary social and educational issues and are even less familiar with "radical" perspectives (King and Ladson-Billings, 1990). My students' explanations of persistent racial inequity consistently lack evidence of any critical ethical judgment regarding racial (and class/gender) stratification in the existing social order; yet, and not surprisingly, these same students generally maintain that they personally deplore racial prejudice and discrimination. Wellman (1977) notes, however, that this kind of thinking is a hallmark of racism. "The concrete problem facing white people," states Wellman "is how to come to grips with the demands made by blacks and whites while at the same time *avoiding* the possibility of institutional change and reorganization that might affect them" (p. 42). This suggests that the ability to imagine a society reorganized without racial privilege requires a fundamental shift in the way white people think about their status and self-identities and their conceptions of black people.

For example, when I broach the subject of racial inequity with my students, they often complain that they are "tired of being made to feel guilty" because they are white. The following entries from the classroom journals of two undergraduate students in an education course are typical of this reaction[2]:

> With some class discussions, readings, and other media, there have been times that I feel guilty for being white which really infuriates me because no one should feel guilty for the color of their skin or ethnic background. Perhaps my feelings are actually a discomfort for the fact that others have been discriminated against all of their life because of their color and I have not.

> How can I be thankful that I am not a victim of discrimination? I should be ashamed. Then I become confused. Why shouldn't I be thankful that I have escaped such pain?

These students' reactions are understandable in light of Wellman's insights into the nature of racism. That white teacher education students often express such feelings of guilt and hostility suggests they accept certain unexamined assumptions, unasked questions, and unquestioned cultural myths regarding both the social order and their place in it. The discussion of the findings that follows will show how dysconscious racism, manifested in student explanations of societal inequity and linked to their conceptions of black people, devalues the cultural diversity of the black experience and, in effect, limits students' thinking about what teachers can do to promote equity.

THE FINDINGS

Since the fall academic quarter 1986, I have given the student teachers in my Social Foundations course statistical comparisons such as those compiled by the Children's Defense Fund (Edelman, 1987) regarding black and white children's life chances (e.g., "Compared to White children, Black children are twice as likely to die in the first year of life"; see Harlan, 1985). I then ask each student to write a brief explanation of how these racial inequities came about by answering the question: "How did our society get to be this way?" An earlier publication (King and Ladson-Billings, 1990) comparing student responses to this question in the fall 1986 and spring 1987 quarters identifies three ways students explain this inequity. Content analysis of their responses reveals that students explain racial inequity as either the result of slavery (Category I), the denial or lack of equal opportunity for African Americans (Category II), or part of the framework of a society in which racism and discrimination are normative (Category III). In the present article I will again use these categories and the method of content analysis to compare student responses collected in the 1986 and 1988 fall quarters. The responses presented below are representative of 22 essay responses collected from students in 1986 and 35 responses collected in 1988.

Category I explanations begin and end with slavery. Their focus is either on describing African Americans as "victims of their original (slave) status" or they assert that black/white inequality is the continuing result of inequity that began during slavery. In either case, historical determinism is a key feature; African Americans are perceived as exslaves, and the "disabilities of slavery" are believed to have been passed down intergenerationally. As two students wrote:

I feel it dates back to the time of slavery when the Blacks were not permitted to work or really have a life of their own. They were not given the luxury or opportunity to be educated and *each generation passed this disability on* [italics added]. (F6–21)[3]

I think that this harkens back to the origin of the American Black population as slaves. Whereas other immigrant groups started on a low rung of our economic (and social class) ladder and had space and opportunity to move up, Blacks did not. They were perceived as somehow less than people. This view may have been passed down and even on to Black youth. (F8–32)

It is worth noting that the "fixed and universal beliefs" Europeans and white Americans held about black inferiority/white superiority during the epoch of the Atlantic slave trade, beliefs that made the enslavement of Africans seem justified and lawful, are not the focus of this kind of explanation. The historical continuum of cause and effect evident in Category I explanations excludes any consideration of the cultural rationality behind such attitudes; that is, they do not explain *why* white people held these beliefs.

In Category II explanations the emphasis is on the denial of equal opportunity to black people (e.g., less education, lack of jobs, low wages, poor health care). Although students espousing Category II arguments may explain discrimination as the result of prejudice or racist attitudes (e.g., "Whites believe blacks are inferior"), they do not necessarily causally link it to the historical fact of slavery or to the former status of black people as slaves. Rather, the persistently unequal status of African Americans is seen as an *effect* of poverty and systemic discrimination. Consider these two responses from 1986 and 1988:

Blacks have been treated as second class citizens. Caucasians tend to maintain the belief that Black people are inferior . . . *for this reason* [italics added] Blacks receive less education and education that is of inferior quality . . . less pay than most other persons doing the same job; [and] live in inferior substandard housing, etc. (F6–3)

Because of segregation—overt and covert—Blacks in America have had less access historically to education and jobs which has led to a poverty cycle for many. *The effects described are due to poverty* [italics added], lack of education and lack of opportunity. (F8–7)

In addition, some Category I and Category II explanations identify negative psychological or cultural characteristics of African Americans as effects of slavery, prejudice, racism, or discrimination. One such assertion is that black people have no motivation or incentive to "move up" or climb the socioeconomic ladder. Consequently, this negative characteristic is presumed to perpetuate racial inequality: like a vicious cycle, whites then perceive blacks as ignorant or as having "devalued cultural mores." The following are examples of Category II explanations; even though they allude to slavery, albeit in a secondary fashion, the existence of discrimination is the primary focus:

Blacks were brought to the U.S. by Whites. They were/are thought to be of a "lower race" by large parts of the society . . . society has impressed these beliefs/ideas onto Blacks. [Therefore] Blacks probably have lower self-esteem and when you have lower self-esteem, it is harder to move up in the world. . . . Blacks group together and stay together. Very few move up . . . partly because society put them there. (F6–18)

> Past history is at the base of the racial problems evident in today's society. Blacks have been persecuted and oppressed for years. . . . Discrimination is still a problem which results in lack of motivation, self-esteem and hence a lessened "desire" to escape the hardships with which they are faced. (F8–14)

In 1986 my students' responses were almost evenly divided between Category I and Category II explanations (10 and 11 responses, respectively, with one Category III response). In 1988 all 35 responses were divided between Category I (11) and Category II (24) responses, or 32% and 68%, respectively. Thus, the majority of students in both years explained racial inequality in limited ways—as a historically inevitable consequence of slavery or as a result of prejudice and discrimination—without recognizing the structural inequity built into the social order. Their explanations fail to link racial inequity to other forms of societal oppression and exploitation. In addition, these explanations, which give considerable attention to black people's negative characteristics, fail to account for white people's beliefs and attitudes that have long justified societal oppression and inequity in the form of racial slavery or discrimination.

DISCUSSION

An obvious feature of Category I explanations is the devaluation of the African American cultural heritage, a heritage that certainly encompasses more than the debilitating experience of slavery. Moreover, the integrity and adaptive resilience of what Stuckey (1987) refers to as the "slave culture" is ignored and implicitly devalued. Indeed, Category I explanations reflect a conservative assimilationist ideology that blames contemporary racial inequity on the presumed cultural deficits of African Americans. Less obvious is the way the historical continuum of these explanations, beginning as they do with the effects of slavery on African Americans, fails to consider the specific cultural rationality that justified slavery as acceptable and lawful (Wynter, 1990). Also excluded from these explanations as possible contributing factors are the particular advantages white people gained from the institution of racial slavery.

Category II explanations devalue diversity by not recognizing how opportunity is tied to the assimilation of mainstream norms and values. These explanations also fail to call into question the basic structural inequity of the social order; instead, the cultural mythology of the American Dream, most specifically the myth of equal opportunity, is tacitly accepted (i.e., with the right opportunity, African Americans can climb out of poverty and "make it" like everyone else). Such liberal, assimilationist ideology ignores the widening gap between the haves and the have nots, the downward mobility of growing numbers of whites (particularly women with children), and other social realities of contemporary capitalism. While not altogether inaccurate, these explanations are nevertheless *partial* precisely because they fail to make appropriate connections between race, gender, and class inequity.

How do Category I and Category II explanations exemplify dysconscious racism? Both types defend white privilege, which, according to Wellman (1977), is a "consistent theme in racist thinking" (p. 39). For example, Category I explanations rationalize racial inequity by attributing it to the effects of slavery on African Americans while ignoring the economic advantages it gave whites. A second rationalization, presented in Category II explanations, engenders the mental picture many of my students apparently have of equal opportunity, not as equal access to jobs, health care, education, etc., but rather as a sort of "legal liberty" that leaves the structural basis of the racial status quo intact (King and Wilson, 1990). In effect, by failing to connect a more just opportunity system for blacks with fewer white-skin advantages for whites, these explanations, in actuality, defend the racial status quo.

According to Wellman, the existing social order cannot provide for unlimited (or equal) opportunity for black people while maintaining racial privileges for whites (p. 42). Thus, elimination of the societal hierarchy is inevitable if the social order is to be reorganized, but before this can occur, the existing structural inequity must be recognized as such and actively struggled against. This, however, is not what most of my students have in mind when they refer to "equal opportunity."

Category I and Category II explanations rationalize the existing social order in yet a third way by omitting any ethical judgment against the privileges white people have gained as a result of subordinating black people (and others). These explanations thus reveal a dysconscious racism that, although it bears little resemblance to the violent bigotry and overt white supremacist ideologies of previous eras, still takes for granted a system of racial privilege and societal stratification that favors whites. Like the whites of Dred Scott's era, few of my students even think of disputing this system or see it as disputable.

Category III explanations, on the other hand, do not defend this system. They are more comprehensive, and thus more accurate, because they make the appropriate connections between racism and other forms of inequity. Category III explanations also locate the origins of racial inequity in the framework of a society in which racial victimization is *normative*. They identify and criticize both racist ideology and oppressive societal structures without placing the responsibility for changing the situation solely on African Americans (e.g., to develop self-esteem) and without overemphasizing the role of white prejudice (e.g., whites' beliefs about black inferiority). The historical factors cited in Category III explanations neither deny white privilege nor defend it. I have received only one Category III response from a student at the beginning of my courses, the following:

> [Racial inequity] is primarily the result of the economic system . . . racism served the purposes of ruling groups; e.g., in the Reconstruction era . . . poor whites were pitted against Blacks—a pool of cheap exploitable labor is desired by capitalists and this ties in with the identifiable differences of races. (F6–9)

Why is it that more students do not think this way? Given the majority of my students' explanations of racial inequity, I suggest that their thinking is impaired by dysconscious racism—even though they may deny they are racists. The important point here, however, is not to prove that students are racist; rather, it is that their uncritical and limited ways of thinking must be identified, understood, and brought to their conscious awareness.

Dysconscious racism must be made the subject of educational intervention. Conventional analyses—which conceptualize racism at the institutional, cultural, or individual level but do not address the cognitive distortions of dysconsciousness—cannot help students distinguish between racist justifications of the status quo (which limit their thought, self-identity, and responsibility to take action) and socially unacceptable individual prejudice or bigotry (which students often disavow). Teacher educators must therefore challenge both liberal and conservative ideological thinking on these matters if we want students to consider seriously the need for fundamental change in society and in education.

Ideology, identity, and indoctrination are central concepts I use in my Social Foundations of Education course to help students free themselves from miseducation and uncritically accepted views that limit their thought and action. A brief description of the course follows.

THE CULTURAL POLITICS OF CRITIQUING IDEOLOGY AND IDENTITY

One goal of my Social Foundations of Education course is to sharpen the ability of students to think critically about educational purposes and practice in relation to social justice and to their own identities as teachers. The course thus illuminates a range of ideological interests that become the focus of students' critical analysis, evaluation, and choice. For instance, a recurring theme in the course is that of the social purposes of schooling, or schooling as an instrument of educational philosophy, societal vision, values, and personal choice. This is a key concept about which many students report they have never thought seriously. Course readings, lectures, media resources, class discussions, and other experiential learning activities are organized to provide an alternative context of meaning within which students can critically analyze the social purposes of schooling. The range of ideological perspectives considered include alternative explanations of poverty and joblessness, competing viewpoints regarding the significance of cultural differences, and discussions of education as a remedy for societal inequity. Students consider the meaning of social justice and examine ways that education might be transformed to promote a more equitable social order. Moreover, they are expected to choose and declare the social changes they themselves want to bring about as teachers.

The course also introduces students to the critical perspective that education is not neutral; it can serve various political and cultural interests, including social control, socialization, assimilation, domination, or liberation (Cagan, 1978; Freire, 1971; O'Neill, 1981). Both impartial, purportedly factual information as well as openly partisan views about existing social realities such as the deindustrialization of America, hunger and homelessness, tracking, the "hidden" curriculum (Anyon, 1981; Vallance, 1977), the socialization of teachers, and teacher expectations (Rist, 1970) allow students to examine connections between macrosocial (societal) and microsocial (classroom) issues. This information helps students consider different viewpoints about how schooling processes contribute to inequity. Alongside encountering liberal and conservative analyses of education and opportunity, students encounter the scholarship of racial educators such as Anyon (1981), Freire (1971), Kozol (1981), and Giroux and McLaren (1986), who have developed "historical identities" (Boggs et al., 1978) within social justice struggles and who take stronger ethical stances against inequity than do liberals or conservatives. These radical educators' perspectives also provide students with alternative role models; students discuss their thoughts and feelings about the convictions these authors express and reflect upon the soundness of racial arguments. Consequently, as students formulate their own philosophical positions about the purposes of education, they inevitably struggle with the ideas, values, and social interests at the heart of the different educational and social visions that they, as teachers of the future, must either affirm, reject, or resist.

Making a conscious process of the struggle over divergent educational principles and purposes constitutes the cultural politics of my Social Foundations course. In this regard my aim is to provide a context within which student teachers can recognize and evaluate their personal experiences of political and ethical indoctrination. In contrast to their own miseducation, and using their experience in my course as a point of comparison, I urge my students to consider the possibilities liberatory and transformative teaching offers. To facilitate this kind of conscious reflection, I discuss the teaching strategies I myself model in my efforts to help them think critically about the course content, their own world view, and the professional practice of teaching (Freire and Faundez, 1989). To demonstrate the questions critical, liberatory teachers must ask and to make what counts as "school knowledge" (Anyon, 1981) problematic, I use Freire's (1971) strategy of developing "problem-posing" counterknowledge. For example, I pose biased instructional materials as a problem teachers address. Thus, when we examine the way textbooks represent labor history (Anyon, 1979) and my student teachers begin to realize all they do not know about the struggles of working people for justice, the problem of miseducation becomes more real to them. Indeed, as Freire, Woodson (1933), and others suggest, an alternative view of history often reveals hidden social interests in the curriculum and unmasks a political and cultural role of schooling of which my student teachers are often completely unaware.

Analysis of and reflection on their own knowledge and experience involves students in critiquing ideologies, examining the influences on their thinking and identities, and considering the kind of teachers they want to become. I also encourage my students to take a stance against mainstream views and practices that dominate in schools and other university courses. Through such intellectual and emotional growth opportunities, students in my course reexperience and reevaluate the partial and socially constructed nature of their own knowledge and identities.

My approach is not free from contradictions, however. While I alone organize the course structure, select the topics, make certain issues problematic, and assign the grades, I am confident that my approach is more democratic than the unwitting ideological indoctrination my students have apparently internalized. For a final grade, students have the option of writing a final exam in which they can critique the course, or they may present (to the class) a term project organized around an analytical framework they themselves generate.

TOWARD LIBERATORY PEDAGOGY IN TEACHER EDUCATION

Merely presenting factual information about societal inequity does not necessarily enable preservice teachers to examine the beliefs and assumptions that may influence the way they interpret these facts. Moreover, with few exceptions, available multicultural resource materials for teachers presume a value commitment and readiness for multicultural teaching and antiracist education that many students may lack initially (Bennett, 1990; Brandt, 1986; Sleeter and Grant, 1988). Teacher educators may find some support in new directions in adult education (Mezirow,

1984) and in theories of adult learning and critical literacy that draw upon Freire's work in particular (Freire and Macedo, 1987). This literature offers some useful theoretical insights for emancipatory education and liberatory pedagogy (Heaney, 1984). For example, the counterknowledge strategies I use in my Social Foundations course are designed to facilitate the kind of "perspective transformation" Mezirow (1984) calls for in his work. It is also worth noting that a tradition of critical African American educational scholarship exists that can be incorporated into teacher preparation courses. Analyses of miseducation by Woodson (1933), DuBois (1935), and Ellis (1917) are early forerunners of critical, liberatory pedagogy. This tradition is also reflected in contemporary African American thought and scholarship on education and social action (see Childs, 1989; Gordon, 1990; Lee et al., 1990; Muwakkil, 1990; Perkins, 1986).

As Sleeter and Grant (1988, p. 194) point out, however, white students sometimes find such critical, liberatory approaches threatening to their self-concepts and identities. While they refer specifically to problems of white males in this regard, my experience is that most students from economically privileged, culturally homogeneous backgrounds are generally unaware of their intellectual biases and monocultural encapsulation. While my students may feel threatened by diversity, what they often express is guilt and hostility. Students who have lived for the most part in relatively privileged cultural isolation can only consider becoming liberatory, social-reconstructionist educators if they have both an adequate understanding of how society works and opportunities to think about the need for fundamental social change. The critical perspective of the social order offered in my course challenges students' world views as well as their self-identities by making problematic and directly addressing students' values, beliefs, and ideologies. Precisely because what my students know and believe is so limited, it is necessary to address both their knowledge (that is, their intellectual understanding of social inequity) and what they believe about diversity. As Angus and Jhally (1989, p. 12) conclude, "what people accept as natural and self-evident" is exactly what becomes "problematic and in need of explanation" from this critical standpoint. Thus, to seriously consider the value commitment involved in teaching for social change as an option, students need experiential opportunities to recognize and evaluate the ideological influences that shape their thinking about schooling, society, themselves, and diverse others.

The critique of ideology, identity, and miseducation described herein represents a form of cultural politics in teacher education that is needed to address the specific cultural rationality of social inequity in modern American society. Such a liberatory pedagogical approach does not neglect the dimension of power and privilege in society, nor does it ignore the role of ideology in shaping the context within which people think about daily life and the possibilities of social transformation. Pedagogy of this kind is especially needed now, given the current thrust toward normative schooling and curriculum content that emphasizes "our common Western heritage" (Bloom, 1987; Gagnon, 1988; Hirsch, 1987; Ravitch, 1990). Unfortunately, this neoconservative curriculum movement leaves little room for discussion of how being educated in this tradition may be a limiting factor in the effectiveness of teachers of poor and minority students (King and Wilson, 1990; Ladson-Billings, 1991). Indeed, it precludes any critical ethical judgment about societal inequity and supports the kind of miseducation that produces teachers who are dysconscious—uncritical and unprepared to question White norms, white superiority, and white privilege.

Myths and slogans about common heritage notwithstanding, prospective teachers need an alternative context in which to think critically about and reconstruct their social knowledge and self-identities. Simply put, they need opportunities to become conscious of oppression. However, as Heaney (1984) correctly observes: "Consciousness of oppression can not be the object of instruction, it must be discovered in experience" (p. 118). Classes such as my Social Foundations course make it possible for students to reexperience the way dysconscious racism and miseducation victimize them.

That dysconscious racism and miseducation of teachers are part of the problem is not well understood. This is evident in conventional foundations approaches and in the teacher education literature on multiculturalism and pluralism that examine social stratification, unequal educational outcomes, and the significance of culture in education but offer no critique of ideology and indoctrination (Gollnick and Chinn, 1990; Pai, 1990). Such approaches do not help prospective teachers gain the critical skills needed to examine the ways being educated in a racist society affects their own knowledge and their beliefs about themselves and culturally diverse others. The findings presented in this article suggest that such skills are vitally necessary. The real challenge of diversity is to develop a sound liberatory praxis of teacher education that offers relatively privileged students freedom to choose critical multicultural consciousness over dysconsciousness. Moving beyond dysconsciousness and miseducation toward liberatory pedagogy will require systematic research to determine how teachers are being prepared and how well those whose preparation includes critical liberatory pedagogy are able to maintain their perspectives and implement transformative goals in their own practice.

Notes

1. It should be noted that dysconsciousness need not be limited to racism but can apply to justifications of other forms of exploitation such as sexism or even neocolonialism—issues that are beyond the scope of the present analysis.

2. I want to thank Professor Gloria Ladson-Billings, who also teaches at my institution, for providing these journal entries. See her discussion of student knowledge and attitudes in *The Journal of Negro Education*, 60, 2, 1991.

3. This and subsequent student comment codes used throughout this article identify individual respondents within each cohort. "F6–21," for example, refers to respondent 21 in the fall 1986 academic quarter.

References

Angus, I., and S. Jhally (Eds.). (1989). *Cultural politics in contemporary America*. New York: Routledge.

Anyon, J. (1979). Ideology and U.S. history textbooks. *Harvard Educational Review, 49,* 361–386.

———. (1981). Social class and school knowledge. *Curriculum Inquiry, 11,* 3–42.

Ayers, W. (1988). Young children and the problem of the color line. *Democracy and Education, 3*(1), 20–26.

Banks, J. (1977). *Multiethnic education: Practices and promises.* Bloomington, Ind.: Phi Delta Kappa Educational Foundation.

Bennett, C. (1990). *Comprehensive multicultural education: Theory and practice.* Boston: Allyn & Bacon.

Bloom, A. (1987). *The closing of the American mind.* New York: Simon & Schuster.

Boggs, J., et al. (1979). *Conversations in Maine: Exploring our nation's future.* Boston: South End Press.

Brandt, G. (1986). *The realization of anti-racist teaching.* Philadelphia: The Falmer Press.

Cagan, E. (1978). Individualism, collectivism, and radical educational reform. *Harvard Educational Review, 48,* 227–266.

Childs, J. B. (1989). *Leadership, conflict, and cooperation in Afro-American social thought.* Philadelphia: Temple University Press.

Cox, G. O. (1974). *Education for the Black race.* New York: African Heritage Studies Publishers.

DuBois, W. E. B. (1935). Does the Negro need separate schools? *Journal of Negro Education, 4,* 329–335.

Edelman, M. W. (1987). *Families in peril: An agenda for social change.* Cambridge, Mass.: Harvard University Press.

Ellis, G. W. (1917). Psychic factors in the new American race situation. *Journal of Race Development, 4,* 469–486.

Freire, P. (1971). *Pedagogy of the oppressed.* New York: Harper & Row.

Freire, P., and A. Faundez (1989). *Learning to question: A pedagogy of liberation.* New York: Continuum.

Freire, P., and D. Macedo (1987). *Literacy: Reading the word and the world.* South Hadley, Mass.: Bergin & Garvey.

Gagnon, P. (1988, November). Why study history? *Atlantic Monthly,* pp. 43–66.

Ginsburg, M. (1988). *Contradictions in teacher education and society: A critical analysis.* Philadelphia: Falmer Press.

Ginsburg, M., and K. Newman (1985). Social inequalities, schooling and teacher education. *Journal of Teacher Education, 36,* 49–54.

Giroux, J., and P. McLaren (1986). Teacher education and the politics of engagement: The case for democratic schooling. *Harvard Educational Review, 56,* 213–238.

Gollnick, D., and P. Chinn (1990). *Multicultural education in a pluralistic society.* Columbus, Ohio: Merrill.

Gordon, B. (1985). Critical and emancipatory pedagogy: An annotated bibliography of sources for teachers. *Social Education 49*(5), 400–402.

———. (1990). The necessity of African-American epistemology for educational theory and practice. *Journal of Education 172,* (3), pp. 88–106.

Harlan, S. (1985, June 5). Compared to White children, Black children are . . . *USA Today,* p. 9-A.

Heaney, T. (1984). Action, freedom, and liberatory education. In S. B. Merriam (Ed.), *Selected writings on philosophy and education* (pp. 113–122). Malabar, Fla.: Robert E. Krieger.

Hirsch, E. D. (1987). *Cultural literacy: What every American needs to know.* New York: Houghton Mifflin.

Howard, B. C. (1857). *Report of the decision of the Supreme Court of the United States and the opinions of the justices thereof in the case of Dred Scott versus John F. A. Sandford, December term, 1856.* New York: D. Appleton & Co.

Kozol, J. (1981). *On being a teacher.* New York: Continuum.

King, J., and G. Ladson-Billings (1990). The teacher education challenge in elite univeristy settings: Developing critical and multicultural perspectives for teaching in a democratic and multicultural society. *European Journal of Intercultural Studies 1*(2), 15–30.

King, J., and T. L. Wilson (1990). Being the soul-freeing substance: A legacy of hope in Afro humanity. *Journal of Education 172*(2), 9–27.

Ladson-Billings, G. (1991). Beyond multicultural illiteracy. *Journal of Negro Education* 60(2), 147–157.

Lee, C., et al. (1990). How shall we sing our sacred song in a strange land? The dilemma of double consciousness and complexities of an African-centered pedagogy. *Journal of Education* 172(2), 45–61.

Mezirow, J. (1984). A critical theory of adult learning and education. In S.B. Merriam (Ed.), *Selected writings on philosophy and adult education* (pp. 123–140). Malabar, Fla.: Robert E. Krieger.

Muwakkil, S. (1990). Fighting for cultural inclusion in the schools. *In These Times* 14(37), 8–9.

O'Neill, W. F. (1981). *Educational ideologies: Contemporary expressions of educational philosophy.* Santa Monica, Calif.: Goodyear.

Pai, Y. (1990). *Cultural foundations of education.* Columbus, Ohio: Merrill.

Perkins, U. E. (1986). *Harvesting new generations: The positive development of Black youth.* Chicago: Third World Press.

Ravitch, D. (1990). Diversity and democracy. *The American Educator* 14, 16–20.

Rist, R. (1970). Student social class and teacher expectations. *Harvard Educational Review* 40, 411–451.

Searle, C. (Ed.). (1975). *Classrooms of resistance.* London: Writers and Readers Publishing Cooperative.

Shor, I. (1980). *Critical teaching in everyday life.* Boston: South End Press. Sleeter, C., and C. Grant (1988). *Making choices for multicultural education: Five approaches to race, class and gender.* Columbus, Ohio: Merrill.

Stuckey, S. (1987). *Slave culture: Nationalist theory and the foundations of Black America.* New York: Oxford University Press.

Vallance, E. (1977). Hiding the hidden curriculum: An interpretation of the language of justification in nineteenth-century educational reform. In A. Bellack and H. Kliebard (Eds.), *Curriculum and evaluation* (pp. 590–607). Berkeley, Calif.: McCutchan.

Wellman, D. (1977). *Portraits of White racism.* Cambridge: Cambridge University Press.

Woodson, C. G. (1933). *The miseducation of the Negro.* Washington, D.C.: Associated Publishers.

Wynter, S. (1990, September 9). *America as a "world": A Black studies perspective and "cultural model" framework.* [Letter to the California State Board of Education.]

22

WHEN IS A SINGING SCHOOL (NOT) A CHORUS? THE EMANCIPATORY AGENDA IN FEMINIST PEDAGOGY AND LITERATURE EDUCATION

Deanne Bogdan

This paper addresses the conundrum of why, for some of us, the more we become sensitized to the imperatives of democratic education and student ownership of their own learning, the harder they can become actually to accomplish in a classroom. This is especially true in literature education and feminist/critical pedagogy, where personal and social transformation are implicit and explicit goals. Underlying the ethical aims of feminist pedagogy and literature education is the accepting of the Other on the Other's own terms.[1] In classrooms full of real readers reading, this principle, which informs what Elizabeth Ellsworth has called "a pedagogy of the unknowable,"[2] plays itself out in the interstices between authority and trust, academic rigor and personal empathy, community and fracture, professional and political responsibility. Recently Deborah Britzman has analyzed her student teachers' attempts to implement critical/feminist pedagogical methods in English education at the secondary school level, detailing the complexity of the tensions and contradictions that mark "not just what it means to know and be known, but how we come to know and come to refuse knowledge."[3] To espouse a liberatory agenda is often to embark on a "pedagogical encounter" that, in Britzman's words, is simply "scary."

> More often than not, things do not go according to plan: objectives reappear as too simple, too complicated, or get lost; concepts become glossed over, require long detours, or go awry. . . . In short, pedagogy is filled with surprises, involuntary returns, and unanticipated twists.[4]

My reflections arise out of my more recent experiences teaching at my home institution, the Ontario Institute for Studies in Education, which is a graduate department of education. In contrast to Britzman's grade ten class, our students are mature adults, many of them seasoned, successful teachers in their own right, who bring to the learning environment highly diverse personal, professional, and disciplinary backgrounds. But even within this milieu, the very heightening of consciousness about the changing intellectual and political premises of English studies, heavily influenced by critical/feminist pedagogy, can threaten at any given moment to break down into solipsistic world views and group alienation.

References to "the Singing School" in my title (with apologies to Yeats and Northrop Frye)[5] and whether or not it is a "Chorus" signal the tension between what an instructor perceives to be happening and what may in fact be happening with respect to the learning taking place. For me, "the Singing School" has become a metaphor for what we might think of as a "dream class," that is, one in which achieving the objectives of a course becomes seamlessly incorporated into the process itself, and where the joy of teaching is indistinguishable from being a student of the students' learning.[6] The apotheosis of my dream class was my women's literature and feminist criticism class of 1988, which accepted my invitation to embark with me on a collaborative experiment to explore the feminist critique of Romanticism, a subject in which I am not a specialist. In thinking and writing about the sheer exuberance of that experience since then, I have tried in vain to isolate the factors that might account for what had seemed so successful to us all in working across difference. Was it that the more democratic collaborative setting had allowed me to comfortably shed my role as "expert"? Was it the carefully sequenced readings and exercises? Was it that the students enjoyed reader-response journal writing, for most of them a "first" in graduate education—or were we all just nice people?[7] And how accurate, in any case, is the absence of factional strife or the presence of a mutually reinforcing class dynamic as a barometer of productive learning?

By contrast, the first time I taught women's literature and feminist criticism (in hindsight probably the most transformational event in my professional life), the tenor of the class was totally the reverse of that of the Singing School. It was no euphonious chorus. Bent on taking literature personally and politically at any cost, that group of highly sophisticated but combustible readers literally mutinied against the strictures of the traditional culture of literary critical interpretation in repudiating the offensive sexist bias in John Updike's short story "A & P," becoming what at the time I thought were literary "illiterates" by reversing the norms of what was deemed "naive" and what, "educated."[8] Yet in my discussions with those students since then, we've concluded that, in the depths of all that anguish, none of us ever stopped thinking feelingly or feeling thinkingly about what we were doing and why. Psychic suffering *can* be a powerful condition of learning, but it's not that simple either. That incursions into the inner life are necessary effects of my coming to know does not give teachers licence to perform the "god trick and all its dazzling—and, therefore blinding— illuminations"[9] on unsuspecting students. Professional hubris, an occupational hazard of all teaching, which by its very nature invokes change, is especially pertinent to English studies and feminist pedagogy, whose mandate espouses liberation, whether that liberation be from the "hegemony" of The Great Tradition to the "freedom" of discourse theory, or simply toward a more egalitarian classroom.

Over the twelve years that I've been teaching at the graduate level, in both feminist literary criticism seminars and in mainstream philosophy of literature courses, I have moved from a performance pedagogical mode and a fairly tightly structured curriculum to a more decentered classroom and a syllabus constantly open to revision. But that doesn't mean that I can tell any better when a class is "working" and when it isn't. How do I know that what looks like everyone riding our communal bicycle is not really a coercive regime masking silences and erasing hostilities? And conversely, given that my role is so fraught with paradox, especially in a feminist class, where I am invariably cast as "the bearded mother" (expected to be both supportive emotionally and rigorous scholastically),[10] how do I know that something quite wonderful is not happening to someone? What am I, for instance, to make of the remark of one of my best students who sincerely thought she was paying me a compliment with, "I really love your class. It makes me sick to my stomach"? By this I take her to mean that she was involved in what Shoshanna Felman calls "self-subversive self-reflection,"[11] a process in which her presuppositions about the conditions of her own learning were continually being thrown open to question by herself and by others whose intellectual training, political temper, and disciplinary affiliations differed markedly from hers. Though this polylogue can be productive, it can also precipitate dialogic impasse, especially in an interdisciplinary class, when one hears statements such as, "I understand where you are coming from, but have you read X?" (a book or article intended to correct what is presumed by the questioner to be Other's misguided ideology about what should count as knowledge).

Accepting the Other on the Other's own terms entails self-subversive self-reflection about our own paths of identification; it also foregrounds the ethical importance of what Northrop Frye called the "direct" or "participating" response[12]—to literature and to fervently held assumptions about one's own life. In the literary educational enterprise there is, of course, no substitute for knowledge *about* texts and their theoretical implications. *What* people say, *how* they respond, is doubtless important; but, *that they do* in this or that way is in some respects a prior consideration. That is to say, performative utterances situate students as moral beings, who in turn form the social fabric of the classroom community. This is a crucial point when dealing with the personal and the political implications of response to literature, inasmuch as the pedagogical importance of cultural codes cannot claim epistemic privilege over students' affective lives. While discourse strategies may improve conceptual understanding, they do not necessarily alter autobiographical significance, which I suggest is an educational value in need of further theorization within both feminist pedagogy and the philosophy of literature education. That is to say, while my literary interpretation may be "better" than yours, and my analysis of classroom dynamics possibly more astute, I, nevertheless, cannot make you mean.[13] The ontological force of this dictum is a logical extension of politicizing and privileging "direct" literary response at the same time (a contradictory endeavor, as we'll see).

It was this problematic of reeducating the imagination that I consciously undertook when I returned to the classroom after a year's sabbatical during which I completed a book addressing issues related to canon, curriculum, and literary response.[14] In designing the course (a mainstream course dealing with literature and values in education, also taught for the first time), I wanted to replicate the structure of my own argument in the book as well as to let the phenomenology of my journey in the feminist critique of Frye's concept of the educated imagination unfold, as I intended that it would for my reader. Since the book was still in press and I felt uncomfortable about distributing the manuscript, I combined sequenced ancillary readings that had informed my own thinking in writing the book with class discussion and twenty-minute lectures from the text of my manuscript.

The class (twelve women and three men), composed mostly of high school and community-college English teachers, began as another "dream" Singing School, and ended, if not in a nightmare, in the purgatorial twilight zone of bruised identities and painful oppositional stances between the majority, who "got" it, and the minority who "didn't." I focus on this in order to highlight the complexities of how bringing the personal and the political simultaneously into the discussion of response to literature might help us think about the discrepancies between what we think is happening in front of us and what in fact might be going on. When, indeed, is a Singing School not a chorus? When is feeling sick to your stomach an indication, not of the "natural" part of coming to consciousness, but of the oppressive effects of too much consciousness at the wrong time and in the wrong circumstance? And when might it be producing what Teresa de Lauretis calls a "genuine epistemological shift"?[15] When does honoring the Other on the Other's own terms bridge the intrinsic and extrinsic value of literary education and when is it simply the arrogant admonition by those who presume to "know" of those who would know better? And does it matter whether it is one or the other?

Let's first look at what made me think last year's Singing School was tuneful. My sense of it as a "dream class," the feeling that it was going swimmingly or that the class was teaching itself, was confined to the first half of the course, where the students quickly took hold of my clear-cut conceptual framework. (The course examined the interdependence of the why, what, and how of teaching literature under the rubric of a "meta-problem," which juxtaposes the issues of justifying the teaching of literature [why], canon/curriculum/censorship [what], and the classroom treatment of reader response [how]). The promise of seriously working across difference came early when one of the men, Kevin, signed up to do a seminar on Julia Kristeva's concept of abjection later on in the course.[16] As time went on, I consulted with the students about revising the balance between new content and digesting what had gone before. At about the half-way point, another student, Ellen, conducted a lucid account of my taxonomy of Frye's developmental theory of reader response. Here she used a tape of John Updike reading his "A & P," the "invidious" piece that had been the site of the previous rebellion in my women's literature and feminist criticism class. Now, however, reactions were multiple: some students were chuckling with obvious enjoyment, others were grim, still others, pensive. No one, it seemed, was unengaged. The presenter herself had intentionally adhered to Frye's structure, a hierarchy of "pre-" to "post-critical" response, with "autonomous" at the top; describing her initial feminist resistant response to the story as an angry, and therefore "negative" and "lesser" stock response, she acknowledged that it had become more "refined" to a "fuller," more "literary" one as she saw herself moving through her "raw experience" to an understanding of the story as a whole in a "greater appreciation of the human condition." (Later, after reading Sandra Lee Bartky, she observed that she was probably able to do this because she was a younger feminist and had not experienced "the double ontological shock" Bartky describes.)[17] As people began to discuss the conditions of their responses more openly, I had the feeling that this was just about the ideal class. They were doing double-takes all over the place, but really communicating. What possibly could have been better?

There was, however, a nagging doubt that just maybe the class was beginning to feel set-up by the agenda of the course, which remained largely hidden from them. Ellen's presentation had in a way become a perfect foil for the following week's seminar, in which we dealt with my feminist subversion of my taxonomy. But the effect on her of that reversal and indeed of the feminist cast of the rest of the course was quite emotionally devastating, as it was for some other students. I began to ask myself whether, in the very actualizing of my pedagogical project, I had helped produce at least one casualty of its very efficacy. If so, what did that mean about my respect for my students' learning? Shouldn't students be subjects, not just objects, of their own transformations? Who is responsible for the psychological cost of such transformations? And what right did I have to do what I was doing at all? I went to the next seminar convinced that my book manuscript would still be the informing principle of the rest of the course, but not the *controlling* principle. That is, I resolved to reserve more discussion time in order to diffuse any latent hostility generated by my possibly manipulating the students into enlightenment (I had to give them more power), to loosen my hold on the structure, stop lecturing, and focus on student presentations of the secondary material without my intervention except as just another member of the class.

This proved to be yet another paradox of decentered teaching. There was no way I could divest myself of my authority, already established by the heuristic I'd set up at the beginning and reinforced by my own invisible manuscript as a major component of the course content. Even more worrisome to me was that I was increasingly becoming identified with a more rigid ideological stance toward the course material than I in fact held. At the same time, coincident with my decentering, the majority of the women and one of the three men had begun to evince their profeminist concerns more overtly; others complained that in the second half of the course there was a loss of continuity in the conceptual framework, which, of course, only I could provide. Little wonder that I felt the class was polarizing badly and that its exploratory intent seemed to have become submerged in a "search for answers."

The Updike episode had opened up the possibility of a *poetics of refusal* that had taken seriously the negative effects of the close proximity of some literary content to the lived lives of readers. These students had extended that discussion to include how being very close to the bone of real experience also affected their critical temper and their own teaching practices. Though the positive exchange in the class, as well as the students' final papers, persuaded me that the self-subversive self-reflection of most of them had indeed produced heightened sensitivity to the Other, anger, silence, and denial also surfaced. These came to the fore when another woman, Clare, did a forceful reading *with* the grain, of Robin Morgan's *The Demon Lover: The Sexuality of Terrorism.*[18] Clare's intent was to "put on" Morgan's polemic in relating social and cultural processes to systemic misogyny. That seemed to tap into the deep but covert rage felt by some of the, until then, more "detached" feminists, who now were able to recover their voice—and did, with vehement recognition scenes. Ellen, however, did not join that chorus, but became noticeably upset, excusing herself in tears at the break. A few days later she confessed her anxieties about remaining in graduate school: the course had triggered her feelings of futility about academic work, and she thought that perhaps she should return to high school teaching. Having become alienated from literature as a living force in her life through doing an M.A. in a highly conservative English department, she had relished the prospect of our trek into theory; but now she had second thoughts about its value if such negativity as was being expressed in the class was still rampant after so many years of feminism. A staunch feminist as an undergraduate, she'd expected that by now feminism would have "moved ahead to something more inclusive." This, in face of the fact that figuring in her present crisis was her grief over the murder of one of her own female students. Ironically, though, Ellen's path of identification, which she confirmed in her final paper, was with the two "outsider" men in the class, both of whom were feeling embattled. One was Kevin, who told me that he was surprised to encounter so much feminist content in a course that wasn't advertised in that way.

Kevin was also full of contradictions. In his seminar on Kristeva, while he bravely grappled with her complex notion of abjection, something that he acknowledged he could understand only intellectually from his privilege as a white, heterosexual male, he ended his presentation by bringing in Robert Bly's *Iron John*,[19] thereby positioning himself as victim. And in the discussion period, he deliberately interpolated the term "terrorist" to describe what he referred to as "militant feminism." This, he said after class, was a strategic move to address the by now palpable feminist agenda of the course. When another woman, Jennifer, rewrote "A & P" from the viewpoint of "the witch about fifty, with rouge on her cheekbones and no eyebrows"[20] as a way of expressing her "epistemic privilege,"[21] her feelings of being "Othered" by Updike, Kevin simply dug in his heels, insisting that the portrayal of the males in Jennifer's rewrite didn't remotely resemble him or any guy he knew.

Perhaps Ellen and Kevin were in part both trying to find their own "safe house" in face of their loss of a certain conceptual security, which had been provided by the structural framework of the course set up at the beginning, and in face of their pedagogical loss of the bearded mother. It is worth mentioning that in this class these losses coincided with the introduction of explicitly feminist content, which complicated the meta problem with what we might call the "feeling, power, and location problems."[22] What seems clear about Ellen and Kevin is that they were both thrown up against their own resistance—Ellen as one who already knew too much and perhaps wanted to know less, at least for now, and Kevin as one who couldn't cope with his own awareness of what he didn't yet know. Yet by the end of the course this playing field looked profoundly unequal: whereas Kevin was voluble, Ellen fell silent. It's difficult to assess here who "got" it and who "didn't"; moreover, what is the "it"? Did Ellen "get" "it" and just couldn't bear to feel "it," yet again, in her solar plexus? Did Kevin have to fill up the space because he couldn't hear "it," or because he could? Does he remain an "unreconstructed male"? Is that my business? What *I* perceived was that Ellen was experiencing Bartky's "double ontological shock" more or less alone, and that Kevin's feelings were being taken care of by me and the rest of the class. When is honoring the Other on the Other's own terms truly emancipatory and when might it mask a false integrity?

This year, when I teach the course again, the students will be in possession of the text of my book; my feminist project will be more visible to them from the start; and my pedagogy will consist almost exclusively of small groups reading and re-writing each other's short papers in response to the primary and ancillary texts. That might mitigate, but will not eliminate, the incessant transferring and withdrawing of powerful psychic projections that necessarily abound when the personal and political contexts of literary response form part of the agenda of a literature classroom in grade ten English or a graduate seminar in literature education. Once we credit transformation of any kind as a legitimate goal of our teaching, literature ends up with more relevance to life than many of us who entered the profession as a partial escape from life originally bargained for. One can only be where one is in literary criticism, but to be wherever one is today is indeed a "perilous undertaking,"[23] in which the resistances of students like Ellen and Kevin have become a new body of content—inchoate, untidy, but nonetheless sacred, matter.

Does this mean that teachers of literature are the unwitting "mental health paraprofessionals" that Clara Park (in *Uses of Literature,* one of the volumes of the 1973 *Harvard English Studies*) said that we perforce become?[24] As someone professing to be a philosopher of literature education, not a clinical psychologist or bibliotherapist, I can't say that I'm really up for this.[25] But as a practitioner of feminist pedagogy, I do not find the alternatives wholly satisfactory either. Returning to uncritiqued notions of "literariness" and universalist paths of identification, innocent of political awareness, is certainly not an option for me. That only makes it easier for some to move from prefeminist or precolonial unconsciousness to appropriation without ever having to pass through comprehension. Even abandoning transformational agendas altogether—teaching the theory wars or navigating students through endless textual undoings and remakings—cannot blanket over the still monumental significance of the intervention by "words with power"[26] in the emotional lives of people who really might be changed by what they learn in school.

Felman suggests that "the most far-reaching insight psychoanalysis can give us into pedagogy" is the realization that "the position of the teacher is itself the position of one who learns, of the one who teaches nothing other than the way [s]he learns. The subject of teaching is interminably—a student; the subject of teaching is interminably—a learning."[27] And, she argues, this knowledge is a fundamentally *literary* knowledge in that it is knowledge *"not in possession of itself."*[28] A knowledge not grounded in mastery but always in the process of becoming is especially germane to the educational aim of meeting the Other on the Other's own terms. This pedagogy of the unknowable does not disclaim knowledge; it *"knows it knows but does not know the meaning of its knowledge."*[29] Within this context, students' resistance to knowing is perhaps one of the best teaching tools we have. As Felman, Frye, and others before them have observed, teaching is impossible; that is why it is difficult.[30] What, then, are we to do? In coming to solutions, we might keep in mind the thoughts of the young Polish pianist Krystian Zimmerman, who gave a master class in Toronto last spring. In concluding his remarks to the audience and to the five students whose sparkling performances he'd unabashedly acknowledged his admiration for, he said, "Of course, we study the text, and then improvise around it. The rest is up to you. But the most important thing is to do [sic] mistakes, as many as possible and as soon as possible."[31]

Ellen did decide to remain in graduate school, and even won a scholarship. In her final paper, she reflected on our various mistakes when she responded to the optional question I asked about the experience of the course as a whole:

My unusually emotional response to this course was of considerable concern to me, hence the amount of time spent analyzing my feelings and discussing the situation with friends. I have concluded that mine has been a rather ironic and yet educational experience. What I have encountered, I think, is a very real feeling, power, and location problem within a course where [these problems were] not only recognized but apparently sympathized with . . . What I am left with primarily are not feelings of alienation . . . or cynicism . . . (although these feelings do exist still); rather, I have become more profoundly aware of just how complex perception, communication, and inter[personal]relations are and just how difficult it is *not* to make assumptions, to disempower someone or to silence opposition in a group setting. I am also much more aware of how emotions, social contexts, and personal meanings and experiences affect learning, which has been traditionally seen as [only] an intellectual activity.

Here Ellen has named for herself what David Bleich has called the "affective [inter]dependency" of the classroom.[32] Perhaps a Singing School can still be a chorus, if dissonance be part of resonance.

Notes

This paper was first presented at the Forty-Ninth Meeting of the Philosophy of Education Society, New Orleans, March 1993. It appears in the Proceedings of that conference and is slightly revised here; I wish to express thanks to the proceedings editor, Audrey Thompson, for permission to reprint. As well I am grateful to Wendy Burton, James Cunningham, Hilary Davis, and Alice Pitt for their comments and suggestions on an earlier draft, and to members of 1485S who gave me permission to excerpt their work.

1. Contemporary literary theory has propelled the profession beyond unproblematized Arnoldian or Leavisite assumptions about the liberatory nature of English studies. But teaching to or for theoretical understanding does not erase the question of the powerful impetus for personal change inherent in all teaching. This is especially true of literary reading. Shoshanna Felman reminds us that any "reading lesson is . . . not a statement; it is a performance. It is not theory, it is practice . . . for (self) transformation." *Jacques Lacan and the Adventure of Insight* (Cambridge: Harvard University Press, 1987), p. 20. The rapprochement between English studies and feminist/critical pedagogy has been underscored by numerous authors, including Janice M. Wolff, who introduces her article "Writing Passionately: Students' Resistance to Feminist Readings" with the assertion that "ideological consciousness-raising is very much part of [her] faculty's concerns." *College Composition and Communication* 42 (4) (December 1991): 484. I read this paper after having completed my own, and would like to note the resemblance of its themes to this one, in particular, resistance as an instrument of learning, the gendered character of students' resistant responses, and the teacher as one who does not know.

2. Elizabeth Ellsworth, "Why Doesn't This Feel Empowering? Working through the Repressive Myths of Critical Pedagogy," *Harvard Educational Review* 59 (3) (August 1989): 318.

3. Deborah P. Britzman, "Decentering Discourses in Teacher Education: Or, the Unleashing of Unpopular Things," *Journal of Education* 173 (3) (1991): 75.

4. Ibid., p. 60.

5. "The Singing School" is the title of the second chapter of Northrop Frye's *The Educated Imagination* (Toronto: Canadian Broadcasting Company Publications, 1963), pp. 12–33. The original citation is taken from Yeats's "Sailing to Byzantium" (quoted in Frye, p. 12).

6. See Marion Woodman, Kate Danson, Mary Hamilton, and Rita Greer Allen, *Leaving My Father's House: A Journey to Conscious Femininity* (Boston and London: Shambhala Press, 1992), p. 167.

7. See Deanne Bogdan, "Joyce, Willie, and Dorothy: Literary Literacy as Engaged Reflection," *Proceedings of the Forty-Fifth Annual Meeting of the Philosophy of Education Society*, San Antonio, Texas, April 14–17, 1989, ed. Ralph Page (Normal, Illinois: University of Illinois Press, 1990), pp. 168–182.

8. See Deanne Bogdan, "Judy and Her Sisters: Censorship, Identification, and the Poetics of Need," *Proceedings of the Forty-Fourth Annual Meeting of the Philosophy of Education Society,* San Diego, California, March 25–28, 1988, ed. James M. Giarelli (Normal, Illinois: Philosophy of Education Society, 1988); John Updike, "A & P," in his *Pigeon Feathers and Other Stories* (New York: Knopf, 1962).

9. Donna Haraway. "Situated Knowledges: The Privilege of Partial Perspective," *Feminist Studies* 14 (1988): 584.

10. Kathryn Morgan, "The Perils and Paradoxes of Feminist Pedagogy," *Resources for Feminist Research* 16 (1987): 50.

11. Shoshanna Felman, *Jacques Lacan*, p. 90.

12. Northrop Frye, *The Critical Path: An Essay on the Social Context of Literary Criticism* (Bloomington: Indiana University Press, 1971), p. 28.

13. See Susan Leslie Campbell, "Expression and the Individuation of Feeling" (Ph.D. diss., University of Toronto, 1992), p. 291; also Felman, *Jacques Lacan*, p. 119. In her response to Charles Taylor's Inaugural Address to the University Center of Human Values at Princeton, Susan Wolf makes a related point about the justification for widening the canon. See Charles Taylor's *Multiculturalism and the Politics of Recognition, with Commentary by Amy Gutmann*, ed. Steiner C. Rockefeller, Michael Walter, and Susan Wolf (Princeton, N.J.: Princeton University Press, 1992), pp. 79–85.

14. See Deanne Bogdan, *Re-educating the Imagination: Toward a Poetics, Politics, and Pedagogy of Literary Engagement* (Portsmouth, N.H.: Boynton/Cook-Heinemann, 1992).

15. Teresa de Lauretis, *Technologies of Gender: Essays on Theory, Film, and Fiction* (Bloomington: Indiana University Press, 1987), p. 10.

16. Julia Kristeva, *Powers of Horror: An Essay on Abjection,* trans. Leon S. Roudiez (Oxford: Blackwell, 1982).

17. Bartky defines the "double ontological shock" as "first, the realization that what is really happening is quite different from what appears to be happening; and second, the frequent inability to tell what is really happening at all" (1979, 256). Sandra Lee Bartky, "Towards a Phenomenology of Feminist Consciousness," in *Philosophy and Women*, ed. S. Bishop and M. Weinzweig (Belmont, Calif.: Wadsworth, 1979), p. 256.

18. Robin Morgan, *The Demon Lover: On the Sexuality of Terrorism* (New York: Norton, 1989).

19. Robert Bly, *Iron John: A Book About Men* (New York: Addison-Wesley, 1990).

20. Updike, p. 187.

21. Uma Narayan, "Working Together Across Difference: Some Considerations on Emotions and Political Practice," *Hypatia* 3 (2), (1988): 34.

22. See Bogdan, *Re-educating the Imagination*, pp. 140–148.

23. Clara Clairborne Park, "Rejoicing to Concur with the Common Reader: The Uses of Literature in the Community College," in *Uses of Literature*, ed. Monroe Engel, *Harvard English Studies 4* (Cambridge: Harvard University Press, 1973), p. 231.

24. Ibid., p. 242.

25. Toronto high school teacher Brian Fellow, in an article titled "Sex, Lies, and Grade 10," describes his reader-response approach to a literature lesson on the poem, "Lies," by Yevgeny Yevtushenko. According to Fellow, the theme of this poem is "Do not lie to the young." As a way of exploring its meaning with his class, Fellow wrote on the board three columns: "The Best Lies, The Best Liars, and The Best Liees." The result was not an interpretive discussion about the poem as what we might call a "greater appreciation of the human condition" in the abstract but the palpable and painful coming to terms with the social problem of sexual pressure experienced by the girls from their boyfriends, some of whom, as attested to by one of the girls, tell the worst lie—"I love you." Such was the gravity of the unspoken crisis in that instance that the girls in the class ended up proposing the startup of a support group "like Alcholics Anonymous." *The Glove and Mail,* Toronto, Ontario, October 20, 1992, p. A32. Surely Percy Bysshe Shelley would be surprised to see this particular context for poets as the unacknowledged legislators of the world. I am not suggesting that this poem not be taught according to a reader-response model. I am simply pointing to the deep social effects that literature has in the lives of readers and that it has always claimed to have.

26. See Northrop Frye, *Words with Power: Being a Second Study of 'The Bible and Literature'* (Harmondsworth, England: Penguin, 1990).

27. Felman, *Jacques Lacan,* p. 88.

28. Ibid. p. 92.

29. Ibid.

30. Ibid., p 69; Northrop Frye, *The Stubborn Structure: Essays on Criticism and Society* (London: Methuen, 1970), p. 84.

31. See also Felman, *Jacques Lacan,* pp. 78–79, 89.

32. David Bleich, *The Double Perspective: Language, Literacy, and Social Relations* (New York: Oxford University Press, 1988), p. 94.

INDEX

CONTRIBUTORS

Madeleine Arnot (previous MacDonald) is Lecturer in the Department of Education, University of Cambridge. She has published widely on theories of gender and class relations in education. Recent publications include *Gender and the Politics of Schooling* (edited with G. Weiner) and forthcoming, *Feminism and Social Justice in Education: International Perspectives* (coedited with K. Weiler) and *Feminism Politics and Educational Reform*.

Deanne Bogdan is Associate Professor in the Department of History and Philosophy of Education at the Ontario Institute for Studies in Education, University of Toronto. Her publications include *Beyond Communication: Reading Comprehension and Criticism* (edited with Stanley Shaw) and *Re-Educating the Imagination: Toward a Poetics, Politics, and Pedagogy of Literary Engagement*.

Bonnie Thornton Dill is Professor of Women's Studies at the University of Maryland at College Park. Formerly Professor of Sociology and Founding Director of the Center for Research on Women at Memphis State University, she has published in such journals as *Signs*, *Feminist Studies*, and the *Journal of Family History*. In 1993 she received the American Sociological Association's Jessie Bernard Award for her work at the Center for Research on Women.

Elizabeth Ellsworth is an Associate Professor in the Department of Curriculum and Instruction and a Women's Studies Program Affiliate at the University of Wisconsin-Madison. Her work includes *Becoming Feminine: The Politics of Popular Culture* (edited with Leslie G. Roman and Linda Christian-Smith) and *The Ideology of Images in Educational Media: Hidden Curriculum in the Classroom* (with Marianne H. Watley).

Carol Gilligan is the author of *In a Different Voice: Psychological Theory and Women's Development*. She is Professor in the Human Development and Psychology Program at Harvard University, Graduate School of Education, and a founding member of the Harvard project on Women's Psychology and Girl's Development. Her most recent publication is *Meeting at the Crossroads: Woman's Psychology and Girls' Development* with Lyn Mikel Brown.

Maxine Greene is William F. Russell Professor of Educational Foundations, Emerita at Teachers College, Columbia University. Known for her interdisciplinary writing in education and the arts, multiculturalism, and women's lives, her publications include *Teacher as Stranger*, *Landscapes of Learning*, and *The Dialectic of Freedom*, as well as *Existential Encounters for Teachers* and *The Public School and the Private Vision*.

Madeleine Grumet is Dean, Brooklyn College, City University of New York. She has published widely in reconceptualist curriculum theory, in phenomenology, and in feminist studies. Her work incudes *Bitter Milk: Women and Teaching*; she also edits a series of feminist theory and education for SUNY.

Barbara Houston is Associate Professor, Philosophy of Education, at the University of New Hampshire. She has published numerous articles on gender, the ethics of care, and feminist pedagogy in Canada and the US. Among her work is "Sex, Gender, and Identity" In *Atlantis: Canadian Journal of Women's Studies* and recently, "In Praise of Blame" in *Hypatia*.

Joyce E. King is Associate Professor and Director of Teacher Education at Santa Clara University. She has written *Black Mothers to Sons: Juxtaposing African American Literature with Social Practice* (with C. A. Mitchell) and "Diasapora Literacy and Consciousness in the Struggle Against Miseducation in the Black Community" in the *Journal of Negro Education*.

Patti Lather is Associate Professor, Educational Policy and Leadership, at Ohio State University, where she teaches qualitative research and feminist pedagogy. Her work includes *Getting Smart: Feminist Research and Pedagogy With/in the Postmodern, Within/Against Feminist Research in Education* and "Fertile Obsession: Validity After Poststructuralism" in *Sociological Quarterly*.

Nona Lyons, Director of Teacher Education at Brown University, is interested in human development and learning and the intellectual dimensions of decision making and conflict negotiation. Her publications include "Two Perspectives: On Self, Relationships, and Morality" in *Harvard Educational Review* and *Making Connections: The Relational Worlds of Adolescent Girls at Emma Willard School* (edited with Carol Gilligan and Trudy Hanmer).

Jane Roland Martin is Professor of Philosophy, Emerita, at the University of Massachusetts, Boston. She is widely published in philosophy of education and is the author of *Reclaiming a Conversation: The Ideal of the Educated Woman, The Schoolhome: Rethinking Schools for Changing Families*, and *Changing the Educational Landscape*, a collection of her own essays on women and curriculum.

Barbara McKellar, originally from the Caribbean, is one of a handful of Black teachers and teacher educators in Great Britain. At the time of the writing of her article, she was employed in the Department of Education, South Bank University, London. Since that time she has worked in school administration.

Sue Middleton is a Senior Lecturer in Education Studies at the University of Waikato, Hamilton, New Zealand. Research and teaching interests include feminist educational theory, life-history methods, education policy as discourse, and the sociology of women's education. She is the author of *Educating Feminists*, editor of *Women and Education in Aerotearoa*, and coeditor (among several volumes) of *Feminist Voices*.

Linda J. Nicholson is Professor of Philosophy of Education works in Women's Studies at the State University of New York at Albany. She is the author of *Gender and History: The Limits of Social Theory in the Age of the Family* and the editor of *Feminism/postmodernism*. She also edits the book series "Thinking Gender" for Routledge.

Nel Noddings is Lee Jacks Professor of Child Education, School of Education, Stanford University. Her books include *Caring: A Feminine Approach to Ethics* and *Moral Education, Women and Evil, The Challenge to Care in Schools: An Alternative Approach to Education*, and *Educating for Intelligent Belief or Unbelief*.

Jo Anne Pagano is Associate Professor of Education and of University Studies at Colgate University. Among other topics, she has published on feminist theory and teaching. Her books are *Exiles and Communities: Teaching in the Patriarchal Wilderness* and *Preparing Teachers as Professionals* (with James Anthony Whitson, Landon Beyer, and Walter Feinberg).

Dianne Smith is Assistant Professor, Curriculum and Instruction, at the University of Missouri-Kansas City. Related work by her includes "African American Women Teachers and Sexual Abuse," in Joy James and Ruth Farmer (eds.), *African American Women in (White) Academe.* In addition, she has recently written a paper titled "Womanism and Me: I Know That I Know Why the Caged Bird Sings."

Lynda Stone is Assistant Professor, Philosophy of Education, University of Hawaii at Manoa (Honolulu). Her related work includes "Feminist Educational Research and the Issue of Critical Sufficiency," in Peter McLaren and James Giarelli (eds.), *Critical Theory and Education Research*; and "What 'Certain Knowledge' Means for Women," in Wendy Kohli (ed.), *Critical Conversations in Philosophy of Education: From Theory to Practice and Back.*

Patricia J. Thompson is Professor, Division of Professional Studies, at Herbert H. Lehman College of the City University of New York. Among her published work is "Home Economics in a Hestian Voice," in Dale Spender and Cheris Kramarae (ed.), *The Knowledge Explosion*: and *Bringing Feminism Home*, as well as her earlier *Home Economics and Feminism: The Hestian Synthesis.*

Valerie Walkerdine is Professor of the Psychology of Communications in the Department of Media and Communications, Goldsmiths' College, University of London. Among her books are *Counting Girls Out* (with The Girls Mathematics Unit) and *Schoolgirl Fictions.* She has recently completed a volume on young girls and popular culture. She is also an artist and filmmaker.

Ruth E. Zambrana is an Associate Professor of Social Welfare at the UCLA School of Social Welfare. She has conducted research and published in areas of maternal and child health and children and adolescents, with a specific focus on low-income and Latino populations. A second area of research is women and education, using a cross-cultural, comparative approach.